PARTNERSHIP FOR CHANGE
Australia–China Joint Economic Report

ANU Press

East Asian Bureau of Economic Research, ANU, Canberra

China Center for International Economic Exchanges, Beijing

August 2016

PRESS

Published by the ANU Press, East Asian Bureau of Economic Research and the China Center for International Economic Exchanges

© East Asian Bureau of Economic Research, China Center for International Economic Exchanges 2016

ISBN 9781760460648 (print)
ISBN 9781760460655 (ebook)

A CiP catalogue record of this book is available from the National Library of Australia

Contact

Inquiries regarding the licence and requests to use material in this document for commercial purposes are welcome at:

East Asian Bureau of Economic Research
Crawford School of Public Policy
The Australian National University
Acton ACT 2601
Phone: +61 2 6125 6411
Email: peter.drysdale@anu.edu.au

This title is also available online at press.anu.edu.au

Design and artwork by Kylie Smith
Printed by Prinstant, Canberra

Contents

Foreword

This Report is the product of a joint study undertaken by the East Asian Bureau of Economic Research (EABER) in the Crawford School of Public Policy at The Australian National University (ANU) and the China Center for International Economic Exchanges (CCIEE) in Beijing. We were privileged to guide this work through to its completion over the past year.

There are few more important economic relationships for Australia than the one it has with China. Merchandise and services trade with China now accounts for more than a quarter of Australia's overall trade. Chinese investment in Australia is growing fast. For many Australian businesses, the Chinese market represents an enormous potential growth market. For China, Australia has been a reliable provider of high-quality inputs from iron ore to education. But as China's growth model and policy focus changes, there are big adjustments that will have to be made in the relationship and new opportunities that are emerging for both countries.

Capturing the economic potential of the relationship will depend on how both the public and private sectors in Australia and China engage up close and shape the relationship. Getting the most out of the relationship for both countries will require a functional understanding among policymakers, corporate leaders and the broader community of the changes that will shape China and the regional and global environment in the next 10 years.

This is a critical moment in a once-in-a-generation transition. This is a vital opportunity for both countries to think about how to shape the future course of our relationship in a deliberate way, establishing some common reference points rather than simply muddling through.

What are the dynamic forces within China that are driving its new growth model? Our joint study looked both back at what has worked in the past and forward to what might yield the best results for the future of the Australia–China relationship, after the conclusion of the China–Australia Free Trade Agreement and in the context of the big changes that are taking place in the relationship.

This Report seeks to define the potential of our trade and investment relationships, economic cooperation efforts and other interactions, and to produce a tangible macro- and micro-level roadmap of the future relationship. We have also tried to identify where the economic relationship is likely to develop, looking at the sectors and activities in which trade and investment ties are likely to concentrate, and which industries will thrive and which will decline under China's new growth model.

The kinds of economic interactions and government policies that have underpinned the bilateral relationship thus far are the starting point: whether these are appropriate or sufficient as the economic relationship changes and diversifies is the question on which this Report has focused.

The Report identifies key policy changes in China and Australia that will be necessary to promote a deeper economic partnership, not only bilaterally but also through their regional and global cooperation. Situating these reforms within the broader context of the Chinese reform agenda (for example, financial and capital account liberalisation and deregulation) and the economic challenges facing Australia, this Report has set out detailed conclusions for Chinese and Australian policymakers, with clear priorities for action.

This is an independent joint study by leading think tanks in China and Australia, but it has also had the warm support of both governments and the cooperation of the key economic ministries and other agencies in both countries. It also marshalled broad Chinese and Australian participation and input from business, from governments at all levels, from leading research institutions, and from the wider communities of both countries.

The Report also engaged a top team of experts in both China and Australia to guide and assist in the preparation of the Report and its argument. We are very grateful for the support and advice of these very busy people in the completion of our work.

The Australian Group of Experts included: Dr Ian Watt, formerly secretary of the Department of the Prime Minister and Cabinet; Professor Gary Banks, Chief Executive and Dean of the Australia and New Zealand School of Government and formerly chair of the Productivity Commission; Professor Allan Gyngell, Director of the Crawford Australian Leadership Forum at the ANU and formerly director-general of the Australian Office of National Assessments; Dr Heather Smith, Secretary of the Department of Communications and the Arts; and Dr Phil Lowe, recently appointed to be the next Governor of the Reserve Bank of Australia; and with advice from Professor Ross Garnaut and Dr Geoff Raby, both former Australian ambassadors to China, along with other expert inputs.

The Chinese Group of Experts included: Professor Huang Yiping, Vice-President of the National School of Development at Peking University and advisor to the People's Bank of China (PBoC) Monetary Policy Committee; Dr He Fan, Chief Economist of the Chongyang Institute of Finance at the Renmin University of China, Senior Economics Fellow at the Institute for New Economic Thinking in New York, and Chief Economics Commentator at Caixin Media; Professor Zhang Yunling, Director of International Studies at the Chinese Academy of Social Sciences and a member of the Foreign Affairs Committee of the Chinese People's Political Consultative Conference; Dr Chen Wenling, CCIEE Chief Economist; Mr Liu Zuozhang, former minister-counsellor at the Chinese Embassy in Australia; Dr Zhu Baoliang, Director of the Economic Forecasting Department of the State Information Center; and Professor Fan Gang, a faculty member at the HSBC Business School of Peking University and Secretary-General of the China Reform Foundation; with advice and input from Mr Zhao Jinjun, former president of the China Foreign Affairs University and former Chinese ambassador to France; Ms Hu Xiaolian, President of Export-Import Bank of China and former deputy-governor of the PBoC; and Mr Xu Chaoyou, Director of the CCIEE Department of External Affairs and formerly of the Ministry of Foreign Affairs (MFA).

The Report has benefited from the valuable support of the leaders of CCIEE and the ANU — Mr Zeng Peiyan, Chairman of the CCIEE, and Professor Brian Schmidt, Vice-Chancellor of the ANU.

This study would not have been possible at the Australian end without the generous support of business sponsors who first engaged with the ANU through an Australian Research Council Linkage Grant project on Chinese overseas direct investment. Our deepest gratitude goes to Rio Tinto, and especially Tim Lane; to MMG, and especially Troy Hey and Andrew Patterson; and to Corrs Chambers Westgarth, especially John Denton.

The success of this project has been made possible by the commitment and cooperation of public service leaders on both sides. In Australia, the Report received cash and substantial in-kind support from the Treasury, who took carriage of this Report in the Australian public service. Chris Legg, John Karatsoreos and Lachlan Carey were constantly involved in advancing the Report, and we also thank Leesa Croke, Adam McKissack, Jyoti Rahman, John Swieringa, Nan Wang, Justin Iu, Vera Holenstein, Hui Yao, Adam Hawkins and Aaron Van Bridges for their support.

Key official supporters of the project in Australia also included the Reserve Bank of Australia, particularly Ivan Roberts, Eden Hatzvi and Chris Ryan; the Department of Prime Minister and Cabinet, particularly Martin Parkinson, David Gruen, HK Yu, Jason McDonald, Hugh Jeffrey, Alistair MacGibbon, Luke Yeaman, Jay Caldwell, Andrew Forrest, Erny Wah and Anna Engwerda-Smith; the Department of Foreign Affairs and Trade, particularly Peter Varghese, Jan Adams, Justin Brown, Brendan Berne, Graham Fletcher, Frances Lisson, Michael Muggliston, James Wiblin, Jason Robertson, Michael Growder and Kevin Thomson; the Department of Defence, particularly Dennis Richardson, Marc Ablong and Scott Dewar; the Office of National Assessments, particularly Richard Maude, Rod Brazier and Jonathan Olrick; Austrade, particularly Bruce Gosper, David Landers, Mark Thirlwell and Kelly Ralston; Tourism Research Australia, particularly George Chen and Janice Wykes; the Australian Bureau of Agricultural and Resource Economics and Sciences, particularly Sheng Yu; and Frances Adamson in the Prime Minister's Office.

The Chinese side would like to extend their deep thanks to those who contributed to the success of the Report from the Chinese government. At the Chinese Embassy in Canberra, they include Ambassador Cheng Jingye, Charge D'Affaires Cai Wei, Minister-Counsellor Huang Rengang and First Secretary Li Fang. In China, they include Zhao Wenfei at the MFA; Li Chao at the National Development and Reform Commission; Fang Hao at the Ministry of Commerce; Qin Yuexing at the Ministry of Finance; and Huang Xinju at the PBoC.

This Report also benefited greatly from consultations conducted with a wide range of institutions and individuals in Australia and China undertaken throughout course of its writing. We would especially like to thank former prime ministers Bob Hawke, Paul Keating, John Howard, Kevin Rudd, Julia Gillard and Tony Abbott for their advice and support.

From Australian state governments we would like to offer special thanks to Martin Hamilton-Smith and Jing Li in South Australia; Simon Phemister and David Latina in Victoria; and Susan Calvert and Matthew Rudd in New South Wales.

Our principal supporters within the Australian business community were the Global Engagement Taskforce of the Business Council of Australia (BCA). We extend special thanks to John Denton, Lisa Gropp, Jason Chai and the many leading companies engaged with this process through the BCA both in Australia and in China, including the China Development Bank.

From the business community we would also like to thank: the Australia China Business Council, with special thanks to John Brumby, Sean Keenihan, Cameron Brown, Daniel Bisignano, Moyi Zheng, Aaron Duff and Jette Radley; Tracy Colgan, Vaughn Barber, Glenn Campbell, Nick Coyle and Oliver Theobald at the Australian Chamber of Commerce Beijing; Amy Auster and Martin Foo at the Australian Centre for Financial Studies; Stephen Joske at Australian Super; Paul Bloxham at HSBC; Andrew Charlton at AlphaBeta; Mick Keogh at the Australian Farm Institute; Nick Bolkus at Bespoke Approach; and Timothy Coghlan at the Australia China Fashion Alliance.

From the academic and research sphere we would like to thank: Jenny McGregor, Mukund Narayanamurti, Bernardine Fernandez and Clio Zheng at Asialink; Bob Carr, James Laurenceson, Thomas Boak and Hannah Bretherton at the University of Technology Sydney;

Hans Hendrischke and Wei Li at the University of Sydney; Christine Wong and Anthony Garnaut at the University of Melbourne; Peter Cai at the Lowy Institute for International Policy; Linda Jakobson at China Matters; Chris Heathcote, Bill Brummitt and Mar Beltran at the Global Infrastructure Hub; Julia Evans at the Australian Academy of the Humanities; Jean Dong at the Australia China OBOR Initiative; and John Lee at the Institute for Regional Security

We are especially thankful for the submissions prepared by the Australia China Business Council; Edward Kus, Ellen Egan and Merric Foley at the Australia–China Young Professionals Initiative; Henry Sherrell at the Migration Council Australia; Sally Loane at the Financial Services Council; and Belinda Robinson at Universities Australia.

The Report would not have been completed without the dedicated professionalism of the task forces at the ANU and CCIEE who assisted with drafting the Report. On the Australian side this included Shiro Armstrong, Amy King, Ryan Manuel, Paul Hubbard, Adam Triggs, Jiao Wang, Owen Freestone and Neil Thomas. On the Chinese side this included Zhang Yongjun, Liu Xiangdong, Chen Yingchun and Lin Jiang.

There were many other people within our respective institutions that provided important input during the drafting process. Academics at the ANU, including Dong Dong Zhang, Paul Gretton, Richard Rigby, Ligang Song, Hugh White, Philippa Dee, Peter McDonald, Zhao Zhongwei, Frank Jotzo, Stephen Howes, David Vines and Anastasia Kapetas, provided valuable contributions in their respective fields of expertise. The ANU secretariat including Tom Westland, Rosemary Tran, Alison Darby, Patrick Deegan, Rosa Bishop, Sam Hardwick, Michael Wijnen, Nawaaz Khalfan, Patrick Williams, Hitonaru Fukui, Owen Hutchison and Luke Hurst provided editorial advice, research support and logistical assistance.

We would be remiss if we did not extend our warm thanks to Neil Thomas, who coordinated the Australian end of the work on the Report, and Zhang Yongjun, Liu Jun and others who coordinated the project at the Chinese end. Their devotion to this task was essential to its successful completion.

This Report is the result of a significant and unprecedented exercise in bi-national collaboration. We have sought to provide common reference points in how we can conduct our relationship and principles to which we can appeal when facing the inevitable uncertainties that we shall have to manage around profound change. We are convinced that the effort that this Report has called forth in both our countries to think through the future of our bilateral economic relationship together is in itself an encouraging harbinger of what Australia and China can hope to achieve together over the coming decades.

Peter Drysdale

August 2016

Zhang Xiaoqiang

List of acronyms

AALD	Australian–American Leadership Dialogue
ABC	Agricultural Bank of China
ABS	Australian Bureau of Statistics
ACACA	Australia–China Agricultural Cooperation Agreement
ACC	Australia–China Council
ACCCI	Australia–China Chamber of Commerce and Industry
ACJER	Australia–China Joint Economic Report
ACOLA	Australian Council of Learned Academies
ACRI	Australia–China Relations Institute
ACT	Australian Capital Territory
ACYA	Australia–China Youth Association
ACYD	Australia–China Youth Dialogue
ACYPI	Australia–China Young Professionals Initiative
ADB	Asian Development Bank
ADS	Approved Destination Status
AEC	ASEAN Economic Community
AFTA	ASEAN Free Trade Area
AIIB	Asian Infrastructure Investment Bank
AJBCC	Australia–Japan Business Cooperation Committee
AJPPPD	Australia–Japan Public-Private Policy Dialogue
AMPC	ASEAN Master Plan for Connectivity
AMRO	ASEAN Plus Three Macroeconomic Research Office
ANZ	Australia and New Zealand Bank
ANZSOG	Australia and New Zealand School of Government
ANZUS	Australia New Zealand United States Security Treaty
APEC	Asia Pacific Economic Cooperation
APRA	Australian Prudential and Regulation Authority
ARENA	Australian Renewable Energy Agency
ARF	ASEAN Regional Forum
ARFP	Asia Region Funds Passport
ASEAN	Association of Southeast Asian Nations
ASIC	Australian Securities and Investments Commission
ASX	Australian Securities Exchange
ATC	Australian Trade Commission
ATSE	Australian Academy of Technological Sciences and Engineering
AWIC	Australia Week in China

BCA	Business Council of Australia
BCIM	Bangladesh–China–India–Myanmar Economic Corridor
BIS	Bank of International Settlements
BIT	Bilateral Investment Treaty
BRICS	Brazil Russia India China South Africa
CBA	Commonwealth Bank of Australia
CCB	China Construction Bank
CCIEE	China Center for International Economic Exchanges
CEFC	Clean Energy Finance Corporation
ChAFTA	China–Australia Free Trade Agreement
CISA	China Iron and Steel Association
CITIC	China International Trust and Investment Corporation
CMBA	Chinese Medicine Board of Australia
CMI	Chiang Mai Initiative
CMIM	Chiang Mai Initiative Multilateralization
CNTA	China National Tourism Administration
CPEC	China–Pakistan Economic Corridor
CPPCC	Chinese People's Political Consultative Conference
CSIRO	Commonwealth Scientific and Industrial Research Organisation
CSRC	China Securities Regulatory Commission
DAF	Department of Agriculture and Food (Western Australia)
DIBP	Department of Immigration and Border Protection (Australia)
DDPP	Deep Decarbonisation Pathways Project
DFAT	Department of Foreign Affairs and Trade (Australia)
DSDBI	Department of State Development, Business and Innovation (Victoria)
DSGE	Dynamic Stochastic General Equilibrium
EABER	East Asian Bureau of Economic Research
EAS	East Asia Summit
EGA	Environmental Goods Agreement
EIA	Energy Information Administration
EPG	Eminent Persons Group
ESM	European Stability Mechanism
EU	European Union
FASIC	Foundation for Australian Studies in China
FDI	Foreign Direct Investment
FinTech	Financial Technology
FIRB	Foreign Investment Review Board (Australia)
FSC	Financial Services Council

FTA	Free Trade Agreement
FTAAP	Free Trade Area of the Asia Pacific
GATT	General Agreement on Tariffs and Trade
GBP	Pound Sterling
GCI	Global Competitiveness Index
GDP	Gross Domestic Product
GNI	Gross National Income
GTAP	Global Trade Analysis Project
GVA	Gross Value Added
HELP	Higher Education Loans Program
HKMA	Hong Kong Monetary Authority
HLD	High-Level Dialogue (Australia-China)
IBRD	International Bank for Reconstruction and Development
ICBC	Industrial and Commercial Bank of China
ICT	Information and Communications Technology
IEA	International Energy Agency
IFA	Investment Facilitation Arrangement
IMF	International Monetary Fund
IPCC	International Panel on Climate Change
IPO	Initial Public Offering
IT	Information Technology
ITA	Information Technology Agreement
KBC	Knowledge-Based Capital
LED	Light Emitting Diode
LNG	Liquefied Natural Gas
MFN	Most Favoured Nation
MoC	Memorandum of Cooperation
MOFCOM	Ministry of Commerce (PRC)
MoU	Memorandum of Understanding
MSR	Maritime Silk Road
NAB	National Australia Bank
NAFTA	North American Free Trade Area
NAIF	Northern Australia Infrastructure Facility
NDRC	National Development and Reform Commission (China)
NICM	National Institute for Complimentary Medicine (Australia)
NIE	New Industrialised Economy
NLA	National Library of Australia
NLC	National Library of China

OBOR	One Belt, One Road
OECD	Organisation for Economic Cooperation and Development
PBoC	People's Bank of China
PLA	People's Liberation Army (China)
PPP	Purchasing Power Parity
PSC	Production Sharing Contract
PTA	Preferential Trade Agreement
RBA	Reserve Bank of Australia
RCEP	Regional Comprehensive Economic Partnership
RFA	Regional Funding Arrangement
RMB	Renminbi
RQDII	Renminbi Qualified Domestic Institutional Investor
RQFII	Renminbi Qualified Foreign Institutional Investor
SASAC	State-owned Assets Supervision and Administration Commission (China)
SBLF	Australia–China Senior Business Leaders Forum
SDR	Special Drawing Rights
SEC	Securities and Exchange Commission (USA)
SED	Strategic Economic Dialogue (Australia–China)
SOE	State-Owned Enterprise
SSO	Sydney Symphony Orchestra
STEM	Science Technology Engineering Mathematics
TCM	Traditional Chinese Medicine
TFA	Trade Facilitation Agreement
TPP	Trans-Pacific Partnership
TRIM	Trade-Related Investment Measure
TTIP	Transatlantic Trade and Investment Partnership
UKTI	United Kingdom Trade and Investment
UN	United Nations
UNCTAD	United Nations Conference on Trade and Development
US	United States
VECCI	Victorian Chamber of Commerce and Industry
WA	Western Australia
WOFE	Wholly Owned Foreign Enterprise
WTO	World Trade Organization

List of figures

List of tables

List of boxes

EXECUTIVE SUMMARY

Executive Summary

Australia and China: forging a comprehensive strategic partnership for change

Australia and China, two vastly different nations, already have a huge and joint political, economic and social investment in the success of their bilateral relationship.

Taken to a higher level, as this Report recommends, this investment in the relationship can have a dramatic additional impact on both economies and societies.

This unique partnership stems from a deep alignment of interests that, short of highly negative policymaking, cannot be undone.

The relationship is already large and will undergo a huge change. The scale and complexity of the relationship is growing because of the increased role of services and investment, as well as its political and security dimensions.

These circumstances laid the foundation for support from both governments for an independent joint study of developments in the relationship in the decade ahead and how to strengthen the bilateral framework and the policy settings for managing it.

This Report is the product of an independent study jointly led by the China Centre for International Economic Exchanges in Beijing and by the East Asian Bureau of Economic Research at The Australian National University. Its aim is to define a framework for policymakers and for stakeholders in business, media, research institutions and the community; a framework that enables Australia and China to harness the opportunities that are arising from the profound transformations in their economies.

Why Australia and China are important to each other

China has for some years been Australia's largest trading partner and one of its most important bilateral relationships. It is now widely understood that Australia's economic growth and continued rising living standards are strongly linked to China's economic success.

In the Chinese policy community, there is wide understanding and clear acknowledgement of the economic and political advantages of open, secure and competitive access to Australian iron ore, coal and other raw materials.

As China's economy matures and its middle class expands, China is also enjoying the added dividend of access to Australian agriculture, institutions and services — everything from infant formula to vitamins, butter to beef, education to tourism, as well as advanced science, technology and research capabilities. Australia's open society provides Chinese investments with security in a stable and well-functioning market economy that guarantees transparent recourse to political, legal and regulatory institutions.

These new avenues of commercial exchange are a two-way street. Both Australia and China gain from growing and diversifying their economic relationship through new flows of tourists, students, investors and migrants. For more than a decade, China has been the world's main economic growth engine. Despite recent slowdowns, China will remain a key driver of global growth in the coming decade. If China's reform agenda succeeds, it can achieve annual GDP growth of around 6 per cent a year over the next 10 years.

But it is obvious that the impact of China's growth on Australia over the next 10 years will be very different from in the past. Australia will no longer only be a remote supplier of raw materials. It can be a palpable and distinctive presence in Chinese daily life, particularly for the urban middle classes whose aspirations and incomes will continue to expand for several decades.

The newly emerging partnership between Australia and China has a significant and valuable extra dimension. Australia is not only economically enmeshed with East Asia, giving it a high stake in China's success. It also has strong economic, cultural and strategic links to the United States, and therefore a compelling interest in a positive relationship between the United States and China.

Australia's geopolitical and geo-economic position and its multicultural society are thus unique assets in shaping China's links with the West.

Chinese and Australian prosperity has depended on the liberal, rules-based global system. Both countries have a compelling interest in the successful adaptation of the institutions of global governance to the economic and security challenges of the 21st century. A deeper partnership between China and Australia can be a powerful force for the strengthening and developing of these institutions. Australia's longstanding commitment to global institutions, its deep engagement with the economies of Asia and its historical ties with Europe and North America are complementary to China's status as a major economic power and its declared willingness to help supply and shape the international public goods of the 21st century in the task of reforming and strengthening the regional and global frameworks of cooperation and governance.

This adds significant weight to Australia's support for China's growing role in the provision of international public goods, such as the Asian Infrastructure Investment Bank (AIIB). Both countries have a common commitment to China's participation in global institutions and rules.

Benefits of closer economic partnership

China is shifting its growth drivers from investment, exports and heavy industry to consumption, innovation and services. China's growth slowdown does not threaten this transformation; it is a symptom of it.

This transformation will, by itself, lead to fast growth in trade between Australia and China in real terms, much of it in services. Even in a pessimistic scenario, in which average Chinese growth is below 5 per cent over the next 10 years, our estimates suggest that Australian exports to China would still grow by 28 per cent and Chinese exports to Australia by 20 per cent. A 'baseline' scenario has Australian exports growing by 72 per cent and Chinese exports by 41 per cent over the same period.

The biggest gains, however, would be realised if Australia and China work to implement the supply-side reforms recommended in this Report. If this reform agenda is prosecuted successfully, Australian exports to China will grow by 120 per cent in real terms, and Chinese exports to Australia by 44 per cent. For China, this is conditional on the implementation of a reform agenda that embraces financial and factor reform, state-owned enterprise (SOE) reform, increased openness to foreign investment and capital account liberalisation. For Australia, it means increased competition in sheltered industries, openness to foreign investment and skills, and facilitating investment in social and physical infrastructure.

Increased trade and investment will mean higher national incomes, more employment and more tax revenue for both China and Australia.

The structural changes in the Chinese economy presage a change in the structure of trade. The profound complementarity stemming from Australia's energy and resource abundance and China's industrialisation will remain a key pillar of the relationship, but will be increasingly augmented by services such as education and tourism, with inbound tourism from China set to treble by 2025. Education and tourism services will jump from 8 per cent to almost 20 per cent of Australian exports to China in 2025 in even the "business as usual" scenario. Machinery and equipment will jump from just below 20 per cent of Chinese exports to Australia to 28 per cent.

Chinese production is shifting from a model based on adaptation and imitation of goods, services and technologies developed elsewhere to a model based on domestic innovation. This is being driven by a substantial investment in China's innovation ecosystem. Australia's high-quality tertiary education sector (already a major services exporter to China) and its commitment to its own National Innovation and Science Agenda make it a natural partner in this transformation. Australia's experience in building a highly developed financial system can also be of value to China, where a sophisticated financial system will be crucial for allocating capital to the most innovative and efficient firms. China sees special benefit in the partnership with Australia for trialling reforms in investment policy and services markets as well as seeking greater alignment with Australia in its geopolitical interests in Asia and the Pacific.

In short, there is every reason to believe that the Australia–China relationship will become more, not less, important to both countries as the Chinese economy continues to change and upgrade.

For Australia, this means enhanced long-term economic capacity through opportunities for new trade and productivity-boosting innovation as well as through improving national infrastructure and the development of regional Australia.

For China, this means a sustainable path through middle-income status on its way to becoming a high-income economy through economic upgrading and diversification.

Towards a new policy framework

The need for an upgraded policy framework is broadly accepted in both countries.

That is why both governments have financially and institutionally supported the production of this Report and provided the necessary access to allow wide consultations with the key economic ministries and agencies on both sides, as well as with subnational governments, key research institutions, business leaders and community figures.

Creating an upgraded framework is a complex task: it will require building a new set of national capabilities in both countries. These will best be founded on past experience and achievements.

In the 1980s, Australia and China established what they called a 'model relationship' between two economies with different political and social systems and at different stages of development. This was the two countries' first significant joint effort at building a framework for their relations. This principle should continue to guide the bilateral relationship to higher levels.

Australia embraced China's openness and reform as a critical factor in regional prosperity and stability. China embraced the partnership with Australia as a crucial part of its opening policy, and Australia assumed a key role in China's foreign economic strategy. This path-breaking partnership opened market-based resources trade, foreign investment and regional cooperation with China — leading to positive engagement with China in APEC and working together on China's accession to the WTO.

Australia and China have since worked to strengthen regional economic cooperation through APEC, the ASEAN Plus frameworks and the East Asia Summit in order to secure the framework of political confidence and security necessary to economic prosperity.

Australia and China already have a Comprehensive Strategic Partnership, agreed in 2014, which guarantees high-level attention to the bilateral relationship through an annual Leaders Meeting, Strategic Economic Dialogue, and Foreign and Security Dialogue. Australia and China also have the China–Australia Free Trade Agreement (ChAFTA), which delivers significant trade liberalisation and opens the door in both countries to new and wider access to investment and the services sector. Indeed, ChAFTA has the potential to serve as a key agent in transforming the commercial relationship between the two countries in the coming decade.

But the full opportunity of these arrangements is far from being realised — both countries must now provide for the comprehensive setting of strategic bilateral objectives in a forward agenda. This will depend on new frameworks for institutionalising active collaboration on policy development and reform.

China is now building regional and global institutions that are commensurate to its place in the international economic system. China's lead on the AIIB and the One Belt, One Road (OBOR) initiatives represent China embedding its interests jointly with others partners to bolster infrastructure investment and regional connectivity.

Australia has worked closely with China in the IMF and other international economic bodies to support these Chinese initiatives. Australia is a founding member of the AIIB, and participates in OBOR through programs including the development of Northern Australia. There has been close collaboration in the G20 on shared agendas for global growth and reforming the multilateral trading system.

Managing new dimensions of the relationship: policy framework and programs

How are Australia and China going to manage their increasingly complex relationship — a relationship in which China is by far the biggest economy in Asia, is the second-largest economy in the world, is deeply enmeshed in a complex relationship with the United States, and is projecting growing political confidence?

Close cooperation with Australia should be an integral part of the next phase of China's economic reform and opening. Collaboration on service sector reform, financial restructuring and capital account liberalisation will help China realise its growth potential. As an advanced regional services-based economy, Australia is a natural partner and a promising test bed for China in its reform effort.

This Report outlines the key ideas and programs for dealing with this question. The conclusions that follow are envisaged as a long-term agenda of cooperation for bilateral relations, and will require careful consideration by both governments and other stakeholders in the relationship over the decade ahead.

This Report shows that, in order to realise the opportunities and counter the risks to bilateral growth, the Australian and Chinese governments should sensibly elevate their relationship to the unique level of a *Comprehensive Strategic Partnership for Change*. Leadership at the highest level should signal the priority attached to development of the relationship.

In particular:

- The new *Comprehensive Strategic Partnership for Change* that the Report recommends would build on ChAFTA and the current annual Leaders Meeting, and parallel ministerial meetings, through establishing *joint policy working groups* that support this work and other policy initiatives stemming from the leaders' dialogues and advance ongoing policy development and reform: for example, in the negotiation of a new *Agreement on Investment* within the framework of ChAFTA or on access to services markets and other issues (see below).

- Joint policy working groups can work, as needed, with state and provincial authorities, business sectors, research institutes and community-based interests on specific initiatives to advance the trade, investment, financial, regional and global reform agendas of both countries.

  - These working groups can assist in effecting the bilateral commitments to further investment liberalisation and expanded access to services markets made under ChAFTA.

  - The two countries should also establish a working group for dialogue and cooperation on the *maritime economy*, as this is a particular area of potentially productive collaboration between Australia and China. Both countries are maritime powers with common interests in seaborne supply routes and many other maritime issues.

- Both governments should aim, over the decade ahead, to draw on precedent from their other bilateral relationships and embed their new partnership into a *comprehensive bilateral Basic Treaty of Cooperation*.

  - This treaty would lock in the practice and principles for cooperation, and: commit to regular high-level government dialogues; set out the principles for managing the relationship that are enunciated in this Report; institutionalise official bilateral exchanges and technical cooperation programs between economic and foreign affairs ministries, including branches of the military; include policy approaches between federal–state governments in Australia and central–provincial governments in China; provide for the comprehensive setting of strategic bilateral objectives in a forward agenda; enfold the agreements, mechanisms and reforms of the ChAFTA arrangement; and entrench cooperation on improving educational, cultural and people-to-people exchange.

- Both countries should nurture the capacities necessary for new high-level engagement through establishing by treaty agreement a new and well-resourced bi-national Australia–China (Ao–Zhong) Commission in the form of a statutory entity that operates independently of both governments.

  - The Commission will boost the level and range of policy, research, scientific, technology, education, cultural and people-to-people exchanges between the two countries. Its nearest parallel in Australian experience is the treaty arrangement between Australia and the United States that established the Australian–American Fulbright Commission after World War II.

- Within the framework and provisions of ChAFTA, Australia and China should move to negotiate a comprehensive *Agreement on Investment* — incorporating a 'negative list' approach, effective national treatment of foreign investors, respect for rule of law, resource access guarantees, and greater mobility of people — ahead of Chinese agreements with the European Union and the United States. The *Agreement on Investment* can serve as a model for a regional investment regime in East Asia. Investment flows from China to Australia and from Australia to China will play a critical role in the development of the new economic relationship from exchange, to investment, and now to partnership.

  - This will not be achieved if the broader community does not grasp the benefits of foreign investment in both Australia and China. In Australia, this means accepting equal treatment for Chinese investment and reconsidering attitudes towards state-owned investors from all countries. In China, it means building respect for rule of law to make investments secure and predictable for all domestic and international parties.

- The *reengineering of the bilateral architecture* that is proposed should be aligned with the Australian government's National Innovation and Science Agenda and the Chinese government's innovation priority in its 13th Five Year Plan.

  - This would see the prioritisation of bilateral cooperation in future opportunities in research and development, capital sourcing, STEM collaboration, research commercialisation, tech landing pads, the digital economy, and exchanges between Australian and Chinese entrepreneurs and investors.

- Australia and China should attach top priority to the conclusion of a high-standard agreement on trade and investment liberalisation and ongoing economic cooperation arrangements in the Asia Pacific under the Regional Comprehensive Economic Partnership.

- The two countries' shared interest in the G20 and constructive participation in global economic governance should focus on China's role in mutual support among the major currencies; securing the international financial safety net to protect against the spread of financial crises; connecting reform to economic growth; and intensifying efforts to reform the multilateral trading system.

- Importantly, China and Australia should instigate top-level regional dialogues with Japan, South Korea, India, the United States and other key players in the region on the energy transformation that is necessary to mitigate climate change and other environmental issues. This is a fruitful area for regional coalition building on an issue in which China, as it seeks to reconcile increasing energy use with its environmental ambitions, and Australia, as a major energy supplier to the region, have a major stake. It is also an area in which cooperation with other Asia Pacific countries could be very productive politically.

If these steps are taken, the Australia–China relationship will be taken to a wholly new level. While fully respectful of each other's existing relationships (such as Australia's ANZUS relationship with the United States), the new partnership will be a powerful force for the stability and prosperity of the region, and indeed for the global system. It can serve as a principal vector of Australian and Chinese engagement within a rapidly changing world. Nurtured carefully and imaginatively by governments, businesses, research institutions and other stakeholders on both sides, this deeper partnership could become one of the most strategically vital and productive bilateral relationships that either country has in the world.

概要

中国和澳大利亚：打造与时俱进的全面战略伙伴关系

中国和澳大利亚两个极度不同的国家共同在政治、经济和社会方面做出了巨大的努力，塑造了相当成功的双边关系。

如报告所述，通过双方付出更多努力，把双边关系提升到更高水平，将有助于两国的经济和社会健康发展。

中澳之间这种独特的伙伴关系植根于双方深厚的利益互补性，除非受极端负面政策的影响，这种关系不可逆转。

中澳关系相当重要并面临改变。由于服务业、投资以及政治和安全层面的重要性日益凸显，这一关系的广度和复杂性还在继续增加。

这些因素为中澳两国政府支持开展一项有关未来十年两国关系前景并为此制定双边管理的框架和政策设置的独立联合研究提供了前提。

这份报告是由中国国际经济交流中心和澳大利亚国立大学东亚研究所联合完成的独立研究成果。其目的是为决策者和商界、媒体、研究机构、社团组织等利益相关者提供一个中澳合作框架，使得两国能够充分把握各自经济转型中的机会并相向而行。

为什么中国和澳大利亚对彼此很重要

多年来，中国一直是澳大利亚最大的贸易伙伴及其最重要的双边关系国之一。众所周知，澳大利亚的经济增长和持续提升的生活质量与中国经济的成功息息相关。

中国领导人也清晰地意识到，借助建立开放、安全、竞争的经济政治安排，可以从澳大利亚便利地获取铁矿石、煤炭和其他原材料。

随着中国消费者的成熟和中产阶层的壮大，中国正从澳大利亚农业、服务业部门和公共机构分享红利，享受包括婴儿奶粉、维他命(类营养品)、奶酪、牛肉、教育、旅游、先进科技和研发能力等产品或服务。竞争开放的澳大利亚向中国投资者提供了一个安全稳定、良性运转的市场制度，通过保持对政治、法律和监管机构的公开透明，保障投资的安全。

中澳之间商业交流渠道是双向的。随着游客、学生、投资者和移民持续涌现，中澳经贸关系日益增进和多样化，两国均从中获益良多。近十多年来，中国已经成为世界上重要的经济增长引擎。尽管近期增速放缓，未来十年中国仍将是世界增长的关键驱动力。如果中国正在实施的全面深化改革方案取得成功，未来十年中国仍能取得约6%的年均GDP增速。

显然，未来十年中国经济增长对澳大利亚的影响将与过去大不相同。澳大利亚将不再仅仅是个遥远的原材料供应地，而是显著地存在于中国人的日常生活中。尤其是那些未来几十年需求和收入持续增长的城市中产阶层，他们将会明显感受到澳大利亚的存在。

中澳新型伙伴关系具有格外重要的价值内涵。澳大利亚与东亚地区经济上相互依存，更高度依存于中国的成功。它还与美国有着很强的经济、文化、战略联系，从而在塑造良好的中美关系方面具有不可比拟的优势。因此，澳大利亚对中美间(能否)保持良好的关系有着非常切身的利益。

因此，澳大利亚地缘政治经济地位及其多元文化社会成为强化中国与西方国家关系的独特资源。

中国和澳大利亚的繁荣建立在自由的、基于规则的全球体系之上。两国有共同的重大关切，依靠全球治理机制来成功应对21世纪经济和安全领域的挑战。进一步深化中澳伙伴关系有助于强化和完善全球治理机制。澳大利亚是全球治理机制的坚定参与者，不仅与亚洲经济深度融合，并且与欧洲、北美颇具历史渊源，有助于中国巩固主要经济大国地位，也有助于中国推进区域合作框架和全球治理体系的改革发展并达成增加21世纪国际公共品供给的良好凤愿。

中国正成长为国际公共品的提供者。深化中澳关系可以极大地增加获取澳方支持的分量，如澳大利亚是中国倡议的亚洲基础设施投资银行的积极支持者。在推动中国参与全球治理机制和规则制定上，两国有着共同的追求。

建立更加密切经济伙伴关系的好处

中国经济增长的动力正从投资、出口和重工业向消费、创新和服务业转变。中国经济增长放缓并不会威胁到这一转型，反而是经济转型的一种表征。

实际上，这一转型本身将会带来中澳贸易的快速增长，尤其是在服务业领域。据估计，即便在最坏的情景下，即未来10年中国经济增长降低到5%以下，澳大利亚对华出口仍将增长28%，而中国对澳出口也将增长20%。在基准情景下，即未来10年中国经济增长平稳，澳大利亚对华出口将增长72%，而中国对澳出口将增长41%。

然而，如果中澳能共同努力实施本报告建议的改革措施，双方收益将会最大化。如果这些改革措施得以成功实施，澳大利亚对华实际出口将增长120%，而中国对澳出口将增长44%。就中国而言，这一改革议程包括：金融和要素(市场)改革、国有企业改革、加大对外商投资开放程度和资本账户自由化。对澳大利亚来说，这意味着提升受保护产业竞争程度，加大外商投资和技能开放，推进社会和物理基础设施投资便利化。

对中澳两国来说，贸易和投资规模的增加意味着更高的国民收入水平、更多的就业机会和更多的税收收入。

中国经济结构的改变预示其贸易结构的改变。中澳全面的互补关系来自于澳大利亚丰富的能源资源供应和中国的工业化。今后这仍将是维持两国互补关系的重要支柱，与此同时，教育、旅游等服务业领域的发展将进一步夯实这一互补关系。即使依据基准情景预测，到2025年,中国到澳洲的游客将增加三倍，教育和旅游业将从现在占澳大利亚对华出口的8%增加到2025年的近乎20%，机器和设备将从现在占中国对澳出口的20%以下上升到28%。

中国制造将从模仿改造别国的货物、服务、和技术的模式转变为自主创新驱动的模式。这种转变背后的驱动力来自于中国对其创新生态体系的大量投资。澳大利亚高品质的高等教育行业（现已是重要的对华出口服务部门））及其"国家创新和科学进程"战略，使其自然成为中国创新驱动转型中的良好伙伴。成熟的金融系统可以把资本有效配置到最具创新能力和效率最高的企业。澳大利亚在建立高度发达的金融系统方面拥有丰富经验。这对中国极具借鉴价值。从投资政策、服务市场改革试验和在亚太地区寻找与澳方地缘政治利益的更大交汇点等方面，中国从双边伙伴关系中也能找到特定利益。

简言之，无论从哪个方面来看，随着中国经济的持续变化和不断升级，中澳关系对两国的重要性都只会增加而不会降低。

对澳大利亚来说，这意味着通过把握贸易和促进生产力的创新、通过改进全国性基础设施和增加地方发展所带来的机会，增强其经济长期发展的能力。

对中国来说，这意味着通过转型升级和多样化发展，寻找到一条由中等收入迈向高收入经济体的可持续发展之路。

通向全新的政策框架之路

亟需一个升级版的政策框架是中澳两国广泛认可的。

这也是两国政府对本报告给予资金和机制安排支持的原因。为此，两国政府还提供必不可少的便利支持，允许与关键的政府部门和代表处、地方政府、研究机构、商界领袖和民间代表等进行广泛和必要的咨询。

创建一个升级版的政策框架是一项复杂的工程。它意味着要在每个国家建立一套新的国家能力。这最好是基于以往取得的经验和成就之上。

20世纪80年代，中澳这两个不同政治社会制度和不同发展阶段的经济体建立起了所称的"模范关系"。这是两国首次联合做出重大努力来建立两国关系框架。这一努力应得以继续，以引领两国关系迈向更高水平。

澳大利亚接纳中国的改革开放，并视其为区域繁荣和稳定的关键因素。中国愿意与澳大利亚建立伙伴关系，视其为对外开放政策的重要部分，并视澳大利亚为中国开放型经济战略中的关键角色。这一开创性的伙伴关系开启了中澳之间基于市场规则的资源贸易、双向投资和区域合作进程，也为中国积极参与APEC和加入WTO作出了贡献。

自此中澳两国继续携手并进，通过APEC、东盟加（ASEAN+）框架和东亚峰会来加强区域间经济合作，以便建立政治互信和地区安全的框架来保障经济繁荣。

2014年中澳建立了全面战略伙伴关系，通过年度领导人会晤、战略经济对话、外交安全对话等机制确保对两国双边关系的高度重视。中澳两国也达成了中澳自贸协定（ChAFTA），它极大地推动双边贸易自由化、更广泛的投资便利化和服务业市场开放。事实上，中澳自贸协定具有促进未来十年两国商业关系转型关键引擎的潜力。

但这些机制所提供的各种机会远未完全实现。在未来议程中，两国必须对双边战略目标进行综合考量。这需要设计一个全新的框架，促使双方在改革和政策制定方面的积极合作制度化。

中国正在建立与自己在国际经济体系中的地位相称的区域性和全球性架构。中国提议的亚洲基础设施投资银行和"一带一路"倡议代表了中国正在将自身利益与其伙伴国利益相融合，加大基础设施投资支持力度，促进区域内和区域间的互联互通。

澳大利亚与中国密切合作，在IMF和其他国际经济组织中支持中国的这些倡议。澳大利亚是亚洲基础设施投资银行的创始成员国，而且通过开发北澳的项目方式参加"一带一路"倡议。在G20框架下，两国密切合作，为推动全球增长和多边贸易制度改革分享议程。

提升两国关系的新视角:全新的政策框架和规划要点

中澳两国如何处理好日益复杂的双边关系？两国关系的复杂性在于：中国目前已是亚洲最大的经济体、世界第二大经济体，并且政治自信日益增强，但与世界第一大经济体美国之间有着盘根错节的关系。

中国应把与澳大利亚的密切合作视为其新一轮改革开放战略中不可分割的一部分。两国在服务业开放、金融体制改革、资本账户开放等领域的合作将有助于中国实现其增长目标。作为以服务为主的发达经济体，澳大利亚可以成为中国改革开放的天然伙伴和试验温床。

本报告阐述了如何处理好日益复杂的中澳关系这一议题的关键理念和规划。以下结论是为两国合作的远景议程而设计，在未来十年里，需要两国政府及其他利益相关者深思细酌。

本报告建议，为了更好地把握发展机遇和抵御增长风险，中澳两国政府应把双边关系提升到与时俱进的全面战略伙伴关系这一特殊高度。两国最高层领导人应该优先明确提升两国关系的重点。

具体如下：

- 本报告建议的"与时俱进的全面战略伙伴关系"应建立在中澳自贸协定和已有年度领导人会晤以及平行部长级对话基础之上，通过建立联合政策工作组以支持这一工作，以及由此产生的的政策倡议，并推进实施正在进行的政策和改革措施：例如在中澳自贸协定下开展双边投资协定谈判、开放服务市场准入及其他议题（见下）。

- 根据需要，联合政策工作组可以和州/省政府、商界、研究机构、社会团体一起工作，就两国关心的具体的贸易、投资、金融、区域和全球改革议程等问题提出倡议。

  o 这些工作组可以协助落实中澳自贸协定所做的有关投资自由化和服务市场准入方面的双边承诺。

  o 海洋经济是两国间极具合作潜力的一个领域，双方都是海洋大国，在海运路线和其他许多海洋议题上有着共同的利益。两国应为促进在海洋经济方面的对话与合作设立一个工作组。

- 两国政府应致力于在未来十年汲取各自双边关系的经验，并把中澳新型伙伴关系纳入一个全面、友好、合作的双边条约里。

  o 这一条约将规定合作原则与做法，包括：定期政府高层对话；设定本报告建议的两国关系管理原则；推动经济、外交、军事等部门官方交流和技术合作项目制度化；加强中澳各自中央-地方政府或联邦-州政府之间的接触；在前瞻性政策议程中提供全面的双边战略目标设定；包含中澳自贸协定安排中的各项协议、机制和改革措施；强化日益改善的教育、文化和人员交流方面的合作。

- 两国应培育全新的高层次接触所必需的能力，为此可通过条约协议建立起一个全新的资源充沛的中澳委员会，该委员会以法定实体的形式存在，独立于两国政府之外。

  o 该委员会将提升两国在政策、研究、科学、技术、教育，文化和人员交流等方面的层次和幅度。澳大利亚方面与此最相似的经验是二战后澳大利亚和美国以条约协议的形式建立起的澳-美富布赖特委员会。

- 在中澳自贸协定的框架和条款范围内，中澳两国应该着手开展全面的投资协定谈判。该协定应包括"负面清单"管理、赋予外国投资者有效的国民待遇、尊重法律和规则、保证资源获取权和人员更频繁自由的流动。该投资协定应先于中欧、中美双边投资协定签署，并使其成为东亚区域投资协定的蓝本。中澳之间的双向投资将对构建中澳新型伙伴关系发挥关键的作用，包括从交易、投资到现在的伙伴关系中的各个环节所起的作用。

  o 但是如果中澳广大民众不能认识到外国投资带来的好处，以上的各种讨论都无法实现。在澳大利亚，这意味着要对中国投资者提供同等待遇，并重新审视对各地国有投资者的态度。在中国，这意味着建立起遵法守规的制度，让国内外所有投资者都能得到安全、可预期的投资保障。

- 本报告建议的重构中澳双边框架应与澳大利亚"国家创新和科学进程"战略以及中国"十三五"规划中的创新驱动战略保持一致。

  o 今后双边合作的机会应重点放在研发、集资、科技-教育-数学合作领域、研究成果商业化、技术孵化平台、数字经济、企业家和投资者交流等方面。

- 在区域全面经济伙伴关系（RCEP）的框架下，中澳两国应把建设高水平的贸易投资协定和亚太地区持续的经济合作放在首要的位置。

- 中澳两国在G20框架下的共同利益和在全球经济治理中的建设性参与应着重强调以下几个方面：中国在主要货币互持中扮演的角色，构建国际金融安全网以防范金融危机的蔓延，将改革与经济增长结合起来，加大多边贸易体制改革力度等。

- 非常重要的是,中澳两国应在能源转型议题上推动与日本、韩国、印度、美国和其他区域伙伴开展高水平的区域对话。能源转型是应对气候变化和解决其他环境问题必不可缺的一环。在这一领域，建立区域合作机制将大有作为。中国正在寻找解决能源消耗增长和环境保护约束之间矛盾的良方，澳大利亚则是本区域主要的能源供应国，两国对此都有切身利益。这也是一个可与亚太国家开展合作的领域，并且能在政治领域取得较多收获。

如果以上建议得到采纳，中澳关系将迈上一个新的台阶。在彼此充分尊重各自既有关系的同时（如澳大利亚与美国的澳新美关系），中澳新型伙伴关系将成为区域乃至全球体系稳定和繁荣的重要力量。它还可以作为中澳国民接触一个快速变化世界的主要矢量之一。在双方政府、商界、研究机构和其他利益相关者悉心而富有想象力地培育下，中澳两国更加深化的伙伴关系将成为世界双边关系中最具战略重要性和最富成效的双边关系之一。

CHAPTER 1
Strategic importance of the relationship

KEY MESSAGES

There is no economic or geopolitical future for China, Australia or the world that would not be improved by China's sustained and balanced economic growth. And yet the future direction of Chinese growth will be very different from that over the past four decades. The forces of change that have already unleashed a wave of consumption growth are affecting the relationship with Australia profoundly. Economic reform and liberalisation can intensify the ongoing change in the structure of the Chinese economy and, while these changes imply a less heavy reliance in Australia on the resource sector for economic growth, there are opportunities for growth that will require substantial repositioning of policy and commercial strategies by both countries and the development of a still closer relationship between the two countries.

The structural transformation of the Chinese economy as it grows toward high-income status will be fuelled by domestic reforms that make the allocation of resources more efficient and by the opening of the capital account, a step that should be undertaken incrementally and with due caution. China will reorient its economy towards domestic consumption. Australia's challenge, meanwhile, is to counteract the fall in real incomes that has resulted from the fall in commodity prices as Chinese demand slows, and to invest in filling the infrastructure gaps that will act as a brake on productivity and income growth if left unaddressed.

The recent history of the growing ties between the two countries shows that the determined pursuit of a deeper relationship yields tangible benefits. The institutions and policy frameworks that have emerged to provide structure for the relationship in recent years provide a strong starting point for the next phase of the Australia–China partnership.

Both countries have invested heavily in their partnership. The path-breaking record of the Australia–China partnership in opening the resource trade, foreign investment, regional cooperation initiatives and China's accession to the WTO provides a legacy on which to build new international standards into their bilateral trade, investment and all other dealings. Their high-level Comprehensive Strategic Partnership and ChAFTA are major institutional assets (embodying mutual trust and practical commitment) that can be deployed to manage change over the decades ahead. Still closer engagement and institutional arrangements are needed to capitalise on the opportunities that these foundations present.

ChAFTA is a blueprint for initial change, not an end-point in the bilateral relationship. A joint work plan for achieving change will not only define progress in the bilateral trade, investment and commercial relationship over the coming decade; it will also provide the foundation for Australia and China pushing liberalisation and reform in the Asian region and setting out the pathway towards reform and strengthening of the global trade and economic systems. Precedent exists in institutional frameworks such as the 1976 Basic Treaty of Friendship and Cooperation between Australia and Japan for a comprehensive bilateral treaty to provide an overall guiding structure for the Australia–China relationship as it matures.

The scale and significance of developments that are now taking place — especially in China through its transformation towards a high-income economy — recommend deeper bilateral institutional arrangements between Australia and China. These would build on existing bilateral frameworks with bold new bi-national initiatives, including in the areas of investment, tourism, people movement, science, and educational exchanges. They will need to capture opportunities in the relationship, and manage the inevitable risks and processes that are a consequence of large-scale change.

Both countries should work together to strengthen the established regional economic cooperation arrangements and to secure the framework of political confidence and security within which economic prosperity can be attained. But there are gaps in regional policy strategies that Australia and China must now work more actively with regional partners to fill. The Australia–China relationship is anchored in global institutional and political arrangements. Australia has a direct and important stake, in partnership with China, in working to ensure China's success in the assumption of its role of shared leadership in global economic affairs.

In the coming decade, Australia's relationship with China will be a top policy priority. Trade with China accounts for almost a quarter of Australia's overall trade, with China absorbing almost a third of Australia's total merchandise exports (DFAT 2016e). China is the fifth-largest source of foreign direct investment into Australia and for many Australian businesses China represents an enormous growth market (ABS 2016f). While Australia is China's seventh-largest source of imports, Australia is also a major and reliable source of strategic industrial raw materials and high-quality inputs, from iron ore to education, which China needs to fuel its industrialisation and urbanisation. The relationship between Australia and China is integral to their other important international relationships.

With remarkable success in the achievement of higher incomes and wages in China, the pace of growth is slowing as ready supplies of low cost labour are exhausted. The shift in China from export- and investment-led growth to growth based on domestic demand, and especially domestic consumption, has contributed to the decline of the Australian resources boom.

As China's growth model and focus shifts and Australia seeks to define a prosperous economic future less reliant on its resource base, big changes are bound to occur in the relationship. Some big changes have already taken place and new opportunities are emerging for both countries. The transformation towards productivity and innovation-led growth, financial market reform and capital account openness will propel China's deeper integration into the global economy. A richer China with a more open services industry will gain new standing among the major economies of the world. Australia's shift to more human capital-driven growth, together with the changes in China, provide the opportunity to forge new complementarities between the two countries, profoundly reshaping their bilateral relationship over the decade ahead.

As production in some of China's heavy, resource and energy-intensive industries is peaking, the price of Australia's exports of commodities such as iron ore and coal has fallen. As economic rebalancing towards consumption and service sector-led growth continues, the share of heavy industry in the Chinese economy will inevitably decline. Yet Chinese demand for resources and energy will remain large as urbanisation continues in China and Australia's share in China's resource imports, which has risen as prices have fallen, is likely to stay high. As one of the world's leading and most competitive suppliers of a range of industrial inputs, Australia will remain a major anchor in China's external resource security. Increasingly, however, the trade relationship will diversify beyond commodities into a wider range of goods and services. The two countries' investment and financial integration will become deeper and more sophisticated. Australia can aim to become a major supplier of knowledge, skills and products supporting China's next stage of development, which involves an emphasis on high value-added industries, innovation and clean production processes. Industrial restructuring and upgrading in China will see China's machinery and equipment exports become more important to Australia and will diversify Chinese investment into tourism, finance and infrastructure.

Australia and China have played a key role in economic cooperation in Asia and the Pacific, regions which include economies that are the fastest-growing and most dynamic centres of global economic activity. Through regional and multilateral forums, both countries have worked closely to promote development, stability and stronger regional cooperation. They have a deep intersection of interest in strengthening established regional arrangements, such as APEC, the ASEAN Plus frameworks and the East Asia Summit, and in global institutions, especially the G20. They also have a shared interest in securing the framework of political confidence and security within which economic prosperity can be attained.

The growth of China's importance in the world economy has occurred very rapidly and has brought with it new capacity, responsibilities, expectations and challenges in managing its interdependence with the rest of the world.

The Chinese economy accounted for less than 3 per cent of global GDP in 1980 (OECD 2013a). It is now the second-largest economy in the world in nominal terms, accounting for 13 per cent of global GDP in current US dollars, and its GDP is larger than that of the United States in real purchasing power parity terms (World Bank 2016). China became the single largest contributor to global growth in 2007 and has maintained that position ever since (Yueh 2015). China is the world's largest goods trader and is also the world's second-largest importer of goods and services, making it a major element in global demand for traded goods and services (Austrade 2015a; World Bank 2016).

Until recently, China was mainly a rule-taker in the global economic system. Since the late 1970s it has benefited enormously from opening its economy and participating in the post-Bretton Woods system. China's role in global economic governance remained passive, constrained by the small size and low capacity of its economy. Now China is growing out of this stage and is therefore becoming more active in the provision of global public goods. The transition to joining the ranks of global rule-makers is not automatic or easy for either China or the global system. But China is now actively participating in global governance and actively assuming its international responsibilities and duties. An important opportunity is China's chairing of the G20 in 2016.

Australia has a direct stake in working, in partnership with China, to ensure China's success in the assumption of its role of shared leadership in global economic affairs. There is special value in the development of this partnership because of Australia's unique role in the region as well as its closeness to the United States. The value of the partnership includes the chance of working with China in the development of its contribution to the provision of international public goods, both through established international institutions such as the IMF, the WTO, the World Bank and new international institutions such as the AIIB. It also includes Australia's working together with the established and emerging powers to build new platforms to coordinate a range of global economic policies within the G20 and to manage the challenges to sustainable growth from climate change and other environmental issues.

This is a critical moment in a far-reaching global economic transition. Australia and China have a vital opportunity to define how they will shape the future course of their relationship in a deliberate way, establishing some common reference points to help manage it purposefully, as they have with some success in the past, rather than muddling through in the future.

Capturing the full benefit of the economic relationship will depend on how both the public and private sectors in Australia and China engage in and develop the relationship. Managing the risks and uncertainties that can impact on the economic relationship will be important. As a starting point, getting the most for both countries will require a functional understanding among policymakers, corporate leaders and the broader community of the changes that will shape China and Australia in the next 10 years. This Report can play a role in this. The understanding that has been built through this work can be embedded in institutional forms to help facilitate better management of the relationship. ChAFTA represents a major step in putting in place stronger institutional arrangements for the development of trade and investment links. But a relationship of the kind that will be required by the changes in both economies, their economic cooperation in the region and their partnership in global affairs in coming decades, demands substantial joint policy initiative and strengthened institutional frameworks (both government and private).

In 1976, Australia signed a Basic Treaty of Friendship and Cooperation with Japan, an agreement which set out the principles underpinning their bilateral relationship, defined key areas of cooperation, and pledged to enshrine and preserve the principle of non-discrimination in economic relations. Since its signing, the Treaty, and the mutual confidence that it gave both Japan and Australia, has provided the framework within which closer ties have forged. The opportunity for evolving a similar framework to underpin the Australia–China relationship should not be passed up. ChAFTA can provide the beginnings for such a framework.

Economic transformation in China and Australia

China

The Chinese economy is undergoing a major transformation after nearly 40 years of high-speed economic growth. China's rapid economic rise has been fuelled by market-oriented reforms and economic liberalisation that helped reduce the distortions in resource allocation in the economy. The reform was more thorough in the goods market than in factor markets for land, labour, capital and energy, which remained under tighter state control. This growth model encouraged investment in manufacturing capacity and infrastructure.

With real GDP growth at around 10 per cent per annum from the 1980s, manufacturing output is now larger than that in any other economy in the world. China accounted for a quarter of world manufacturing output by 2015, up from less than 3 per cent in 1990. Chinese consumption has dominated the global markets for industrial raw materials (World Bank 2016). The expansion of the iron and steel industry, for example, which produced over 800 million tons of crude steel in 2015, or more than six times as much as it did in 2000, lifted the Chinese share in world iron ore consumption from 14 per cent in 2000 to an estimated 65 per cent in 2015 (Figure 1.1). This surge in Chinese demand drove a more than five-fold rise of prices in the years from 2000–2008 in the scramble for additional supplies of iron ore (RBA 2012).

Australia's established competitiveness in international resource and energy markets, relative geographic proximity and close engagement since China's economic opening in the 1970s, made Australia a natural and complementary partner in China's trade and industrial transformation. Australia has been an anchor in Northeast Asian resource security and a pioneer in the export of high quality resources to China. Australia became China's principal supplier of imported iron ore, coal and a range of other industrial raw materials over these years. In 2015, Australia supplied 64 per cent of China's imported iron ore, for example, compared with the 43 per cent it supplied in 2010 (Ng 2016). The relationship with China saw massive investment in the Australian resource sector in the first decade of the 21st century, and strong growth in Australia throughout the global financial crisis when growth in other industrial economies languished.

While China's investment-led growth delivered astonishing outcomes, it also led to structural imbalances that increasingly threatened sustainable growth and stability.

China's reforms now aim to remove those distortions, especially in the financial market, and nurture consumption- and service-led growth. The Chinese government is also implementing measures to close down capacity in heavy industries, such as iron and steel, that does not embody best-practice production technology or environmental protection. This entails substantial costs of adjustment and the need to manage economic as well as social dislocation. The focus of growth is now on the 'new economy'. The change in gear from double-digit to single-digit growth is expected to put the economy on a more sustainable, but still relatively high, long-term growth trajectory over the coming decade.

Figure 1.1: Chinese and global steel production

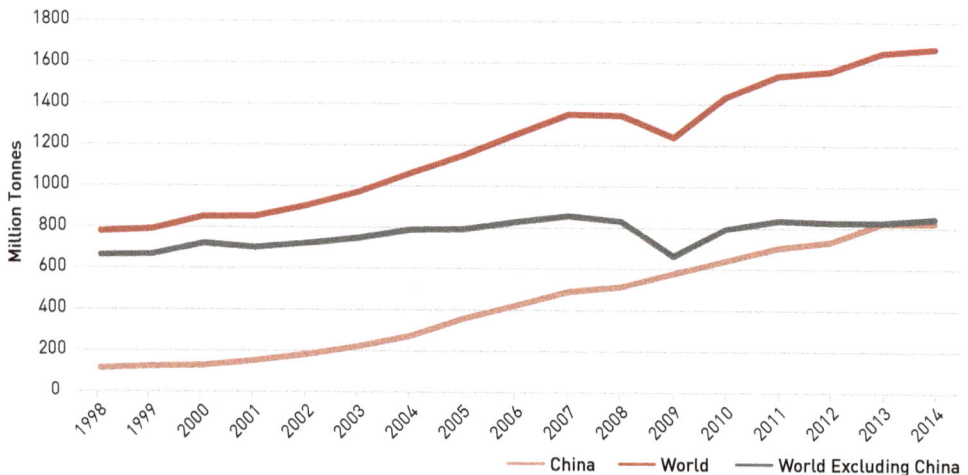

Source: World Steel Association 2015.

Among the national economic policy commitments that are likely to have the most profound effect on China's relations with Australia and other countries is the Chinese government's 13th Five Year Plan commitment to build an open economic system, deepen financial system reform, liberalise financial markets and accelerate the realisation of Chinese capital account convertibility.

Capital account liberalisation is essential to making China's renminbi a truly global currency and increasing China's role in international finance. Inclusion of the renminbi in the IMF's Special Drawing Rights basket is a first step in this process. For the renminbi to become a truly international currency, however, China needs to have an open capital account. But the significance of capital account liberalisation is much more wide-ranging than renminbi internationalisation.

Financial reform and capital account liberalisation are central to rebalancing the Chinese economy and fostering innovation and productivity growth. Market reforms and market-determined interest rates and exchange rates will correct the misallocation of capital that has until now favoured particular regions, state-owned enterprises and the state banking sector, and crowded out financing and investment from the more dynamic private sector. Healthy and well-managed financial institutions are at the heart of financial and economic stability. These changes will help China to move through the so-called 'middle-income trap' and to become a high-income society. Capital account liberalisation could also assist with geopolitical stability in the region through greater economic and financial integration.

The scale of China's cross-border trade and investment payments and the importance of using market mechanisms (in particular a fully flexible exchange rate and a robust and more efficient financial market) to manage the interaction between the domestic and international economies effectively require the move to an open capital account.

Liberalising China's capital account is an enormous challenge and it will take time. The nervousness in international markets about Chinese stock market volatilities and the move to a new foreign exchange rate regime with more flexibility against a currency basket over the past year is a harbinger of the difficulties in managing this policy change. The overriding lesson of financial history around the world is that transitions are never easy or smooth. This has been no less true in China than it has been in other economies that are in the process of profound transformation. There has to be policy trial and error, and there will inevitably be some missteps, but all countries have an interest in ensuring that China's reforms succeed.

The process of capital account liberalisation needs to be incremental, built on robust institutions and markets, and carefully staged and timed to avoid potentially substantial financial and foreign exchange risks. This is not just a technical economic challenge. Integration of China into international capital markets requires China to have a much more open, transparent and predictable set of institutional arrangements to build international confidence in dealing in Chinese financial assets, and this will push at the envelope of political reform.

The trajectory of growth is slowing in this transition. Manufacturing and export growth is slowing. While China will remain a big exporter, export growth is likely to slow as the structure of exports is upgraded. The massive urbanisation that has already taken place in China will continue as the rate of urbanisation — now at 56 per cent of the population — still lags behind that in many developing economies with similar income levels, let alone that in advanced economies (CCTV 2016). This requires continuing, albeit slower, expansion of infrastructure investment. New investment will also be driven by the need for clean energy and environmental protection.

Higher Chinese wages as the labour market has tightened, as well as the removal of some distortions that favoured investment rather than consumption, have meant that growth is increasingly driven by consumer demand. This trend has been underway for some time, with consumption now overtaking investment as the main growth driver (Prasad 2015). Services already account for over 50 per cent of national output, while manufacturing has fallen towards 30 per cent (Figure 1.2).

The constraints on labour mobility, and inter-provincial fiscal and income disparities, continue to bifurcate the geographic pattern of Chinese economic development, meaning that inner provinces have lower incomes and lower rates of urban development. If economic constraints with a negative geographical impact were relaxed, these inner provinces could become a source of strong potential future growth. The timing of policy and institutional reforms that reduce these distortions will affect the impact of future growth on China's external economic relations, including with Australia.

China's 'new normal' growth path — with its structurally declining but still relatively high growth rate, partially tightening labour market, shift to consumption-led growth, and steady shift to services away from manufacturing — will fundamentally change China's interaction with the international economy.

There will continue to be growth opportunities in the Chinese market over the next decade as new business opportunities emerge. China's growth will likely remain at more than twice the global average growth rate. Despite moderating rates of growth, China will continue to make a sizeable contribution to global growth, as it will be growing off a much larger base than a few years ago. Seven per cent growth in China now is equivalent to an addition to income of 10 per cent just five years ago. China's growth rate was 6.9 per cent in 2015, much lower compared to growth of 10.6 per cent in 2010, but in both years China still added RMB3.8 trillion to global GDP (in constant 2010 RMB). Since 2008, China's contribution to global GDP each year has been equivalent to an economy around the size of Mexico or three-quarters the size of Australia.

Figure 1.2: Sectoral value added as a percentage of Chinese GDP

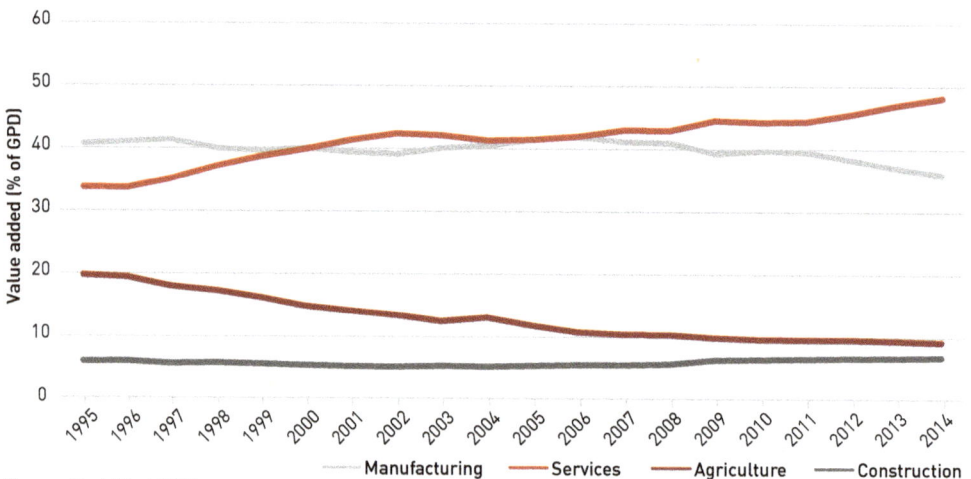

Source: World Bank 2016.

As Figure 1.3 suggests, the IMF expects that China will continue to add more each year to global GDP over the coming decade (in US dollars). China is likely to remain the biggest contributor to global GDP growth for the next five years, adding more to global output than the United States, or more than India and all of the other Asian economies put together.

The huge scale of China's economy today, nonetheless, needs to be understood in the context of its ambitions for growth in the future. China's per capita income is still not high, being only 24 per cent of that of the United States or 34 per cent of the OECD average (OECD 2014a). Chinese policymakers have to manage the transition to higher incomes and keep closing this gap in the coming decades.

Australia

China's remarkable expansion through the first decade of the century brought strong growth in Australia's mining sector. Growth in Western Australia approached growth rates in China during some of these years. Australian income growth and household living standards benefited from the terms-of-trade-induced strength of the Australian dollar as import prices fell. Half the rise in Australian incomes during the mining boom resulted from the boost to Australia's terms of trade (Downes et al 2014). It was not only the Australian mining sector that benefited from Chinese growth: Australia's education exports and tourism services grew strongly, accompanied by sharp rises in China's share of these markets (Austrade 2015b). China's share of Australian exports grew strongly and is higher than that of other major export customers (Figure 1.4). While the economy as a whole unambiguously benefited from the mining boom, some sectors, such as trade-exposed manufacturers, saw demand for their products fall because of Australia's elevated exchange rate. As dramatic as they were, these changes were part of a long-term structural adjustment in the Australian economy that was already well underway and would have substantially occurred even without the mining boom.

Figure 1.3: China's GDP growth (RHS) and its contribution to global output (LHS), 1990–2020

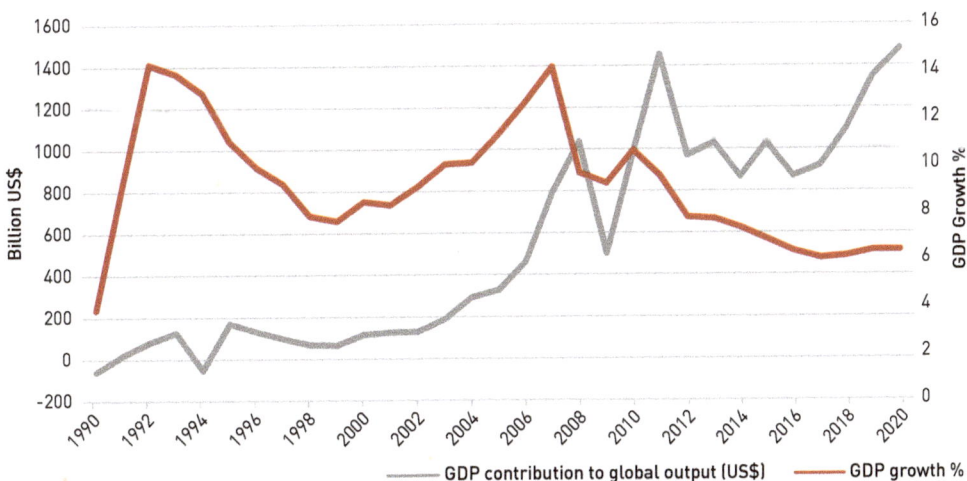

Source: IMF 2015.

Figure 1.4: Exports to China as a share of total exports, Australia and other major exporters

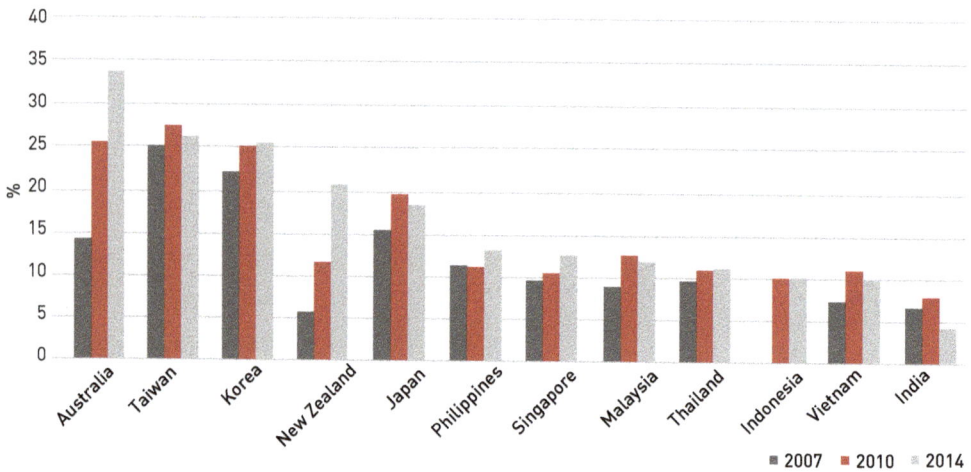

Source: Gruenwald, Conti and Rana 2016; UNCTAD 2015.

Slower growth in Chinese demand for, and increased global supplies of, industrial raw materials have sent iron ore and other commodity prices dramatically lower. The drop in prices has caused the share of commodities in China's imports to contract. But Australia has increased its share in China's imports of industrial raw materials (although import values have dropped sharply) because Australia continues to be one of the world's most competitive suppliers of commodities like iron ore. New energy projects, in the gas and uranium sector, will also come on stream in the near future. But growth in resource exports to China is unlikely to return to the rate seen during the 2000s, and prices are likely to remain subdued.

As in past commodity cycles, prices have fallen (along with the terms of trade) as new mines have come online in Australia and around the world, dragging Australian real incomes down at the same time. This trend is likely to continue, although there is likely to be volatility around this trend. Australia will overcome this drag on income growth only through its own economic transformation and through lifting productivity across the whole economy.

Successful adjustment and sustained growth over the coming decade will require a shift in Australia's economic structure back to a more normal trajectory: away from an abnormal expansion of the resource sector (even if energy demand continues to grow) towards resumption of growth in the share of services, high-end manufacturing and high value-added agricultural production. This structural change, as well as Australia's strong population growth through migration, will need large-scale renovation of urban infrastructure, investment in inter-urban transport and communications (because of growing urban congestion and national connectivity deficiencies), new infrastructure investment and integrated land use planning in the north of the country (because of the location of new agricultural and development opportunities there), and investment in innovation, research and education.

These changes, through a relatively flexible labour market and responsive capital market, are already taking place, but major challenges remain in undertaking tough reforms that make the economy more flexible and help to restructure and upgrade industry. Moreover, the markets in which these opportunities lie for Australia are fiercely contested internationally and Australia does not have the same established advantage as it has in natural resources. Unless

Australia's private and public sector investment becomes smarter, and unless Australia can mobilise capital at home and from abroad to invest more efficiently in infrastructure, it is unlikely to achieve the 3 per cent GDP growth that it has commonly enjoyed over the past few decades. It will not be an easy task — total productivity growth has been stagnant for some years — and while there are signs of improvement, it needs to improve further.

How effectively these changes are managed will shape the future of the Australia–China economic relationship.

Strategic partnership for change

In managing the change anticipated over the coming decade, both the public and private sectors can draw upon substantial assets that already exist in the established bilateral relationship. The Australia–China relationship is distinguished by a history of political commitment at the highest levels, since diplomatic recognition, to a partnership that has embraced China's openness, its reform and its economic rise. Development of the relationship has also been facilitated by Australia's open economy, strong institutions and rich mineral endowment, Chinese perceptions of Australia's business-friendly environment, as well as Australia's good standing with other countries. Though they have different political and social systems, both countries accept this difference and respect each other's achievements, including the remarkable elevation of living standards and improvement in social conditions through economic reforms and liberalisation that both countries have put in place over the past four decades.

The deep complementarity of the established economic relationship and the high political commitment to its development by both countries provide a secure foundation on which to build a new and dynamic partnership.

Australian and Chinese political leaders have invested heavily in the relationship and are now committed to its elevation as a strategic partnership through regular high-level leadership dialogues.

Maintaining the closeness in the relationship at the top leadership level is a priority for both governments. It is a signal of political trust and good intention in the partnership.

ChAFTA is in place — the most open and liberalising such arrangement that China has entered into with any developed economy and one which goes further in its partner country liberalisation than Australia's previous agreements.

What do the big changes in the structure of both economies mean for their bilateral relationship and its management over the coming decade?

As consumer incomes rise and preferences shift, the new patterns of Chinese consumption will drive higher growth in imports of recreational services (like tourism), educational services, health services and financial services. The consumption and import of high value foodstuffs, in which Australia has a strong comparative advantage, are expected to grow rapidly over the next few decades. For example, the real value of beef consumption in China is projected to rise 236 per cent between 2009 and 2050 (ABARES 2014). ChAFTA opens the door wider to grow the trade in markets for high value goods and services. ChAFTA offers the prospect of significant gains in Australia's share in markets for imports across the board, from dairy products and health products to education and tourism (see Chapter 3).

ChAFTA opens the door to new opportunities in the services trade, in investment, in tourism and in the commodity trade; but there are many obstacles to realising these opportunities that still need to be overcome. The obstacles have to do with how commercial parties relate to regulatory institutions beyond national borders. They also have to do with building deeper private bilateral business networks and associations to facilitate business between the two countries. There is a review process built into ChAFTA — in this sense, ChAFTA is a living agreement. Yet the nature of the arrangement embedded in the agreement is that it is reactive to specific problem solving — rather than strategic in its purpose, seeking opportunities through the agreement and beyond (see Chapters 4, 5 and 6).

As China's industrial upgrading gathers pace, Australia's imports from China will be increasingly dominated by higher-value appliances, equipment and machinery. Many of China's exports, of course, involve substantial value-add from other countries in the region, including Japan, South Korea and the United States. A large proportion of Japanese brand imports, from example, now arrive in Australia via China.

China's commitment to freeing up investment abroad in the past decade (the 'going out' strategy) saw Australia emerge as a leading destination for Chinese outbound direct investment. The reforms that are now being put in place in the financial market have already seen Chinese banks and non-financial enterprises lift investment in Australian assets. In the coming decade, these reforms and wider liberalisation of the capital account could fundamentally change the structure of economic relations between the two countries.

Financial market reform and capital account liberalisation will also fundamentally change China's standing and role in the global economy — and its influence and importance in the Australian economy. It will increase the size and range of Chinese assets held by Australian institutions and corporations, as well as the portfolio of Australian assets held by Chinese institutions and enterprises. It will see China's currency used more extensively in international transactions and borrowing. Chinese households and institutions, not only enterprises, will increase the portfolio of assets they hold in Australia and elsewhere.

Arrangements that build confidence in undertaking foreign investment in each country are a priority. Despite the progress made in ChAFTA, there remains confusion about the treatment of Australian and Chinese investors under the other country's foreign investment regimes. Policies that enshrine no discrimination against the same class of foreign investment across foreign investment sources and entrench the national treatment principle need to be the anchors of each foreign investment regime. Mechanisms for direct collaboration in sharing information and data on investment and investor activities need to be put in place between the relevant agencies in each country.

The new phases of Chinese and Australian growth and their changed international circumstances require a new model of economic collaboration which encompasses an update and overhaul of the institutional arrangements that support Australia–China engagement.

An institutional framework that dynamically drives bilateral strategic engagement, promoting the new opportunities for trade and investment in the relationship through and beyond ChAFTA, will provide substance at the working level to the strategic partnership between the two countries at the top.

The task is to capitalise on and manage change. It will require energising and deepening the institutional arrangements that are already in place between Australia and China to:

build trust around common interests in economic and political relationships; manage the uncertainties that inevitably arise through change; and develop the up-close commercial and business engagement needed as the structure of the economic relationship shifts towards services and consumers.

This is a national task for each country. It is also a bi-national task that embraces new undertakings and agreements.

The framework of a new model for economic collaboration would include joint mechanisms and working groups that build upon established partnerships in government such as the Comprehensive Strategic Partnership, the Strategic Economic Dialogue and the Joint Ministerial Economic Commission at the leader and ministerial levels, as well as official agency partnerships such as that between the Australian Treasury and China's National Development and Reform Commission (NDRC) and the ties that are growing between the Reserve Bank of Australia (RBA) and the People's Bank of China (PBoC). These partnerships should draw upon business and outside expertise, as required, to:

- advise in the development of the Comprehensive Strategic Partnership dialogues;
- support joint taskforce or working group activity on issues flowing from the dialogues or other bilateral initiatives;
- work with state and provincial authorities in developing initiatives in the relationship;
- encourage programs of research within and beyond government on all aspects of the relationship;
- engage with the business sectors in both countries in undertaking its work;
- promote joint training and the development of long-term working associations in key areas among the officials of both countries; and
- reflect upon community interests and concerns.

This framework would also include a bi-national initiative to establish an Australia-China (Ao–Zhong) Commission for boosting high-level research, scientific, political and community exchanges to build the capacities in both countries for comprehending and realising the opportunities in what will become an increasingly up-close relationship. This bi-national government effort will be partnered by business, government departments, states and provinces, as it is in a similar though less comprehensive way than envisaged here by the Australian–American Fulbright Commission.

These arrangements will underpin the Australia–China Strategic Partnership for Change. The initiatives and standards that both countries develop pragmatically within that framework should also be consistent with their international and regional ambitions and responsibilities.

This framework will take time to put in place, but this process can begin immediately.

It will require institutional innovation in building the capacity for engagement step-by-step in each bureaucracy, through training and exchange. But this Report demonstrates the will and the incentive to make it work, in the interests of both countries. It will require partnership with the business, academic and think tank sectors. The framework must be guided by enunciation of the understandings and principles identified in this Report to which both partners aspire in the conduct of their relationship. The collaboration established between the China Center for

International Economic Exchanges (CCIEE) and the East Asian Bureau of Economic Research (EABER) and their government and non-government partners in both countries through this Report provides a natural and useful foundation for continuing this initiative.

Strengthening the framework for national government institutions to develop the relationship will be ineffective if it is not complemented by ongoing initiatives at the state and provincial level, and by building capacities through educational and research institutions and across the community. Much of the interaction between Chinese and Australian business and governments in each country takes place at the local level. Much of the community engagement takes place through state and provincial level programs and through sister-city relationships and educational exchanges delivered at the grassroots level. The people-to-people associations established through these programs are frequently the foundations of business and community partnerships that drive initiative and the development of the relationship. The sharp growth in tourism between the two countries is full of potential to strengthen people-to-people links, understanding and appreciation of each other's culture, circumstance and country.

There is a range of models of successful engagement across levels of government and across the community — through the organisation of state and provincial level programs, business associations, youth and professional dialogues, academic institutions and programs, cultural and artistic communities, and community and school-level exchanges. These are targets for development and promotion through the national and bi-national initiatives headlined above (see Chapters 3, 5 and 6).

Opportunities and risks

A critical element in the success of the Australia–China relationship over the coming decades will be the understanding of, and managing the uncertainties from, the huge changes taking place in both economies. These are changes that will transform both societies — with the national ambition in China to be on the way to living standards equivalent to some advanced countries by the end of this period — although their course is impossible to predict exactly. In 2025, China's economy will be much bigger than it is today and its institutions will continue to evolve from what they are today. Australia will also have changed significantly. A premise in the conduct of the relationship is commitment to shared ambitions for national change and to engage bilaterally in regional and global affairs in a way that manages effectively the adverse consequences of unforeseen or unwelcome change that will inevitably occur from time to time. The principles and common understandings outlined in this Report, and the arrangements and institutions that it recommends, are designed to manage both proactive engagement and unexpected shocks. The management of adverse change becomes easier when both countries are closely engaged and have the best access to information and analysis that is possible through such arrangements.

The opportunities in the relationship with an economy the size of China's are huge for many of Australia's biggest corporations, including an increasing number of firms and enterprises that were not touched by China's earlier growth phase. Nonetheless, they have to manage the risks of cyclical and structural change in the Chinese economy, as they do in other markets. Chinese policymakers used to worry about over-dependence on Australian suppliers of iron ore in the up-phase of the commodity boom, although those anxieties have subsided in its down-phase. Insurance against risk from high levels of resource trade dependence, of course, is provided by deep and intensely competitive international markets for these commodities (including energy). Chinese enterprises that undertake large-scale investment in Australia, especially when such investment is new or unfamiliar, inevitably face the same risks that other large-scale investors, Australian or foreign, have to face in the Australian or other markets. These risks are a normal part of any commercial relationship.

There are also risks associated with policy and institutional uncertainties. In economic and political systems that are evolving as rapidly as those in China, these risks are an important part of commercial calculation. In Australia, even though there are robust market and legal institutions, there are residual risks that relate to political, policy and institutional uncertainty, although most of them are legally contestable by foreign as well as national entities. China's accession to the WTO as well as its ongoing massive economic and legal reform serves to ameliorate these risks in China. An important objective in the development of the relationship, nonetheless, is to reduce governance-related uncertainties for enterprises and persons doing business in the other country. A goal in the relationship over the longer term should be to embed these protections in a comprehensive agreement or basic treaty between the two countries.

There is strong precedent for such a treaty framework. The Basic Treaty of Friendship and Cooperation between Australia and Japan, signed in 1976, committed both countries to cooperate on issues of mutual concern. Following decades of popular unease and political caution in the Australia–Japan relationship, this Treaty had a large and analytically measurable impact on growing the overall bilateral economic relationship even after the resources phase of bilateral exchange began levelling off (Drysdale 2006). It improved what were then politically controversial investment flows and led to consequent improvements in people movement, services trade and regional cooperation. The Australia–Japan Report that led to and was associated with the conclusion of the Treaty changed the institutional structures though which both countries engaged with each other, and laid a framework of collaboration on economic issues that led to the formation of APEC. Applying a similar approach to the Australia–China relationship could yield similar economic and political benefits.

The macroeconomic risks of volatility in China's larger economy can be managed within the macroeconomic and flexible exchange rate policies that cushion the domestic impact in Australia of such international economic shocks. Focusing on building stronger balance sheets of financial institutions and companies, both state-owned and private, is a foundation for crisis prevention and crisis resolution.

Systemic failures such as financial market crisis, should they occur in China as they did in the United States during the global financial crisis, will need to be managed through domestic and international mechanisms that provide lines of credit and regulatory disciplines to ameliorate or avoid them. The adequacy of these mechanisms is discussed in Chapter 8. Active partnership with China in regional and global economic cooperation, and in diplomacy to secure dynamic political stability in Asia and the Pacific, are key instruments for handling these risks.

Partners in regional and global affairs

More than on any other factor, economic and political stability in the 21st century will depend on how global governance adapts to the rise of China and other emerging economies, and to the role they play in shaping the architecture of global governance in the future. Australia and

China have a deep strategic interest in ensuring this international transition takes place in a manner that is constructive and benefits China, regional economies including Australia, and the world at large.

Strong, inclusive, rules-based and market-promoting global institutions are important to economic prosperity in both Australia and China. Both countries have benefited greatly from global institutions that were put in place at the end of World War II. The United Nations framework and the Bretton Woods-inspired economic institutions continue to serve as the foundations of global governance and have provided a framework for global stability and economic prosperity.

The system of global governance that these institutions underpin is not static. It must continue to evolve so as to comprehend new issues and stakeholders. The rapid change in the structure of the world economy and depth of global integration that has been delivered by economic openness and the communications and transportation revolution, has created enormous pressure to change and strengthen institutions for global governance. The global financial crisis saw the G20 Summit emerge as the preeminent forum for guiding this change.

No country alone can dictate this change: it must be forged through a consensus among all the countries that are affected and feel the need for change. But there are some areas in which collaboration between China, Australia and their partners in global institution-building will be of special importance in the coming decades.

Global governance is in part the result of what large economies do between themselves to manage their interaction with other economies and polities, as well as being the result of cooperative or collective action among the economic powers, large or small. In many ways China's own choices in international economic policy strategy now exert influence on the shape of global economic governance alongside the actions and initiatives China takes directly in collaboration with other countries through international forums and institutions. The relationship between Australia and China will thus be shaped by China's own economic policy strategies alongside the commitments that are made by both countries in global and regional settings. Australia and China have in the past, and should seek even more actively in the future, to be strategic partners in both theatres. There is no more obvious example of this in the past than China's choice to seek accession to the WTO and conform to its multilateral obligations. Bilateral political initiatives opened up trade with China before WTO accession. But participation in the WTO, not narrowly bilateral arrangements, is the cornerstone of the large and confident trade relationships that Australia and other countries have with China today. This system is under some challenge and both countries have a profound economic and political interest in working together and with partners to ensure that preferential regional and bilateral arrangements do not corrode the multilateral framework that is anchored in the WTO.

China's economic integration into the East Asian and global economy has occurred within a global framework that promotes free trade and investment. Australia has prospered under the same framework. Cooperation in the Asia Pacific region has been significantly directed to reinforcing global goals and objectives, such as when APEC was founded, to lend weight to trade liberalisation in the interests of Asia's emerging economies and agricultural exporters such as Australia. Regional cooperation in Asia and the Pacific fostered market-led integration. Asian economic cooperation has been inclusive, has avoided discriminatory arrangements that weaken the global system and has led regional political cooperation.

Figure 1.5: Asia's weight in the global economy

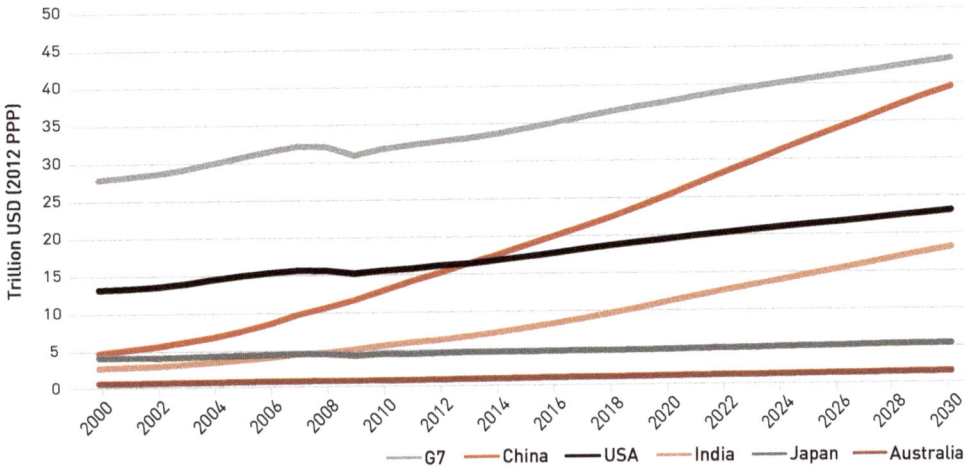

Source: Hubbard and Sharma 2016.

With the huge change that has taken place, and that will take place over the coming decade, in the structure of regional and global economic power (Figure 1.5), there is a need to rethink the role of regional cooperation as a pillar that supports an inclusive global economic system and manages new economic and political challenges.

APEC and the ASEAN Plus regional arrangements provide the foundational framework for regional cooperation. These arrangements and their evolution have been consensus-driven. They are characterised by inclusiveness, in terms of the global dimension of their agendas and their routine openness to dialogues with others. These principles are an enduring foundation for regional cooperation.

With the global processes of trade reform stalled and proliferation of preferential bilateral and regional FTAs, an immediate priority is to ensure new and existing trading arrangements such as the Trans-Pacific Partnership (TPP), Regional Comprehensive Economic Partnership (RCEP) and Free Trade Area of the Asia Pacific (FTAAP), are inclusive and complementary. In this context, both Australia and China have a large stake in the success of the ASEAN Economic Community (AEC), which was established before the TPP was signed. The AEC will be further developed in parallel with TPP domestic ratification processes. There is a crucial opportunity to simultaneously conclude RCEP and advance openness of the regional trade regime by strategic commitments to comprehensive trade and investment liberalisation that is supportive of the goals of ASEAN and inclusiveness across the Pacific and the world. The economic imperatives for cooperation have become more important and, so far, the flexibility of Asian regional arrangements provides an opportunity to connect existing arrangements in ways that allow them to address new challenges and opportunities.

The shift towards a more complex, multipolar order has created some new tensions, and different political allegiances have become a complicating factor.

The major challenges now facing the international community require innovative solutions promoted by effective regional coalitions that include China and the United States and thereby manage the US–China relationship, which is arguably the most important bilateral relationship in the world.

Four forces underscore the need for power-sharing, cooperation and policy adaptation in our region over the coming decade: transition in the geopolitical order; the shift in the structure of the financial geography of the region; the opportunities of changing technology; and the impact of climate change.

Geopolitically, territorial disputes and strategic rivalries have opened up tension in the Asia Pacific region. Managing competing interests in the South China Sea exemplifies the challenge there is as China projects its peripheral power. This is a testing time in which it will be critical to exert common sense on the shared interest between the United States and China in maintaining maritime security and regional stability, while managing strategic differences.

Australia's role as a historical ally of the United States, combined with its geographical position in Asia and its deep interest in its economic relationship with China, opens a space for its leaders to play a vital role as an interlocutor with a compelling and sincere interest in the peaceful accommodation of China as a new power within the regional and global order.

Two major developments in the transition to a new financial geography of the Asia Pacific underline the need for greater regional cooperation. The first was China's move to establish the AIIB as an additional channel of development finance. The bank's creation came in the context of US delay in the implementation of the 2009 G20 agreement to widen IMF reform, including expanding China's voting rights in the IMF, and the obstacles to contributing additional equity to multilateral financial institutions to fill the huge gap in development financing. In 2015, the IMF agreed to include the renminbi in the Special Drawing Rights basket. The AIIB offers opportunity for proactive Australian partnership with China in building experience in the provision of an important international public good, and investment in infrastructure designed to promote regional economic integration. It is an opportunity that can now be actively embraced.

The second event was divergence in industrial countries' quantitative easing strategies, with the US Federal Reserve beginning to reverse easing and the European Central Bank and Bank of Japan both still committed to further aggressive easing. This divergence in monetary policy between the major reserve currency countries opens the prospect of a phase of dollar strengthening. As the Bank of International Settlements has pointed out, the Latin American debt crises of the 1980s and the Asian financial crisis of the 1990s were both associated with periods of strengthening of the US dollar. A strong dollar — particularly when the US economy is no longer the engine of import growth it was in the past — creates huge tensions and a dollar trap for emerging markets. Capital flows back to advanced markets tend to put a deflationary pressure on emerging asset markets. This will put pressure on regional economies and will require their close cooperation in the region.

Regarding technology advancement, technological disruption has proved more pervasive and damaging of traditional economies than was anticipated because it diffused power to new centres and weakened incumbents. Asian and Middle Eastern oil-producers' wealth is being undercut by innovations in shale oil and renewable energy technologies. These are issues on which there is a close intersection of interests between Australia and China, and their regional partners. As robotisation reduces the need for cheap and unskilled labour, governments around the world are finding it difficult to generate new jobs for growing populations of unemployed youth and low-skilled workers. At the same time, non-state players are using technology to create centres of social change or disruption or conflict that cannot be dealt with by national power with conventional tools. These are also issues on which both countries can encourage both regional and global dialogue.

Climate change is also responsible for major social upheaval, resulting in a high-pressure year for global governance institutions in the lead up to the Paris agreements. As water stresses, air pollution and El Nino effects became more marked across the world, global opinion swung enough to help the Paris COP21 negotiations on climate change reach consensus in December 2015. This outcome helpfully embeds concerted unilateral mitigation and is a testament to the urgency of consensus and cooperation in the war on pollution and climate change. The new consensus provides a basis for Australia and China to work with regional partners in developing cooperative strategies on putting in place the institutional, technological and policy innovations needed to address these problems.

Two priority areas for collaboration, building on China's G20 presidency this year, are developing a more cohesive global financial safety net and strengthening the multilateral trading system. While these priorities relate to trade and finance, other important areas for collaboration are on global energy governance and climate change. Australia and China's active participation within the G20 is crucial to all of these ambitions and both countries have incentives to bolster the G20 and build its role as the preeminent forum for global economic cooperation. Collaboration also needs to extend beyond the G20, for example in developing a new and proactive role for the WTO now that preferential arrangements are overtaking the multilateral trading system and trade liberalisation at the border is no longer the primary problem in the promotion of more open and contestable international markets. The question of how different regional arrangements such as the TPP, RCEP, AEC and the proposed FTAAP affect the global trading system are matters that the G20 should consider in the area of international trade.

The G20 is, however, the premier forum through which China can articulate its economic policymaking strategies and intentions. This is more important to other economies, which now need more information and analysis of developments in the Chinese economy to incorporate into the formation of their own economic strategies. This is not about securing China's place against other countries. The steps that China takes today will be of importance to Indonesia, India and Africa, with the lasting legacy of a more robust global system.

In the context of the big forces currently shaping the financial geography of the region and of the world, a more cohesive approach to the issue of infrastructure investment needs to be taken with a focus on improving intermediation between infrastructure investment opportunities and global savings (particularly from Asia and the big pension and superannuation funds in advanced economies) as well as project preparation and prioritisation. More sensitively, the G20 and regional dialogues provide an opportunity to open informal political dialogue on some of the stresses of technological progress, like energy transformation and cyber security.

The current pressures in international financial markets reinforce China and Australia's interest in a strong, inclusive and responsive global financial safety net, centred on the IMF. Fragmentation has presently reduced the safety net's capacity and agility to respond to crises, which reduces market confidence, acts to constrain trade and investment flows, and discourages economic openness

On trade, there is an opportunity to advance global trade reform and economic cooperation through leadership in Asian reform and liberalisation. While Australia and China cooperate at all levels of the global trading system, both countries gain the most from the multilateral trading framework and from trade liberalisation when it is multilateral rather than bilateral or preferential. Australia and China have a particular interest in ensuring the global trading system supports regional and global value chains by facilitating trade and investment flows across all borders, not just those confined to particular bilateral or regional arrangements, and working with regional economies in defining a pathway to globalise achievements in regional liberalisation and reform.

The East Asian members of the G20 can step forward in defining what role the region can play in reshaping global trade governance and ensuring a sustained and effective recovery.

There is opportunity to use regional arrangements such as RCEP to raise the standard for cohesive regional agreements, to push for better collaboration between the WTO and regional agreements, and to deliver ambitious commitments under the Trade Facilitation Agreement by giving the structural reforms that have been pledged in the G20 growth strategies a stronger trade focus.

Finally, on energy, the G20 has developed high-level principles on energy collaboration under the leadership of Australia, China and the United States. Existing institutions and mechanisms, like the International Energy Agency (IEA) and the stockpiling obligations under its treaty, are dramatically weakened through excluding China and other emerging market economies. But these countries, quite rightly, will want a say in the rules and norms that apply to them. Among other things, the G20 recognised the importance of making international energy institutions more representative and inclusive of emerging and developing economies. China can build on these small steps and, along with thinking about low-emissions transformation of energy, use its G20 host year to bolster global energy security through reforms to global energy governance.

CHAPTER 2
The economic transformations in China and Australia

KEY MESSAGES

The Australia–China economic relationship is entering a new phase, shaped by the big changes now underway in both economies, which are seeing the services sector and innovation emerge as larger drivers of growth.

The Chinese economy is in the midst of a major transformation after decades of rapid heavy industrial growth. It is now shifting towards the services sector and advanced manufacturing, industries that will be crucial in sustaining China's progression to a high-income economy. At the same time, China's large and increasingly wealthy middle class will drive massive growth in consumer spending in the coming years.

- To support this transformation, China must prioritise supply-side reforms that allow inefficient industries to shrink and more dynamic and innovative sectors to grow. This will require financial market reforms to improve the efficiency of investment, more private sector involvement in a number of state-dominated sectors and supporting the manufacturing sector to move up the global value chain.

- China's transformation will have profound implications for Australia and the rest of the world as rising demand from China's huge middle class creates vast new export markets in areas from financial services to food. Likewise, China's transition towards a more open capital account will continue to reshape the global investment landscape, as Chinese savers look for investment opportunities abroad and foreign investment expands into new sectors of China's economy.

In Australia, the end of the mining investment boom and steep commodity price falls have also necessitated structural change towards broader drivers of growth, especially given competitive pressures in the region. This has sharpened the policy focus on lifting Australia's productivity, especially in the large services sector, which experienced a relative decline against international benchmarks over the past decade.

- A better productivity performance will be crucial for Australia to capture a share of emerging export markets and support higher living standards. Among other things, this will require removing protection for less productive firms, greater competition in sheltered services industries and facilitating cost-effective investment in new infrastructure, including by attracting further Chinese investment.

While the Australia–China relationship will continue to be underpinned by the traditional areas of complementarity including commodity trade, new areas for trade, investment and broader cooperation are emerging. Besides the growing prominence of the services sector in both economies, this also reflects the broader shift towards innovation-driven growth, which will require highly-skilled workforces capable of developing and absorbing new technologies.

The Australia–China economic relationship is entering a new phase, shaped by the very big changes that are now taking place in both economies. While the dynamic of these changes is difficult to predict exactly, some things are clear.

In China, the structure of the economy is shifting towards the services sector and higher-value manufacturing, and these new drivers of growth will be crucial in sustaining China's progress beyond middle income. Household consumption is becoming a more important source of demand, underpinned by rising wages and incomes.

China's economic transformation will have far-reaching implications for the world, given China now accounts for about one-sixth of global output and global income, and has a fast-growing middle class that is projected to reach 630 million people by 2022 (World Bank 2016; Barton 2013). As Chinese consumers demand an increasingly broad range of goods and services, vast new export markets will open up in areas such as professional services, health and aged care, and agricultural products.

For China, the development of more advanced manufacturing industries will allow its export sector to move up the global value chain, while stronger transport and infrastructure connectivity with the region can support demand for China's traditional manufacturing exports.

Meanwhile, China's ongoing financial sector reforms and capital account liberalisation will continue to recast the global investment landscape over the next decade. According to World Bank projections, China's share of global investment flows could increase dramatically over the next two decades, as China's domestic rates of investment moderate and its huge pool of domestic savings looks offshore for broader investment opportunities (World Bank 2013).

China's economic trajectory over the coming decade may not be smooth. A change of the kind to which Chinese policymakers have committed is unprecedented, and managing the economy's transformation presents a range of difficult challenges for policymakers. Among other things, China must push ahead with supply-side structural reforms that facilitate industrial restructuring, allowing outdated firms and industries to exit and encouraging new and innovative firms to flourish. Further financial market reform will be crucial to this shift, by allowing more productive businesses in emerging sectors to secure finance for investment. Facilitating more private sector involvement within industries currently dominated by state-owned enterprises (SOEs) — such as energy, utilities, transport and banking — will be similarly important.

After decades of economic growth driven by increasing the number of workers and the amount of capital, these supply-side structural reforms will be necessary to promote greater efficiency and achieve sustained increases in multifactor productivity, and therefore incomes, over the next decade.

Much as in the past decade, the Chinese economy will continue to have a large influence on Australia's economic prospects in the coming decade.

Australia capitalised on the China-led increase in global commodity demand in the last decade, thanks to an abundance of economically proven mineral reserves, a globally competitive mining industry and policy settings that facilitated a large-scale expansion of the resources industry.

However, Australia's income growth has now slowed, partly as a result of China's economic transformation towards less resource-intensive growth. In the next decade, Australia will need to broaden its export base beyond mining by tapping into the fast-growing market for consumer and commercial services that is currently emerging in China and across the region, while cementing its position as a reliable, low-cost supplier of a broad range of energy and industrial commodities.

Succeeding in these new markets for services in the region will not be easy. Australia will face fierce competition from service suppliers globally, without the natural and geographic advantages it possesses in minerals production. Australia will need to reinvigorate its economic reform agenda to help drive innovation and productivity, particularly in Australia's large services sector where productivity lags behind the global frontier in many cases. Improving product market efficiency throughout the services sector, including by strengthening and extending competition policy, will be essential if Australia is to expand its service exports and maintain prosperity in the next decade.

For both China and Australia, driving internal economic reform will also require engaging further with the rest of the world. In China's case, this means allowing the Chinese economy to become more closely integrated with global financial markets as a way of improving the allocation of capital internally, and opening up its expanding services sector to greater foreign trade, investment and technologies.

For Australia, increasing contestability in currently sheltered service and infrastructure markets will help attract a wider range of Chinese and other foreign investment. As a relatively small, open economy, this will be critical in financing new infrastructure and Australia's broader investment needs.

In both Australia and China, the services sector is becoming a larger driver of growth, especially in professional service areas and in the information economy, where new technologies are fundamentally changing the way business is being done across the world (Box 2.1).

BOX 2.1: THE GLOBAL RISE OF THE INNOVATION ECONOMY

China and Australia, like the rest of the world, are looking towards innovation and the information economy as key drivers of investment and growth in the coming decade.

Rapidly emerging disruptive technologies are reshaping the way consumers and businesses interact, including through the advent of the sharing economy, the growing capacity to collect and analyse 'big data' and through the shift towards knowledge-based capital (KBC).

KBC includes investment in digital information (software and data), innovative property (patents, copyrights, trademarks and designs) and organisation-specific competencies (brand equity, training and organisational capital). The OECD estimates that investment in KBC now represents almost half of all investment in the United States and other advanced economies (OECD 2013b).

KBC will be a key factor in spurring new sources of growth, by allowing firms and organisations to prosper in a competitive global economy and create high-wage employment. This is particularly relevant for Australia and China as they look to replace the traditional sources of export growth over the past decade. As the OECD notes: 'KBC allows countries and firms to upgrade their comparative advantage by positioning themselves in high value-added industries, activities and market segments'. New, innovative firms are also becoming the main drivers of employment creation, with 'high-growth' firms accounting for up to half of all jobs growth even though they only account for around 5 per cent of all businesses (OECD 2012).

That said, the rise of KBC is creating new challenges for policymakers and businesses, not least the difficulties involved in measuring economic activity associated with KBC. For example, the rise of KBC has made a country's intellectual property regime even more important, a point highlighted in Australia's recent Review of Competition Policy.

KBC businesses are already driving massive innovation in the Australia–China relationship through innovative delivery of goods and financial services via e-commerce that is leapfrogging old barriers to economic integration. What we see so far is just the tip of the iceberg (see Chapter 3).

Both countries are rightly focused on fostering an innovative business climate that supports new and dynamic firms to expand and create employment. Their leaderships opened a new dialogue about their countries' innovation strategies in April this year. As part of this, policymakers must ensure that local workforces have the skills and capabilities to tap into the latest technologies and business practices developed abroad. But there are deeper trends driving the global environment in which information and big data businesses are reshaping the world economy and international business, and these trends will need to be on their agenda for cooperation over the coming decade.

Although merchandise trade — including in commodities — will remain a foundation, the China–Australia economic relationship will increasingly be defined by each country's transition towards more services- and innovation-based economies, and the bilateral collaborations that can help bring this about.

This will mean greater trade in services, but also a broadening of people-to-people engagement to share technologies, business practices and institutional know-how as each country navigates its reform challenges. These areas for greater business and government collaboration are discussed in following chapters.

This chapter sets the economic context for the rest of the Report. It begins with a summary of China's rise and impact on the global economy over the past few decades, with the next section focusing on China's influence on commodity markets and Australia. It first examines the economic transition that is now occurring in China and the implications for Australia and the rest of the world. This includes a discussion of the key economic reforms that will be required in both countries to help sustain economic growth and prosperity over the next decade.

China's rise and its impact on the world economy

China's economic transformation since 1978 has been remarkable. At the commencement of the reform period, China's GDP per capita was less than 5per cent of the United States' (The Conference Board 2015). According to World Bank Development Indicators, since 1978, China's economy has grown in size by an annual average rate of around 10 per cent and is now almost 30 times larger than it was in 1978 (World Bank 2016). This reflects a substantial increase in labour productivity, which has risen from 3per cent of the US level in 1978 to more than 20 per cent now (The Conference Board 2015).

This performance has resulted in China rapidly catching up to higher-income economies, which, combined with a huge population, has seen China's share of global output and income rise from less than 5 per cent in 1990 to 17 per cent today (Figure 2.1).

While unique in scale, China's economic convergence broadly matches the previous experience of other Asian economies such as Japan and South Korea. Indeed, the principle factors behind China's success are similar to those that have driven economic convergence elsewhere in Asia. These include very high rates of physical capital accumulation and mass mobilisation of labour towards an export-oriented manufacturing sector, supported by ongoing improvements in human capital and technological catch-up.

The scale and speed of China's economic rise over the past four decades also reflects the size and demographic profile of China's population, which saw the working-age population grow significantly faster than the overall population. This coincided with the mass movement of rural surplus labour from the low productivity agricultural sector to higher productivity industrial and service sectors.

China's export-oriented growth model has underpinned a large and rapid expansion in its international trade and integration with global markets since 1978.

Figure 2.1: China's share of the global economic aggregates

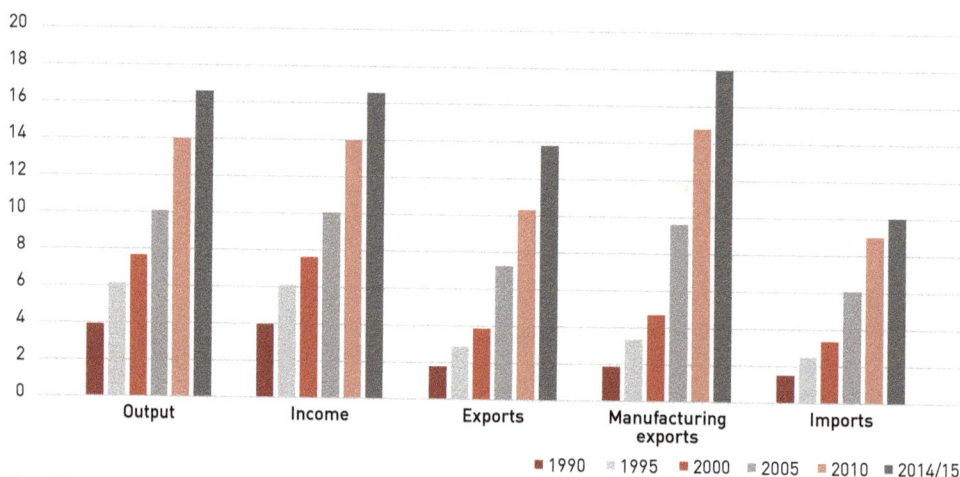

Note: Exports and imports figures are merchandise only.
Source: World Bank 2016; WTO 2016a.

In the past 15 years alone, China's exports have expanded more than 10-fold, facilitated by accession to the WTO in 2001. Having surpassed both the United States and Germany, China is now the world's largest exporter by value, accounting for 12 per cent of global merchandise trade (Figure 2.1).

Greater international openness allowed China to absorb foreign technologies and know-how, driving improved productivity across the broader economy. A more open economy also increased competitive forces domestically, promoting efficiency and innovation in trade-exposed sectors.

Figure 2.2: Investment as a share of GDP

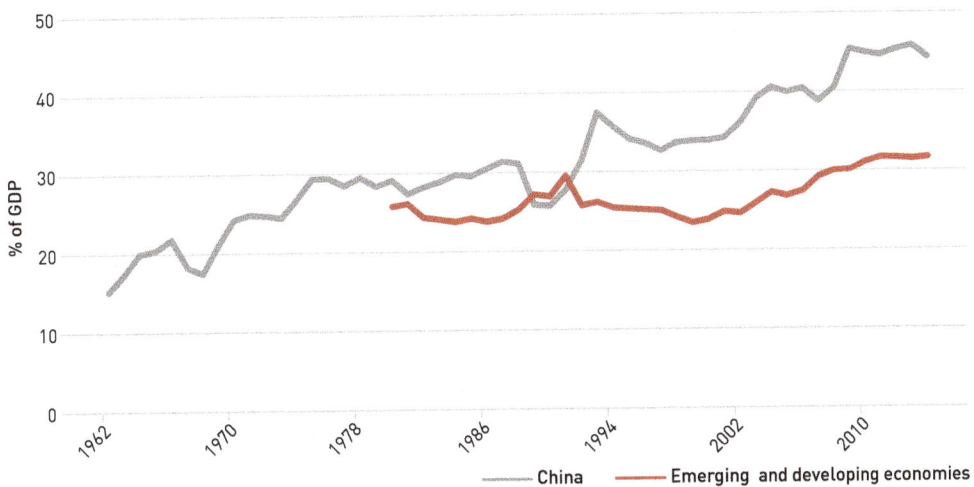

Source: World Bank 2016.

Since the mid-1990s, China's rapid economic convergence has reflected very large investments in physical capital. China commenced the reform period with relatively low capital per worker, allowing for initially large labour productivity gains and high returns on investment. Growth in the capital stock is estimated to have averaged 10 per cent annually from the 1980s, accounting for significantly more than half of GDP growth over this time (Wu 2014).

These trends have resulted in China's investment as a share of GDP reaching very high levels, both historically and even compared with other emerging economies (Figure 2.2).

China's elevated rates of investment have been supported by government policies that have incentivised property development and infrastructure investment, and expansions in manufacturing capacity. This includes the structure of the financial system, which has channelled subsidised capital from savers to large private and state-owned enterprises, and an exchange rate regime in previous decades that encouraged exports over domestic spending. China's very high rates of investment have been supported by very high rates of national saving (Box 2.2).

The impact of China's rise on global commodity markets and Australia

It is not just the rapid growth and transformation of the Chinese economy that has affected opportunities globally; it is also the sheer scale of China's impact that has mattered to the world economy.

The unprecedented scale of China's industrialisation has resulted in China's consumption of metals, other raw materials and energy expanding massively over recent decades. China is now the world's largest user of a range of industrial and energy commodities including steel, copper and coal (Figure 2.4).

BOX 2.2: CHINA'S HIGH RATES OF NATIONAL SAVING

China's vast stock of savings, together with its capital account controls, has played an important role in high rates of investment. Saving as a share of GDP rose from less than 40 per cent in the 1980s to a peak of 50 per cent in the late 2000s. While the national saving rate has eased in the past few years to around 48 per cent, it remains very high by historical and international standards (Figure 2.3).

The household sector has made a significant contribution to higher rates of national saving, reflecting a growing working-age population with an increasing capacity to save. Incomplete domestic financial markets and restricted access to foreign financial assets have also encouraged high household saving rates, as has the limited state provision of social security and health insurance.

Corporate saving has also made a large contribution to China's high rates of national saving. A flexible dividend policy has allowed SOEs to retain and then reinvest most of their profits, rather than distributing dividends to the state. Financial underdevelopment has also made it difficult for the private sector, especially small businesses, to access intermediated financing, inducing higher saving rates in that sector.

Planned reforms to financial markets (including interest rates) and to the regulation of SOEs, as well as the broader provision of social infrastructure, should support higher household consumption and corresponding declines in household and corporate saving rates. Likewise, China's ageing population is likely to play a part in reducing saving rates, as an increasing share of China's adult population moves into retirement age and begins to draw down savings.

Figure 2.3: National saving by sector

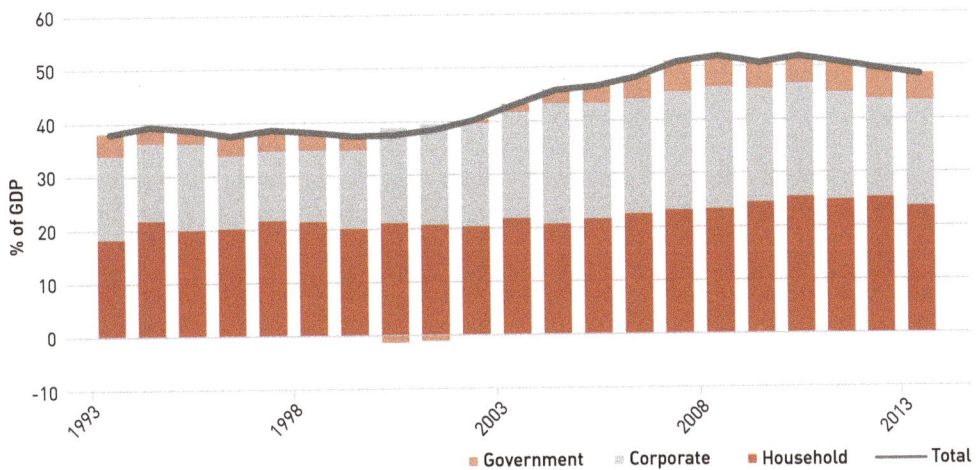

Source: China National Bureau of Statistics 2015.

China's growth in steel consumption has been particularly dramatic over the past two decades, driven by rising investment in steel-intensive buildings and infrastructure, as well as large expansions in the manufacturing sector. China is now the largest steel consumer, accounting for 45 per cent of global steel usage in 2015 (World Steel Association 2015). China's increasing steel requirements necessitated a massive expansion in its steel industry, which is estimated to have produced over 800 million tonnes of crude steel in 2015 — more than six times as much as it did in 2000 (Figure 2.5).

Figure 2.4: China's share of global commodity consumption

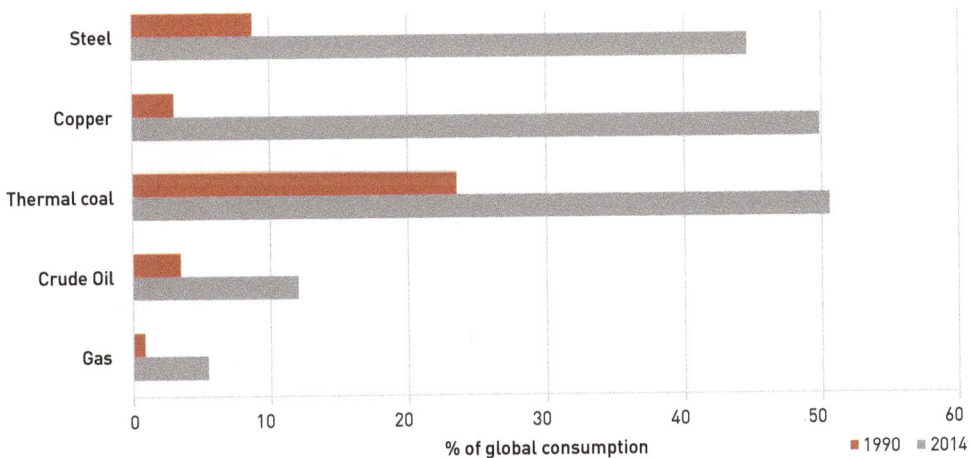

Source: World Steel Association 2015; World Bank 2015; BP 2016.

China's increasing production of steel has had flow-on effects to its demand for the raw ingredients used in steelmaking, namely iron ore and metallurgical coal. Most notably, China's share of world iron ore consumption rose from 14 per cent in 2000 to an estimated 65 per cent in 2015.

While having large quantities of its own resources, China has become increasingly reliant on imported inputs as strong commodity demand has drawn in lower-cost, higher-quality commodities from abroad. Trade dependency continues to rise as commodity prices fall, and the share of imported industrial inputs in domestic consumption is at an all-time high.

Figure 2.5: China's steel production

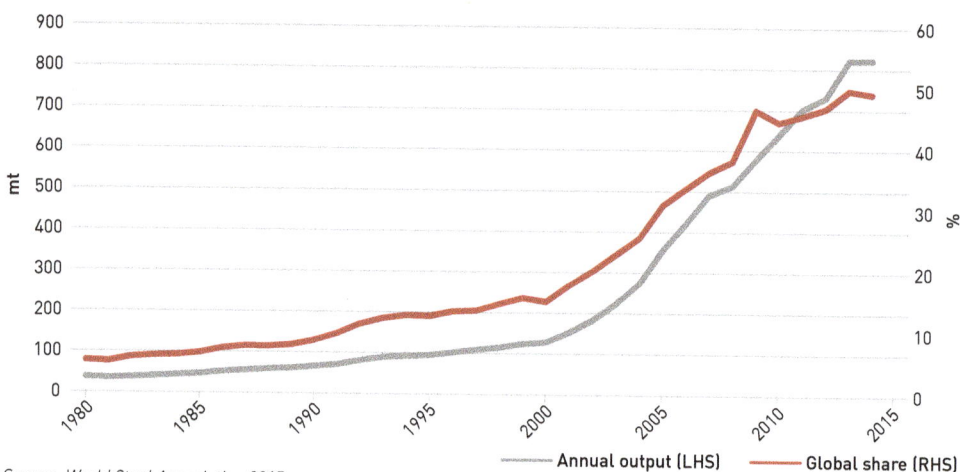

Source: World Steel Association 2015.

Responding to the sharp rise in global commodity prices and growth in China's demand for raw materials, Australia's mining industry invested heavily in new export capacity over the past decade (Figure 2.6). This investment was initially concentrated in the iron ore and coal sectors, but was followed by an even larger investment in liquefied natural gas (LNG) capacity, which will make Australia the largest exporter of LNG within a few years. At its height in 2013, the mining industry's share of private investment in Australia reached one-third, more than triple the typical historical share.

There was a lag in the response of investment and capacity to rising prices because of its gestation period. But as this new capacity came on line, Australia's export volumes of these products almost doubled compared to the previous decade. In the iron ore market, Australia now accounts for almost one-third of global production and one-half of seaborne trade, significantly higher than a decade ago.

Almost all of Australia's additional iron ore supply has been absorbed by China, with Australia increasing its share of Chinese imports to over 60 per cent as less efficient global supply has been displaced, including within China itself. Australia's share of China's coal imports has also increased, from around 10 per cent in 2009 to around one-third now (Figure 2.7).

By 2018, the mining industry's capital stock will be almost four times larger than it was in 2004, a massive investment in new capacity that will underpin Australia's mining exports for decades to come.

Extensive reserves of iron ore, coal and other commodities meant that Australia was well positioned from the outset to benefit from China's rising commodity demand. But the mere existence of these natural resources did not guarantee Australia's success. Instead, Australia owes its success to the competitiveness of its mining industry as well as the flexibility of the wider economy that allowed resources to be efficiently reallocated to expand the minerals sector.

Figure 2.6: Mining investment in Australia

Panel A: By commodity type

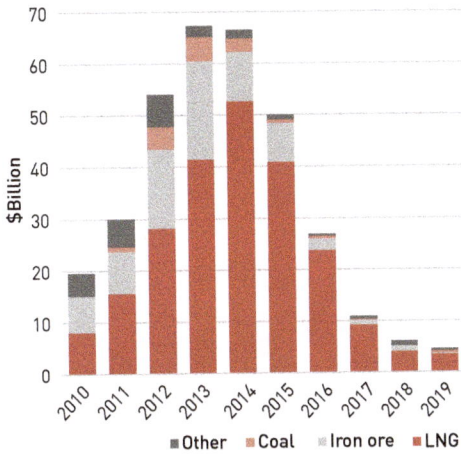

Panel B: Share of total private investment

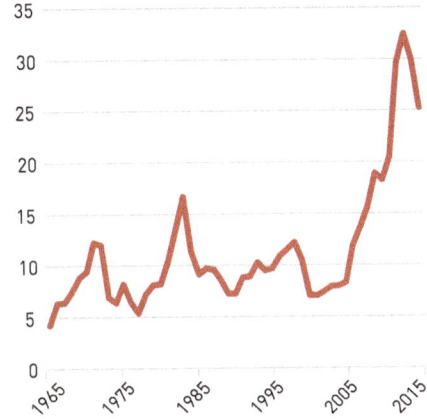

Sources: Government of Australia 2014.

Australia's well-established macroeconomic policy frameworks, including a floating exchange rate, played an important role in accommodating the expansion in Australia's mining capacity with limited disruptions to the broader economy. Along with a sufficiently flexible labour market, these settings helped inflation expectations to remain anchored when the terms of trade rose sharply, avoiding many of the macroeconomic difficulties that arose in previous terms of trade booms in Australia (Gruen 2011).

Figure 2.7: Australia's share of Chinese commodity imports

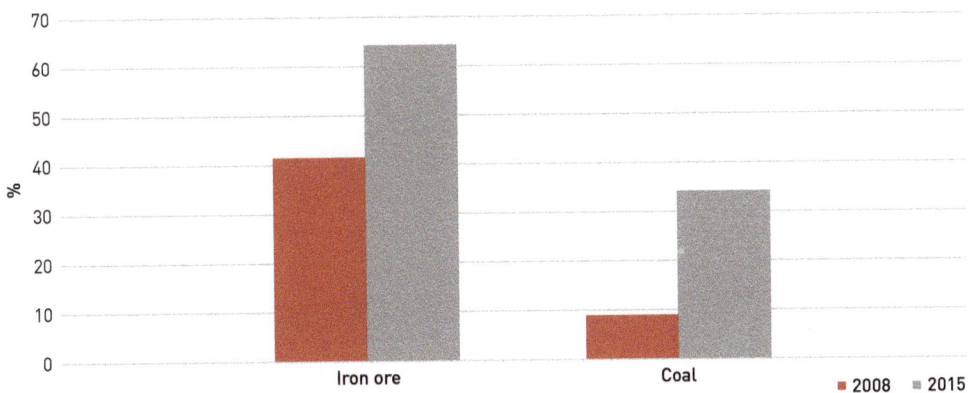

Source: China National Bureau of Statistics 2015.

China's economic transformation to new drivers of growth

After almost four decades of rapid growth, the Chinese economy is undergoing a major transformation, brought about by a combination of internal and external economic forces.

On the external front, substantially slower growth in international trade has seen a corresponding moderation in demand for China's traditional, labour-intensive manufactured exports in recent years (Figure 2.8). This slowdown partly reflects China's already significant market share in some global manufacturing segments, as well as a more fundamental shift in global trade towards information and services, consistent with the rise of e-commerce globally.

Figure 2.8: Growth in global trade

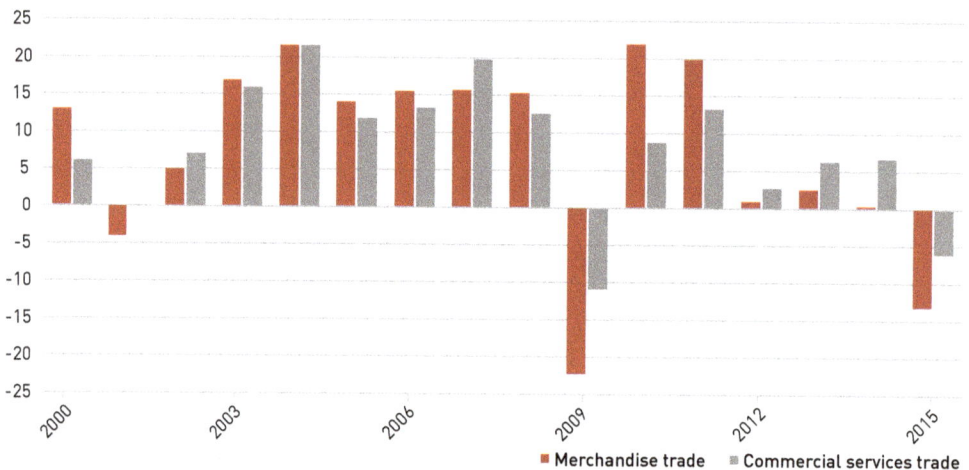

Source: WTO 2016a.

Domestically, as wages and incomes rise, household consumption is emerging as a more important driver of economic activity. At the same time, China's growth drivers in recent decades — investment in physical capital and labour-intensive manufactured exports — are slowing. The lower growth in investment in these sectors reflects oversupply in the property market and the excess capacity that has emerged across segments of the manufacturing sector, and the lower profitability in these sectors.

Demographic forces and labour market dynamics are also playing their part in China's shift away from factor-driven growth towards more balanced growth. After growing strongly for nearly four decades, China's working-age population is now shrinking, which is directly reducing China's growth potential via lower growth in the labour force.

China's ageing population has implications that go beyond the impact on aggregate economic growth. For example, there will be an extra 110 million people aged over 65 by 2030, which will increase the demand for aged-care services and put pressure on China's still developing social safety net.

In the labour market, the slower growth in the labour force and shrinking pool of surplus rural labour is contributing to higher wages. Higher wages combined with a significant appreciation of the real exchange rate over the previous decade is helping to shift the composition of demand from exports and investment towards consumption. This is being supported by a shift in economic resources towards consumers, illustrated by the uptick in the wage and household sector shares of GDP in recent years (Figure 2.9).

Similarly, consumption expenditure has now overtaken investment spending as the main contributor to economic growth. While this partly reflects slower growth in investment in recent years, the contribution from household consumption also rose in 2015 (Figure 2.10).

Within consumption, the shift towards services, as well as discretionary goods, is occurring as Chinese households become wealthier. This changing pattern of demand is giving rise to faster employment growth in the services sector. Over the past two years, employment in China's services sector has grown strongly and now accounts for a little more than 40 per cent of employment across the economy, up from 30 per cent a decade ago (WTO 2016).

The appreciation of China's real exchange rate is also encouraging employment creation in China's non-traded services sectors, which ultimately will be at the expense of employment in China's export-oriented sectors. This dynamic is consistent with the experience of other emerging economies such as Japan in the 1970s and 1980s where increases in the real exchange rate reinforced a shift towards domestically oriented industries such as education, health and financial services (Dorrucci et al 2013).

While investment as a share of GDP has fallen in recent years, and may fall further, China's transformation towards services, higher-end manufacturing and the digital economy will still involve substantial new investment in these growing industries. For example, China's entry into new, higher-technology manufactured segments will require large-scale investment in plant, equipment and human capital, as illustrated by the recent plan to establish a semi-conductor industry in China.

Figure 2.9: Wages and household disposable income

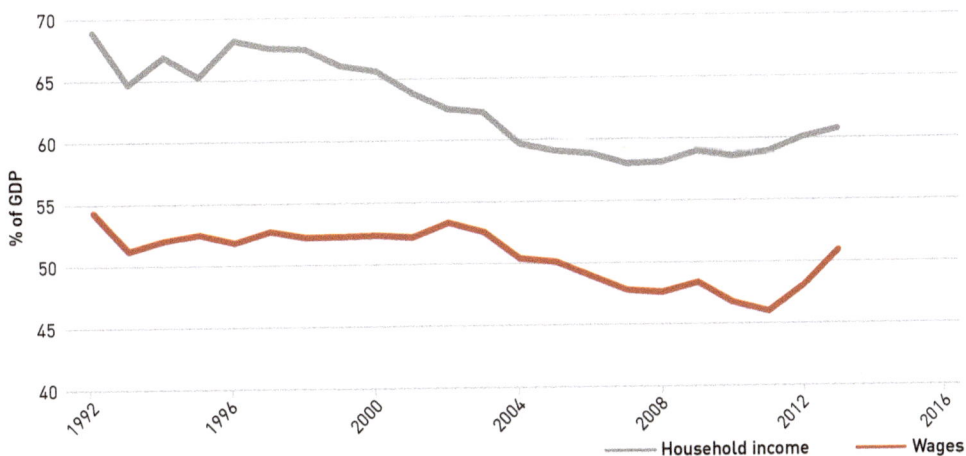

Source: China National Bureau of Statistics 2015.

The types of assets attracting investment are also likely to evolve as China's industry becomes more advanced. This reflects the greater need for investment in innovation and information technology as Chinese industry develops, in line with the global trend towards knowledge-based capital (OECD 2013b). For China, this means a greater proportion of investment is likely to be directed towards intangible assets, such as digital information, computer software and research and development to support China's progression into higher-technology manufacturing (Box 2.3).

Figure 2.10: Contributions to China's GDP growth

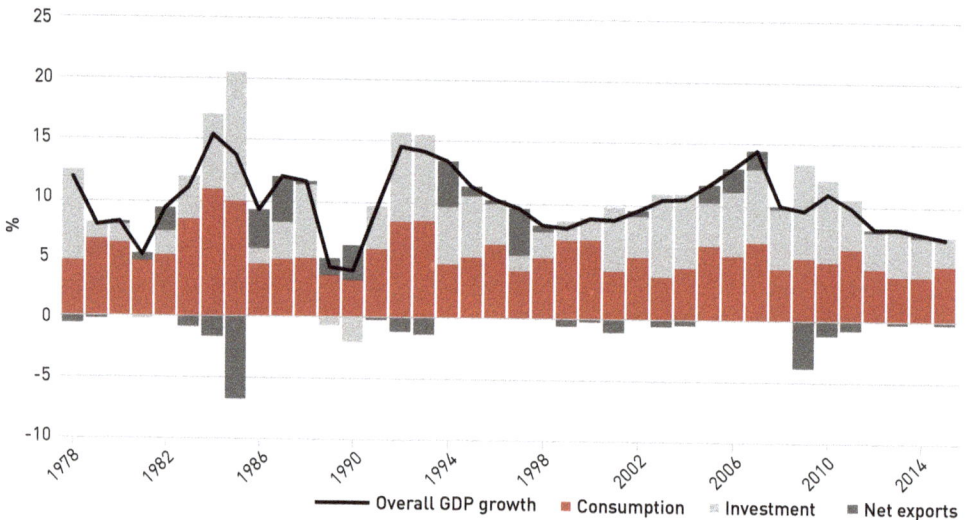

Source: China National Bureau of Statistics 2015.

That is not to say that investment in traditional forms of physical capital will not remain essential in supporting China's continued urbanisation and raising the quality of life in urban centres. This includes further investment in public transport networks and urban amenities, which in many cities remain underdeveloped. Notwithstanding the current areas of oversupply, continued urbanisation will also require substantial new investment in residential and commercial building over the coming decade.

Reforms to assist China's economic transformation

To sustain economic growth in the next decade, China's policy environment will need to support the shift in activity towards the services sector, higher-tech manufacturing and energy transformation to address environmental challenges. It will also need to allow economic resources to shift towards these more innovative and fast-growing sectors of the economy.

This focus on lifting multifactor productivity recognises that the long period of factor-driven growth China has experienced over the past 40 years can no longer be sustained. This reflects falling rates of return and the build-up of excess capacity in significant parts of the industrial sector, a shrinking working-age population as well as broader quality of life considerations, including reducing the pollution-intensity of growth. In this context, China's economic performance over the coming decade will depend in large part on whether China can improve upon the limited growth in multifactor productivity achieved since 2007 (Figure 2.13).

BOX 2.3: CHINA'S PROGRESSION TOWARDS HIGHER-END AND VALUE-ADDED MANUFACTURING

The pace and scale of China's rise as a manufacturing exporter has been truly remarkable. Since accession to the WTO in 2001, China's share of global manufacturing exports has grown from 5 per cent to 18 per cent, making a strong contribution to economic growth both directly and through technology spillovers to the wider economy.

However, growth in China's exports of traditional, labour-intensive manufacturing products has slowed in recent years, reflecting a range of factors — including that global markets may have reached saturation point for these products. For example, China's share of international clothing exports has remained at almost 40 per cent in recent years, having risen continuously over the previous few decades (WTO 2016).

In the next decade, China will therefore need to build upon its traditional export categories by continuing to progress into higher-technology manufacturing, following in the footsteps of countries such as Japan. This process has been underway for some time, with the share of medium- and high-tech manufacturing in China's merchandise exports now substantially higher than what it was 20 years ago (Figure 2.11).

Figure 2.11: China's export mix 1995–2015

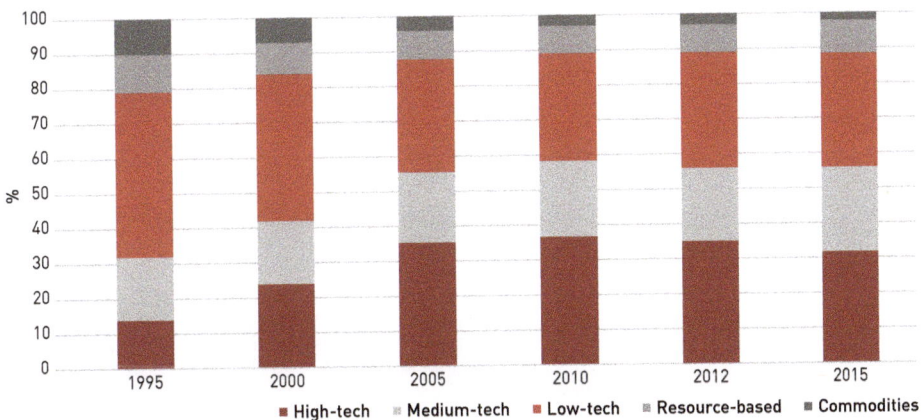

Source: OECD and United Nation's Comtrade database.

At the same time, China's manufacturing sector will need to capture a larger share of the gross value of its manufacturing exports, by moving up the value chain in line with the Made in China 2025 initiative, an official initiative aimed at promoting advanced manufacturing. This will be essential if China's export sector is to continue to make a strong contribution to economic growth over the next decade. Again, there are signs that China is already making progress in this respect, having captured a larger share in the global value chain across many manufacturing sub-categories over the past two decades (Figure 2.12). This includes particularly large increases in the domestic economy's share of the value-added of computers, electrical machinery and appliance exports.

Figure 2.12: Domestic value-added share of China's gross exports

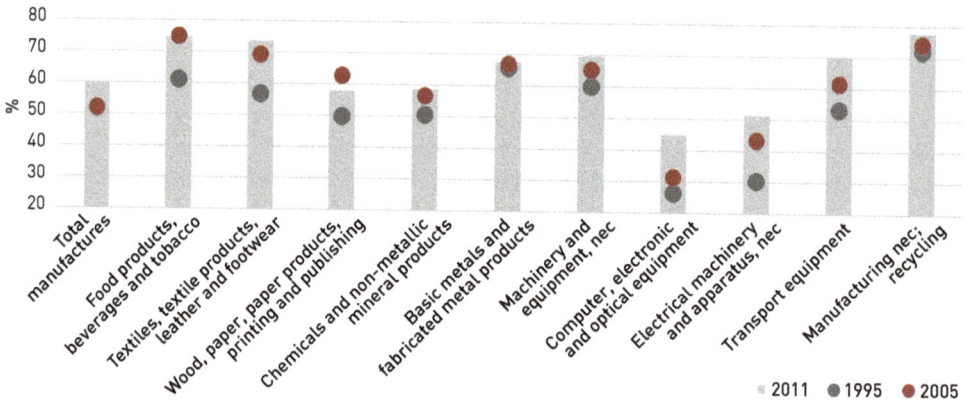

Source: WTO and OECD 2016.

While China's progression to a more advanced and higher-income economy will not be straightforward, the 13th Five Year Plan recognises these economic imperatives, building upon the reform strategies as set out in the Third Plenum of the 18th Party Congress in late 2013. This includes the need to support greater household spending, improve the efficiency of investment, encourage a more innovative science-led economy and expand into higher-technology manufacturing (Box 2.4).

Figure 2.13: Contribution to China's GDP growth

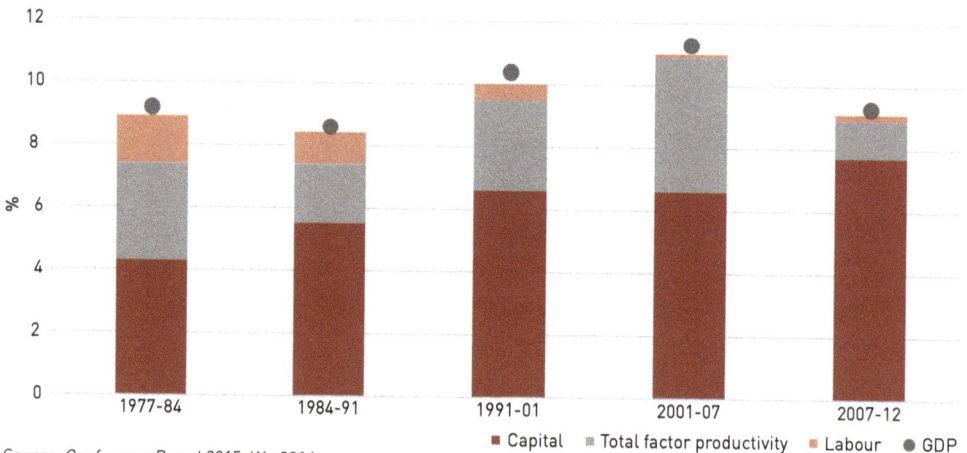

Source: Conference Board 2015; Wu 2014.

Most importantly, the Plan's focus on supply-side structural reforms recognises the need to encourage an expansion in China's more dynamic private sector while limiting further investment in those parts of the economy that are now experiencing over-capacity. This will encompass a broad range of reforms including opening up monopoly industries to private sector participation, reducing government involvement in a number of sectors still dominated by SOEs and improving market exit mechanisms.

Financial market reforms will also play a role in allowing more dynamic and efficient firms to expand by providing better access to finance at lower rates. This will require pushing ahead with banking sector reforms, including liberalising interest rates, as well as encouraging a greater role for non-traditional banking (including through emerging online credit providers) and direct equity financing.

BOX 2.4: CHINA'S ECONOMIC TRANSFORMATION AND THE 13TH FIVE YEAR PLAN

The 13th Five Year Plan ('the Plan') presents a roadmap for China's economic transformation towards a higher income economy. The Plan prioritises a range of areas including: improving development quality and efficiency; supply-side structural reforms; better matching supply and demand; encouraging a more innovative economy; fostering more coordinated, green and inclusive economic development; and accelerating institutional reforms to support China's continued economic development. The Plan focuses on the three economic goals of lifting household consumption, transforming industry towards services and higher value-added manufacturing, and promoting the development of an innovation- and talent-based economy.

Strengthening consumption-led growth. China will promote consumption to become a more important contributor to economic growth. This encompasses policies that promote an industry structure that better reflects demand from Chinese consumers for higher-quality products and encourages an expansion in China's consumer-oriented services industries, including health and aged care. Consistent with a greater domestic capacity to produce higher-end consumer products, Chinese consumers will be encouraged to consider switching their spending from overseas to domestic markets.

Encouraging the services sector and higher-end industry. China will lift the share of the services sector in the economy and encourage higher-end manufacturing. While aggregate demand will be adjusted appropriately, the emphasis will be on supply-side structural reforms that enable the Chinese economy to meet the Chinese people's growing material, cultural, ecological and environmental needs. Consistent with the 'Made in China 2025' initiative, the transition into higher end manufacturing will allow Chinese industry to capture a large share of value chains. To help accelerate the development of a modern service sector, these parts of the economy will be exposed to greater foreign competition. The 'Internet Plus' action plan will help to promote better and broader use of the internet, with greater access to information and better information networks facilitating the adoption of more efficient production methods and organisational structures within industry.

Fostering scientific and technological innovation. China will aim to improve multifactor productivity, underpinned by scientific and technological innovation, investment in human capital and greater entrepreneurship. Market reforms will be undertaken to ensure that research and innovation is geared towards the most valuable areas, supported by closer collaboration between researchers and industry. While absorbing and integrating foreign innovation will remain important, the Plan prioritises ways of encouraging locally generated technologies and new ideas, to help generate self-sustaining economic development.

At the same time, the Plan highlights the need to address distortions in policy and institutional arrangements and the need to promote further competition among firms in some industries as part of a generally open and contestable market system.

Capital account liberalisation can also assist, by providing another channel through which Chinese firms can access finance at market rates, while also subjecting domestic providers of finance to external competition.

Besides having the potential to improve China's efficiency of investment, capital account liberalisation can also support the shift to household consumption. As the constraints on outbound investment are loosened further, Chinese households will be able to invest in a wider range of assets with higher risk-adjusted returns. This will be reinforced by establishing market-determined interest rates and a more market-determined exchange rate, helping to reallocate income towards the household sector.

Although it is in China's longer-term interests, the transition to new drivers of growth will take time, and the pace of economic growth may moderate more than anticipated in the transitional period. Alternative growth scenarios are examined in later chapters (see Chapters 3 and 6) to consider the effect of different Chinese growth trajectories and structures on the Australia–China economic relationship. For example, China's progression into higher-tech manufacturing, which is a difficult transition in its own right, may not occur quickly enough to offset the impact of slower growth in traditional manufacturing segments. Likewise, China's concern about the environmental impact of heavy industry and the mining sector may weigh further on industrial production as new policies in these areas begin to take effect.

During this transition, China must strike the right balance between policies that support near-term growth and policies that promote the economy's longer-term growth potential.

In particular, excessively loose monetary stimulus to support short-term growth would have the potential to encourage higher borrowing and leverage in the corporate sector, which could create fragilities in the financial system and undercut longer-term reforms to improve the efficiency of investment. China should be extremely careful in managing financial risks associated with high levels of total debt, which reached 237 per cent of China's GDP in the first quarter of 2016, from 148 per cent at the end of 2007. Deleveraging is one of five top priorities for the work of the government for 2016. Deleveraging will help China achieve more sustainable growth in the longer term but can put downward pressure in the short term.

Implications of China's transition

Implications for the global economy

First and foremost, the sheer size of the Chinese economy means opportunities to do business with China will continue to expand even if aggregates rates of economic growth are lower. The IMF projects China's growth rate to remain more than twice the global average in the next few years, while its contribution to global growth will be much larger than it was 10 years ago given it is now a significantly larger share of the world economy.

But the transformation underway in the Chinese economy means that China's impact on the world economy will be very different from what it was in the last decade. The increase in per capita consumption, urbanisation and the emergence of the services economy, as well as the further liberalisation of financial markets in China's economy, will fundamentally change how China interacts with the rest of the world.

The larger role for consumer spending and the shift to a more services-based economy will provide China's trading partners with vast export opportunities in new areas of the Chinese economy. China's middle class is projected to reach 630 million people by 2022, providing a huge and expanding market for international providers of consumer goods and services, in areas spanning healthcare, education and food (Barton 2013).

China's demand for high-value foodstuffs is expected to rise dramatically over the coming decades, with the consumption of beef and other meats doubling or even tripling according to some projections (Hamshere et al 2014). While the majority of this increased food demand will be met by expanding China's domestic production, there will be significant unmet demand that international food exporters will be able to exploit.

Likewise, the opening up of China's domestic services sector will present new opportunities for foreign investors, in areas such as finance, insurance and the utilities sector.

The share of China's labour-intensive manufacturing segment is likely to decline going forward. However, building greater connectivity and infrastructure projects with Asian and European exports markets via the infrastructure investment projects associated with the One Belt, One Road (OBOR) initiative can support demand for China's traditional export categories.

The OBOR initiative can also assist in absorbing China's construction capacity (including for infrastructure), while simultaneously supporting economic and trade networks across participating economies.

BOX 2.5: THE OUTLOOK FOR CHINA'S STEEL DEMAND

Having grown strongly over the previous decade, China's apparent steel consumption fell by 3 per cent in 2014 and is estimated to have fallen by another 5 per cent in 2015. This raises the question of whether China's steel consumption has peaked or whether this weakness reflects mainly cyclical factors that will give way to further increases in China's steel consumption over the coming decade. This question will have important implications for China's large steel industry as well as iron ore producers in China and overseas.

In the past, large rises in China's steel demand were driven by construction investment and demand from the manufacturing sector, which are the main users of steel (Table 2.1).

Table 2.1: China's steel usage by purpose (percentage of total)

	2000	2010	2014
Construction	56	56	55
Machinery	15	18	19
Automobile	6	7	7
Home Appliance	3	1	1
Rail	2	1	1
Energy	7	4	5
Shipping[a]	3	5	2
Other	8	8	11

Source: Reproduced from Hamshere et al 2016. [a] *Shipping is defined as the sum of the 'container' and 'shipbuilding' categories.*

The large contribution from the construction industry reflects the substantial steel requirements associated with China's urbanisation, including for high-density residential and commercial buildings and for urban infrastructure such as railways, highways and bridges.

China's increased steel consumption over recent decades has been supplied by expansions in its domestic steel industry. Over the decade to 2013, China's domestic steel production increased almost four-fold to around 820 million tonnes. This has had flow-on effects to iron ore and metallurgical coal — the raw ingredients used by China's steelmakers — with demand for these inputs also growing strongly. In the case of iron ore, China's domestic supplies, while substantial, are of relatively poor grade and located in less accessible parts of the country. This has meant that China has increasingly turned to the seaborne market, including Australian supply, to accommodate its growing iron ore needs (Figure 2.14).

In recent years, the downswing in the housing market, combined with weaker conditions in China's manufacturing sector, have both contributed to lower demand for steel. This has resulted in China's steel consumption falling over the past two years. Steel production was flat in 2014 and fell by 2.3 per cent in 2015 despite a strong increase in steel exports.

In the nearer term, the outlook for China's steel demand will depend in large part on the state of China's housing market, where there is significant oversupply across a number of regions. Growth in real estate investment, which is an important driver of overall steel demand, is therefore likely to remain weak until these pockets of unsold housing are absorbed by the market.

Similarly, excess capacity in the manufacturing sector is weighing on producer prices and profitability, and this will continue to limit manufacturing-related investment, and therefore steel usage in this sector, until this excess capacity is absorbed.

Notwithstanding continued strength in infrastructure-related steel usage, these factors mean that China's steel industry is likely to face continued challenging demand conditions in coming years. As a result, China's demand for iron ore is also likely to grow at a significantly slower rate than in the previous decade, although there may be scope for low-cost global suppliers such as Australia and Brazil to expand their market share.

Figure 2.14: China's steel production and iron ore imports

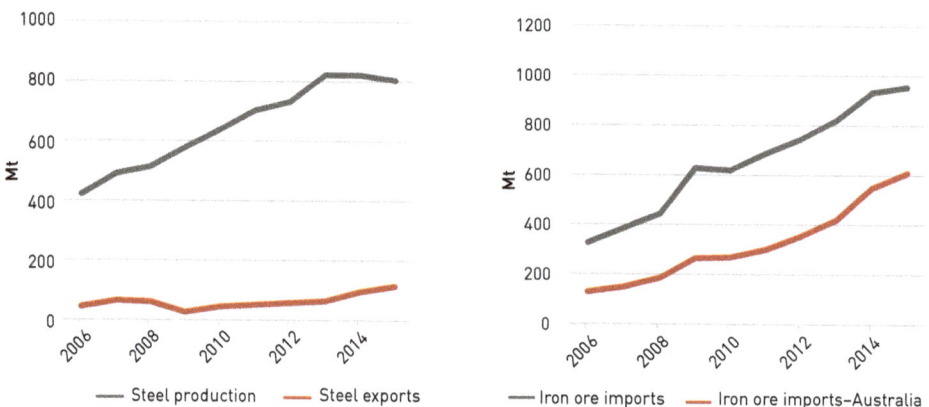

Source: Roberts et al 2016.

China's economic transition is also likely to result in less resource-intensive growth than in the last decade. Already, slower growth in industrial production and real estate investment has coincided with significantly slower growth in China's demand for steel and other commodities in recent years. While some of this weakness may prove to be cyclical rather than structural, the outlook for China's steel demand remains a central source of uncertainty for global steel and iron ore markets (Box 2.5).

Beyond the near term, China's steel and broader metal usage will be underpinned by a number of longer-term drivers, notwithstanding the rebalancing currently underway in the economy. These include further urbanisation, with China's urbanisation rate of just 55 per cent suggesting that the need for investment in new construction is still substantial. Likewise, China's public infrastructure remains underdeveloped in a number of areas, including urban amenities and national transport networks. With rising incomes, Chinese households will also demand a growing number of durable goods, including motor vehicles (with China's per capital vehicle usage still low by international standards) and home appliances.

There are also downside forces that could affect China's steel industry and its demand for iron ore. This includes the policy objective of consolidating the steel industry to help eliminate excess capacity and improve environmental outcomes, which is a growing focus for authorities. The potential for greater use of scrap steel could also significantly alter the outlook for China's demand for iron ore, noting that scrap usage in China remains low by international standards.

While the outlook for China's steel production and iron ore demand is highly uncertain, Australia has some of the lowest-cost iron ore producers in the world and will therefore remain a major source of China's iron ore imports in the coming decade.

Implications for the Australian economy

For the Australian economy, the slower growth in China's commodity demand in recent years has contributed to a more challenging global environment just as the investment phase of the mining boom has neared completion. Combined with large increases in global supplies, softer global demand has resulted in Australia's commodity export prices falling sharply in recent years. This has reduced Australia's terms of trade and growth in national income, with Australia facing the prospect of lower growth in incomes over the coming decade unless productivity growth can be lifted above historical averages (Figure 2.15).

While growth has been slow in recent years, established macroeconomic policy frameworks, including a freely floating exchange rate, have served Australia well in managing the downswing in global commodity prices, reinforcing the positive role these mechanisms played in cushioning the Australian economy from the Asian financial crisis in the late 1990s and the global financial crisis in late 2000s. Likewise, Australia's labour market, while still over-regulated in some areas, has been flexible enough to allow the necessary adjustments in real wages to take place in recent years, helping to sustain employment growth.

But Australia, like China, is now searching for new sources of growth as the old ones fade, and the structure of the Australian economy is reverting back to a more normal pattern of growth in which the services sector will again be the main driver of growth.

Australia's services sector, which accounts for around three-quarters of output, comprises a diverse range of industries. This spans traditional areas such as utilities and goods distribution, services to households such as healthcare and recreation, as well as services mainly directed towards other businesses such as professional services (Figure 2.16).

Figure 2.15: Growth in Australia's national income

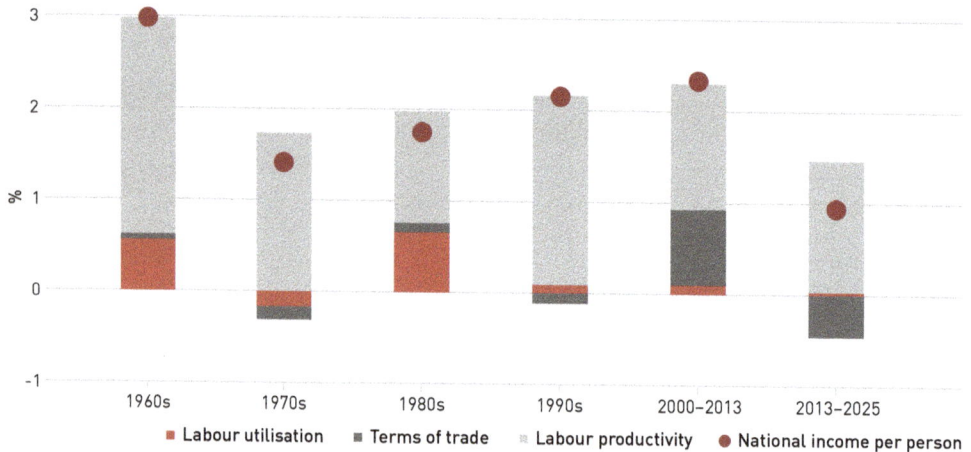

Legend: ■ Labour utilisation ■ Terms of trade ▪ Labour productivity ● National income per person

Note: Growth in GNI per capita also reflects a generally small contribution from net foreign income, which is not shown.
Source: Government of Australia 2014.

Figure 2.16: Australia's industrial composition

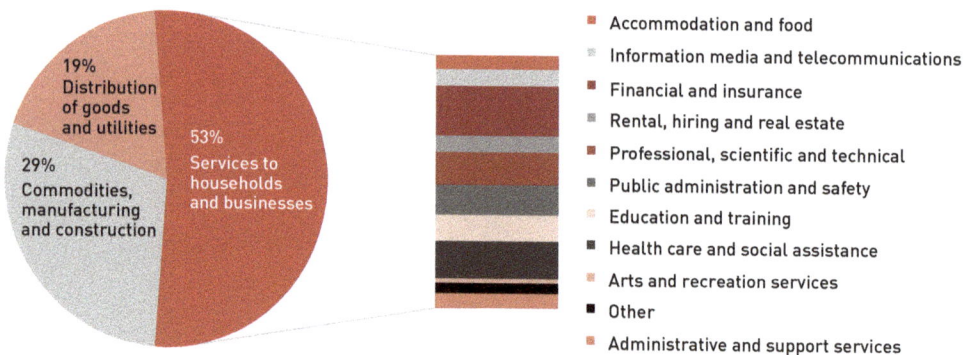

- 19% Distribution of goods and utilities
- 29% Commodities, manufacturing and construction
- 53% Services to households and businesses

Legend:
- ■ Accommodation and food
- ▪ Information media and telecommunications
- ■ Financial and insurance
- ■ Rental, hiring and real estate
- ■ Professional, scientific and technical
- ■ Public administration and safety
- ▪ Education and training
- ■ Health care and social assistance
- ▪ Arts and recreation services
- ■ Other
- ■ Administrative and support services

Source: ABS 2015a.

While it is impossible to predict exactly which industries will prosper in the coming decade, China's transition towards a more consumer-driven economy will undoubtedly see China's imports tilt towards services and higher-value food. The ongoing liberalisation of China's financial markets, as well as latent demand of Chinese households and firms for a broader range of investment and credit products, will present a raft of opportunities for Australia's financial services sector. These opportunities are discussed further in Chapter 5.

Export opportunities are likely to extend well beyond financial services. Supported by ChAFTA, there will also be opportunities for providers of other services to access the growing Chinese market in areas such as education, tourism, healthcare, accounting and legal services.

However, unlike the experience of the last decade, Australia will have no particular natural advantages in capturing these new export markets, and will face formidable competition from other advanced, service-based economies.

In fact, productivity in some of Australia's service industries lags well behind the global frontier, partly reflecting a relatively poor performance over the past decade. This picture is consistent with measures of Australia's relative international competitiveness, which also point to an underlying deterioration over the past decade (Box 2.6).

BOX 2.6: AN ASSESSMENT OF AUSTRALIA'S COMPETITIVENESS

The World Economic Forum provides a useful cross-country assessment of competitiveness based on its rating on 12 categories (or 'Pillars') that have been found to correlate with a country's longer-term productivity performance (World Economic Forum 2015). These 12 Pillars include a country's institutions, infrastructure and market efficiency, with scores in each of the 12 categories aggregated to form an overall global competitiveness index (or GCI).

Australia's overall GCI ranking has fallen over the past decade, from 16th to 21st. While slipping across most categories, Australia's drop in the areas related to market efficiency (in both goods and labour markets) has been starkest (Figure 2.17).

Figure 2.17: Australia's competitiveness ranking

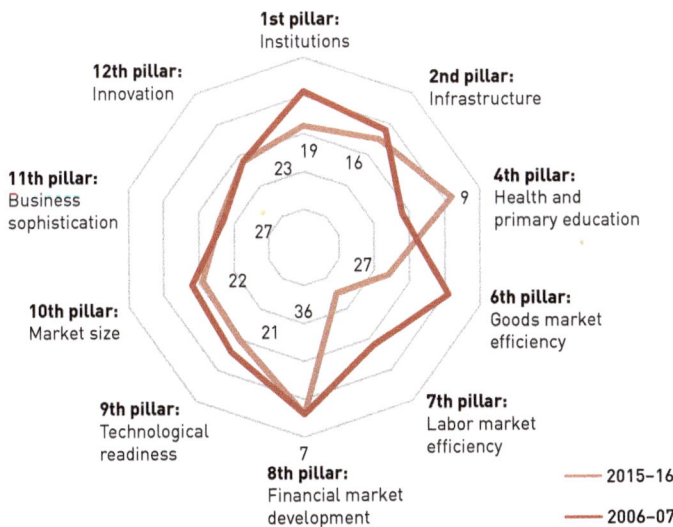

Note: Points further from the origin denote a higher/better ranking.
Source: World Economic Forum 2015.

In the area of goods market efficiency, the fall in Australia's ranking reflects lower scores on indicators of domestic competition, partly offset by increased scores relating to foreign competition. The lower ranking on labour market efficiency reflects increasing costs associated with redundancies and hiring, and little progress over the past decade in strengthening the link between productivity and pay outcomes in employment agreements.

Australia's ranking on infrastructure has also fallen, reflecting lower scores for road and air transport infrastructure, partly offset by increases in the quality of electricity infrastructure and a more comprehensive mobile phone network.

While the GCI is only one measure of competitiveness, these movements in Australia's GCI performance highlight some areas where reform efforts should be focused, namely in product and labour market efficiency as well as certain categories of infrastructure. In the categories in which Australia's score has improved most — health and primary education — it is important that increased public spending in these areas is allocated efficiently, to ensure that higher spending translates to better outcomes.

To compete effectively in emerging export markets, Australia will therefore need to undertake further reforms to drive productivity performance, particularly in the services sector. This will require exposing the domestic economy to increased international competition, through eliminating remaining trade barriers and addressing the relatively high regulatory burden imposed on businesses engaging in international trade, as noted in the World Bank's *Ease of Doing Business* measure for Australia.

Strengthening and extending national competition policy throughout the domestic services sector will also be needed, especially in Australia's large human-services sector, where competitive forces and consumer choice are generally lacking (Box 2.7).

BOX 2.7: REFORM PRIORITIES ACROSS AUSTRALIA'S SERVICES SECTOR

With the terms of trade returning towards historical averages, the focus of policymakers is now on improving the productivity of Australia's services sector as a way of maintaining economic growth and prosperity.

This focus reflects the large weight of the services sector in the Australian economy (more than 70 per cent of output and 80 per cent of employment) and its underperformance in key areas relative to global productivity benchmarks.

For example, Australia's Productivity Commission found that productivity in Australia's retail industry is almost 40 per cent below the United States', while researchers based at the RBA have found below-par productivity growth in the financial services, education and wholesale industries over the past decade.

Recognising this productivity challenge, the Harper Review of Competition (2015) highlighted the need to cultivate more competition in product markets, particularly across the services sector. The Review emphasised the need for policy settings to be flexible in order to allow new entrants possessing disruptive technologies or lower-cost products into the Australian market, including in the 'sharing economy' and through online provision. As part of this, the Review identified intellectual property law as an area where policy frameworks needed to be reassessed to ensure that the existing regime is not preventing new ideas and technologies from being efficiently dispersed across the economy.

The Review also emphasised the potential for efficiency improvements in human services, including those provided by governments, such as health, education and community services. While already significant, the ageing of Australia's population means that human services are expected to become an even larger part of the economy, underlining the benefits that could accrue in these areas from increased competition and contestability as well as greater consumer choice.

Competition reform will not only help Australian businesses to compete in fiercely contested service export markets, but will also be important in achieving productivity growth across the non-traded segments of the services sector. Better productivity performance in Australia's non-traded sector will, in turn, free up resources to cope with the demands of an ageing population and to further improve living standards over the next decade.

As noted in Box 2.6, there is also room for Australia to significantly improve its infrastructure, with further investment needed in areas like transport networks to support growing urban populations. Additional public spending in these areas needs to be accompanied by a more rigorous approach for selecting projects, to avoid wasting public resources (Infrastructure Australia 2016).

As a relatively small, capital-importing economy, Australia will also need to ensure that policy settings remain supportive of foreign investment in infrastructure and other parts of the economy. China's move towards capital account liberalisation will fundamentally change the availability of funds within the international capital market. China's vast pool of savings could help underpin Australia's investment needs over the next decade, but only if the foreign investment regime and broader policy frameworks continue to make Australia an attractive destination for both direct and portfolio capital inflows. Improving infrastructure delivery for existing assets will be a priority, including through more efficient pricing in the areas of transport and water infrastructure (Infrastructure Australia 2016). Similarly, with a relatively small population, Australia needs to ensure that the local workforce has the capabilities and nimbleness to capitalise on new and emerging technologies. In part, this means building upon the emerging culture of start-up businesses and entrepreneurship, and encouraging greater commercialisation of research ideas, consistent with Australia's National Innovation and Science Agenda (Australian Government 2016).

Partners in economic transformation

For both China and Australia, the past decade saw economic prosperity reach new levels, as each economy successfully navigated the global financial crisis to extend already long periods of unbroken economic expansion.

But global economic circumstances have changed, and the sources of growth that underpinned rising incomes in the last decade will need to change also. The challenge in the next decade will therefore be to unleash new sources of growth, especially in each economy's services sector and in other areas where new technologies are rapidly emerging.

To achieve this, both countries will need to extend and deepen reform in those areas of the economy that have remained protected from domestic and international competition, which will be the main recipe for driving productivity growth and innovation.

In China, opening up domestic capital markets to the rest of the world will be crucial in supporting domestic financial market reforms to improve the allocation of capital and to underpin further increases in incomes. Reforms to reduce the role of SOEs, including those operating in the banking sector, will also be needed, as will further trade liberalisation of China's services sector. Together, these policies can assist China to rebalance towards more consumer-oriented growth, and support the economy's transformation towards the services and higher-technology manufacturing sectors.

In the economic transition, China also needs to balance the short-term goal of supporting a slowing economy with fiscal and monetary policy measures, which may contribute to the rise of total debt, and the long-term objective of achieving more balanced and sustainable growth, which will require a proper management of financial risks.

As China's capital account becomes more open, its investment links with the rest of the world are likely to grow dramatically, which has the potential to profoundly affect Australia and the rest of the world.

As a country reliant on foreign investment, Australia needs to be ready to embrace the expansion in Chinese outbound investment, including in infrastructure where Australia will need to finance new projects in areas like transportation to support growing urban populations and living standards.

More broadly, Australia will need to increase contestability across markets, including in significant parts of the services sector that are currently protected from domestic and international competition. Foreign participation will be important to success in this endeavour. Among other things, this will involve extending reform in areas such as competition policy and labour market regulation and breaking down remaining barriers to international trade.

CHAPTER 3
Trade in goods and services

KEY MESSAGES

Australia and China are and will remain deeply complementary bilateral trading partners. The bedrock of this trade has been China's demand for Australia's mineral and energy exports. The structural transformation of China's economy implies a structural change in the composition of bilateral trade.

Modelling undertaken for this Report indicates that while Australia will continue to supply China with minerals well into the future, the relative importance of high value-added goods and services in Australia's export basket will increase. This transformation will, by itself, lead to fast growth in trade between Australia and China in real terms, much of it in services. Australian companies can be a source of the high-quality food and health products that Chinese consumers increasingly demand. Even more promising is the expansion of the services trade beyond education and tourism, to services such as healthcare and finance, where Australian experience and expertise can assist with the development of China's own services sector. China, meanwhile, will continue to move up the value chain into higher value-added manufacturing and services.

Even in a pessimistic scenario, in which average Chinese growth is below 5 per cent over the next 10 years, the modelling suggests that Australian exports to China would still grow in real terms by 28 per cent and Chinese exports to Australia would grow by 20 per cent. A 'baseline' scenario has Australian exports growing by 72 per cent and Chinese exports by 41 per cent over the same period. But there will be much stronger outcomes — growth of 120 per cent in Australia's exports and 44 per cent in China's — if the two countries succeed in their ambitions for supply-side structural reform.

- The potential of Australia–China trade will not be realised automatically. Australia does not enjoy the same natural advantage in services as it does in resources. Deeper, broader engagement at all levels of society will be necessary. Domestic regulatory reforms in both China and Australia will be necessary if both countries are to make the most of the opportunities.

- Recognition of professional qualifications, starting with traditional Chinese medicine and engineering, will add new trade potential. One reform that offers large potential gains would be to establish recognition of professional services qualifications from the other jurisdiction. By the end of 2017, the side letter to ChAFTA on skills assessment and licensing is due for review. To help make the most of this review, the Australian and Chinese governments should coordinate engagement between accrediting regulatory bodies.

- E-commerce channels are now providing a channel for Chinese consumers to find niche products and services. Regulators on both sides should cooperate, particularly concerning food and healthcare products, to encourage mutual recognition of standards that allow this trade to be scaled up.

- Reflecting the nature of regional and global supply chains, extending the tariff reductions committed to in ChAFTA through to RCEP negotiations will help sustain China's industrial up-skilling.

- In order to capitalise on demand from Chinese tourists, Australia could consider removing restrictions on domestic aviation services that make international routes to the country less commercially attractive. This would not only have positive direct impacts on the competitiveness of the aviation industry in Australia, but would encourage more flights from China that would boost Australia's tourism industry.

- At the national level, the Strategic Economic Dialogue provides a mechanism alongside ChAFTA for high-level official engagement. The Australia–China State/Provincial Leaders Forum and sister-city relationships provide more local channels for engagement.

- Within the community, the Chinese diaspora in Australia is a valuable agent for building engagement and trust, as are civil society organisations and peak business groups.

Economic prosperity in Australia and China depends on international trade. Trade allows countries to specialise in areas of comparative advantage, encourages them to exploit economies of scale, and obliges them to compete with the best the world has to offer in foreign and domestic markets. By increasing competition, trade boosts productivity, fuels innovation, makes consumers better off through improved choice and lowers input prices for producers.

Australia and China are deeply complementary trading partners. Australia has a large natural resource base relative to its population. Australia therefore specialises in the production of primary goods for export, and uses the proceeds to purchase labour-intensive and other manufactured goods. Conversely, China has a large labour supply, but relative to its population has smaller endowments of natural resources and accumulated capital. For this reason, China's industrial development was built on labour-intensive production, which it exchanges with Australia for imports of scarce resources.

In 2014, Australia and China each imported an equivalent of 21 per cent of their GDP, and exported 20 and 24 per cent respectively (OECD 2016). China is now Australia's largest trading partner. It became Australia's single largest source of goods imports in 2006 (replacing the United States, Figure 3.1A) and the largest market for goods exports in 2009 (replacing Japan, Figure 3.1B). The total value of bilateral trade, including goods and services, was in 2015 A\$156 billion (ABS 2015b). In 2009–2010, China overtook the United States as the largest overseas purchaser of Australian services. The value of Australia's services exports to China increased from A\$1.1 billion in 2000–2001 to A\$8.8 billion in 2014–2015, as China's share of Australia's services exports rose from 3 per cent to 14 per cent (ABS 2016c).

The relationship is naturally asymmetric because of the relative size of the two countries. Australia is only China's seventh-largest import source and 14th-largest export destination (DFAT 2016c). Even though Australia is already an economically developed country, its entire population is roughly the same as that of Shanghai. The Chinese economy inevitably dwarfs Australia in scale, despite its much lower levels of per capita income.

This asymmetry means that even small changes in China's economy can have profound impacts on Australia. By contrast, Australian policy choices or economic performance have little impact on China, which has no shortage of other countries competing to supply its huge domestic market. For this reason, Australia needs to ensure that its policies enable flexible markets that can adapt quickly, allowing domestic businesses to remain competitive in response to changing global circumstances. Waiting for global agreements, or holding out on economic liberalisation as a bilateral negotiating tactic, would mean missed opportunities for Australia.

Australia's role as a low-cost, high-quality and reliable provider of raw materials needed for China's growth makes Australia a much more important trading partner than could be expected based on scale alone. Beyond this, Australia can assist China in its own economic transformation to a services-based economy. This is an area where Australian experience may be helpful. Australia's services sector accounts for more than 70 per cent of its real gross value added (ABS 2016e). Outside of mining, the fastest-growing industries in Australia over the last 25 years have been in knowledge-oriented industries such as information media, telecommunications, finance and professional services. There has also been substantial growth in major services industries such as education and tourism (ABS 2016e).

Australia's merchandise trade by trading partner

Figure 3.1A: Export share

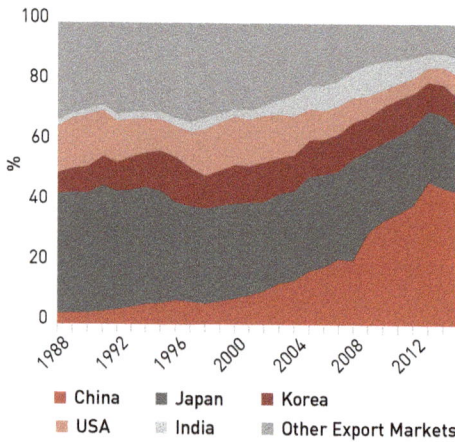

Figure 3.1B: Import share

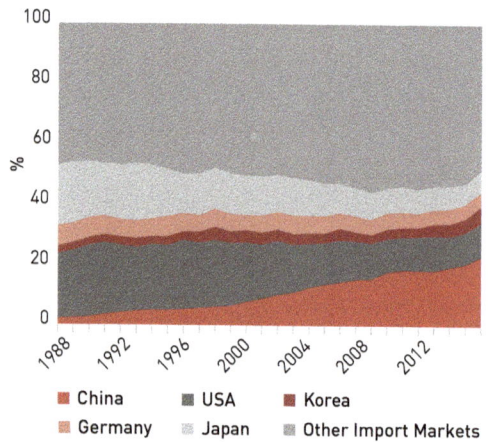

Source: Calculated from ABS 5368.0 2016a.

ChAFTA, which came into force in December 2015, will lower the costs of bilateral trade across resources, manufacturing and services. But ChAFTA is, in many respects, like opening a door. The opportunities of this open door will not be fully realised until further work is done. The two countries therefore need to use the platform established by ChAFTA to develop their respective economic strengths in a mutually beneficial way. In addition to an overarching Joint Commission which is scheduled to meet at least annually to review overall implementation, ChAFTA creates committees dealing with investment, trade in services, financial services, movement of natural persons, trade in goods, sanitary and phytosanitary measures, technical barriers to trade and intellectual property.

Through these forums, ChAFTA should be thought of as a living document that can facilitate many of the policy suggestions from this Report. In particular, Australia can help meet the changing needs of China as it shifts to a more sustainable model for economic development, moving up the value chain with a larger services sector and a growing middle class. The goal of this is not to create any artificial trade preference between Australia and China, but to create an environment in which both countries can more easily develop their respective advantages for mutual benefit. That benefit can extend beyond bilateral trade, and Australia and China can jointly pursue trade strategies that expand regional integration to spread the gains from trade through countries involved in the Regional Comprehensive Economic Partnership (RCEP), and eventually a Free Trade Area of Asia and the Pacific (FTAAP) (see Chapter 7).

The resources trade

The unprecedented scale and speed of China's urban construction, as well as China's dominance in manufacturing, have demanded tremendous mineral and energy resources, particularly steel (Garnaut 2012). The main inputs to steel are iron ore and metallurgical coal, both of which Australia has in abundance at high quality and low cost. Prior to the 2000s, Australia's main exports to China had been agricultural, with iron ore accounting for just 15 per cent of the value of Australian exports to China in 2001 (DFAT 2011).

Australian iron ore helped fuel China's investment boom in the early 2000s. While the global financial crisis caused a brief slump in 2008, the resources-intensive nature of China's investment-led growth helped Australia avoid the recession that gripped other advanced economies. As iron ore prices peaked in 2011, Australia's iron ore exports were worth A$44 billion, or 57 per cent of the total value of Australian exports to China. By the end of 2015, the iron ore price had fallen to one-quarter of its peak, in response to increased global supply and slowing demand growth in China. However, increased export volumes and the declining value of the Australian dollar mean that the total Australian dollar value of iron ore exports has remained well above historic levels (Figure 3.2) and Australia's total share of China's iron ore imports has been increasing.

Figure 3.2: Iron ore price and export value

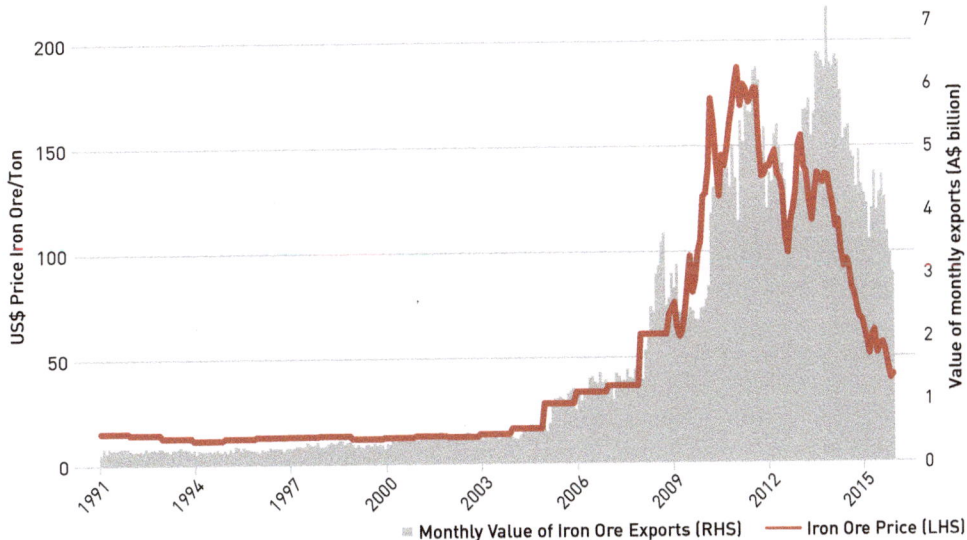

Source: Price, IndexMundi - China import Iron Ore Fines 62% FE spot (CFR Tianjin port), US Dollar per Dry Metric Ton, Monthly Export, and Australian Bureau of Statistics cat no. 5368.0 Table 12B 2016a.

The prices of commodities are determined through the interaction of global demand and supply, including the recent effects of Chinese investment overseas to expand that supply while reducing the resource-intensity of growth on the demand side through improved efficiency. Because the price of commodities impacts both Australia and China greatly, better understanding price determinants and the effect of supply responses should be one of the priorities for joint academic research between Chinese and Australian academic, government and business partners.

Whatever the fluctuations in global prices, the sheer volume of Chinese resource demand will keep resources as the bedrock of bilateral trade for decades. Even at slower rates of economic growth, the size of the base to which that growth applies means that overall demand will still increase by a significant amount in absolute terms. There are still hundreds of millions of Chinese who will move to cities. This migration, coupled with higher levels of income and consumption for urban residents, could sustain Chinese demand for apartments, highways, railways, bridges and cars (Berkelmans and Wang 2012; Wilinks and Zurawaski 2014). Although China's richest cities suffer from traffic congestion, overall car ownership in China is low. A continued shift in manufacturing from textiles, clothing and footwear to higher value-added electronics and machinery will also support resource demand. China produced 603 kilograms of steel per person in 2014, but peak steel demand could reach 700–800 kilograms per person in the mid-2020s depending on the spread of automobile ownership, the prevalence of high-rise construction and the pace of technological change (McKay et al 2010). China's steel producers operate in a highly competitive market — continued reliance on market mechanisms to deal with any short-term overcapacity in steel production is the best way to make sure that the supply will adjust to meet demand (Hubbard 2015).

Much of these resources will continue to be imported. China's dependence on imported iron ore rose from 50 per cent in 2005 to 81 per cent in 2015. Australia's share of these imports rose from 41 per cent in 2008 to 64 per cent in 2015 (Russell 2016). As prices have fallen, Australian iron ore producers increased their share of the Chinese market. In fact, even as China's steel production declined by 2.3 per cent in 2015, the volume of Australia's iron ore exports to China increased by 9.8 per cent (Roberts et al 2016).

Chinese demand for Australian resources extends well beyond iron ore. The composition of China's resource consumption is likely to change as its manufacturers move up the value chain and its middle class continues to grow (Box 3.1). For example, greater demand for whitegoods, consumer electronics and lightweight electric vehicles will increase demand for Australian copper and bauxite (the mineral from which aluminium is produced), and require more thermal coal, gas and uranium for power generation. Australia supplies half of China's imports of metallurgical coal, another key ingredient in steel. ChAFTA is already assisting Australian resource exporters, having eliminated the tariff on metallurgical coal in December 2015. It also removes Chinese tariffs on steaming coal, copper, aluminium, nickel, zinc and titanium, either immediately or over a four-year period. This could reduce costs of delivering Australian minerals and energy to China by A$600 million per year (Minerals Council of Australia 2016).

> ## BOX 3.1: MORE THAN ORE
>
> China's consumption of copper and aluminium has increased by 16 per cent annually over the past decade, making it the world's largest consumer of both commodities. In 2014, China bought 46 per cent of Australia's copper exports, worth A$1.8 billion, and 74 per cent of Australia's total nickel exports, worth A$0.6 billion. China's machinery, automobile and home appliance industries are key drivers of aluminium demand. Australian exports of aluminium oxide to China make up 89 per cent of total world aluminium oxide exports. And Australian exports of aluminium metal to China are 19.1 per cent of total world aluminium exports (Minerals Council of Australia 2016). As China increases production of more sophisticated manufacturing goods its demand for aluminium will also increase. The scale of China's aluminium smelting capacity makes it difficult for other nations to compete for supply of the primary metal, but Australia remains a major supplier of the bauxite and alumina required to feed those smelters.
>
> China's imports of LNG will grow as China seeks cleaner energy sources by reducing dependence on coal. Australia is currently one of the world's three largest uranium exporters, and has had an agreement since 2006 to allow uranium exports to China. While trade statistics on uranium are not publicly available, the volume of Australian uranium exports to China (around 500 tons a year) is reportedly less than exports to the United States, the EU, Japan or South Korea (World Nuclear Association 2016).

Australia was China's second-largest supplier of coal in 2015, after Indonesia. Australia supplied 35 per cent of China's total import tonnage (Figure 3.3A). Australia is China's largest supplier of liquefied natural gas (LNG), supplying 28 per cent of China's rapidly growing imports in 2015 (Figure 3.3B).

Figure 3.3: Chinese imports from Australia and rest of world

Figure 3.3A: Coal (Tons)

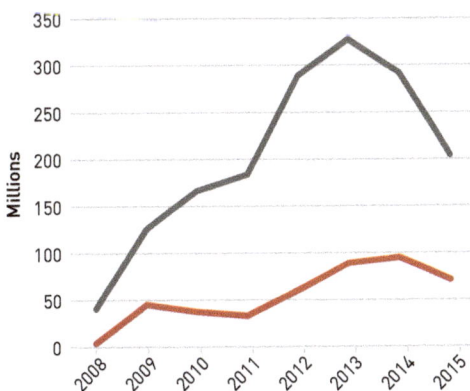

Figure 3.3B: LNG (Tons)

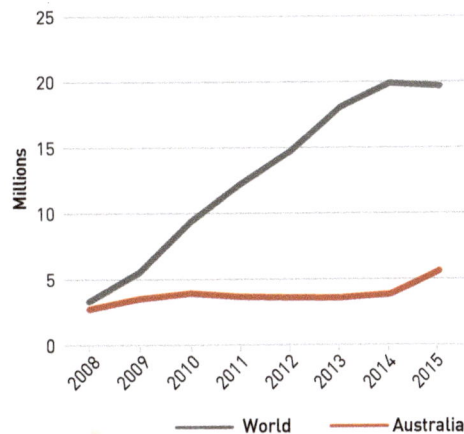

Source: China General Administration of Customs 2016.

Projections across a range of commodities suggest that food and LNG are likely to rise in importance as a share of Australia's exports to China, while iron ore and base metals are likely to fall as a share of total commodity exports (Table 3.1).

Table 3.1: Actual and projected exports of commodities to China

Share of commodity exports to China by value (per cent)				
	2005	2015	2025	2035
Growth scenario	Actual	Estimated	Projection	Projection
Iron ore	47.3	57.9	51–51.5	43–47.5
Base metals	25.1	13.2	13	12–13
Coal	4.3	8.7	9.5–10	11–13
Natural gas (LNG)	0.0	5.4	10	12–14
Food	5.8	8.6	9	9.5–11

Source: Roberts et al 2016.

The Australia–China resource trade relationship echoes the evolution of the Australia–Japan relationship since the 1960s. While Australia's resources trade is private, since 1976 there has been an official treaty-level recognition between Australia and Japan of each country's 'mutual interest in each being a stable and reliable supplier', discussed further in Box 3.2 (Dee 2006). The 2014 Japan–Australia Economic Partnership Agreement affirmed this principle in a chapter that ensures the stable supply of energy and minerals. This commitment is important, because while global trade disciplines are strong with respect to restricting import bans, multilateral rules against export restrictions are not as robust.

BOX 3.2: RESOURCE SECURITY AND GLOBAL TRADE

All economies require access to energy and mineral resources for industrialisation, urbanisation and growth. To ensure stability of their own economy, some countries adopt policies to ensure resource stability, which may include strategic stockpiles of resources or, in extreme cases, policies tending toward autarky. But these policies are often insufficient to meet demand, and can only be done at very high cost. They forgo the gains that can be had from global trade on open markets consistent with comparative advantage.

But international trade is not without its risks. Raw materials may be abundant in, or need to transit through, politically unstable or dangerous parts of the world.

The resource partnerships between Australia and the countries of Northeast Asia over the last 60 years is a powerful example of how resource security can be achieved through open markets, in a stable geopolitical setting and in the context of mature political relationships. The ability of downstream resource users to invest directly into Australia's resources adds the reassurance that resources will be available, while expanding supply for global markets.

As pointed out in Chapter 1, the geographical orientation of the Chinese economy has changed fundamentally, from being continentally self-contained to being the largest maritime economy in the world. Import dependence has grown as commodity prices have fallen and high-cost domestic supplies become less attractive industrial inputs. The reductions in costs and gains in efficiency from increased reliance on international markets have freed up capital for investment elsewhere in the Chinese economy and made better use of state resources. This development has naturally and steadily drawn China into the maritime economy, including the construction of huge sea freight capacities, interest in maritime scientific and weather research, and concern about securing international supplies. As it is one of the world's largest maritime resource suppliers, Australia reciprocates these interests.

Policy thinking about the implications of China's maritime economy has failed to keep pace with this change. The major effort to redress this deficiency that is now under way in China would be assisted by collaboration between Australia and China on the implications of growing resource dependency for resource security, maritime resource development and protection, maritime scientific and weather research, and Australian participation in China's Maritime Silk Road initiative. Working together on these and other joint interests in the maritime economy, given both countries' deep mutual interests in this subject, should be seen as a top priority for both governments. The initiative can commence under the established framework for cooperation between China's National Development and Reform Commission (NDRC) and the Australian Treasury, and bring in other agencies and research organisations as it develops. This could include building on the excellent cooperation between both countries on Antarctic research.

Resource security is important for China in ensuring ongoing inputs for its economic growth. This does not mean security from international markets. A treaty-level commitment between Australia and China not to arbitrarily restrict Australian resource exports would help reinforce China's confidence in the ability of open markets to provide resource security while reducing costs and improving efficiency through increased competition. This would both be good for China as a recipient of Australian raw materials, and good for the Australian resources industry, which could make long-term plans with confidence. This commitment would be the core of the proposed Australia–China Comprehensive Strategic Partnership for Change.

Agricultural trade

Even before China's reform and opening in the late 1970s, the postwar Australia–China trade relationship had begun in agriculture, with large-scale Australian wheat exports to China from 1960 (Wilczynski 1965). Mineral exports to China overtook agricultural exports in the 2000s, but Australia still plays an important role in China's agricultural market. China has also become a significant exporter of agricultural products to Australia. The location of the two countries in different hemispheres means that counter-seasonal products can be traded to fill domestic supply gaps. The proximity of the two countries allows for products to reach markets quickly and in quality condition. And Australia's track record as a safe and reliable source of high-quality produce shows that it can help meet the food safety demands of Chinese consumers.

Australia's exports of agricultural primary products to China grew steadily through the 2000s before more than doubling in value between 2009–2010 and 2013–2014, when they reached A$9.6 billion. In 2010–2011, China overtook Japan to become the most important export destination for Australian agricultural primary products. China's share of Australia's total agricultural exports grew from 6.4 per cent in 2000–2001 to over 20 per cent in 2014–2015 (Austrade 2016b).

Australian exports of wool and grains to China were each worth more than A$2 billion in 2014–2015 (Figure 3.4). Australia is China's largest source of wool imports. Australian beef exports to China have grown, from a low base, at a rate of more than 200 per cent a year and were worth more than A$736 million in 2014–2015. China is Australia's second-largest market for dairy exports, which grew an average of 20 per cent annually over the past five years (and were worth A$295 million in 2014–2015) (Australia–China Business Council 2015). Australian wine exports have focused on the Chinese market for more than a decade. China's wine import industry was valued at A$2.1 billion in 2014–2015. Australia is China's second-largest wine supplier by value, with exports valued at A$269 million in 2014–2015 (DFAT 2014b). China has also tapped the expertise of foreign winemakers and has been expanding its own domestic production over this time, which is why growth opportunities for Australian winemakers come from focusing on the premium market rather than bulk wine exports.

Agricultural trade has grown despite Chinese tariff barriers and non-tariff measures. WTO data show that while China's trade-weighted average tariff rate in 2013 was just 4.6 per cent, it was 13.5 per cent for agricultural goods (WTO 2016b). ChAFTA removed some of these barriers. For example, tariffs on beef that previously ranged from 12–25 per cent are being eliminated (DFAT 2014b). Under ChAFTA, the Australian dairy industry will now receive even more favourable treatment than that negotiated by New Zealand with China in their 2008 free trade agreement.

One of the key drivers for opening up China's agriculture to further trade is to ensure long-term food security through access to open markets. Chinese agriculture still tends to be relatively small-scale and non-commercial, although there are now major agricultural operations in the private and public sectors that are expanding their influence in China and abroad. As more arable land passes into urban use, Australia's highly productive firms and extensive land can buttress China's food supplies. In the same way that Australia has proved to be a reliable partner for Chinese energy and minerals demand, so too can Australia be a valuable partner in supplementing China's food security.

Developing the capacity necessary to meet China's demand, even at the margin, will require significant investment in Australian agribusiness, some of which may be financed by Chinese investors, as discussed in Chapter 4 (Australia–China Business Council 2014).

Volume growth is not the only indicator of potential. Australian agriculture also offers premium opportunities to serve China's growing middle-income consumers. Moreover, according to the BCG China Consumer Survey 2016, food safety tops the list of consumer concerns, ahead of health care, education and the environment. The results are particularly stark for younger Chinese consumers, with 63 per cent of those aged between 18 and 25 expressing dissatisfaction with food safety (Walters and Kuo 2016).

Since 2004, both countries' dairy industries have been involved in an official dialogue (DFAT 2012). But moving from formal dialogue to large-scale delivery of new supply will require investment, services and infrastructure. A 2012 joint report between the Australia and Chinese ministries responsible for trade and for agriculture identified the construction of breeding facilities, as well as dairy farms, as possible opportunities for Chinese investment in Australian agribusiness.

Part of the premium value of Australian food products in China is Australia's track record in supply-chain management and food safety. For Chinese investors, partnering with recognised Australian brands and businesses can help them realise the full value of their output. For Australian businesses, partnering with Chinese investors helps with distribution channels within China, whether directly to retail consumers or as inputs for other parts of the Chinese food industry.

Despite these opportunities, investors in Australia from China face a much stricter threshold for investment in agribusiness (A$55 million) compared to other sectors (where the threshold is over A$1 billion) or compared to other FTA partners from Chile, New Zealand and the United States, as well as other TPP members should the TPP come into force. While this screening threshold does not necessarily prevent investment going ahead, it adds extra costs and risks to investments that would expand trade and develop rural Australia. Barriers to Chinese investment are considered in Chapter 4.

New opportunities for bilateral trade

The mining boom benefited Australians directly employed in the resource sector, boosted government tax receipts and increased the purchasing power of Australians overseas through a stronger Australian dollar. Australian households could afford to import more, and much of this import demand was met by China. By 2014–2015, almost one-third of Australia's imports of elaborately transformed manufactures — a category that includes clothing, motor vehicles, machinery and paint — came from China, up from just 10 per cent in 2000–2001 (ABS 2002; DFAT 2016c).

But the high Australian dollar also reduced the competitiveness of other Australian exports, particularly in manufacturing. Indeed, the rapid rise of Chinese manufacturing, with hundreds of millions of low-cost Chinese workers entering the global economy for the first time, inhibited wage growth in the lower end of manufacturing around the world.

The boost in Australia's national income from the resources boom cushioned Australia from some of the costs that come with industrial restructuring. However, Australia now faces significant policy challenges if it is to maintain its living standards while adjusting to much lower commodity prices. In particular, Australia's resource endowments and position in Asia provide limited competitive advantage to Australian business when compared to competitors in other developed markets in Europe and North America.

The flexibility of Australia's floating exchange rate regime, which allows the dollar to fall in value as commodity demand eases, is an important channel for making non-resource sectors more competitive. But policymakers need to make sure that labour markets are flexible enough to enable creation of jobs in emerging industries, that workers are able to acquire the skills required to find new employment in emerging industries, and that faster-growing regions receive adequate infrastructure investment. The removal of obstacles to Chinese capital to develop Australia's productive capacity in areas of growing Chinese demand would be of benefit to both countries and strengthen their overall relationship (see Chapter 4).

Figure 3.4: Australian agricultural exports to China (A$ million, 2014–2015)

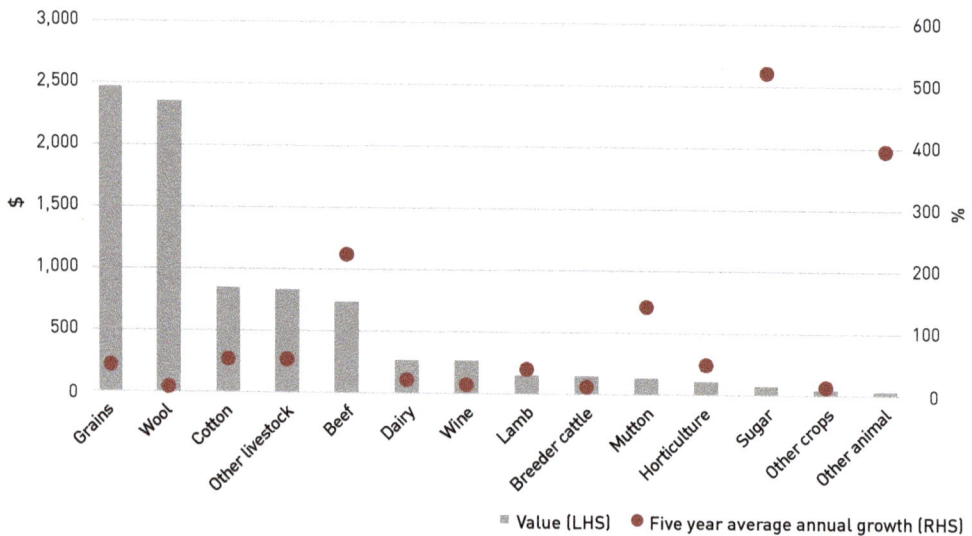

Note: Free on board value, Grains includes oilseeds and pulses.
Source: ABARES 2016.

As ChAFTA comes into effect, over 86 per cent of Australia's goods exports to China (by 2014 value) will enter duty free. This will increase to 94 per cent by 2019 and 96 per cent by 2029 (DFAT 2016d). This is an important opportunity to diversify Australia's exports to China. In 2014, more than 85 per cent of Australia's goods exports to China were in unprocessed primary products and gold.

Comparing this figure with Australian exports to high-income Northeast Asian economies shows that while primary exports comprise an important share of exports to these other countries, there is also a large role for processed primary products, especially foods (Figure 3.5). This suggests that there is a significant opportunity for Australian agribusiness to transform raw unprocessed food and livestock into safe and respected brands of high-quality food, wine and dairy products to export to China in the future. Australia is also a large potential source of ingredients used in Traditional Chinese Medicine (TCM).

The value of Chinese online retail sales of goods and services in 2015 was RMB3.9 trillion (US$592 billion), an increase of 33.3 per cent compared with 2014. This growth is due primarily to lower prices, greater product variety, better product information, more reliable seller reputations and faster delivery times compared to traditional retail shopping. The pent-up demand for quality Australian goods in China is evident in the growing volume of Australian goods retailed directly and indirectly in China through e-commerce channels.

Chinese consumers demand foreign goods for their quality. According to Nielson research, Chinese online shoppers imported US$16.3 billion of foreign products in 2014 (Burbank 2014). In 2014, Australia Post and the Chinese e-commerce giant Alibaba agreed to a deal that allows Australian brands to sell directly to Chinese consumers through leading Chinese online retailer TMall (ABC News 2014) (Box 3.3). Popular purchases from Australia include health food products, infant formula, cosmetics, organic foods and sheepskin boots. An advantage of this arrangement is that it guarantees to the Chinese consumer the authenticity of the good and provides a guaranteed supply chain for sellers.

Figure 3.5: Australian goods exports to Northeast Asian economies

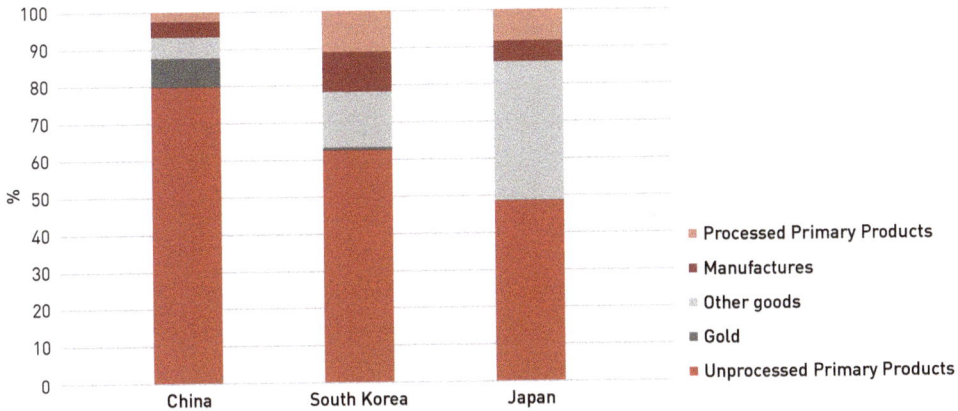

Note: The export of 'other goods' includes confidential uranium exports.
Source: DFAT 2015c

The opportunities presented by the internet and e-commerce need to be closely studied. Government agencies responsible for innovation policies on both sides should partner with industry to identify and remove barriers to the full adoption of this new technology. Moreover, the policies that affect cross-border e-commerce need to be carefully communicated on each side. For example, sudden recent changes to the enforcement of China's Customs and Duties Law were mistakenly but avoidably perceived by some as a crackdown on foreign competition, rather than the closing of a tax loophole (Manuel 2016).

Although changes to China's e-commerce market were widely anticipated, the rollout of these changes was conducted without adequate consultation with key stakeholders. This resulted in confusion in the market, and led to adverse impacts on suppliers. This has been a learning experience. These guidelines have since been revised and a grace period allowed in order to minimise unintended consequences and allow for sellers and suppliers to adjust to these changes. Closer cooperation between Australian and Chinese customs authorities could help ensure that these kinds of actions are better communicated and understood. It could also ensure that regulations are commonly understood and consistently applied between all stakeholders.

Even outside e-commerce channels, there is a strong flow of health food products that are bought at retail outlets in Australia and posted to China (Battersby and Zhou 2015). Small-scale retail can be attractive partly because of the high number of Chinese with friends and relatives in Australia, and because these low-value personal imports into China avoid the need to undergo the often-onerous product and food-safety testing that would be required for commercial imports. While formal tariff barriers are reduced under ChAFTA, the need for product testing and certification within China increases the costs of larger-scale trade in agriculture and processed food products. Therefore, Australian companies can also be successful in complementing e-commerce delivery channels with a traditional 'bricks and mortar' presence (see Box 3.4).

Removing barriers to, and lowering the cost of, commercial-scale imports, as well as guaranteeing the integrity of bilateral supply chains and product quality, should be a priority for Australia–China trade cooperation. When the enforcement of domestic standards on imported goods is more rigorous than it is for locally produced goods, this constitutes a de facto trade barrier. There are opportunities to reduce these discrepancies, based on an overarching principle that the purpose of such regulations is to protect domestic consumers, not domestic producers. Indeed, one reason for the popularity of e-commerce in Australia–China trade is Australian producers of food and nutritional products not being able to access Chinese consumers through traditional channels because of high tariffs and protracted product registration and accreditation processes.

BOX 3.3: ALIBABA GROUP OPENS NEW MARKETS FOR AUSTRALIAN EXPORTERS

Alibaba Group has provided an electronic bridge for Australian exporters into new Chinese markets.

The value of China's e-commerce market exceeded US$600 billion in 2015. Of this, Alibaba accounted for around US$485 billion in e-commerce sales, or over 80 per cent of the total. This figure makes Alibaba Group the largest retail e-commerce company in the world. By the 2020 fiscal year, Alibaba aims to be the first company to have a retail market scale of over US$1 trillion.

Australian exporters have achieved success by tapping into Alibaba Group's e-commerce platforms including Tmall, Tmall Global, 1688.com, Taobao and Alibaba.com.

Australian products are increasingly popular on Chinese e-commerce channels. Alibaba sees strong and growing demand for a range of products such as dairy, premium foods, healthcare, skincare, and mother and baby products.

Each year, Alibaba runs the largest shopping festival in the world, the Double 11 Shopping Festival, on 11 November. In 2015, Australia ranked fifth among 41 countries globally on Tmall Global, with one Australian vendor, Chemist Warehouse, recording sales worth RMB10 million (over A$2 million) in just the first 46 minutes of the Festival.

Alibaba Group has also forged a strategic partnership with Australia Post. Australia Post's Tmall store provides a solution for exporters, particularly small and medium enterprises, to access some of the 420 million active Chinese consumers across Alibaba Group's platforms.

Alibaba Group plans to open an office in Australia at the end of the 2016 to better support its Australian clients and assist more Australian companies in accessing the Chinese market.

To level the playing field further, China could unilaterally recognise Australia's high food safety and quality standards, and expedite the approvals of Australian food exports to China. This would be a win–win policy: it would benefit Chinese consumers through lower prices and benefit Australian producers through lower transaction costs. Both countries should aim to ensure that Chinese consumers can access safe products at low cost from around the world. The relevant chapter of ChAFTA on sanitary and phytosanitary measures can help ensure that quarantine rules do not pose an unnecessary obstacle to trade. However, there are opportunities to go further in building trust and understanding on both sides, including through direct exchanges of officials.

BOX 3.4: BLACKMORES' CHINA ENTRY STRATEGY

Blackmores is a market leader in the natural vitamin, herbal and mineral supplements market in Australia, with strong market positions throughout Asia.

Blackmores launched in China in 2012 and has established itself as a premium natural health brand with Chinese consumers. Before launching in China, Blackmores spent more than two years researching the market. This involved extensive use of the services of Austrade and DFAT to understand the regulatory environment, to meet relevant Chinese government agencies, to connect with industry organisations and to assess potential partners and market-entry models.

Unlike many foreign firms who saw rapid growth in China's vitamins and dietary supplements market as a short-term trading opportunity, Blackmores' relationship with China has been positioned for the very long term. The company established a Wholly Owned Foreign Enterprise (WOFE) in Beijing and subsequently established branch offices in Shanghai and within the Shanghai Free Trade Zone.

Blackmores has absorbed from its long history and experience in other Asian markets — the company has been in Thailand and Malaysia for 40 years — that success in the region requires the recruitment of strong locally engaged teams in each market who are responsible for its brand. Since 2012, Blackmores has built a team of 30 staff in China with offices in Beijing, Shanghai and Guangzhou, with another soon to open in Chengdu.

Blackmores distributes through the traditional 'bricks and mortar' retail trade, has an extensive online presence and over 3200 offline distribution points covering first-tier and second-tier cities. The company has a wide-ranging presence on all major Chinese e-commerce platforms (domestic and cross-border), including Tmall and JD.com as well as strategic partnerships with VIP.com and Netease. The company serves more than 20 key e-retailers and thousands of Taobao and WeChat stores through Free Trade Zone distributors. Blackmores has also undertaken broad channel expansion to cover chain pharmacy, independent pharmacy, health and beauty stores, supermarkets, hypermarkets, medical, TV shopping, duty free outlets, department stores and corporate sales.

Blackmores strongly supported the entry into force of ChAFTA, which strengthens the long-term commercial ties between Australia and China. ChAFTA not only delivered the elimination of tariffs on Australia's pharmaceutical, vitamin and health supplement products but also contains a built-in agenda to address non-tariff barriers to trade between Australia and China.

This situation could be improved by the increased sharing of technical expertise between regulators in Australia and China, including staff exchanges. Such exchanges would help build capacity, familiarity and trust with each other's regulatory systems.

The next stage for bilateral trade

The opportunities for both China and Australia are large, if policymakers are proactive in pursuing the reforms necessary to achieve them.

ChAFTA offers a framework through which Australia–China initiatives in reform and liberalisation across all areas — merchandise trade, services trade and investment — can be advanced. The bilateral liberalisation of commodity market access delivers some immediate benefits. These benefits are important to the growth of agricultural trade, for example, but they will also be dependent on improving the bilateral investment regime and achieving the liberalisation of complementary services. Given the big shift in the structure of the Australia–China relationship that this Report highlights, many of the potential gains from ChAFTA will only be realised through securing reform and opening of trade in services as well as reform of investment policies. It is difficult, in any case, for liberalisation of trade in services to be narrowly bilateral and only providing special if limited benefit to either Australia or China in each other's market. Reform that increases the productivity of services markets requires comprehensive domestic institutional reform. But ChAFTA opens the door to trialling services reform with Australia in China and has the potential to be at the leading edge of China's economic reform program. There is potential for ChAFTA to deliver benefits beyond the border for domestic reform in both countries.

Modelling undertaken for this Report bolsters this case. First, the gains are estimated from the full preferential merchandise trade liberalisation that is potentially available under the ChAFTA framework, using standard GTAP techniques (Gretton 2016). (In Chapter 4, this will be extended to consider the gains to be had from liberalisation that is more comprehensive, including services and investment). The present simulation shows that the removal of all tariffs preferentially between China and Australia yields modest but important output gains to each country. In the long run, it could increase Australia's GDP by 0.22 per cent and lift China's GDP by 0.11 per cent (Table 3.2). This simulation measures the maximum possible gain under a fully comprehensive ChAFTA agreement, not the gains from the agreement that is currently in place. It presumes that the two countries will move to 100 per cent bilateral tariff removal in their merchandise trade, and that there are no negative effects imposed by rules of origin or other regulations to enforce preferences. The ChAFTA agreement currently in place is in fact still subject to carve-outs and product-specific rules of origin and will not yield these gains fully, but this measure can be regarded as the outer limit to potential gains from ChAFTA-focused merchandise trade liberalisation.

Table 3.2: Simulated effects of reducing remaining tariffs to zero

	Australia		China	
	GDP	Gain as proportion of full world MFN liberalisation	GDP	Gain as proportion of full world MFN liberalisation
Simulation	per cent change	per cent of full gain	per cent change	per cent of full gain
Australia–China bilateral	0.22	23	0.11	4
Australia unilateral	0.56	60	0.03	1
China unilateral	0.12	13	2.28	78
RCEP open liberalisation	0.88	94	2.37	81
World MFN liberalisation	0.94	100	2.94	100

Source: Gretton 2016.

By way of comparison, and to define the parameters of gains from using ChAFTA as a lever for broader regional and multilateral liberalisation, modelling is done to simulate liberalisation through a comprehensive Asian free trade agreement — RCEP. And, as a benchmark, an estimate is made of the benefits to Australia and China from multilateral merchandise trade liberalisation.

If RCEP brings comprehensive merchandise trade liberalisation based on open regionalism, Australia's GDP could increase by 0.88 per cent and China's by 2.37 per cent. If all tariffs were removed globally, Australia's GDP could increase by 0.94 per cent and China's by 2.94 per cent. Australia can achieve 60 per cent of that global merchandise trade liberalisation scenario by unilaterally removing tariffs. China can achieve 78 per cent of the global scenario by removing its tariffs. These scenarios are simply simulated to estimate the different magnitudes of potential gains under alternative trade policy strategies.

The structure of bilateral trade

Not only is the volume of trade between China and Australia set to increase, its structure will change as well, depending on the ways in which the Chinese economy itself is transformed.

The growth trajectory of China's economy will be one of the biggest stories in the global economy over the next decade. Not only will it matter for the living standards for Chinese people, it will also impact on China's trade with Australia and the rest of the world.

Taking into account possible developments in both economies as well as in the rest of the world, what is the structure and scale of Australia–China trade likely to look like in the next 10 years? To answer this question, growth and its structure over this period is modelled under three different sets of assumptions using GTAP (Sheng 2016).

In the period until 2020, International Monetary Fund (IMF) growth projections are used, after which three growth scenarios for China are projected using United Nations population projections and the global competitiveness index as a proxy for quality of institutions. In the first 'business as usual' case, China's GDP grows at an average annual rate of 5.0 per cent a year from 2021 to 2025 with annual average labour productivity growth of 5.2 per cent offsetting an annual average decline in the working-age population of 0.2 per cent (Table 3.3).

An optimistic, or reform-based, scenario would see Chinese institutions converge upwards to the quality of South Korean institutions, with growth then averaging 6.1 per cent to 2025. A final, stagnation case would see growth fall to 3.1 per cent per year as Chinese institutions converge downwards towards the quality of Turkish institutions. The growth rate to 2020 is from the IMF and is the same for all three projections, at 6 per cent from 2016–2020.

The structure of bilateral Australia–China trade is projected to 2025 under the three growth scenarios. The world is split into 12 regions and 16 sectors, which are comprised of 10 manufacturing, two agricultural and four service sectors. The results are shown graphically in Figure 3.6.

Table 3.3: Decomposition of Chinese GDP growth under three growth scenarios

	Historic 2011–2015	IMF Outlook 2016–2020	Projection 2021–2025
Business as usual			
Growth	7.5	6.0	5.0
Productivity	7.3	6.3	5.2
Working population	0.2	−0.3	−0.2
Reform scenario			
Growth	7.5	6.7	6.1
Productivity	7.3	6.9	6.3
Working population	0.2	−0.3	−0.3
Stagnation			
Growth	7.5	5.0	3.1
Productivity	7.3	5.8	3.3
Working population	0.2	−0.3	−0.2

Source: Hubbard and Sharma 2016.

Under the business as usual scenario of an average of 5.73 per cent growth per year from 2016–2025, Australian exports to China grow from US$84.0 billion in 2014 to US$145 billion in 2025, or 72 per cent in constant value terms over the decade. Chinese exports to Australia increase from US$41.0 billion to US$58.0 billion, or 17 per cent. Total Australian exports increase from US$295 billion to US$535 billion while total Chinese exports increase to US$4.04 trillion from US$2.58 trillion. China's share in Australian exports falls slightly to 27.1 per cent (from 28.5 per cent) while Australia's share in China's exports falls from 1.6 per cent to 1.43 per cent.

Figure 3.6: Real growth in exports from China and Australia under three Chinese growth scenarios

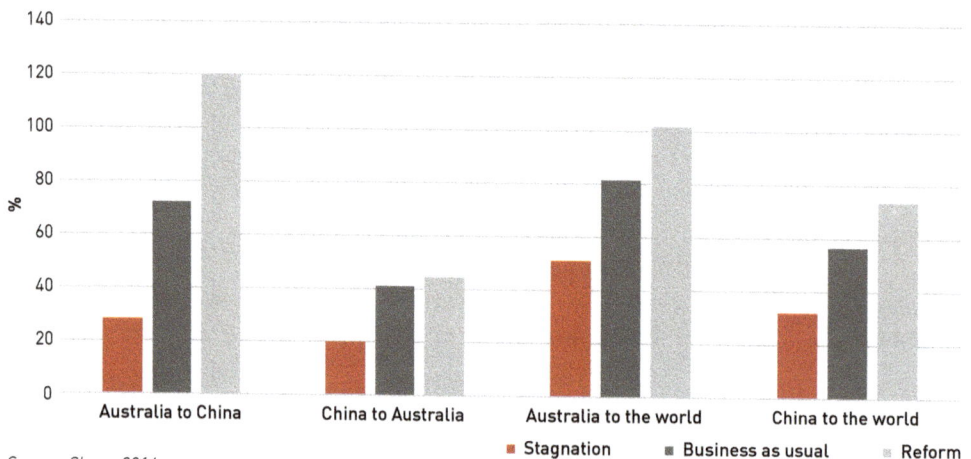

Source: Sheng 2016

The extraction sector, which includes metals, minerals and various other natural resources, is the largest sector for Australia comprising of 70.6 per cent of exports to China and 46.6 per cent of total exports in 2014 (Table 3.4). The relative importance of this sector falls in 2025 to 58.7 per cent of Australia's exports to China and 36.0 per cent of total exports.

The growth in Australia's exports to China is driven mainly by services, which more than double as a proportion of total trade, led by transport, telecommunications, computer and information services. Currently the Australian services export sector is largely education and tourism, with education accounting for 4.9 per cent of Australian exports to China (of the 8.0 per cent that the transport, travel and tourism sector accounts for). Under the business as usual scenario, education and tourism grow to 11.9 per cent of Australian exports to China, of the 19.6 per cent that the broader transport, travel and tourism sector accounts for. Agricultural exports also rise substantially.

Table 3.4: Actual and projected shares of exports by sector

	2014				2025 Business as usual			
	Aus to China	Aus Total	China to Aus	China Total	Aus to China	Aus Total	China to Aus	China Total
Grains and Crops	2.5	4.5	0.4	1.4	3.0	4.8	0.3	0.9
Livestock and Meat Products	4.8	6.0	0.5	0.7	6.4	6.9	0.5	0.6
Mining and Extraction	70.6	46.6	2.3	2.1	58.7	36.0	1.5	0.9
Processed Food	0.6	1.9	1.2	0.9	0.8	2.5	1.1	0.7
Textiles and Clothing	0.0	0.2	21.7	16.3	0.0	0.2	20.0	15.0
Leather, Wood and Paper products	0.6	0.9	4.5	3.1	0.5	0.7	4.7	3.4
Petroleum and Chemical products	8.2	8.7	14.1	12.1	6.3	8.5	10.7	8.6
Metal products	2.9	4.4	9.0	7.2	2.2	3.2	7.8	6.1
Motor vehicles and transport equipment	0.1	1.6	4.8	4.1	0.1	1.8	5.3	4.5
Electronic equipment	0.2	0.9	14.1	22.2	0.1	0.2	15.1	26.0
Other machinery and equipment	0.7	2.9	19.6	18.4	0.5	3.3	27.9	25.7
Other manufacturing	0.0	2.9	3.0	2.5	0.0	3.8	2.1	1.8
Utilities and construction services	0.1	0.4	0.1	0.6	0.1	0.5	0.1	0.6
Transport, travel and tourism	8.0	12.9	3.7	3.7	19.6	19.7	2.2	2.0
Financial, insurance and business	0.5	1.8	0.4	1.1	1.1	2.5	0.2	0.7
Other services	0.3	3.3	0.6	3.6	0.6	5.2	0.5	2.6
Bilateral trade share (% of trade with world)	**28.5**		**1.6**		**27.1**		**1.4**	

Source: Sheng 2016.

Table 3.5: Actual and projected share of exports by sector in alternative scenarios

	2025 Reform				2025 Stagnation			
	Aus to China	Aus Total	China to Aus	China Total	Aus to China	Aus Total	China to Aus	China Total
Grains and Crops	3.4	4.8	0.1	0.3	2.8	4.6	0.3	0.9
Livestock and Meat Products	10.3	8.0	0.0	0.0	6.2	6.5	0.5	0.5
Mining and Extraction	62.2	41.5	0.4	0.2	59.1	39.1	1.2	0.6
Processed Food	0.7	2.3	0.8	0.5	0.8	2.4	1.1	0.8
Textiles and Clothing	0.0	0.2	16.5	10.7	0.0	0.2	21.1	15.5
Leather, Wood and Paper products	0.5	0.9	2.5	1.7	0.5	0.8	4.7	3.4
Petroleum and Chemical products	3.2	7.3	12.9	9.5	6.6	8.1	10.2	8.2
Metal products	1.5	2.7	8.3	5.9	2.5	3.3	7.4	5.8
Motor vehicles and transport equipment	0.1	1.7	2.1	1.7	0.1	1.7	5.0	4.3
Electronic equipment	0.1	0.3	14.2	21.6	0.1	0.3	16.5	27.4
Other machinery and equipment	0.2	2.4	34.8	28.9	0.7	3.4	27.1	25.1
Other manufacturing	0.1	4.0	0.8	0.6	0.1	3.8	1.9	1.6
Utilities and construction services	0.1	0.4	0.1	0.6	0.1	0.4	0.1	0.6
Transport, travel and tourism	16.8	17.3	3.1	2.5	18.8	18.3	2.1	2.0
Financial, insurance and business	0.9	2.2	0.3	0.8	1.1	2.3	0.2	0.7
Other services	0.1	4.0	3.1	14.5	0.6	4.8	0.5	2.6
Bilateral trade share (% of trade with world)	**31.1**		**1.3**		**24.1**		**1.4**	

Source: Sheng 2016.

Under the China reform scenario, total Australian trade and Chinese trade are larger than the business-as-usual scenario. Chinese exports increase to US$4.48 trillion, compared to the US$4.04 trillion case under the business-as-usual scenario. Chinese exports to Australia are roughly the same under both scenarios, at US$59.1 billion in 2025. Total Australian exports are projected to be US$595 billion in 2025, larger than the business-as-usual case and driven mostly by the increase in exports to China. Australian exports to China increase from US$84 billion to US$185 billion, or just over 120 per cent, in constant value terms.

Australia's exports to China are projected to be US$185 billion in 2025 under the reform scenario compared to US$145 billion a year given business as usual. Under the stagnation scenario with Chinese growth significantly contracting after 2020, Australian exports to China are projected to be US$107 billion, still a 28 per cent increase in constant value terms. Yet total Chinese exports will be over US$1 trillion less in 2025 under this scenario.

The structure of Australian exports to China does not change significantly under each scenario because under all scenarios the impact of structural change in the Chinese economy is powerful. The mining and extraction sector will be less important, while services and agriculture will grow in importance in all circumstances (Table 3.5). The total share of each country in the other's trade will not change greatly in any scenario: the share of China in Australia's exports will decline slightly from 28.5 per cent in 2014 to 27.1 per cent in the baseline case and increase to 31.1 per cent in the reform case; and the share of Australia in China's exports will fall from 1.6 per cent in 2014 to 1.4 per cent in the former case and 1.3 per cent in the latter.

The share of textiles and apparel in China's exports to Australia was 22 per cent in 2014. That is projected to fall to 20 per cent under the business-as-usual scenario and 17 per cent under the reform scenario. If growth in China stagnates, the share is projected to be 21.1 per cent. Electronic equipment, with a share of 14.2 per cent in 2014, exhibits a similar pattern. The share of textiles and apparel in China's total trade tells a similar story: higher growth scenarios indicate successful industrial transformation and upgrading, with low-skilled manufacturing becoming less important. A failure to transform the structure of the Chinese economy results in the growth stagnation scenario.

Education services will be a major Australian export to China under all three growth scenarios, accounting for between 10 per cent of total exports in the stagnation scenario and close to 12 per cent in the reform scenario. Even if growth stagnates in China, education exports will triple to US$12 billion in 2025. Under the reform scenario, education exports will be as high as US$18.6 billion.

The transformation of China's trade with Australia

China's industrial up-skilling is already underway, as shown by the shifting composition of Chinese exports to Australia. Twenty-five years ago, Chinese exports to Australia were predominantly lower value-added goods such as household equipment, textiles, clothing and footwear. Over that time, China's export economy has progressed from being a low-end producer of textiles and assembler of simple goods, to being a high-end producer of far more sophisticated electrical and machinery products.

Much of the lowest-skilled factory work that boomed in China's coastal provinces and special economic zones has now either moved to less-developed inland regions or to other lower-wage countries. While the absolute value of all categories of Chinese manufacturing to Australia has grown, the share contributed by sophisticated engineering products, such as machinery, has risen from less than 10 per cent to almost half of all imports since 1990 (Table 3.6).

Australia's falling barriers to manufacturing imports have assisted this evolution. In 1991, the weighted average of effectively applied tariffs on manufactured imports into Australia was 10.5 per cent; by 2002 it had more than halved to 4.3 per cent, and in 2014 stood at 2.5 per cent (World Bank 2016). ChAFTA will eliminate almost all tariffs on imports of Chinese manufactures after 1 January 2019.

The effective manufacturing tariffs applied to Chinese goods around the world also fell over this period, lowering the cost of China's entry into regional and global production networks. Weighted average tariffs on imports of manufactures were 36 per cent in 1992, falling to 13 per cent in 2001 and 4 per cent in 2014 (World Bank 2016). Lowering the cost of manufactured imports provides cheaper parts and components for subsequent exports of more elaborate goods.

Table 3.6: The changing nature of Chinese manufacturing exports to Australia

	1990		2000		2010		2014	
	A$	Percentage share in total	A$	Percentage share in total	A$	Percentage share in total	A$	Percentage share in total
Simply transformed manufactures	77,509	6.5	461,961	5.4	1,942,412	5.2	2,879,711	5.8
Engineering products	100,168	8.4	1,907,341	22.1	17,255,046	45.8	23,279,101	47.0
Other elaborately transformed manufactures	1,014,804	85.1	6,245,133	72.5	18,494,832	49.1	23,335,877	47.1

Source: DFAT 2015c.

Upgrading Chinese manufacturing through regional supply chains

Chinese manufactured goods are not strictly 'made in China' but rather 'made in Asia', or 'made in the world' once global supply chains involving parts, components and intellectual property are considered. Yet while a contractor in China assembles Apple's iPhone and iPad products, the contribution of Chinese labour to these products' final retail value was less than 2 per cent in 2011 (Kraemer et al 2011). Even for a tiny component such as a Light Emitting Diode (LED) manufactured in China, 28 per cent of the value-added is estimated to come from outside China (UNCTAD 2015). For a product as simple as a rubber tyre made in China, the Chinese share of value added is just under 77 per cent.

The emergence of regional and global supply chains reveals the limits of bilateral trade arrangements that focus only on removing formal tariff barriers among potential export markets (Productivity Commission 2010). When tariffs on intermediate and unfinished goods cascade through many different countries before producing a finished product, the unilateral reduction or removal of import tariffs helps an economy remain a competitive base for global production networks.

Trade agreements that seek to entrench preferential treatment for particular bilateral trade flows further compound these inefficiencies, and encourage other nations to compete on the basis of policy distortions rather than economic fundamentals. In addition, the costs of delays at customs and disruptions to logistics make it difficult to reap the full efficiencies from truly integrated trade.

Broader trade agreements provide the greatest welfare gains, and so multilateral trade liberalisation through the WTO would provide the greatest gain to global welfare. The consolidation of existing bilateral preferential trade agreements into RCEP is a practical intermediate step. RCEP could form the foundation for defining the pathway towards a FTAAP that is not just regionally but globally liberalising.

One promising prospect for improving bilateral trade logistics is China's OBOR initiative, which aims to improve infrastructure connectivity in the region. This should help boost trade by lowering transaction and transport costs. Australian and Chinese cooperation in the AIIB is also a welcome and practical step toward reducing transport costs. The AIIB was founded to help finance infrastructure investment in the region, which could include finance for infrastructure development in Northern Australia under OBOR arrangements. More detailed discussion of areas in which Australia and China can cooperate to advance regional and global economic diplomacy is set out in Chapters 7 and 8 of this Report.

Delivering services to Chinese consumers

China's domestic reform agenda provides a strong case for allowing Australian companies to compete directly in China's services markets. The Decision of the current Central Party Committee's Third Plenum in 2013 — a meeting that introduces a five-year economic reform agenda — focused on the development of the services sector, including finance and healthcare services. This has been encapsulated in the five priorities for the 13th Five Year Plan of innovation, coordination, green development, opening-up and sharing.

The growth of China's middle class is driving growth in the bilateral services trade (Productivity Commission 2015). According to one long-term estimate, the proportion of China's population in the middle class could rise from around 10 per cent in 2009 to over 40 per cent in 2020, and more than 70 per cent in 2030. This equates to over 850 million Chinese people entering the middle class within the next two decades (Kharas and Gertz 2010). This means that Chinese consumers will spend more of their discretionary income on services. Some of these services, such as tourism and education, may be provided to Chinese overseas. But Australia can also assist China in developing its domestic services sector (see also Chapter 5).

The potential for increased services imports in China takes on added significance for Australia given the particularly high contribution of value-added services to the Australian economy. While a large proportion of the profits of the Australian resources boom accrued to overseas investors in mining companies, more services exports translate directly into more Australian jobs. From 2002–2011, from the start to near the peak of the resources boom, the value-added in Australia's services exports actually exceeded that of minerals exports (Kelly and La Cava 2014).

Tourism and education services in Australia

Chinese demand for Australian services has so far been concentrated in travel services for education and tourism (Box 3.5).

In 2015, education-related travel from China to Australia was worth A$4.8 billion (ABS 2016a). There are more than 136,000 Chinese students in Australia, more than one-quarter of the international student population (DFAT 2016b). The long-run significance of this sector is even higher than these statistics suggest given the Australian brand awareness, family tourism expenditure, professional relationships and migration opportunities that accompany international educational exchange. This story is told in greater detail in Chapter 4.

BOX 3.5: CHINESE TOURISM IN AUSTRALIA

In 2015, annual Chinese tourist arrivals to Australia exceeded one million for the first time, accounting for 13.8 per cent of total international arrivals. According to Tourism Research Australia, in the period through to 2025, China will account for 60 per cent of growth in inbound tourism expenditure in Australia. By 2017–2018, China is expected to become Australia's largest tourism market in terms of inbound tourist numbers and tourist expenditure, overtaking New Zealand (Tourism Research Australia 2016).

Chinese visitors have been the driving force behind recent increases in tourist arrivals and spending trends in Australia, with China now Australia's primary source of inbound tourism expenditure (Tourism Research Australia 2014). In 2000, travel from China accounted for just 3.5 per cent of international travel expenditure in Australia; in 2015, it accounted for 22 per cent (ABS 2015b, 2016a). In 2014–2015, total expenditure by Chinese visitors increased by 29.8 per cent in real terms and the number of visitor nights rose 18.8 per cent to 39 million (Tourism Research Australia 2016).

These trends are encouraging, but come alongside potential challenges as well as opportunities for further growth. Since the global financial crisis, the Australian dollar has weakened more sharply against the New Zealand dollar, the Singapore dollar and the Chinese renminbi, than it has against the US dollar or the British pound. This has made Australia relatively more attractive for tourism than other countries in the region in recent years (Terlato 2015). But the short-term nature of such advantages highlights the importance of developing a tourism industry that is robust to global economic uncertainty.

Despite Chinese consumers ranking Australia first out of all countries in 'aspiration', 'awareness' and 'intention' to visit, Australia ranks only 10th in actual visitation, behind more-established competitors such as the United States and France (Tourism Australia 2015b). The expansion of air connections, wider marketing operations in China and the accessibility of tailor-made travel experiences to Chinese visitors will be essential in narrowing this gap (Tourism Australia 2011). Australia's tourism sector must seize the opportunities offered by recent tourist activity and the favourable opinion of Chinese visitors to cement Australia as a premier destination in the longer term.

Tourism Research Australia forecasts the share of Chinese leisure arrivals in Australia to grow from 13 per cent in 2014–2015 to 17.9 per cent in 2017–2018 and 27.2 per cent in 2024–2025. This would see the number of annual Chinese leisure tourist arrivals more than treble from 684,000 in 2014–2015 to 2.6 million in 2024–2025 (Tourism Research Australia 2016).

In 2011, the China National Tourism Administration and the Australian Government signed a Memorandum of Understanding (MoU), continuing Australia's Approved Destination Status (ADS) and committing to support cooperation in tourism through an annual dialogue. Australia and New Zealand were the first Western countries to be granted ADS in 1999 and Australia's delivery of the scheme is highly regarded in China. The official-level Australia–China tourism partnership was reaffirmed in April 2016, with a new MoU on Strengthening Tourism Cooperation being signed as part of Australia Week in China. The 2016 MoU builds on the 2011 agreement and covers industry cooperation, labour and skills development, investment, research and infrastructure.

During the 2016 Australia Week in China, national leaders announced the bilateral Year of Tourism for 2017. Designating 2017 a 'Tourism Year' is an excellent opportunity to increase people-to-people links through tourism. It will focus the Chinese government (and media) on Australia and strengthen the Australia–China tourism relationship. A number of events are planned for 2017, including Australian participation in the Beijing International Film Festival and Chinese participation in the Virgin Australia Melbourne Fashion Festival and Australia's Chinese New Year celebrations.

In order to ensure the current rapid growth in the inbound Chinese tourism market remains sustainable, and the benefits of this growth are distributed beyond Australia's gateway cities of Sydney and Melbourne, the Australian government is striving to increase the geographic dispersion of Chinese visitors. Dispersal spreads the opportunity, prosperity and demand from Chinese tourism, and is being achieved through measures such as improving tourism infrastructure in rural and regional areas and the introduction of a Work and Holiday Arrangement that allows 5000 Chinese participants each year. This program enables Chinese with tertiary education and English skills to experience a working holiday in Australia. It will boost demand for tourism services and help address shortages of bilingual workers available to the tourism industry as the industry seeks to service growing numbers of Chinese visitors.

While Australia is attractive to tourists because of its natural environment, tourism around the world is fiercely competitive. The scope of people-to-people links between China and Australia are a huge asset for Australia. Chinese visiting their friends or relatives in Australia not only strengthened these people-to-people ties, but spent an average of almost A$4000 per visit in 2015 (Figure 3.7). By contrast, Chinese holidaymakers coming to Australia just for tourism spent A$2389 per visit, close to the average spend of all holidaymakers in Australia.

Figure 3.7: Total average spend of foreigners visiting friends and relatives in Australia, 2015

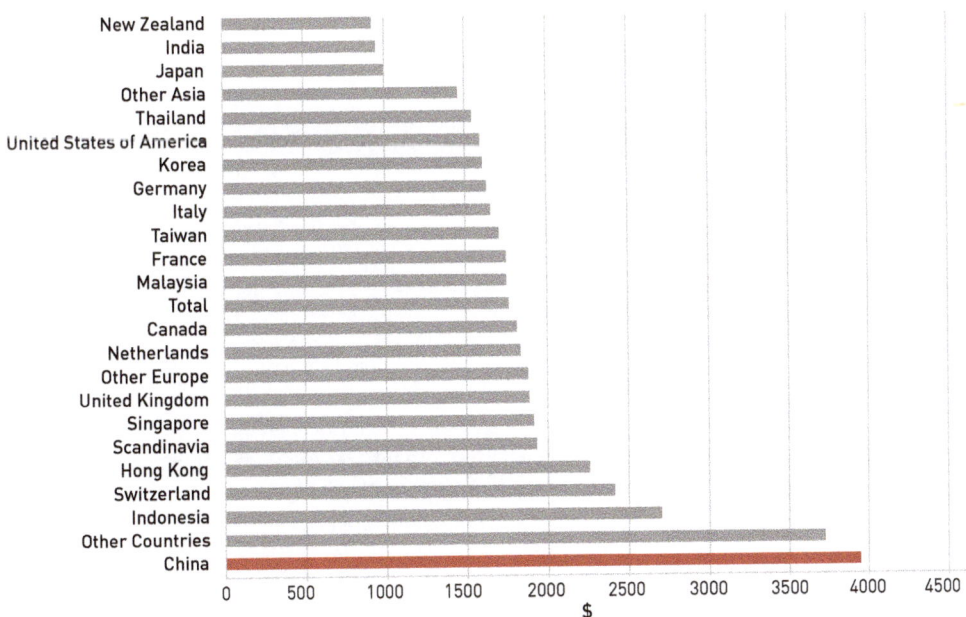

Source: Tourism Research Australia 2016.

When Chinese visitors are not coming to visit friends and family, then Australia will have to compete for Chinese tourists with established destinations in Southeast Asia, Europe and North America. This means that Australian tourism providers need to focus on ensuring a quality experience that is adapted to the Chinese market. But the payoffs from attracting new visitors can be large once the connection between China and Australia is established. In a 2016 survey of 514 recent Chinese visitors to Australia, nearly half were repeat visitors. Three-quarters of surveyed visitors intended to visit again or come back for tertiary education, 48 per cent were interested in real estate investment, while 41 per cent and 24 per cent, respectively, were interested in the further purchase of Australian goods and services in China (LEK Consulting 2016).

The survey found that tourism is a first step to much deeper economic engagement. Chinese visitors' average annual spend on Australian products rose by 40 per cent after visiting Australia. The report recommended that Australian government and businesses need to act to harness the full potential of Chinese tourism and that Australia needs to ensure that: it remains an attractive travel destination so that visitor numbers continue to grow; visa-application processes, where appropriate, are smooth and easy to navigate; Australia's airports and transport facilities are among the world's best; and the Australian workforce grows its Chinese-language capability.

Australia is in an Asian time zone, but Berlin and Paris are both closer to Beijing than Brisbane. This highlights the importance of direct air connections that respond to traveller demands. Many flights from China to Australia still require time-consuming connecting flights, both domestically and via Asia. Authorities in Australia and China signed a milestone air services agreement in January 2015, tripling and in some cases abolishing caps on the number of seats for passengers from some of China's biggest cities (Minister for Trade and Investment 2015). Tourism agreements between South Australia and China Southern Airlines are another way to facilitate this (Williams 2016). But Australia could do more to ensure that profitable routes are available to Chinese carriers. This would include removing restrictions that prevent foreign carriers from flying domestic passengers or cargo on domestic legs of international flights — effectively tripling aviation capacity between Chinese and Australian major gateway locations. The air services agreement also provides for unrestricted access between China and Australian regional airports. While this arrangement has made significant aviation capacity available, China is one of Australia's fastest growing visitor sources and more can be done to ensure aviation capacity will foster future growth in visitation from China.

Removing these restrictions would make it easier for Chinese tourists to see more of Australia, and expand capacity in Australia's domestic aviation markets without requiring additional capital investment from Australian airlines. Given that this reform is directly beneficial to Australia, it should not be contingent on reciprocation in the developing Chinese aviation market. Better connectivity would also further open up the Chinese tourism market to Australians wanting to experience Chinese food, culture and history, as well as economic and social progress (Box 3.6).

To provide better services to Chinese visitors, Australia has improved visa arrangements by reducing documentary requirements and waiving interview requirements. Australia has introduced a three-year multiple entry visa as standard for eligible Chinese business visitors, and eligible Chinese tourists applying through an agent via an online trial. Additionally, Australia is now trialling the online lodgement of visitor visa applications; this service is expected to be rolled out fully by the end of 2016. A trial of 10-year visitor visas for eligible applicants in China is also expected to begin by the end of 2016, along with the implementation of a Chinese language lodgement option. Under the Developing Northern Australia White Paper visa initiatives, Australia began a priority 48-hour processing trial for visitor visa applications from Chinese passport holders in March 2016.

BOX 3.6: AUSTRALIAN TOURISTS IN CHINA

Australian outbound tourism is relatively larger by volume than its inbound tourism (Tourism Research Australia 2016). In 2015, Australian residents made 9.5 million overseas trips, spending a total of A$32 billion abroad. In 2015, Australia ranked 10th in international inbound tourism expenditure, valued at US$23.5 billion (behind Italy but before Hong Kong).

In 2015 Australian residents made 422,800 trips to China, meaning China is Australia's sixth-largest destination market. Those destined for China comprised 4.5 per cent of Australia's total resident departures, behind destinations such as Thailand (5.8 per cent), the United Kingdom (6.3 per cent), the United States (10.7 per cent), Indonesia (11.7 per cent) and New Zealand (13.4 per cent). Tourism Research Australia forecasts that Australian outbound tourism will grow at an average of 3.7 per cent per annum from 2014–2015 to 2024–2025, reaching 13.3 million overseas trips in 2024–2025.

From 2000 to 2015, visits to China have increased from 2.7 per cent to their current 4.5 per cent of Australian international travel (ABS 2016c). The value of goods and services acquired through Australians' travel to China for personal reasons increased by 392 per cent between 2000 and 2015. Over the same years, business and education travel grew significantly, but at slower rates — 203 per cent and 115 per cent respectively (ABS 2015, 2016a).

As of December 2015, Australia is the 16th most common source country of China's inbound tourism. Per capita, it ranks seventh, ahead of Japan, Canada, the United States and the United Kingdom (CNTA 2016).

Air connectivity improvements are a major factor behind the growing numbers of Australian tourists in China, as is the size of Australia's Chinese diaspora and the extent of people-to-people links. Wendy Wu, owner of Australia's largest tour operator to China, took 10,000 passengers in 2013 (up from just 16 in 1994). 'The majority of our customers,' said Ms Wu, 'say they want to go to China because their Chinese neighbours, friends, relatives and colleagues have talked about it and said they had a wonderful time there' (Karnikowski 2013).

Against this backdrop, there should be great potential for China to compete for a larger share of Australian tourism expenditure. Like Australia, China could improve its competiveness through measures facilitating tourist mobility, including more flexible and preferential visa arrangements (see Chapter 4). Many such arrangements would represent reciprocation of existing Australian initiatives. The bilateral Year of Tourism in 2017 also provides an excellent opportunity for China to promote its tourism attractions to Australian tourists. However, these promotions could go beyond traditional realms like food, culture, history and natural scenery, to showcase new attractions including China's state-of-the-art infrastructure in high-speed rail and metropolitan subway systems. These new tourist attractions would not only increase convenience for Australian travellers, but also provide opportunities for more Australians to experience China's economic development and social progress. Deeper community understanding is critical to the building of mutual trust and partnerships and facilitating flows of commercial opportunities between the two economies.

Developing China's services sector

The next step in implementing ChAFTA, which has the potential to help drive the transformation of China's domestic services industry, is to further open up the Chinese services market to competition from Australian companies. The Chinese services market is not as open to foreign competition as Chinese goods markets, and even absent formal barriers to trade, service providers often face stiff 'behind the border' barriers in the form of local restrictions on licensing and professional accreditation. The domestic provision of services often depends on complementary arrangements allowing foreign direct investment, as well as rules facilitating the movement of people.

Much of the hard work in enhancing these sectors requires major domestic policy reforms that are already underway in China. These reforms recognise that the biggest gains from trade liberalisation occur not from market access overseas but from allowing other countries to participate in domestic markets. Australian services providers are not big enough global players that they will be able to swamp Chinese incumbents. Nevertheless, their agility and experience in developed markets can help bring competitive pressure and know-how to Chinese domestic markets, and help prepare Chinese companies for future competition. Australia successfully executed a similar strategy in liberalising its financial markets 30 years ago.

While Australian financial institutions may be able to play a role in delivering financial services directly to Chinese consumers, they have more of a role to play in lowering the costs of trade between Australian and Chinese companies. This includes by supporting settlement or trade directly between the Chinese renminbi and the Australian dollar, providing products to hedge currency risk (particularly as China's foreign exchange regime becomes more flexible), and fostering integration with Chinese payment systems such as UnionPay and Alipay. ChAFTA also created a Committee on Financial Services. Opportunities for cooperation in financial services are further explored in Chapter 5.

ChAFTA removes many 'at the border' constraints on both established and emerging aspects of the trade relationship. The challenge now is to address residual 'behind the border' barriers — the sizeable trade constraints that go beyond the scope of traditional bilateral trade negotiations. The key way to do this will be through ChAFTA's Trade in Services Committee, which will review the state of the services trade within two years and propose measures to increase trade in services. An example of bilateral opportunities is delivering healthcare services to China's ageing population (Box 3.7).

Part of its role is to ensure that the commitments that Australia or China might make to third parties in other negotiations are automatically extended through ChAFTA. Australia's Most Favoured Nation commitment extends to all service sectors. China's is limited to education, tourism and travel-related services, construction, engineering, securities, environmental services, services relating to forestry, computer and related services, and certain scientific and consulting services. This means that if Australia or China extends more favourable access conditions to other trade partners, then suppliers in the other country will automatically receive this better treatment.

One reform that offers large potential gains would be to establish recognition of professional services qualifications from the other jurisdiction. By the end of 2017, the side letter to ChAFTA on skills assessment and licensing is due for review. To help make the most of this review, the Australian and Chinese governments should coordinate engagement between accrediting regulatory bodies, such as Certified Public Accountants Australia and the China Institute for Certified Practising Accountants in the field of accounting, and Australian State Bar Associations and the All-China Lawyers Association in the legal profession. Two other fields that could provide early gains are engineering and TCM (Productivity Commission 2015).

BOX 3.7: HEALTHCARE SERVICES

China's developing healthcare sector is struggling to keep up with the demand placed upon it by China's huge and ageing population (Austrade 2016a). There are over 202 million Chinese who are over 60, representing 15.5 per cent of the population. And this share is projected to increase to 24 per cent by 2050 (Xu 2016).

Australia's healthcare facilities are among the best in the world (Brown and van Nieuwenhuizen 2016), and ChAFTA will give them an advantage against their main competitors in the market: Japan and the United States. Australian exporters have the opportunity to service the Chinese market by providing:

- training and education programs for human resources;

- home care services;

- operation and management of seniors living/retirement villages/resorts;

- conceptual design and planning of institutional aged care, seniors living, retirement villages and resorts;

- quality health care products (that is, functional food, additives and nutrition, healthy food, assisted living and e-health products for the elderly); and

- infrastructure investment and operation (Austrade 2016a).

Traditional Chinese Medicine

China is also contributing to the development of new sectors in Australia. TCM in Australia is still a nascent industry, yet it has succeeded in attracting significant attention from government bodies and business. The range of recent advancements in regulation, collaboration and exchange will only lead to greater opportunities for Australian TCM research, development and export in years to come.

In November 2014, the University of Western Sydney (UWS) and the Beijing University of Chinese Medicine signed a MoU to develop Australia's first TCM integrative clinical service. The Australian prime minister and the Chinese president attended the signing ceremony.

The UWS National Institute for Complementary Medicine (NICM), which will operate the new service, hopes its research will lead to new treatments for outstanding medical needs and new medicines for global export. The NICM will also partner with Chinese researchers to run clinical trials on TCM (CRI 2015). The institution's capabilities should also be of interest to international complementary medicine companies wishing to prepare regulatory filings for other markets, such as in the United States and Europe (ATC 2014; Austrade 2014).

This MoU is one of a range of initiatives in recent years that have made Australia well placed to advance the production, regulation and market access of TCM in the future. In July 2012, Australia became the first Western country to institute mandatory national registration of TCM practitioners, a major institutional step for TCM development and quality control (CMBA 2012).

ChAFTA includes a number of provisions encouraging bilateral TCM collaboration and exchange between regulators, professional bodies and relevant government departments. The agreement encourages the development of mutually acceptable standards for TCM licensing and certification, as well as providing support for personnel movement, granting entry and temporary stay for four years to a quota of TCM practitioners.

In addition to the export of services such as clinical trials, some agricultural and medical bodies are exploring prospects for the Australian export of TCM goods. The Western Australian Department of Agriculture and Food has encouraged the growing of jujubes or Chinese dates, a common food and medicinal product, which can be grown in Australia counter-seasonally to China (DAF 2016). University of Queensland pharmaceutical researchers have pointed to the possibility of the export of cane toad products for TCM use (Milman 2015).

Building trust to achieve potential trade

A business-as-usual approach to the bilateral relationship will not be sufficient to capitalise on its full potential. The resources trade is predominantly conducted through large mining companies on the one side and Chinese SOEs on the other side. But this trade goes beyond the supply of bulk commodities to include targeted marketing, integrated supply chains and cross-cultural human resource management. This trade is built on a foundation of strategic trust to ensure that governments do not arbitrarily interfere with commercial relationships. Going beyond this, in the services trades for example, will require deeper understanding and institutional relations between Australian and Chinese organisations and people.

High-level official engagement

The Australian and Chinese governments have a role to play in removing barriers to trade, catalysing the commercial and social relationships from which beneficial exchanges can emerge, and establishing the institutions and trust required to lower barriers to trade. This is a hard task given the expanding pool of bilateral stakeholders. A larger number of smaller-valued trade transactions mean that industry players will be less organised and find it harder to attract attention at the official level, meaning that governments on both sides will need to take greater effort to consult with business.

At the highest level, a joint commitment to trade liberalisation should be proactive and extend beyond the implementation of ChAFTA. This work can be developed as part of the agenda for the Strategic Economic Dialogue (SED) between the two countries (Box 3.8). This dialogue brings together the Australian Treasurer and Minister for Trade and Investment for annual talks with the Chairman of China's National Development and Reform Commission (NDRC).

BOX 3.8: THE AUSTRALIA-CHINA STRATEGIC ECONOMIC PARTNERSHIP

When then Chinese executive vice premier Li Keqiang visited the Australian prime minister Kevin Rudd in October 2009, he stressed the role of 'dialogue, coordination and cooperation' in building Australia–China relations (Chinese Embassy Australia 2009). The Australia–China Strategic Economic Dialogue (SED), which provides such an opportunity for Australia, was announced in 2013. The first meeting in June 2014 was attended by the Australian Treasurer and Trade Minister, and the Chairman of China's NDRC.

At this inaugural SED in Beijing, the two countries established an Investment Cooperation Framework. The Framework goes beyond ChAFTA and creates new pathways for promoting the export of financial services, two-way investment in new sectors and identifying roadblocks for investors from both countries. There is tremendous opportunity to deepen the relationship at a number of levels, including by expanding services exports from Australia to China and improving investment opportunities.

The second SED, held in Canberra in August 2015, saw the two governments agree to further 'two-way investment to diversify our trade relationship and create opportunities in the services sector' (Treasurer of Australia 2015a).

This high-level political cooperation is practically supported by a MoU for cooperation between the NDRC and the Australian Treasury, which was first signed in 2008 (Australian Treasury 2008). Chapter 6 discusses how to energise these institutions.

While much has been done both in terms of international trade law and bilateral negotiations to remove formal barriers to trade, many of the barriers that remain occur at state/provincial, municipal and more local levels of government. It is often at these levels where national laws have to be implemented, and where local licensing practices and enforcement can have the effect of producing major, if sometimes unintended, barriers to international trade.

The premier forum for bilateral engagement at the state/provincial level is the Australia–China State/Provincial Leaders Forum. The Australian prime minister and the Chinese President opened the Forum. This institution should meet regularly, and possibly establish a standing secretariat that is able to support its work, share knowledge and coordinate the implementation of its commitments and initiatives between different levels of government.

The environment for managing and welcoming foreign investment projects is significantly influenced by how they are managed at the local level. A strong partnership between provincial and state governments, and dialogue with lower levels of governments and community stakeholders assists firms to discover trade opportunities and facilitate the investment that supports trade. Australian states have long had sister state–province relationships with China's most outward-oriented provinces (Table 3.7), and there are more than 70 sister-city relationships. Trade delegations led by the political leaders of Australian states and territories to China can help cement commercial ties (Box 3.9).

This can be taken further — although China only established diplomatic relations with South Korea in 1992, the two countries already have 154 sister-city relationships (Ren 2014). The relationship between Weihai, a town of 600,000 people, in Shandong Province, and Incheon, a city of 3 million in South Korea, is an exemplar of a sister-city relationship. More than 800 South Korean companies operate in Weihai, which is also home to 40,000 South Koreans (Zhao 2015).

State and provincial level governments can further bilateral links through more exchange programs for students, businesspeople and government officials. Victoria is currently taking the lead in establishing a 'Partnerships for Prosperity' strategy with China (Government of Victoria 2016). This involves strengthening cooperation on innovation with its existing sister-province, Jiangsu, as well as formalising a new sister-province relationship with Sichuan. The strategy includes targeted capacity building within business, government and education, as well as cultural engagement. Victoria wants to be the destination for 20 per cent of Chinese investment in Australia by 2026. Over the same timeframe, the Victorian government expects exports to expand, revenue from Chinese tourists in the state to increase, and post-graduate tertiary enrolments from China to grow by a quarter.

Table 3.7: Sister state–province relationships between Australia and China

Australian State or Territory	Chinese Province or Municipality	Relationship established
New South Wales	Guangdong	1979
Victoria	Jiangsu	1979
Tasmania	Fujian	1981
South Australia	Shandong	1986
Western Australia	Zhejiang	1987
Queensland	Shanghai Municipality	1989
Northern Territory	Anhui	2000
Australian Capital Territory	Beijing	2000
Queensland*	Guangdong	2004

Source: ACCCI 2001; AHFAO 2015; GFAO
* refers to a Friendly Cooperative Province rather than a 'sister' relationship.

The American Chamber of Commerce in China (AmCham) conducts annual surveys of China's business environment, and releases an annual white paper for American business (AmCham 2015). Many of the detailed concerns raised by this organisation are likely to reflect the experience of Australian business in China. AmCham finds that foreign companies trading in China report that local regulatory environments and conditions matter. Central policies are not always uniformly enforced across China, and the institutions and infrastructure needed to get products to market, and the financial services required to facilitate trade, are not always well developed beyond China's first-tier cities. In particular, foreign companies often complain that regardless of tariff levels, their export operations become complicated by inconsistent and inefficient customs procedures and regulations at the local level. AmCham reports that there is a perception among foreign businesses that local governments favour local developers with regards to access to land and real estate.

Beyond the first-tier cities, an absence of international schools, multilingual health centres and international financial institutions can make it difficult for non-Chinese speaking foreigners hoping to do business (AmCham 2015). Some areas impose regulations and fees for importing international educational resources, including textbooks. Further opening up of the market for healthcare and education services would make it easier for international providers to offer these services to foreign visitors, therefore facilitating more business and investment connections. At a practical level, even different regional bureaux of the Exit-Entry Administration of China's Public Service Bureau interpret and apply regulations differently. This can cause visa problems for students and professionals.

States and provinces can play a leading role in driving practical cooperation (Box 3.9). Australian state governments already have an on-the-ground presence in China — New South Wales, South Australia, Queensland and Western Australia in Shanghai; New South Wales in Guangzhou; Victoria in Nanjing, Beijing and Chengdu; South Australia in Shandong — which can help deliver this engagement. Victoria's China strategy includes increasing resources for its network of government business offices by A$66 million, including the appointment of a new deputy commissioner responsible for Western China (Premier of Victoria 2016). Tasmania also recently capitalised on a visit by the Chinese President by launching 'Tasinvest', a promotion that attracted over 100 representatives of Chinese companies. Tasmania also signed a MoU on planning and cooperation with the China Development Bank, in order to facilitate Chinese investment in Tasmanian mining, agriculture, tourism and infrastructure (Premier of Tasmania 2014).

State–provincial and sister-city relationships should be forums in which to negotiate and resolve these issues, as well as to recognise professional accreditations (such as real estate broker licenses), and ensure transparency and consistency in granting local licenses and government approvals, including in banking and finance. Australian companies operating in China do not need any kind of preferential treatment, but they do need an assurance that the interpretation of laws and regulations at the local level is not being used to restrict competition. Opportunities for official visits and exchanges of state and provincial government officials, including with judicial and prosecutorial organs, can contribute to the trust and understanding needed to identify and resolve local regulatory discrepancies.

BOX 3.9: STATE AND PROVINCIAL TIES

The first sister state–province relationship was established in 1979 between New South Wales and Guangdong province, and the annual NSW–Guangdong Joint Economic Meeting has been a key component of the relationship. In July 2008, the NSW government also signed a formal MoU with the Financial Services Office of the Shanghai municipal government to strengthen their relationship. Since then, the two cities have held an annual financial services symposium to grow their positions as financial hubs in the Asia Pacific. In June 2012, Guangdong's former party secretary visited Sydney, and in 2015, the NSW Premier Mike Baird hosted the current Guangdong Party Secretary Hu Chunhua, who was then received by the Australian prime minister as a guest of the Australian government in Canberra. Prior to the NSW premier's first official visit to China in 2014, NSW released its own China Engagement Strategy. The premier led a delegation to Guangzhou in November 2015 in order to discuss opportunities under ChAFTA. In April

2016, the NSW health minister travelled to China to promote new opportunities for health care providers and medical device manufacturers under ChAFTA. During this visit, the minister also attended Austrade's Australia Week in China 2016.

The Victoria–Jiangsu Joint Economic Committee first met in 1987. A number of Victorian projects in China have progressed through this Committee, particularly some relating to sustainable urban development. To celebrate the relationship's 35th anniversary, a MoU was signed between Regional Development Victoria and the Jiangsu Foreign Affairs Office in July 2014, launching the Victoria–Jiangsu Regional City Alliance. The alliance aims to strengthen multiple city-to-city trade and investment ties between the two states. Over 60 government and business leaders, including Jiangsu's vice governor, attended the launch. Following his visit to China in 2015, Victorian Premier Daniel Andrews proposed to send every member of his ministry to China before the next state election in November 2018. The premier intends to visit China every year in order to boost trade and explore further investment opportunities.

On top of this, Jiangsu and Victoria have a formal partnership between the Victorian Department of Education and Training and the Jiangsu Provincial Department of Education, and the Hamer Scholarship program for young Victorians to study Chinese language and culture in Jiangsu. Moreover, Monash University was the first Australian university licensed to open a campus in China, in partnership with Southeast University in Suzhou. As part of Victoria's new China Strategy, Victoria will also formalise its new sister-province relationship with Sichuan by the end of 2016.

Tasmania and Fujian province have had an active relationship since 1981. After the 2014 Australia G20 Summit, Chinese President Xi Jinping (a former governor of Fujian) visited Tasmania accompanied by the Fujian party secretary. The Tasmanian premier and the Fujian party secretary signed the Agreement on Establishing the Joint Committee for Cooperation and Development, an organisational body overseeing bilateral exchange, and committed to hold biannual meetings to discuss trade. The delegation was accompanied by representatives from eight Fujian companies, including Xiamen Airlines, the Zijin Mining Group and Xiamen Construction and Development Group. The inaugural meeting of the Joint Committee was held in March 2015 in Fujian and attended by the Tasmanian premier. Tasmania also signed a MoU with Fujian when Chinese President Xi Jinping visited Tasmania in November 2014, establishing a Joint Committee for Cooperation and Development.

In 2013, the South Australia Shandong Cooperation and Development Forum was established, with the inaugural Forum held in Jinan that April. The Forum is chaired by the South Australian premier and the vice governor of Shandong. The delegation included business leaders from the mineral, energy, agribusiness, wine and education sectors. MoUs advancing economic relations were signed with the Shandong Commerce Bureau and the Qingdao Bureau of Commerce. In May 2015, the Governor of Shandong, Guo Shuqing, welcomed South Australia's largest ever trade delegation led by the South Australian Premier Jay Weatherill. The premier released the state's updated China Engagement Strategy in May 2016 (Premier of South Australia 2016).

Western Australia has had a sister state–province relationship with Zhejiang province since 1987. In 1995, the Western Australia–Zhejiang Sister-State Economic Exchange Committee was established to oversee the economic aspects of the partnership. In September 2012, a delegation led by the Zhejiang governor visited Perth to celebrate the 25th anniversary of the relationship. In April 2014, a MoU was signed between the two parties on live cattle exports. The WA minister for regional development led a delegation in August 2015 to China to meet with Zhejiang provincial government officials.

Queensland and Shanghai have maintained a sister state-city relationship since 1989. To mark the 25th anniversary of this relationship in 2014, their two governments agreed to work together on urban development issues, strengthen information sharing in relation to the Shanghai Free Trade Zone, and expand cooperation and exchange.

The Australian Capital Territory (ACT) has had a formal sister-state relationship with Beijing since 2000. The scope of the ACT's engagement with China was expanded in 2014 with an economic cooperation agreement signed by the ACT chief minister and the mayor of Shenzhen.

Grassroots engagement

The next round of trade opportunities in services requires much more sophisticated engagement by tens of thousands of enterprises and entrepreneurs on each side (see Chapter 6). The Australia–China CEO Roundtable is the premier forum for this at the peak business level.

Opportunities exist to improve bilateral capacity in many services industries, including tourism and education, and professional services, where the delivery of high-value products depends on tailoring services to meet the demands of specific consumers. A deep understanding of consumer preferences is essential to providing niche services, and members of Australia's Chinese diaspora community are ideally placed to play a leading role (Box 3.10) This community is growing — the number of Chinese-born Australian residents more than doubled from 2004 to 2014 (ABS 2015b). The estimated Chinese resident population is currently around half a million (ABS 2015b). Ongoing migration from China to Australia (discussed in Chapter 4) helps meet Australian demand for human capital in fast-growing areas. Chinese accountants, advertising and marketing professionals, IT specialists and educators do not just bring technical skills, but also possess up-to-date knowledge of consumer preferences, business practices and market opportunities in China.

Whether Chinese-born, or raised in Australia with an awareness of Chinese culture and sensibilities, the Chinese diaspora community brings with it new and valuable opportunities to tailor local products and services to suit Chinese consumer demands. When Chinese-Australian business leaders make use of their linguistic, networking and entrepreneurial advantages, their colleagues and collaborators gain firsthand experience of the importance of developing culturally specific human capital, and the opportunities presented by China's continued transformation and growth.

> **BOX 3.10: CULTURAL CONNECTIONS AND BUSINESS OPPORTUNITIES FROM THE CHINESE DIASPORA**
>
> Chinese graduates can have transformative effects on Australian businesses. At one medium-sized wine producer in the Adelaide Hills, a Chinese-speaking employee began addressing occasional enquiries from China and translating tasting notes. The employee, a wine business postgraduate, soon took on a permanent position developing the business' 'strategy for China' — a position she had, according to the general manager, effectively created 'for herself'. Now, 36 per cent of that business' total revenue (approximately A$2 million) is accounted for by China.
>
> Chinese-Australian business leaders can play a central role in strengthening and consolidating supply chains. One Chinese-Australian business owner described sourcing cardboard packaging for a client: 'They're so expensive here, but in China it's so cheap … [What's] really important for business is you have to hear the people. You have to know what they're thinking. And you have to know where the need is' (Rizvi et al 2016).

For example, the presence of Chinese workers in the South Australian wine industry has already begun to transform it. Wine producers throughout Australia, especially small- and medium-sized businesses, are keen to capture a share of the growing Chinese market, but they have limited ability to identify market opportunities and adapt to Chinese tastes. Chinese workers can provide the linguistic ability, multicultural business perspective and networking advantages needed to match producers to international consumers. Some recent Chinese graduates have even started their own export-focused wine businesses.

The Australia–China Youth Association (ACYA) and the Australia China Young Professionals Initiative (ACYPI) are exemplar non-government organisations. ACYA is supported by the Australian government through the Australia–China Council and has many institutional partners, particularly in Australian and Chinese universities. ACYA is dedicated to improving people-to-people ties through career and education services. It operates across 22 chapters, 17 in Australian universities and five in Chinese cities, and in 2010 launched the annual high-level Australia-China Youth Dialogue (ACYD).

In October 2015, the ACYPI surveyed more than one hundred of its own members as well as participants in the 2015 South Australia–Greater China Future Leaders Dialogue. More important than the business environment in either Australia or China, participants cited the 'lack of trust in and understanding of the other country' as the most important issue in the bilateral economic relationship. Australia's relationships with Japan and the United States were regarded as the least important issue in the Australia–China relationship (Egan et al 2015).

In its submission to this Report, ACYPI recommended investing in education (particularly secondary, tertiary and ongoing professional development), encouraging development of people-to-people-ties and maintaining an ongoing bilateral dialogue (on economics and other matters) as the key means of building this trust, and developing the relationship-specific human capital that is crucial to providing tailored goods and niche services to each other's markets.

These forms of state–provincial, sister-city and civil society cooperation are an underutilised resource for improving the overall bilateral relationship — as are peak business groups. The role of these bodies could be expanded and formalised into a new Australia–China Leaders Forum, which would be tasked with identifying practical areas for cooperation, and continue building the understanding and trust that is the basis of a true partnership.

Programs of cooperation among different layers of society will also be crucial in the development and maturation of each nation's 'brand' in the other country (Box 3.11).

BOX 3.11: BRAND AUSTRALIA AND BRAND CHINA

A country's 'brand' represents the promise, inherent value and reputation, real or perceived, that its name possesses in the eyes of overseas consumers, tourists, businesspeople and other foreign entities. What is China's idea of 'brand Australia', and, conversely, how do Australians perceive 'brand China', in economic, cultural, political and other senses?

Australia enjoys a positive brand image in China. Many Chinese believe that Australia is a 'friendly' place with pleasant weather and many open spaces. In recent years, Australian consumer products, including food, agricultural goods and health supplements, have become very popular with Chinese consumers as they are considered to be high quality, healthy and most importantly chemical-free, whereas the equivalent Chinese products are not. Australia is perceived as non-threatening, and there are few negative perceptions of the country in most Chinese people's view. But that can change. Incidents such as the problems surrounding Chinalco investments in Australia have an adverse impact on Chinese perceptions of Australia's 'brand', as would problems with Australian goods.

In Australia, there is a wider range of perceptions of China. Australians respect China's achievements in modern development. A recent poll across several countries suggests that 80 per cent of Australian respondents acknowledged China as a rising power. Elements of Chinese culture like Chinese food, kung fu and the hard-working ethic of the Chinese are also widely admired and welcomed in Australia's multicultural society. China's political system evokes anxieties and there are often negative reactions to Chinese investment in Australia, particularly in real estate. However unfairly, China's consumer brands are often perceived as cheap and of inferior quality, even though China now manufactures — and Australia now buys from China — a vast range of world-class products, such as the iPhone. Even though these are sometimes designed in the United States or Japan, they are 'made in China'. Quality whitegoods like Haier and Midea, as well as other foreign brands made in China, prove that China is capable of making world-class consumer products. This could help China enhance its own national brand in the process.

Governments can play a role in building a national brand. Organisations like Austrade and Tourism Australia work to enhance the trade opportunities in China of products and services that play on the Australian brand: milk powder, education and tourism, for example. For Chinese companies, the China Council for the Promotion of International Trade organises Chinese trade delegations to visit other countries. It also manages overseas trade shows for Chinese organisations and assists Chinese companies to attend overseas economic conferences, exhibitions and forums.

Developing a national brand is one way of developing soft power. This can sometimes take the form of cultural diplomacy initiatives, such as the Confucius Institutes set up around the world to promote Chinese culture.

On two recent global soft power rankings Australia was listed as the sixth most effective country at deploying its soft power, behind much more powerful countries such as United States, the United Kingdom, France, Germany and Japan (Monocle 2016; Portland Communications 2016). China lags behind on these rankings, with the country's soft power ranked at 21st and 30th in the Monocle and Portland Communications ranking, respectively. This implies that China's soft power score is out of sync with its overall economic and political accomplishments.

While these rankings are both conducted by Western organisations and may not portray sentiment towards Australia or China across the entire spectrum of cultures, it does ring true that, compared to the size of its population and economy, Australia carries significant weight in terms of soft power.

National brand changes, as countries develop and change. Both the Australian and Chinese governments have a role to play in fostering this familiarity through more people-to-people and cultural exchanges that will reconfigure perceptions and play an important role in the evolution of each countries' national brand in the other country. The nuanced mutual understanding that emerges from this will allow both Chinese and Australian citizens to gain the most in working together on the relationship.

The scope for a maturing and deepening of the bilateral trade relationship is clear. Australia will expand its exports in high value-added goods and services, though its resource abundance will continue to make it an important supplier of energy and minerals to China. However, realising the full potential of this relationship depends on active engagement on the part of public and private sectors in both countries, and on the vigorous prosecution of respective agenda for domestic reform.

CHAPTER 4
Investment, human capital and labour movement

KEY MESSAGES

Two-way flows of investment, people and ideas are essential to advancing economic, political and social ties between Australia and China, and to realise the full potential for expanding trade in higher value-added goods and more sophisticated services. China has become a major supplier of international capital. Australia's resource endowments made it a natural destination for Chinese investment during the mining boom. Australia now faces global competition to attract the foreign capital it needs to service growth in agriculture, tourism and infrastructure.

China's domestic economic transformation is prioritising development of the services sector. In the same way that foreign investment into China's manufacturing sector made China a highly competitive goods producer, foreign investment into services industries will improve quality, reduce costs and further the Chinese reform agenda. The freer exchange of people and ideas will be crucial to strengthening bilateral investment and trade. More can be done to leverage diaspora communities in facilitating economic exchange and in ensuring that Chinese and Australian students, tourists and businesspeople enjoy greater freedom of movement.

The argument in the chapter concludes that:

- The ChAFTA framework opens the opportunity to upgrade the existing Australia–China Bilateral Investment Treaty (BIT) by adopting the principles of national treatment and a negative list on investment access. The early negotiations of a new Australia–China investment agreement in this framework will also assist the progress with RCEP investment protocols and China's BIT negotiations with the United States and the EU.

- Australia's current foreign investment review regime risks deterring beneficial Chinese capital by increasing the costs and the uncertainty of doing business in Australia — especially as capital looking to invest in manufacturing, agriculture, tourism and services is far more mobile compared to that seeking resources investment. Australia should institute a more predictable and transparent investment review process that focuses on ongoing risk management rather than a pre-approval process, and move to a 'notification and compliance' system for commercially certified state-owned enterprises. Foreign investment policy in China is in the early stages of liberalisation. China should approach foreign investment from the perspective of negative-listing and national treatment, and should reconsider sector-specific investment restrictions that apply to both domestic and foreign investors.

- Both sides would benefit from clear frameworks for cooperation on the bilateral movement of people and ideas. A bilateral working party consisting of official, business, tourism and education representatives should be convened to review the adequacy of visa arrangements on both sides. Existing initiatives, such as Australia's Significant Investor Visa program, could be more widely advertised to promote uptake. Both countries should consider making it easier for one another's citizens to live and work in either country.

- For example: Australia should consider relaxing the cap on Chinese working holiday visas; Australian students should be extended more opportunity to access Australian income contingent loans for degree study at top-ranking Chinese universities; and Australia should expand its network of bilingual English–Chinese schools.

Fully realising the potential for trade in higher value-added goods and more sophisticated services requires China and Australia to go beyond a transactional relationship based on resources and manufactured goods, toward a partnership that supports long-term two-way investment and the exchange of ideas and talent in building innovative and more productive economies. While the resources trade remains central, the future relationship cannot be focused only on resources or contained to prescribed sectors. Rather, it is a relationship that in future must encompass connections between all dimensions of the broader economic relationship — trade in goods and services, investment and people-to-people connections.

This chapter considers the benefits from direct investment and from people-to-people connections between the two countries (Box 4.1). Chapter 5 discusses the evolving framework within which portfolio investment and other financial flows will grow and capital markets will integrate more fully.

BOX 4.1: THE BENEFITS OF FOREIGN DIRECT INVESTMENT

Foreign investment helps meet the gap between what domestic residents are able to save, and the productive investment opportunities in the economy. It improves the global allocation of resources by increasing investment in the countries that have lower domestic savings and increasing returns in countries with excess savings.

Investors primarily seek a return on the capital they invest. But investment is also good for workers, as it equips them with more capital and therefore makes them more productive. This increases wages and living standards. Local asset-holders benefit from being able to sell to the highest bidder on the world market, making it more profitable to develop new assets.

The extent of this 'capital deepening' effect applies to all foreign investment, and will be influenced, among other things, by the rates of taxation on capital, the general business environment and the perceived political risk of investing offshore.

The benefits of direct investment go beyond simply providing loans or buying shares in a foreign company, to establishing or buying a controlling interest in the company, injecting not only capital, but also crucial linkages to foreign markets and technologies, which further expands export opportunities for producers and opens up a wider range of cheaper goods for consumers.

Unlike portfolio investment, which can be easily liquidated and transferred in response to financial market fluctuations, direct investment tends to build longer-lived assets that provide returns over years or even decades, including long-term investment in infrastructure. Foreign direct investment (FDI) creates powerful long-term commercial interests in maintaining good relations between countries.

Direct investment abroad delivers benefits that can spill over to the whole economy — including familiarising locals with new production techniques and bringing international standards into domestic production.

Australia's population is low relative to its land area and natural resources. Foreign investment in mines, ports, transport infrastructure, technology, land and factories is essential to transform resource endowments into real wealth. Foreign capital in Australia came first from the United Kingdom, but more recent waves have come from the United States, Japan and now China. Australia has historically run a small, but persistent, current account deficit. That means that Australians invest more than they save, with the difference made up by borrowing from abroad. Reducing foreign investment would mean that many productive investments in Australia could simply no longer be funded. That would lower productivity, and reduce the standard of living and the economic strength of the country.

Despite being a foundation of Australia's economic prosperity, the role of foreign investment is not always fully or widely understood in the community. Concerns in Australia about 'selling off the farm' and shifting profits overseas miss the point that foreign investment enhances the productivity of local labour, lifts wages and increases the value of domestic assets. Investment in infrastructure and better linkages to foreign markets further expand export opportunities for Australian producers, and open up a wider range of cheaper goods for Australian consumers. Australian asset-holders benefit from being able to sell to the highest bidder on the world market, making it more profitable to develop new assets.

Foreign investment has also played a crucial role in China's reform and opening since 1978. Investors from Hong Kong and Taiwan were the first to develop China's emerging coastal trading hubs. FDI helped transplant the rules and institutions of a modern market economy into China. For example, when a special economic zone was established in Shenzhen in 1980, that city was a small fishing town. It is now one of China's largest and wealthiest metropolises.

Despite phenomenally high rates of investment over the past two decades, China has run a current account surplus every year since 1994. This means that, unlike Australia, China does not depend on global savings to meet its investment needs because its own savings are very high. But China's economic growth, particularly in its export-oriented manufacturing sector, has relied heavily on the technology transfer and advanced labour skills that come with FDI.

One way of dealing with persistent current account surpluses was for the Chinese government to allow Chinese companies to invest abroad. This 'going out' policy was launched in 1999 and formally included in China's subsequent Five Year Plans. As well as providing a higher return on Chinese savings than that available on US government debt, the stated goals of this policy are to ensure that China can access the natural resources it needs for economic development, access export markets and acquire foreign technology needed to improve economic capacity in China (Government of China 2006).

More recently, China's OBOR initiative, and its leadership in establishing the multilateral AIIB, seek not just to connect China to foreign markets, but also to build connectivity — and therefore prosperity — across the region. This will provide investment opportunities to expand infrastructure investments in Australia, including reaping the benefits of agricultural investment in Northern Australia.

The benefits of opening up to foreign investment and services

To capture the gains from these policy initiatives, there will need to be further policy engagement of the kind recommended in the argument of this Report.

The economic benefits of China's opening up to foreign capital and to competition in the services sector are very substantial.

In order to give a rough quantification of these benefits, modelling can be used to simulate the effect of services sector and financial market reform that might be set in train by a strong policy commitment to opening up, utilising the GTAP model introduced in Chapter 3 (Gretton 2016).

Domestic reforms across the services sectors would improve the productivity of value-adding labour and capital in production and would be trade liberalising. The modelling suggests, for example, that for every 1 per cent improvement in the productivity of service provision in China, Chinese GDP could be increased by 0.68 per cent, with a small but positive flow-on effect to Australia. The same proportional increase in the productivity of service provision in Australia could generate an increase in Australian GDP of 1.13 per cent.

Barriers to the efficient functioning of the financial system arise for a variety of reasons, including ownership restrictions, government directives on the use of finance, domestic market practices and regulations favouring designated activities, as well as discrimination between foreign and domestic investors. Higher investment costs raise the price of an effective unit of capital used in production and reduce the competitiveness of capital-using activities and potential output. A reduction in the risk premium of investment in China achieved through domestic financial system reforms would lower the rate of return required by domestic and foreign investors to undertake new investment.

The modelling estimates suggest that a 10 per cent reduction in the cost of capital through financial market reform could increase China's GDP by 5.7 per cent above levels that would otherwise be achieved in the longer term. This projection does not necessarily represent the effects of a single policy, but rather a concerted effort to improve the operation of the financial system. The time horizon over which the benefits could be achieved would, in turn, depend on the pace of reform, the rate at which businesses took up new opportunities and the transition of labour to these new activities.

While these projections provide an indication of the potential economic benefits of trade liberalisation and economic reform towards better functioning markets for goods and services and a more efficient financial system in China and in Australia, they do not directly capture all effects. Beyond reducing the risks associated with investment, for example, a well-functioning and efficient financial sector in China should also allocate capital to the most profitable firms and exert pressure on those firms to maintain high standards of corporate governance, affording additional potential productivity benefits. Distributional effects within the Chinese economy could also follow, such as between government-owned or controlled sectors and other sectors within the economy, and between the Chinese economy and other economies. Overall, a lowering of investment risk in China would be expected to raise global economic activity and incomes.

These simulations of the effects of alternative policy directions illustrate the importance of leveraging broader regional and global trade liberalisation agendas to the bilateral agenda, and pressing ahead with a trade liberalisation agenda that goes beyond merchandise trade to include the services sector, the financial sector and investment reform. Capturing these gains will be central to realising the potential of the next phase of Australia–China economic engagement. The rest of this chapter considers in more detail the challenges that policymakers must navigate and the specific reforms that will be necessary for securing the benefits from liberalisation.

Adapting to Chinese FDI in Australia

In the 1980s, China's two largest investments outside of Hong Kong were both in Australia — China International Trust and Investment Corporation (CITIC) invested in the Portland aluminium smelter, and the Chinese Ministry of Metallurgical Industry took a 40 per cent stake in a new iron mine with Rio Tinto at Mt Channar in Western Australia. These two investments operationalised important aspects of China's reform and opening trade and economic strategy. Today, investment from China into the Australian market has diversified into other sectors. Last year, China's outbound investment reached US$118 billion, an increase of 15 per cent on 2014. Australia is a major investment market for China. In 2015, Chinese investment in Australia amounted to US$11 billion — a 33 per cent increase on the year before (Figure 4.1).

The KPMG–University of Sydney database on Chinese direct investment in Australia details the changing trends. With the resource boom over, Australia has fallen back to be only the second-largest destination for Chinese direct investment after the United States. But relative to economic size, Australia is China's most important ultimate destination for foreign investment. With a reduction in Chinese investment in resources as the resources boom ends, 45 per cent of the recorded inbound investment in 2015 was in real estate. The shift away from resources saw private Chinese investors exceeding Chinese SOE investment for the first time in 2014 (KPMG 2016). The 2015 share was 49 per cent SOE, 48 per cent private, 3 per cent SOE–private joint venture.

MOFCOM and MFA identify opportunities for Chinese investment in Australian agriculture, aquaculture, dairy, iron ore, natural gas, coal, bauxite mining and aluminium smelting, shale oil, pharmaceutical production, trade, retail, transport, research, finance, telecommunications and tourism (MFA 2014). The promotion of bilateral investment gives momentum to the development of bilateral trade.

The legacy of the planned economy has meant that all major Chinese investments — whether private or state-owned, domestic or foreign — historically required government approvals. On top of project-level approvals, restrictions on the Chinese capital account have limited the ability of Chinese firms to invest offshore. However, the requirements for project-level investment approvals have been relaxed over time, and as restrictions on the capital account are removed, the flow of Chinese investment is likely to expand dramatically. According to ABS data for foreign investment stocks in 2015, China is only the fifth-largest direct investor in Australia behind the United States, Japan, the United Kingdom and the Netherlands. However, Chinese direct investment in Australia has been increasing rapidly from a low base, growing from A$3.6 billion in 2008 to A$35 billion in 2015 (ABS 2016f).

Figure 4.1: Stock of foreign direct investment in Australia by source (2014 A$ billion)

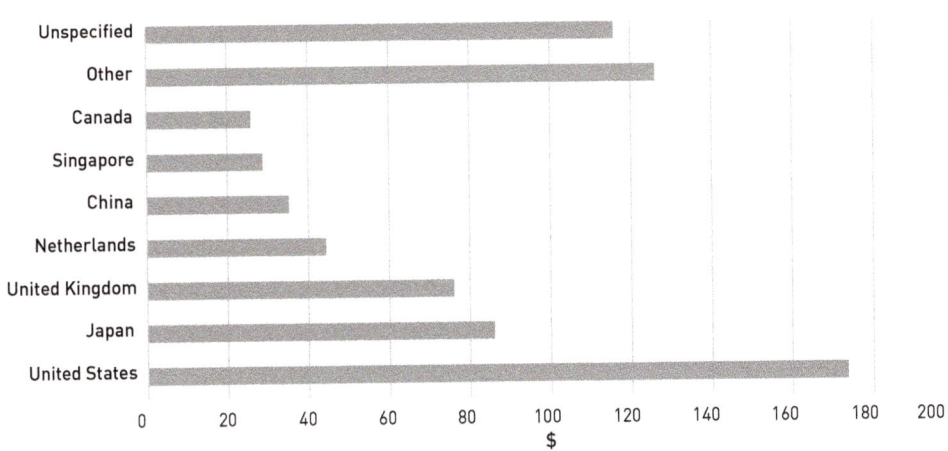

Source: ABS Cat. No. 5352.0, table 2, 2016f.

The speed with which China has expanded its global investment has raised some concerns in the Australian community. These concerns are not new, and not unique to Chinese investment (Box 4.2). The Foreign Investment Review Board (FIRB) process has helped allay popular concerns about new waves of foreign investment in Australia since 1976. But the discretion accorded to the Australian Treasurer to block certain proposals on 'national interest' grounds means that individual cases can become highly politicised. While in practice, the formal power is rarely used, it nevertheless adds to the uncertainty, and therefore the risks, for foreign companies seeking to invest in Australia.

As long as Australia was competing for investment to develop its rich natural resource endowments, this risk may have been trivial compared to the sovereign risks involved in many other resource-rich nations. International capital looking to invest in manufacturing, agriculture, tourism and services is much more mobile. In these sectors, Australia's competitors are advanced economies in Europe, Asia and North America. Amongst its OECD peers, Australia's regime ranks as the sixth-most restrictive based on the OECD's index of foreign equity restrictions, screening and other prior approval requirements, rules for key personnel and other restrictions on the operation of foreign enterprises (Figure 4.2). It is only slightly more liberal than the average of non-OECD members that are assessed. The Chinese inward investment regime, which is discussed later in this chapter, is the most restrictive of all countries surveyed on this measure.

BOX 4.2: POPULAR ATTITUDES TOWARD FOREIGN INVESTMENT

Successive waves of foreign investment in Australia from the United Kingdom, the United States, Japan and now China have all caused community anxieties (Groot 1990). A Gallup poll in June 1972, which referenced British and American investors, reported that almost 90 per cent of Australians would limit the shares that these foreigners could purchase in Australian companies. A survey conducted by the Japanese embassy in 1988 found that 36 per cent of Australians believed that their government should actively discourage Japanese investment. A 1996 Newspoll recorded 56 per cent of Australians agreeing that foreign investment levels were already 'too high'.

Annual surveys conducted by the Lowy Institute for International Policy from 2009 to 2014, after Chinese investment had become prominent in Australia, consistently found that more than half of respondents agreed with the proposition that the Australian government allows 'too much' investment from China (Lowy Institute 2015). An Essential Report from August 2012 suggests that most Australians are wary about investment from any foreign government-related entities — Chinese or otherwise (Lewis and Woods 2012).

A foreign investment study by UTS researchers in 2015 suggests that the Australian public is more concerned about how large the share of an Australian company being bought by a foreign investor is rather than whether that investor is a state-owned entity or whether the foreign investor is from a particular country — although China is preferred significantly less than the United States or Japan (Laurenceson et al 2015).

Community apprehension towards FDI is equally present in China — a Pew Global Attitudes survey found that 50 per cent of Chinese believe that foreign companies buying local companies is 'bad' (Pew Research Centre 2014). However, ACRI-Zogby polling in 2015 found that Chinese business elites view Australia as a more attractive place to invest than Germany, the United States, Singapore, Canada, New Zealand, South Korea and Russia (Zogby Research Services 2015).

Potential investors, and governments, have an important role to play in ensuring that the direct and indirect benefits of foreign investment projects are understood throughout wider communities.

Since ChAFTA came into force, private investments from China in most sectors only require screening when the total project value is above an A$1094 million threshold. This effectively removes much of Chinese private investment from screening. Nevertheless, there are exceptions on a sectoral basis, including media, airports, telecommunications, transport, defence and uranium mining, which are subject to more restrictive thresholds. All applications to invest in residential or vacant commercial land are reviewed, and investments in Australian agribusiness and purchases of agricultural land also have stricter thresholds.

Mandatory screening also applies to investors which are at least 20 per cent owned by a foreign government. This provision has been a longstanding feature of the FIRB process, and is not formally directed at Chinese SOEs. Given that China's resources sectors and public utilities are largely state-owned, these provisions are more likely to affect investors in these sectors who come from China.

Figure 4.2: OECD foreign direct investment regulatory restrictiveness index

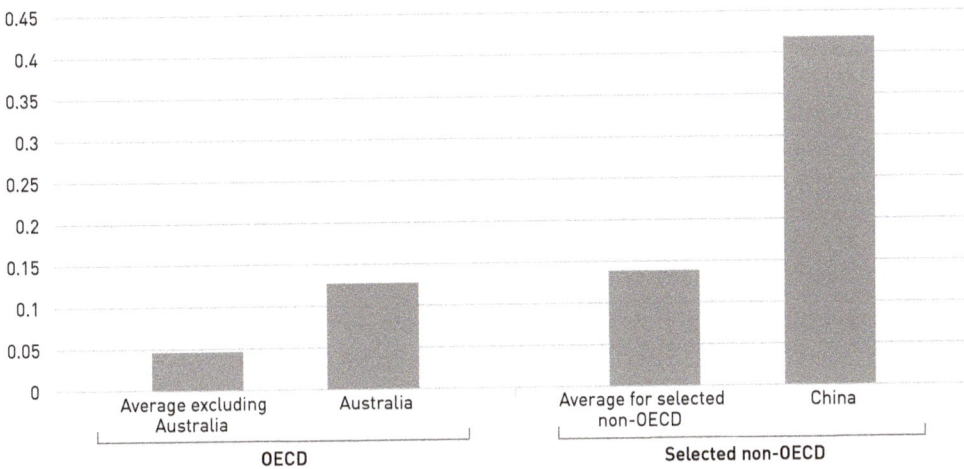

Note: Averages are unweighted. Other non-OECD countries rated by OECD are: Argentina, Brazil, Colombia, Costa Rica, Egypt, India, Indonesia, Jordan, Kazakhstan, Kyrgyzstan, Latvia, Lithuania, Malaysia, Mongolia, Morocco, Myanmar, Peru, Romania, Russia, Saudi Arabia, South Africa, Tunisia and Ukraine.
Source: OECD FDI Regulatory Restrictiveness Index 2014b.

For projects subject to screening, the Treasurer may approve a project subject to conditions. In the past, this has included conditions that proscribe particular corporate structures on foreign investors. Investors who contravene these orders can face civil penalties and possible criminal prosecution, although investors can later apply to change the conditions.

After receiving approval, and subject to any conditions, Chinese investment receives the same treatment as a domestic investor with respect to domestic laws ('national treatment'). Chinese companies face the same competition, taxation, labour, environmental, and workplace health and safety regulations as Australian companies. Investments in publicly listed companies demand even higher standards of corporate governance and transparency. National treatment in this way is subject to robust protection under an impartial legal framework.

Very few foreign investment applications have been explicitly rejected (Australian Treasury 2015). Between 1 July 2008 and 30 June 2014, the Australian government approved 67,582 such applications (the majority being applications to buy real estate) and rejected only 65 applications, mostly relating to real estate. The value of rejected proposals is very low relative to the value of approvals, although in 2010–2011 the government rejected A$8.8 billion (5 per cent) worth of proposals compared to the A$176.7 billion it approved. In 2013–2014, China became the largest source country in terms of volume of investment approvals (14,716), as well as total value of proposed investment (A$27.7 billion).

While the formal rejection rate is low, it is not clear how many investment proposals are withdrawn before a formal rejection is delivered, or more importantly, how many potentially successful investment projects are deterred by the uncertainties of the screening regime. Such uncertainty is rooted in the discretion of the Treasurer to reject projects or apply conditions based on the 'national interest'.

The Australian Government's December 2015 foreign investment policy provides some guidance as to the factors that the government would typically consider. These include national security, competition, tax, the effect on the economy and the community, competition and the character of the investor, along with specific considerations for agricultural investment, investment in residential land and non-government investors (FIRB 2015). However, this policy is not binding on the Treasurer, and additional considerations can be included, as the policy is interpreted on a case-by-case basis. While this may be reassuring for the Australian community, it does so at the cost of uncertainty for potential investors. Specifically, it creates an application risk that does not apply to domestic investors. In particular, as a senior member of government of the day, the Treasurer may only consider the national interest in response to short-term political issues or popular pressure.

As Australia increasingly competes with other advanced economies on the basis of its business environment rather than its natural resource endowments, there is no benefit from the government creating regulatory uncertainty. For the most part, Australian competition law, labour standards, corporate governance and environmental regulations should be enough to ensure that foreign investors follow the same 'rules of the road' as domestic investors in the Australian economy.

The recent high-profile decision to reject an application for a Chinese company to acquire an 80 per cent stake in Australia's largest private land-holding, owned by S. Kidman & Co Ltd on account of its 'size and significance' creates uncertainty for Chinese and other foreign investors (Treasurer of Australia 2016). The property portfolio is Australia's largest in terms of total land area, including 10 cattle stations across four Australian states and territories, covering over 100,000 square kilometres and so collectively accounts for more than 1 per cent of Australia's total land area, and 2 per cent of its agricultural land (Treasurer of Australia 2015). The public explanation given by the Treasurer notes that foreign acquisitions of land this large would not be permitted in many other countries. This would include China.

This Report does not take a view on the merits of the argument in limiting the size of land parcels available for foreign investments. However, this case illustrates well the problem that the current FDI regime does not specify such limits clearly in advance, which would have allowed all parties to proceed with more certainty and avoid the additional costs, delay and uncertainty of the review process. It also suggests that consideration of the benefits of foreign investor acquisitions should be properly judged independently of the choices made by other countries on similar investment acquisitions: it makes no sense to replicate decisions that are damaging wherever they are made. A market environment that allows the free entry and exit of companies, together with sound market regulation and non-discriminatory enforcement of Australian laws, is likely a better guarantee of national economic wellbeing than one-time approvals of business transactions by FIRB in an ad hoc screening process.

Dealing with sensitive sectors

While national treatment for foreign investors looking to come to Australia is a sound principle, there will be some sectors where the Australian government might still reserve the right to impose sector-specific restrictions to guarantee national security or protect other legitimate public policy concerns. Australia already identifies the sectors in which additional restrictions to foreign investment apply (a 'negative list'), but there are no binding principles that the Treasurer must consider when deciding these matters.

The foreign investment regime should provide a clear line between sectors in which foreign investment is welcome (therefore removing application risk), and those in which the government retains discretion. In sectors where discretion is retained, the nature of the national interest considerations being applied should be well specified and defined as tightly as possible. Sector-specific regulators rather than the Treasurer might impose these considerations. Priority development areas might still be designated in which foreign investment in land and agribusiness is accorded less restrictive treatment.

Clearly defining boundaries and providing guidance for potential investors in Australian infrastructure is also important. Given the long-term nature and very large capital requirements of infrastructure investment, this is an ideal candidate for foreign direct investment (Box 4.3). Chinese investment in Australian infrastructure assets has been the cause of public debate in Australia on the grounds that some infrastructure assets may be critical to Australia's national economic and strategic security.

BOX 4.3: INFRASTRUCTURE INVESTMENT IN AUSTRALIA

Prior to 1945, neither the private sector nor the federal government were involved in the provision of infrastructure in Australia: state governments provided the vast proportion of infrastructure. In the postwar years, federal infrastructure investment underpinned Australia's rapid industrial expansion and urbanisation. Since the 1950s, the public investment share of Australia's total infrastructure investment has remained fairly stable at just under 6 per cent of GDP.

Since the mid-1990s, there has been a decline in public sector infrastructure investment. This has been more than offset by private sector investment in infrastructure.

Australia's population is expected to reach over 30 million people by 2031 — with three-quarters of this growth occurring in Sydney, Melbourne, Brisbane and Perth — which will put pressure on urban infrastructure that is already in high demand. In order to address some of these concerns, Infrastructure Australia released an Australian Infrastructure Plan in February 2016, which outlines reforms for improving investment, deliverance and usage of Australia's infrastructure.

The Australian Infrastructure Plan highlights the telecommunications, transportation and energy sectors as well as urban congestion and inter-urban connectivity as key areas for infrastructure investment (Infrastructure Australia 2016). The question for Australia, however, is where will the money come from?

Given the federal government's debt position is expected to worsen, the availability of public infrastructure funding will be increasingly limited. Funding for infrastructure investment from foreign investment should therefore be mobilised to play a much larger role.

This risk management is best approached as a matter of broad policy that ensures ongoing monitoring and mitigation of risks, regardless of the identity of the asset owner. Foreign operators in this area can be legitimately required to notify government of their involvement, and abide by all relevant laws and regulations, including licensing conditions for the operation of key infrastructure. Where the behaviour of a foreign investor breaks the law or threatens national security, then the Australian government should reserve the right to force divestment of the asset.

Such an ongoing, risk-management approach to managing Australian critical infrastructure would be more effective than one-off screening at the pre-establishment phase. Reforms along these lines would therefore enhance the security of Australian infrastructure assets, while reducing the uncertainty that otherwise deters foreign capital.

As more Chinese construction and public utilities look to expand abroad, there is a large opportunity to attract more Chinese capital in infrastructure. The policy direction suggested in this Report should not, of course, be restricted to Chinese investors, or be preferential to them. Where state governments choose to partner with international investors to build or upgrade state infrastructure assets, this can usually be presumed to be in the national interest. One option to explore would be to allow the state government to issue some form of 'conclusive certificate' that an investment is in the state's interest and therefore does not require the same foreign investment approvals that currently apply to for the sale of state government-owned infrastructure assets.

The United Kingdom might provide a useful model for Australia. There is no legislative framework distinguishing foreign from domestic investors in the UK. However, certain sectors have their own regulatory bodies, through which foreign investors may have to apply for authorisation. These sectors include water, gas, financial services, media and defence, all of which require permits to set up or acquire companies. These bodies do not restrict FDI in particular, but enforce a number of obligations, such as the need to notify substantial changes in shareholdings (Box 4.4).

BOX 4.4: FOREIGN INVESTMENT IN THE UNITED KINGDOM

In the last three decades, the UK has consistently been one of the most successful developed countries in attracting FDI (Driffield et al 2013). Rather than pre-screening investors, it relies on strong domestic legal and regulatory frameworks to protect the UK's national interests. In terms of its stock of FDI, the UK ranked third in the world in 2014, behind China and the United States. That year, while global direct investment flows fell by 11 per cent, the UK achieved a 50 per cent increase in its inflows. The UK led Europe in terms of the stock, flow and project volume of FDI (UKTI 2015).

In October 2015, UK Prime Minister and Chinese President announced a 'flagship' GBP6 billion Chinese investment in the Hinkley Point C nuclear plant in Somerset. A Chinese SOE, the China General Nuclear Power Corporation, would bail out the plant's main developer, France's EDF. In the same week, further investment projects were struck in areas as diverse as the automobile industry (Aston Martin), creative industries (BBC World) and property (the Advanced Business Park).

The UK's attractiveness for foreign investors can be partly explained by its low corporate tax rates, as well as additional tax incentives such as research and development and patent credits. The UK's corporate tax rate is under 20 per cent and is the lowest in the G20 and significantly lower than Australia's current 30 per cent company tax and the Australian government's announced target of 25 per cent by 2026–2027. Additionally, the UK does not impose exchange controls that affect FDI and there are no geographical restrictions on the establishment of foreign businesses in the UK (Smith 2012).

Investment from Chinese SOEs

While not explicitly targeted at SOEs from China, the effect of Australia's foreign investment regime to screen all foreign government investment proposals has a disproportionate impact on China. This is because of the still significant legacy of SOEs in all sectors of the Chinese economy, and their continued leading role in resources, finance and public utilities (Box 4.5). In addition to SOEs, China controls large sovereign wealth funds that seek financial returns as part of a diversified, global portfolio. These funds provide an additional and important pool of new international investment capital, whether they come with ownership control through direct investment or without ownership control through equity investment.

BOX 4.5: UNDERSTANDING CHINESE SOEs

Despite the emergence of a dynamic private sector in China that dominates its manufacturing economy, SOEs play an important role in key areas of the Chinese economy, including resources, energy, telecommunications, media and finance. Doing business with China in one of these sectors mostly means having to deal with SOEs.

SOEs are no longer mere instruments of the government, as they were when China began investing overseas in the 1980s (for example, in the Mt Channar project). SOE reforms in the 1990s and 2000s transformed SOEs from ministries and industrial bureaux into market-oriented operations with corporate governance, commercial goals and assessments based on financial performance. Many subsidiaries of SOEs are publicly listed on securities markets in China, Hong Kong or New York. Reforms announced in September 2014 require individual SOEs to be classified according to whether they are pursuing strictly commercial or broader public policy functions.

The largest SOEs in industries that are considered most vital to the national economy, including oil and electricity, are supervised by the central State-owned Assets Supervision and Administration Commission (SASAC). These 106 central SOEs are modern corporate structures with hundreds of subsidiaries. SASAC oversees their investment behaviour, and plays a role in preventing 'destructive competition' between central SOEs in their overseas investments. In practice this means dampening what can sometimes be fierce competition between two or more SOEs competing in the same market. China's provinces each have their own provincial-level SOEs that also operate in highly competitive sectors of the Chinese economy. There are thousands of SOEs that compete both among themselves and with the private sector.

One reason to pay closer attention to SOE investment might be the potential harm to the market environment in the host country. The ability of SOEs to borrow from state-owned banks and the potential for state bailouts leads to fears that SOEs might accept heavy initial losses to drive out private competitors in the host country. In reality, the commercial constraints on overseas investments by Chinese SOEs have become more stringent and the Chinese state is less willing to bankroll and subsidise unprofitable projects.

In addition, some SOEs have very large asset holdings and — in some sectors, including electricity, oil and tobacco — monopolise their segment of the Chinese domestic market. This can improve the credit worthiness of these companies even on purely private international lending criteria. However, this domestic position does not automatically flow through to their behaviour in overseas markets. For example, evidence from SOE investment behaviour in the resources market indicates that they have tended to increase competition and expand supply (Box 4.6). The general application of domestic anti-monopoly provisions regardless of ownership type is the most appropriate response.

But while SOEs do dominate some important sectors of the Chinese economy, state ownership is not synonymous with monopoly. Steel is one of China's largest industrial sectors and it is predominantly state-owned. But the most prominent players are local-level SOEs, which compete fiercely among each other. Using the same measure of industrial concentration as the United States applies to anti-trust provisions (the Herfindahl-Hirschman index), steel is not a concentrated market in China. Moreover, on account of the historic legacy of the planned economy in which almost all industrial production was done by SOEs, they still continue to operate in all kinds of industry sectors. Around half of the assets owned by local SOEs (which account for around half of total state assets) are in un-concentrated manufacturing sectors, in which SOEs compete with private companies (Hubbard 2016).

BOX 4.6: CHINESE GLOBAL INVESTMENTS IN IRON ORE

China's global investments in iron ore provide valuable information about how competitive neutrality works in practice. From 2002 to 2015, China made 30 overseas direct investments in iron ore, with 25 made by SOEs. Chinese state banking institutions provided credit based on international benchmarks, plus a margin, generally making this credit cheaper than international commercial finance.

But did this departure from competitive neutrality harm the market?

These Chinese iron ore investors increased rather than decreased partnership opportunities for non-Chinese iron ore investment. Of these 30 investments, 21 were made by firms with an operating competency in mining. Only one of the investments was made by a specialised iron ore miner. Chinese SOEs most often took minority equity positions in partnership with specialised non-Chinese iron ore miners. Joint ventures and minority acquisitions made up 22 of the 30 investments.

A related concern is that Chinese iron ore miners might attempt to 'lock up' supplies of iron ore using long-term contracts with Chinese buyers, in an attempt to reduce the supply to other steel producers in Japan, Taiwan and South Korea.

But an analysis of 50 Chinese iron ore procurement arrangements shows that only 63.8 per cent of projected iron ore output from Chinese projects was reserved through long-term contracts for Chinese buyers. The effect of China's overseas iron ore investments was therefore to increase supply to the global market (Hurst 2015).

According to FIRB's policy guidance, the Australian Treasurer considers whether a foreign government investment proposal is 'commercial in nature or if the investor may be pursuing broader political or strategic objectives' (FIRB 2015). The Australian government has already received and approved large-scale investments from some of the most strategically important central SOEs, including from the State Grid Corporation of China, China Power Investment Corporation, Minmetals and China's three national oil companies.

The differences between the Australian and Chinese systems of politics and governance (see Chapter 6) can generate community concerns in Australia about SOEs. An upfront and transparent account of ownership structures and corporate governance arrangements is important to showing that an investor has nothing to hide. Over time, good corporate behaviour on the part of SOEs, and familiarity on the part of local communities, should make Chinese investment in Australia's development easier, as it has in the case of other foreign investment from different sources.

This extends beyond companies that are formally state-owned. Private Chinese companies sometimes have close personnel ties or contractual relationships with state, political or military institutions. This is not in any way surprising. The Communist Party of China had 87.8 million members at the end of 2014 (China Daily 2015), including private entrepreneurs, who have been allowed to join the Party since 2002. All SOEs have Party Committees, as do the Chinese operations of many private and foreign companies, including global market leaders from the United States such as Wal-Mart (China Daily 2016).

Rather than apply different rules on the basis of formal ownership requirements, foreign investors in Australia should be judged according to their actual behaviour. Foreign government enterprises investing in Australia could still be expected to notify FIRB of their involvement. But SOEs should have the opportunity to prove their commercial credentials, possibly based on an historical accreditation model (BCA 2014), in which case there would be no need to treat them differently from privately owned Chinese companies. Alternatively, investment proposals from SOEs below the general review threshold could be granted an automatic approval, with automatic conditions imposed in relation to legal or corporate governance standards.

This approach would not provide Chinese SOEs with preferential access; rather it would remove discrimination currently in place that disproportionately deters an important class of potential Chinese investors.

Investment to transform Chinese services

In the 1970s, China's economy was closed to foreign investment. The regime is now significantly more open, and China has become the world's largest recipient of foreign direct investment after the United States. Foreign investment flows into China in 2014 totalled US$128.5 billion (UNCTAD 2015). But investment rules and treatment vary between industries, and the playing field between domestic companies and foreign enterprises seeking to enter Chinese markets is not yet even.

Foreign capital in China has been most welcome in the manufacturing sectors that fuelled China's export-led growth through the 1990s and 2000s. Almost three-quarters of foreign investment in China goes into the manufacturing, wholesale and retail sectors. The largest investors in China are its Asian neighbours, such as Japan, which have particular expertise in supply-chain manufacturing. There is also a large inflow of foreign capital into China's real estate sector.

Four-fifths of the investment from companies registered in China as foreign-funded firms or joint ventures are in coastal provinces. Half of the investment is in three provinces — Jiangsu, Guangdong and Shanghai. This reflects historical patterns in the opening and development of

China's export industries and industrial production. These are all important 'sister provinces' for Australian states (see Chapter 3), highlighting the huge opportunity for state governments to leverage these relationships further.

Foreign direct investment in Chinese companies is also important for China's industrial and regional development priorities. The NDRC and MOFCOM provide sector-based foreign investment guidance. As of 2015, there are 349 industries in which foreign investment is 'encouraged', 38 industries in which foreign investment is 'restricted', and 36 industries in which foreign investment is 'prohibited', with foreign investment in all other industries deemed 'permitted'. The status of new sectors is undefined. Restricted industries include key sectors of interest for Australia, such as finance, health and education. Foreign investment in Chinese media is prohibited.

In 24 of the restricted sectors, additional conditions are imposed that prevent wholly foreign-owned investors from entering the industry. This is usually in the form of a requirement that a Chinese partner must be the majority shareholder. Depending on the scale of investment, inbound investments can be approved or noted at the national and local levels. After this, ordinary business licences must be approved before registering for taxation, customs and foreign exchange.

Businesses seeking to invest in China face a complicated regulatory environment. There are three separate laws that govern the creation of foreign enterprises — the *China Foreign Equity Joint Venture Enterprise Law*, the *Foreign Cooperative Joint Venture Enterprise Law*, and the *Foreign-Invested Enterprise Law*. There are also hundreds of subsidiary and local rules and regulations that affect foreign investors.

Sector- and region-specific barriers to investment, including 'behind the border' regulatory restrictions are treated comprehensively in the American Chamber of Commerce's 2015 (AmCham) White Paper, 'American Business in China'. This Report does not endorse specific recommendations made by AmCham, but instead encourages Australian investors in China to be vocal to both MOFCOM and DFAT to ensure that these provisions are on the radar for ongoing consultations under ChAFTA.

While investment in sophisticated services sectors, such as insurance, finance and law, is significantly more restricted, Australian banks have been in China for a long time (see Chapter 5). But despite China's WTO commitments to open up its banking system to competition, the largest Australian bank in China, ANZ, has just four Chinese branches, two sub-branches and one rural bank (AustCham 2012). Each of the banks, except Westpac, holds stakes in local banks but cannot increase their equity share above 20 per cent. These restrictions inhibit the cross-border financial infrastructure needed to underwrite more trade and investment.

Despite this, Australian direct investment in China has also grown significantly over the past decade. Successful Australian investment so far has been in niche areas including banking, medical devices, biopharmaceuticals and water management, and there is currently active investment in the renewable energy sector (Au-Yeung et al 2012). According to the ABS, there was less than A$500 million of Australian direct investment in China in 2004. By 2015, this stock had grown to over A$14 billion (ABS 2016f). This is well behind Australia's direct investment in the United States, the United Kingdom, New Zealand and even Singapore (Figure 4.3).

Figure 4.3: Recipients of Australian direct investment, 2014 (A$billion)

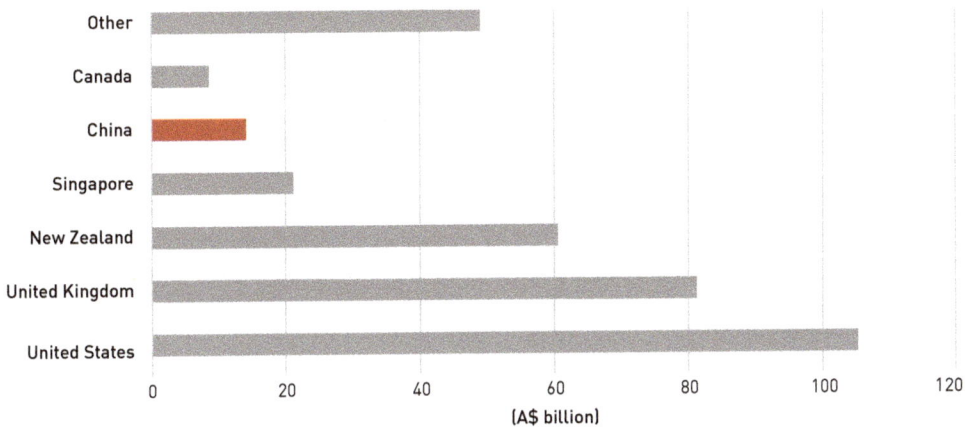

Note: An investment is deemed to be a 'direct investment' where the investor holds at least 10 per cent of equity in the invested entity.
Source: Calculations based on ABS Cat. No. 5352.0 2016f.

Investment in Chinese services sectors

In the same way that foreign investment in manufacturing made China an industrial powerhouse, China now wants to use foreign investment to help drive the transformation of its domestic services sector. Fostering foreign participation and giving full play to the market will help allocate capital more efficiently. This benefits China's economic development, and provides an opportunity for experienced Australian services firms to expand their market in China while contributing to its transformation.

China's overall policy direction in relation to inbound investment is clearly articulated in the November 2013 Decision of the Third Plenum of the Central Committee of the Communist Party of China on Some Major Issues Concerning Comprehensively Deeping Reform ('the Decision'). The Decision commits China to 'stimulate the orderly and free flow of international and domestic factors of production, highly efficient allocation of resources and in-depth market integration, and foster new advantages in participating in and leading international economic cooperation and competition at a faster pace, in order to promote reform through opening up'.

The Decision acknowledges the important role that FDI can play in Chinese economic reform. Specifically, the Central Committee committed to apply 'the same laws and regulations on Chinese and foreign investment' (national treatment for foreign investors), as well as 'keep foreign investment policies stable, transparent and predictable'. Consistent with China's transition to a higher-income services-based economy, the Decision emphasised opening a range of services sectors, particularly 'finance, education, culture and healthcare'.

Chinese authorities have long trialled policy reforms in particular geographic areas as a way of testing them before nationwide implementation. The creation of a Pilot Free Trade Zone in Shanghai, followed by similar zones in Tianjin, Guangdong and Fujian, has provided an additional platform from which to trial the Third Plenum reforms. If these policies are judged to be successful, they should be expanded to a national scale.

The Decision also committed Chinese authorities to 'explore a management model for foreign investors with pre-entry national treatment plus the negative list'. If realised, this would effectively give foreign investors the same rights to invest in China as domestic investors, subject to specified exemptions ('the negative list'). To bring the greatest gains to China's economy, the list of exemptions should be as narrowly specified as possible to core areas of national security and other concerns. In January 2015, MOFCOM released a draft law on foreign investment that would consolidate and replace the existing laws.

This draft law would enshrine the 'negative list' principle and would move Chinese investment approvals away from lists of investments that are 'prohibited', 'restricted' and 'encouraged' toward a presumption that foreign investment is permitted, subject to a well-defined 'negative list' of industries where restrictions are maintained, and a high monetary threshold above which screening is still required. This 'negative list' has also become the basis of China's BIT negotiations with the United States and the EU. After a business is established in China, they are to be accorded national treatment.

The investment law would also introduce an explicit national security test, which would give the State Council the authority to approve, approve with conditions, or reject applications that touch on national defence, key infrastructure (including telecommunications), key commodity resources, investments controlled by foreign governments, or applications that threaten economic stability, public stability or 'any other factor' which the government considers necessary to address.

While these proposed screening arrangements impose restrictions, the law would for the first time allow free investment in and out of sectors that are not listed and that do not touch on broader national security questions. In the continuing revision of the draft law, and when it is implemented, it is recommended that thresholds for review are as liberal as possible and that the list of restricted and prohibited investments is as short as possible. This will maximise its positive effect on transforming China's services sectors.

But a new investment law will not remove all the obstacles to developing China's service industry. Investments in agriculture, energy, transportation, civil aviation, telecommunications, automobiles, tobacco, aerospace, urban infrastructure and large-scale tourism developments are still subject to various additional approvals hurdles that apply to both domestic and foreign investments. Nevertheless, it would be a significant milestone for China's economic development.

Opportunity for an enhanced investment agreement

Both Australia and China have their own domestic policy interests in reforming their treatment of investment flows. These could be pursued unilaterally. Cooperation in the spirit of the Comprehensive Strategic Partnership for Change gives each partner the opportunity to leverage reform through closer policy coordination.

Despite the progress ChAFTA has made, the agreement retains trade barriers in sectors of both the Australian and Chinese economies. These restrictions generally require firms wishing to enter these sectors (Table 4.1) to be owned or managed residents of that country, or run as a joint partnership. Liberalising these sectors can provide commercial opportunities in both countries.

Australia and China have had a BIT since 1988. This has provided the basic legal framework that governs bilateral investment to date. It was adapted to an earlier stage of Chinese development when China was still establishing its basic market system to support the development of its own export manufacturing sectors.

Table 4.1: Remaining barriers to investment

In Australia:	In China:
• Real-estate services	• Legal services
• Telecommunications	• Medical and dental services
• Fishing	• Advertising/market research services
• Professional services (patent attorney, trustee companies, auditor or liquidator, architect (NT), migration agent and customs broker)	• Technical testing and analysis services
	• Agriculture, forestry, hunting and fishing services
	• Mining/oil extraction
• Shipping/freight services	• Photography services
• Aviation	• Convention services
• Banking	• Telecommunications
• Security services (NSW)	• Audio visual/cinema theatre services
• Public transport (NT, ACT and WA)	• Retail
• Biological research (QLD)	• Nature and landscape/environmental protection services
• Wine production (QLD)	• Insurance/banking/securities services
• Tourism (QLD)	• Hospital services (not including Beijing, Tianjin, Shanghai, Jiangsu, Fujian, Guangdong and Hainan province)
• Alcohol and tobacco retail (NT)	
	• Maritime road and aviation transport services
	• Construction and related engineering services

Source: China–Australia Free Trade Agreement, Annex 3 Part 1: Schedule of Non-Conforming Measures 2015.

ChAFTA now provides an appropriate vehicle to foster China's services transformation, and to maintain Australia's status as a preferred destination for mobile investment capital. It also provides opportunity to develop closer linkages between the two countries' agricultural sectors. It includes an agreement to review the BIT within three years, and consider the 'negative list' principle that is the basis of China's BIT negotiations with other partners.

An enhanced investment agreement, which might proceed within the process set up by ChAFTA (though more expeditiously than foreshadowed), would provide commercial certainty to both sides, by removing some of the applications risks and the uncertainty around establishment of new enterprises that currently plague big investment decisions. Both parties would make commitments to undertake the reforms suggested earlier. And both parties would continue to be able to apply domestic laws to protect legitimate interests in sovereignty, public health and security on a non-discriminatory basis.

The conclusion of an enhanced investment agreement could be an appropriate milestone to mark the 30th anniversary of the original 1988 BIT.

There are two major benefits from adopting such an expedited timeline.

First, Australia is an advanced market economy with a highly developed services sector, although it is small relative to the EU and the United States. This makes Australia an ideal 'pilot economy' for China's 'negative list' and 'national treatment' approach before it concludes deals with much larger markets. A successful Australia–China investment agreement could therefore help break the logjam in China's negotiations with the EU and the United States.

Second, an enhanced Australia–China investment agreement, based on the mutual application of the 'negative list' principle, would set the pace for the development norms relating to foreign investment. Unlike trade in goods and services, which is governed by WTO disciplines, there are no well-developed disciplines and norms for FDI flows except those applied at a national level. The principles deriving from a new Australian–Chinese investment agreement could not only serve as a model for further bilateral negotiations with third parties, but also act as the pilot and the template for new multilateral investment liberalisation rules within RCEP. A multilateral arrangement governing investment flows would be superior to bilateral agreements because they establish consistent rules across multiple jurisdictions.

This could help create opportunities for China and Australia to cooperate in India and Indonesia, for example, and to assist regional growth by ensuring that investment flows according to economic productivity rather than political preference. This is a concrete example of the type of engagement envisaged by the Comprehensive Strategic Partnership for Change not just in the bilateral relationship, but also in the region and beyond.

Movement of people

From the earliest days of global trade, the movement of people has been essential to the movement of goods, services and finance. In the future, increased bilateral FDI and the provision of services require opportunities for the two-way exchange of skilled labour. There are currently around 15,000 Australians living, working and studying in the Chinese mainland, many of whom are Australian-Chinese (Australian Centre on China in the World 2015). There is a far greater number of Chinese citizens living, working and studying in Australia (see below). There are many benefits from expanding this two-way flow, both directly in support of trade and investment, and indirectly to build the social trust and cultural understanding that will be crucial to the deeper level of cooperation envisaged by this Report. This does not entail a policy of open borders or mass migration, as both Australia and China understand each other's sovereign right to control their borders and ensure social stability. But there are opportunities to make the bilateral flows of people more conducive to mutual prosperity.

This Report does not attempt to provide an exhaustive treatment of bilateral questions in relation to the issuing of visas and the granting of visa-free status for Australian and Chinese citizens in each other's country. It seeks only to note a few key areas that need to be considered in order to build up the harmonious and friendly social relations that will underpin the next stage in the relationship. There is already an official bilateral working group that considers tourism issues. A bilateral working group, led by government and involving representatives from business, education, tourism and community groups, should be commissioned to review visa issues more broadly and to come up with a specific timetable for the implementation of needed reforms. This would include considering the cost of visas, particularly tourist visas, to ensure that the price charged for visa applications does not exceed the expected administrative costs associated with processing the application.

Permanent migration and citizenship

Chinese have come to Australia since the gold rushes of the mid-19th century and have had a continuous presence ever since. Increased recent migration from China has grown the Chinese diaspora community in Australia (Box 4.7). The 2011 Census recorded 319,000 Australian residents who were born in China, and approximately 865,000 people in Australia reported that they had Chinese ancestry, or 4 per cent of the total population (ABS 2011). This diaspora is a valuable shared asset for the bilateral relationship.

Because of Australia's Chinese diaspora, Mandarin Chinese has become the second-most widely spoken language other than English in Australia. According to the 2011 Census, 336,410 people in Australia speak Mandarin at home. Significantly, the number of Mandarin speakers had increased by over 125,000 since the 2006 Census. More than a quarter-million people speak Cantonese, meaning that over 600,000 Australians already speak a Chinese language.

BOX 4.7: THE CHINESE DIASPORA IN AUSTRALIA

The Australian Council of Learned Academies' (ACOLA) 2015 report *Smart Engagement with Asia* and 2016 report *Australia's Diaspora Advantage* looked at the role of diaspora communities as one aspect of the long-term engagement needed for lasting social, economic and political benefits (Ang et al 2015; Rizvi et al 2016). ACOLA stresses that policymakers must engage with a broadly conceived 'diaspora' that includes migrants, subsequent Australian-born generations, those of mixed cultural heritage, and temporary residents in Australia for work or study.

Diasporas are important, not just because they contribute to social and cultural diversity, but also for the business and professional links that they maintain with their countries of family origin. Diasporas use their language capabilities, cultural understanding and global networks to circulate business, information and resources. Particularly in developing trading relationships with countries where legal protections and market norms are still developing, the informal networks of trust and reputation among diaspora communities are able to facilitate investment and exchange.

Since the days of the gold rush, Chinese diaspora communities have played a continuous role in Australian society. Since 2000, the number of mainland Chinese residing in Australia has grown dramatically — over half of the Chinese migrant population in Australia arrived after 2000. Today, Australia boasts one of the largest Chinese diaspora communities in the Western world. Projections estimate that Australia's Chinese-born population will reach 1.3 million people in 2031.

Four per cent of Australian residents report some kind of Chinese heritage (ABS 2011). This proportion is the same in New Zealand (4.0 per cent; 171,000), much smaller in the US (1.0 per cent; 3.14 million) and England and Wales (0.7 per cent; 393,000), and slightly greater in Canada (4.5 per cent; 1.49 million) (Statistics Canada 2011; Statistics New Zealand 2013). In 2014, 447,400 Australian residents, or 1.9 per cent of the population, were born in China. China is now the third most common country of birth for overseas-born Australians, behind the United Kingdom and New Zealand (ABS 2016d). In Canada, China is the second most common country of birth for recent immigrants, after the Philippines. In New Zealand, China is second to the United Kingdom on this measure.

Migration, tourism, education and investment to Australia all provide a route for Chinese to form permanent bonds with Australia. In 2014–2015, Australia issued 27,872 permanent migration visas to Chinese nationals, making China the second-largest source of new migrants after India (DIBP 2015a). China was Australia's fourth-largest source of newly naturalised citizens in 2014–2015, constituting 7549 (5.5 per cent) of 136,572 new citizens in that year, with more Chinese than New Zealanders taking up Australian citizenship (DIBP 2016a).

But the movement of people between Australia and China can sometimes be problematic. The Chinese *Law on Nationality* does not recognise dual nationality, and some new Australian citizens may not renounce their Chinese citizenship. This means that they may continue to be treated as Chinese citizens when in China, and therefore not be in a position to avail themselves of Australian status and consular assistance in the event of legal issues. This is particularly an issue for Australian businesspeople of Chinese origin conducting commercial activities in China.

Ultimately, it is the responsibility of individuals to ensure that their citizenship status is clear with respect to the laws of both countries, and it is in the interests of both countries to have clear understandings and agreements regarding the rights and legal treatment of their citizens in each other's country (see further discussion in Chapter 6).

Visas for significant investors

The Australian government also provides visas leading to potential residency and citizenship for business owners and investors. These programs are dominated by Chinese investors, who received almost 90 per cent of the Significant Investor Visas granted from 2012 to May 2016.

There are separate streams for business owners and investors in Australia (A\$1.5 million investment threshold) and 'significant investors' (A\$5 million investment threshold). Such investors need to be nominated either by a state government or by Austrade. A new Premium Investment Visa, available only on invitation from Austrade, provides a pathway to permanent residency in Australia after 12 months for an investment of A\$15 million, and is initially targeted at US investors.

These visa types encourage wealthy Chinese to make a permanent connection with Australia. Australia is not the only country that does this. Other developed economies, included the United Kingdom (Box 4.8), also offer visas for potential investors, without trying to direct investment into particular sectors.

BOX 4.8: VISAS FOR INVESTORS AND TOURISM IN THE UNITED KINGDOM

There are numerous visa categories for people involved with FDI projects: investors (those outside the European Economic Area who want to invest GBP2 million in the UK); entrepreneurs (those who want to start a business in the United Kingdom); graduate entrepreneurs (graduates of UK universities with an approved business idea); representatives of overseas businesses; and general visas. Investors from within the EU have the right to live and work in the UK (UKTI 2011). Investment promotion programs such as those offered by UKTI serve to reduce the liability of foreignness faced by overseas investors (Driffield et al 2013). The United Kingdom also extends visas to 'maximise' the spending power of Chinese tourists (Inman et al 2015).

Since July 2015, Australia's investor visas have been linked to the government's innovation policy. This compels substantial investment in venture capital or private equity funds, managed funds or other vehicles that invest in emerging companies. This is intended to direct investment away from areas that already receive large capital flows into riskier and less-established areas.

While it is desirable to have a migration pathway that is open to talented entrepreneurs, managing investment decisions through immigration policy rather than general market provisions risks creating bubbles and distortions rather than developing a sustainable innovation agenda. Therefore, the Significant Investor Visa program should have regular reviews that continue to improve its implementation.

China also provides a visa for significant foreign investors to reside and work permanently in China. In line with China's foreign investment policy, investment thresholds are associated with whether an investment is an 'encouraged' sector and whether it is in Western China (US$500,000 threshold), Central China (US$1 million) or other regions (US$2 million). Permanent residency is also available after a time to high-ranking professionals and university researchers.

But uptake of this visa has been very low. In 2012, only 1202 residency permits were granted to all countries. Unlike Australia's investment visas, which are heavily promoted by Austrade, the website of the Chinese Embassy in Canberra does not provide information about permanent residency opportunities for significant investors. Better publicity and promotion of this visa program could help China attract foreign investment and encourage more investment in services.

Temporary skilled labour flows

One advantage of FDI is the opportunity to share knowledge, business practices and technology across borders by way of the movement of skilled labour. The 1988 Australia–China BIT secured the right of investors from each country to visit the other to carry on investment business, and provides for the appointment of key technical and management roles regardless of nationality. This provides practical support for direct investment on both sides, and provides enough time to allow business professionals to establish professional, personal and cultural bonds between the two countries. The Australian temporary skilled migration program is designed to meet only genuine skills shortages in Australia but given the issues that many Chinese investors encounter in Australia, thought could be given to encouraging more Chinese skilled professionals to utilise this program. The number of skilled Chinese professionals working in Australia under these arrangements, however, is very low. According to the Australian Department of Immigration and Border Protection (DIBP 2016b), from 1 July 2015 to 31 March 2016, 2080 applicants from China were granted temporary work visas. China was the third most popular source of workers after India (8320 grants) and the United Kingdom (5750).

ChAFTA provided more specific commitments, allowing four-year Australian visas to the executives, managers and specialists of Chinese firms operating in Australia, and three-year visas for the Australian executives, managers and specialists of Australian firms in China. In both cases, family visas are also offered. These numbers are also likely to expand through the operation of the Investment Facilitation Arrangement (IFA) that came into force with ChAFTA.

The IFA expanded the scope of temporary skilled labour movement to Australia to meet the labour needs of Chinese-registered companies involved in large infrastructure projects in priority industry sectors, including food and agribusiness, resources and energy, transport, telecommunications, power supply and generation, environment and tourism. Where the Chinese investor cannot meet their demand for skilled labour from the local labour market, they may negotiate with DIBP to import skilled labourers to work in Australia temporarily.

This is clearly a win–win arrangement. While temporary migrant workers are sometimes seen as depriving Australians of jobs, under the IFA they are contributing to projects that in many cases would not have gone ahead but for the foreign investment and the availability of skilled temporary labour. Importantly, the workers are subject to Australian employment standards and assurance of proper implementation of that provision is important. In addition, they create demand for other less-skilled local workers while the project is underway. To bolster community confidence in the scheme, regulating bodies need to have enough resources to be able to assess whether companies are compliant with safeguard obligations.

Tourism

The prospects for the Australia–China tourism trade are discussed in Chapter 3. To realise the potential of this market over the next decade, the promotion of Australia's natural environment needs to be combined with investment in facilities and labour that are adequate to meet the demands of Chinese tourists. An example of a major tourism investment is the A$900 million investment by Chinese companies Wanda and Ridong Group to build three hotel towers on the Gold Coast, an area that is now serviced by direct flights from Wuhan, a city of more than 8 million people.

In addition to increased investment, arrangements facilitating increased temporary movements of tourists are welcome. The Australian government's announcement of a 10-year multiple-entry tourist visa for Chinese tourists is an enabler of this. To facilitate business and tourist exchanges, the Chinese government should extend the same treatment to Australian citizens. At the least, provisions that provide short visa-free entry to China to citizens from Brunei, Japan and Singapore should be extended to Australian citizens on the basis of MFN treatment.

From 1 July 2014 to 30 June 2015, the Australian government granted over 226,812 temporary visas for young people from other countries to work and holiday in Australia for up to one year (these visas can be extended for one more year). These working holiday visas provide valuable opportunities for young people to learn about each other's cultures and gain work experience, often before finalising their longer-term study and career plans. They have been a seedbed of innovation and creativity in Australia's external economic and cultural relations (Figure 4.4).

Agreements were first signed with the UK, Canada and Ireland in 1975. Within Asia, Australia has bilateral agreements with Japan (1980), South Korea (1995), Hong Kong (2001), Taiwan (2004), Thailand (2005), Malaysia and Indonesia (2009) and Bangladesh (2010). At the same time as concluding ChAFTA, Australia and China signed a bilateral agreement allowing 5000 Chinese citizens to come to Australia on working holidays visa each year.

Almost 2900 work and holiday visas were granted to Chinese between the commencement of the program in September 2015 and the end of December (DIBP 2015b). There is enormous demand for the program in China, with the first 1500 visa applications 'filled in minutes' (Minister for Immigration and Border Protection 2015). But based on the grants of working holiday visas to applicants from other countries over the 2014–2015 financial year, the 5000 visa cap means that China would only be the twelfth-largest source of working holidaymakers, accounting for just over 2 per cent of the total.

The 5000 visa cap imposed on China is only around half the number of visas granted to Chinese from Hong Kong, and only one-fifth of the number granted to Taiwanese. Unlike mainland China, both Taiwan and Hong Kong offer reciprocal opportunities for young Australians, and are not subject to a quota.

The quota should be expanded at least six-fold to match the number of working holidaymakers currently accepted from Taiwan. Given the opportunities to expand Australia's domestic tourism industry and to meet the vacationing demands of the new Chinese middle class, this would be a sensible approach both to increase demand for tourism in Australia, and to supply a source of language-equipped and culturally aware seasonal workers to meet that demand.

China should make reciprocal opportunities available for young Australians to live, work and study in China. Steps toward this should commence immediately, and need not wait until the formal review of the bilateral agreement in 2018.

Figure 4.4: Working holiday visas granted from 1 July 2014 to 30 June 2015

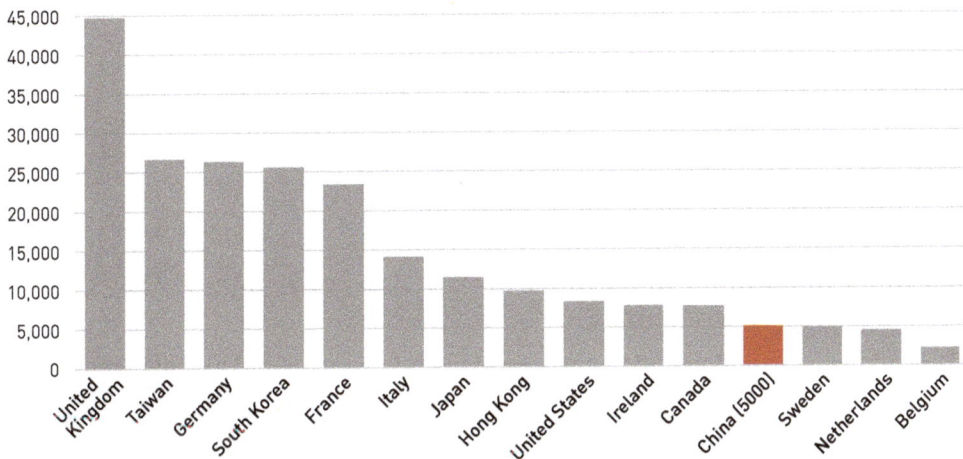

Note: These statistics apply before the Work and Holiday agreement with China came into effect, so the Chinese figure based on the assigned quota is for comparison purposes only.
Source: DIBP 2015b.

Education

Australia and China have a long history of educational exchange. China's first academic exchange agreement with a foreign university after 1978 was established between Peking University and the ANU in December 1980. Since then, the relationship has expanded dramatically. Australian universities have signed over 1200 agreements with Chinese institutions, even more than with the United States (Universities Australia 2014). Scientific exchange and research collaboration is burgeoning (Box 4.9).

Export income related to international education is touted as Australia's third-largest export after iron ore and coal, worth almost A$20 billion per year (Department of Education and Training 2015). Australia is the third-most popular destination for Chinese students after the

United States and the United Kingdom. China has been the largest source of international students to Australia since 2011. Now one-fifth of foreign student visa holders are Chinese, most of whom study at high value-added universities rather than at language or vocational institutes (Figure 4.5).

An example of a new development is the recently established Global Business College of Australia launched in Melbourne by a private Chinese firm. This is the first Chinese-owned educational institution to open in Australia that has students from Australia, China and other countries. It demonstrates the potential for Australia to tap into the expertise (and access to capital) of Chinese educational investors to expand its own education sector.

By contrast, the largest source of foreign students to China in 2014 was South Korea (62,923 students), followed by the United States (24,203) and Thailand (21,296). Around 4700 Australian students studied in China in 2014 (Project Atlas 2016).

Australian education policy encourages both short and longer-term international study experiences. China was the third-largest destination for short-term experiences in 2013, with 2614 Australian undergraduates going, placing it behind only the United States and the United Kingdom. The Australian government's 'New Colombo Plan' mobility program supports over 1400 Australian undergraduates to undertake short educational or work-based placement in China. In 2016, China was the most popular of the 38 possible destinations.

The New Colombo Plan allows for overseas study of up to one year, in addition to six months of internship placements. However, there are fewer opportunities for Australians to access Chinese degree-granting institutions. The China Scholarship Council provides scholarships for overseas students to study degrees at Chinese universities. Private initiatives, such as the BHP Billiton Australia China Scholarships, which provide up to A$60,000 per year for Australians pursuing postgraduate education in China, are most welcome (FASIC 2016). Yet by their nature access to these scholarships will be very limited.

BOX 4.9: COLLABORATIVE RESEARCH AND SCIENTIFIC EXCHANGE

Collaborative research is facilitated through high-level programs such as the Australia–China Science and Research Fund. The Department of Industry, Innovation and Science and the Chinese Ministry of Science and Technology jointly manage this fund. It supports Joint Research Centres, the Australia–China Science Academies Symposia Series, as well as a Young Scientist Exchange Program. The most recent round of joint research grants, between Australian and Chinese universities and government research institutions, covers fields ranging from dairy manufacturing, oceanography, mineral sensing and agriculture. These initiatives concurrently support the Australian government's National Innovation and Science Agenda (Minister for Industry, Innovation and Science 2016), as well as the innovation strategy in China's 13th Five Year Plan.

In 2015, the Australia–China Young Scientist Exchange Program supported 13 Australian researchers visiting China, and 16 Chinese researchers visiting Australia for two weeks. This is intended to develop the potential of early and mid-career scientists as 'science ambassadors' and to catalyse future research collaboration (ATSE 2016).

In 2012, China overtook the United States as the nation with the most formal agreements between domestic higher education institutions and Australian universities.

These agreements include student and staff exchange arrangements and research collaborations (Universities Australia 2014). In April 2015, Australia's Group of Eight universities became the first university umbrella group to sign an agreement with the China Scholarship Council, to increase two-way mobility of students and academics.

The importance of scientific and research exchange to staying abreast with the frontiers of innovation recommends the sharp elevation of these and other exchanges under the new bi-national Australia-China Commission proposed in this Report.

The Australian government's Higher Education Loans Program (HELP), which provides income-contingent loans to Australian tertiary students, also provides loans for expenses for up to two six-month study-abroad experiences that contribute to an Australian degree. To ensure that Australians with strong China skills build a strong foundation for future academic and business relationships with China, overseas HELP loans should be made available for Australian students to enrol in double-structured degree programs at highly regarded Chinese institutions.

This initiative recognises the continued progress of Chinese education. According to the QS World University Rankings, of the top 250 universities worldwide, 11 are in Australia and nine are in China. Because HELP loans are designed to be repaid at threshold incomes, regardless of whether the recipient lives in Australia or not, it would be a lower-cost way of equipping Australian students with China skills.

Figure 4.5: Student visa holders in Australia, 30 June 2015

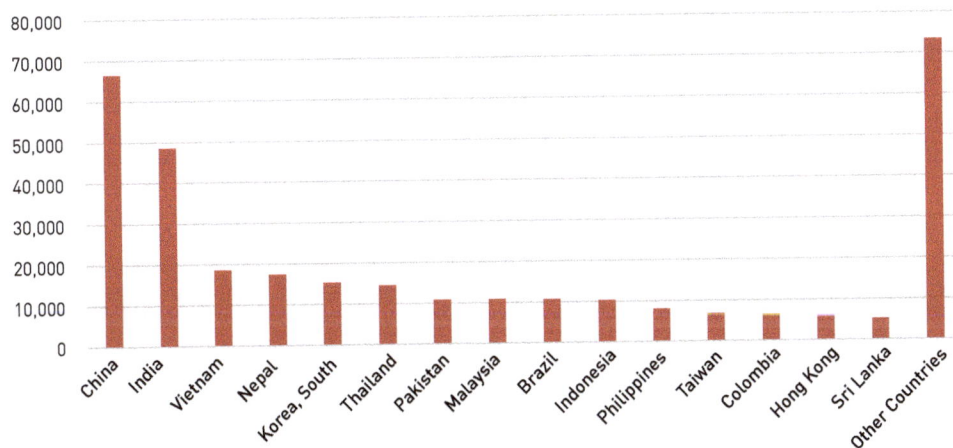

Source: Based on data from DIBP 2015c.

Going the other way, the over one hundred thousand Chinese students who already study at Australian universities each year will continue to build a firm foundation for future bilateral education. Moreover, there are already 36 universities in China that have an Australian Studies Centre, providing an opportunity for ongoing scholarship in China concerning Australia. The proposed Australia–China (Ao–Zhong) Commission can serve to support and facilitate these institutions to develop capacities that allow them to be used as a source of new policy ideas for both governments in the areas of economics, trade, public policy, political science, international relations and the humanities.

Language

While many Chinese learn English throughout their school and tertiary education, Australia cannot expect to have a close relationship with China by relying on English alone. Establishing deep relationships for official, business and social levels requires mutual comprehension of language. This is difficult. Learning Chinese not only involves becoming proficient at the tones of the spoken language, but also committing to memory thousands of Chinese characters that are required for basic literacy. But there are very few young Australians who are involved in this course of study. By their final year of schooling, only 0.1 of Australian students study Chinese, and of these, only around 400 are from a non-Chinese background (ACRI 2016).

All students should have access to appropriate language streams to ensure their efforts and interest can be appropriately rewarded. Those who seek an opportunity to study Chinese in school or university but do not have a background in Chinese outside the classroom may find themselves at a disadvantage if they must compete for grades with students from Chinese backgrounds. By contrast, students who are already proficient in Chinese can be challenged further to ensure they have top-level language skills necessary for professional competence in business, government and education.

One way to help young students achieve proficiency is by attending schools that are formally bilingual in Chinese and English. Only a handful of Australian government primary schools offer bilingual education in which classroom instruction is split between English and Chinese. There are two Victorian primary schools, and one in each of the ACT, South Australia, New South Wales and Western Australia that teach bilingual Chinese–English programs (ACRI 2016). But these are insufficient and ad-hoc when compared to national policy goals — there are more bilingual Japanese–English schools in Victoria than there are Chinese–English schools nationwide.

Given the strategic importance of the Australia–China relationship, the network of bilingual schools teaching Chinese in Australia should be expanded. These could be networked and linked with an equivalent number of bilingual schools in China. It is estimated that in Australia the cost of a bilingual language-program in a primary school is around A$500,000 per year (ACRI 2016). Although running schools is not a functional responsibility of the Australian federal or Chinese central governments, it is appropriate given the strategic importance of this capacity, that a portion of these additional costs is provided from public funds.

The expansion of Chinese-language education suggested here — both through increasing the opportunities to study Chinese for non-native speakers through to high school and the expansion of bilingual school network — also requires an expansion of supply of talented Chinese teachers. ChAFTA does provide a provision for a limited number of Chinese language tutors on up to four-year contracts.

The gains from services and investment policy reforms are additional to, and potentially much more important than, the gains from merchandise trade liberalisation. Using the opening of services sectors in ChAFTA to leverage up productivity-enhancing reforms in these sectors in China and Australia domestically would add considerably to both countries' incomes. And, as discussed in Chapter 5 in detail, financial market reform within the services sector will help intermediate savings to investments where these savings are most productive, improve access to capital and reduce the risk premium on capital investment generally.

CHAPTER 5
Financial integration

KEY MESSAGES

China is at a critical point of its economic transition, committed to continued financial reform and capital account liberalisation while simultaneously managing associated domestic and external challenges. Financial reform, capital account liberalisation and internationalisation of the RMB are interdependent reform processes that are occurring simultaneously. Capital account opening must be sequenced carefully with reforms to strengthen the financial system, maintain macro-financial stability and allow for exchange rate flexibility. Chinese capital and finance are already major forces in international capital markets, creating new opportunities for investment around the globe. The ongoing opening of the Chinese capital account represents a watershed in the financial development of the Asia Pacific economy. Managing this change will require prudent, well-informed and strategic policymaking in China and in each of the region's economies.

If the governments and private sectors of Australia and China position themselves strategically, these reforms offer a once-in-a-generation opportunity to deepen their relationship in financial services and financial flows. Australia has the unprecedented opportunity to export financial services into large and growing Chinese markets, and import increased volumes of Chinese capital to finance investment. China has the opportunity to use Australia as a testing ground as it deepens its financial reforms and opens its economy, gaining access to one of the most developed financial systems in the region and increasing its return on capital. The Australian and Chinese governments should engage with the business sectors of both countries while developing a formal program on financial services, development and reform. It would complement the Strategic Economic Dialogue and engage ministers, officials, regulators and firms in a work program to deepen bilateral financial integration that would be focused on:

- Piloting the select release of regulatory and licensing restrictions on Australian firms in China as a phase-in for regional liberalisation, through expanding the financial services components of ChAFTA.

- Developing a regular dialogue and a mutual recognition framework between financial regulators, and further supporting the development of RMB-denominated assets and securities listings in Australia.

- Reviewing regulatory barriers, including around taxation and the impact of macroprudential regulations and taxation policy to ensure that Australian and Chinese entities are better able to engage with one another in the region.

- Promoting the bilateral and regional opportunities arising from financial technology (FinTech).

- Research between Australian and Chinese institutions on financial services trade and cross-border investment.

- A stronger focus on building financial infrastructure into regional initiatives that seek to improve connectivity — such as One Belt, One Road (OBOR), the Asian Infrastructure Investment Bank (AIIB) and the Asian Development Bank (ADB) including payment systems, credit information, collateral registries and financial institutions, and ensuring China signs on to, and Australia implements, APEC's Asia Region Funds Passport and both countries advocate its use in the region.

China is now at a critical point of its economic transition. It is committed to deepening economic and financial reform in a challenging domestic and external environment. Economic growth has slowed as a result of both cyclical and structural factors. The global economy is experiencing a prolonged period of below-trend growth after the global financial crisis, which is impacting adversely on external demand and creating macroeconomic conditions that make China's reform agenda more challenging but even more essential. Against this background, the Chinese government is aiming to advance reforms while maintaining a stable macroeconomic environment.

The 13th Five Year Plan states that China's financial system reform aims to complete the establishment of financial institutions and market mechanisms, to promote the healthy development of capital markets, to establish monetary policy transmission mechanisms, to deepen reforms of the financial regulation framework, to raise the efficiency of financial services in serving the real sectors, and to effectively mitigate financial risks.

These reforms — however completely they are implemented — will profoundly shape the future of the Australia–China economic relationship. They will have implications across economic, political and social dimensions. But if the governments and private sectors in Australia and China position themselves strategically, these reforms offer a once-in-a-generation opportunity to deepen the relationship in financial services, financial flows and two-way investment which, at present, is nascent compared to the relationship in merchandise trade. In 2015, China accounted for 31.8 per cent of Australia's merchandise exports but just 11.1 per cent of Australia's financial services exports (ABS 2015a).

The earlier reform challenge of fully integrating Chinese commodities markets into international commodities markets, accomplished after China's entry into the WTO in 2001, took the time and determined leadership of former premier Zhu Rongji and former assistant minister and director-general of the International Relations Department of the Ministry of Foreign Economic Relations and Trade, Long Yongtu. Opening China's financial system is similarly an ambition that will not be achieved quickly. It will require political commitment at the highest levels.

Financial services are the largest single component of the Australian economy. With A$6.4 trillion in assets, the fourth-largest superannuation system in the world, a robust regulatory framework, the fourth most-traded currency in the world, some of the largest banks in the world by market capitalisation, and one of the least restrictive financial industries in the region, Australia has a clear comparative advantage in exporting financial services into the region (Auster and Foo 2015). Investing in deeper links and greater engagement with growing Chinese markets offers an immense opportunity to the Australian financial services industry.

As the world's largest saver, China will play a major role in shaping the global financial system into the future as its international investment position deepens and it allocates its savings globally. The role of Chinese capital in the global economy is poised to grow substantially. Based on the historical experience of other countries, China will become one of the world's largest cross-border investors by the end of this decade, with offshore assets tripling by 2020 (Hanemann and Huotari 2016). In the same way China's trade surplus has shaped the global trading system in the past few decades, China's outbound capital will profoundly shape the global financial system over the coming decades.

For China, Australia can help provide the financial products and services in banking, insurance, pension services and wealth management that will be increasingly demanded by the Chinese people as China's reforms deepen. More importantly, Australia offers China the opportunity of a testing ground for reforms that will support its continued opening and financial integration, both regionally and globally. Australia's sophisticated, globally competitive and well-regulated financial markets can act as an effective stepping-stone for China's continued opening to the region. Australia can support China across many of the reforms it is undertaking, including expanding access to insurance, liberalising interest rates, continuing the internationalisation of the renminbi (RMB), raising the proportion of direct financial intermediation, promoting inclusive finance and helping strengthen financial and prudential regulations and the institutions that underpin them.

But building this relationship will not happen on its own. It is an ambition that will not be achieved quickly and will be much more challenging than was the case in building the relationship in merchandise trade. Australian and Chinese governments and private sectors need to strategically position themselves and build the policy infrastructure necessary to foster this relationship.

There are a number of measures through which this positioning can be achieved. The Australian and Chinese governments should develop a program of formal engagement on financial services reform. It would complement the Strategic Economic Dialogue (SED) and engage ministers, officials, regulators and firms in a work program to deepen bilateral financial integration.

There are also opportunities for partnership in regional financial cooperation. This includes building a bilateral focus on financial infrastructure in regional initiatives such as OBOR and the AIIB, to improve payment systems, credit information bureaus, collateral registries and financial intermediaries and institutions throughout the Asia Pacific. China should also sign onto, and Australia should implement, APEC's Asia Region Funds Passport. Both countries should advocate its greater use in the region.

These reforms also involve risks that need to be managed. The most significant risk is associated with the sequencing of the reforms. There is a danger of precipitously removing restrictions on capital account transactions before the domestic financial system is able to manage the ebbs and flows of foreign capital. Capital account opening must be carefully sequenced with reforms to strengthen the financial system, safeguard macro-financial stability and make the exchange rate more flexible (IMF 2015b). Deepening financial markets and increasing capital flows can also carry risks for the region. These reforms will change the nature of regional financial linkages, as trade liberalisation did two decades ago, with implications not just for finance but also for the flows of trade, capital and people. Finally, there is a risk that slowing growth reduces the momentum for reform, which could then slow growth further and create even greater uncertainty and volatility.

Financial integration is the vital next step in strengthening the relationship between Australia and China. It continues a strong tradition in the Australia–China relationship, exemplified in the history of the relationship (see Chapters 1 and 6). Given the already close economic and trade linkages between Australia and China, Australia has a special role to play in the progressing of reform and financial deepening in China.

Integration to date: Australia, China and the region

Australia and China are highly integrated in two-way merchandise trade, but much less so in financial services and cross-border financial flows. In 2015, China accounted for almost 35 per cent of Australia's merchandise exports, but just 11.1 per cent of Australia's financial services exports (ABS 2015b).

Australia has a services-based economy, with the services sector accounting for around 82 per cent of the economy's real gross value added (GVA) and more than 85 per cent of employment (Auster and Foo 2015). Financial services play a particularly strong role. The financial services industry is the largest single industrial segment in the Australian economy on a GVA basis, generating A$146.4 billion or 8.8 per cent of total output as at March 2016 — slightly more than the mining industry at 8.8 per cent (ABS 2016e).

Despite its low base, China's share of Australia's financial services exports is growing rapidly. For example, exports of insurance and pension services from Australia to China increased from A$5 million in 2000 to A$49 million in 2014 (down from a peak of A$53 million in 2013), and now make up 9.1 per cent of all exports in that category compared to 0.6 per cent in 2000 (ABS 2015b).

Greater financial integration between Australia and China has been facilitated by a combination of official and private-sector engagement. Direct trading between the RMB and the Australian dollar was facilitated by a bilateral agreement signed by the Australian prime minister and the Chinese president in April 2013 in Shanghai. The practical impact of this was to reduce the costs of currency conversion by removing intermediary currencies. This agreement saw an increase in trading between the two currencies in the onshore spot market from US$324 million in March 2013 to over US$3.1 billion in May the same year (Finsia 2014). However, this trade has come back since then.

The use of the RMB for cross-border trade and investment transactions has increased noticeably over recent years and the market for the RMB in a number of jurisdictions outside of mainland China — known as 'offshore centres' — has developed further. This trend is also evident in Australia (Hatzvi et al 2014). The use of RMB by Australian entities has increased, although there remains much scope for further growth. A number of policy initiatives have been recently agreed between the Chinese and Australian authorities designed to allow the local RMB market to develop. These include the establishment of an official RMB clearing bank in Australia and a quota that allows Australian-based entities to invest in mainland China's financial markets as part of the RMB Qualified Foreign Institutional Investor (RQFII) program discussed further below (Hatzvi et al 2014).

Having an official RMB clearing hub means that there will be improved efficiency in processing RMB payments and conversions, there will be better liquidity in the market and, most importantly, this will increase confidence for Australian corporates in dealing with familiar local institutions. Similarly, in 2014, the Australian Securities Exchange (ASX) launched an RMB settlement service, enabling Australian companies to take or make payments in Chinese currency in near real-time, reducing the risk and the cost of doing business with China. These will be crucial steps in driving increased integration between Australia and China.

These developments build on existing initiatives, including the local currency swap agreement between the Reserve Bank of Australia (RBA) and the People's Bank of China (PBoC) signed in 2012 and renewed in 2015, and the RBA's investment of a portion of its foreign currency reserves in RMB-denominated assets. There has also been ongoing engagement on RMB internationalisation between Australian officials (including from the RBA and the Treasury) and the private sector through forums such as the Australia–Hong Kong RMB Trade and Investment Dialogue and the new 'Sydney for RMB Committee', a private sector led initiative (see Hatzvi et al 2014).

These policies and related private-sector initiatives have positioned Australia to take advantage of emerging RMB business opportunities. Sydney, as the main financial centre in Australia, has emerged as a fast, safe and reliable hub for RMB cash and securities settlement in the Asia Pacific region. But despite these initiatives, the Australian uptake for RMB settlement by importers and exporters remains low. The RBA has identified several reasons for this, including shortcomings in the availability of instruments allowing hedging in RMB, unfamiliarity around the RMB trade settlement process and administrative difficulties and concerns regarding payment delays and rejections (Weir and Walsh 2014). A more recent survey of Chinese firms found that awareness and use of RMB for trade settlement remains low, although the number of those using RMB trade settlement that reported payment difficulties had fallen significantly (Weir and Walsh 2015).

Financial integration in the Asia Pacific

The financial integration of Australia and China needs to be considered in the context of a changing financial landscape across the Asia Pacific. Decades of strong economic growth have generated greater household wealth and increasing cross-border financial flows, leading to significant growth in demand for financial services and products. Bank balance sheets are expanding, household wealth is increasing, ageing populations are demanding more sophisticated services and products, and technology is enabling greater ease of transactions across national borders. All of these trends will impact Australia and China.

Financial integration in the Asia Pacific region is deepening, compared with the advanced economies where financial integration has backtracked since the global financial crisis. While cross-border capital flows as a share of GDP have fallen globally, in Asia the magnitude of cross-border flows is growing faster than GDP, and in many cases external assets and liabilities now exceed GDP (Auster and Foo 2015). The increasing size and sophistication of the financial services sector throughout the Asia Pacific has enabled rising cross-border flows. Cross-border flows in the region are strongest in the areas of bank lending and foreign direct investment, while portfolio investment tends to lag (Auster and Foo 2015).

The financial services industry in Australia employs 450,000 people and is the biggest net contributor to corporate income tax. Australia's financial system has proved to be sound, resilient and well managed. In the aftermath of the global financial crisis and the Asian financial crisis, both the Australian economy and the financial system outperformed most of their peers (Auster and Foo 2015). Australia's financial services industry has significant depth, with assets of around A$6.4 trillion — over four times Australia's nominal GDP (Austrade 2015). Australia's A$2.0 trillion superannuation system is the fourth-largest in the world. This pool of assets is expected to grow to A$7.6 trillion over the next two decades, largely due to the legislated superannuation scheme (Auster and Foo 2015).

Figure 5.1 shows the gross value added of the financial services industry across the region in 2012. It ranges from about 3.3 per cent of economic output in Indonesia to almost 16 per cent in Hong Kong. This graph also highlights the significant differences between Australia and China. For Australia, gross value added is around 8.7 per cent while it is only 5.5 per cent in China. But, unlike Australia, the growth of financial services in China has been substantial, more than doubling from 2005 to 2012 and reaching 8.5 per cent in 2015 (NBS 2016).

Figure 5.1: Gross value added by the financial services industry as a percentage of total output

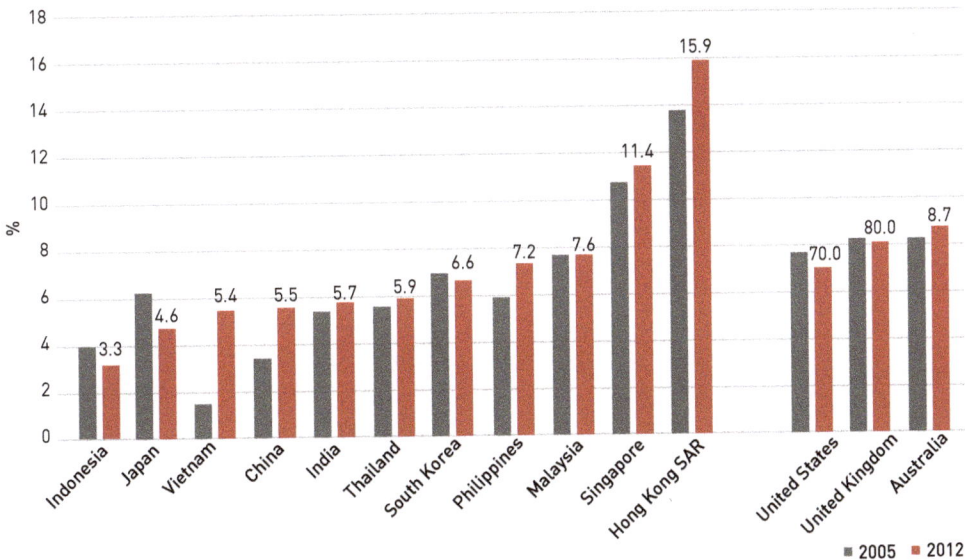

Source: Auster and Foo 2015, using data from Aggregates and Detailed Tables 2013; United States Bureau of Economic Analysis; and United Nations Department of Economic and Social Affairs. Figures for India are at 2005 and 2011 because of a lack of 2012 data.

Despite a high rate of growth, there is still a degree of financial system underdevelopment across the Asia Pacific. Assets under management in the region are only 15 per cent of the global total, and China is only the fifth-largest holder of assets under management in the region, well below its relative GDP share. These underdeveloped financial systems are inefficient in channelling credit to firms and households, and may both inhibit economic growth and reduce the economy's ability to adjust to external shocks.

In addition, the Asia Pacific region remains fairly restrictive in relation to many aspects of cross-border trade in financial services and financial flows. The OECD produces a series of 'trade restrictiveness' indices for services that measure the relative openness of economies by attempting to quantify the effect of relevant laws and regulations.

Figure 5.2: OECD services trade restrictiveness index for commercial banking, 2015

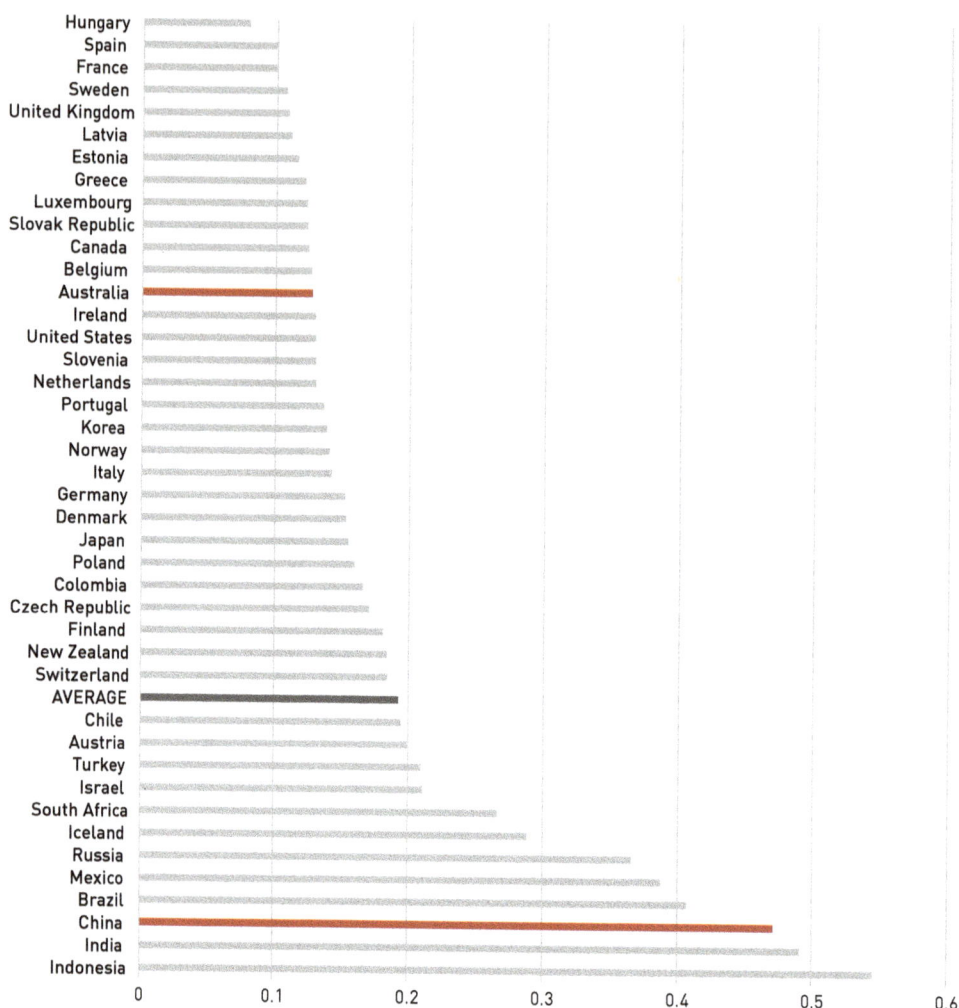

Source: OECD 2015.

In the area of trade in financial services, the OECD evaluates commercial banking (Figure 5.2) and insurance (Figure 5.3). These show Asia has among the most restrictive practices in both commercial banking and insurance, with China, Indonesia and India being the most restrictive. Australia sits well below (less restrictive) the OECD average in both indices, with the largest contribution to restrictiveness coming from Australia's restrictions on foreign ownership and other market entry conditions.

Developments in China's reform agenda and implications for the relationship

The processes of financial reform, capital account liberalisation and the continued internationalisation of the RMB will fundamentally transform the Chinese financial system in the coming years, with the potential to bring significant benefits to the Chinese people.

The 13th Five Year Plan has a special focus on financial reform. This includes accelerating the pace of financial system reform, completing the establishment of financial institutions and market mechanisms, deepening reforms of financial regulation frameworks, raising the efficiency of the financial sector in serving the real economy, further developing capital markets to lower the financing costs of medium, small and micro enterprises, and effectively mitigating financial risks.

Figure 5.3: OECD services trade restrictiveness index for insurance, 2015

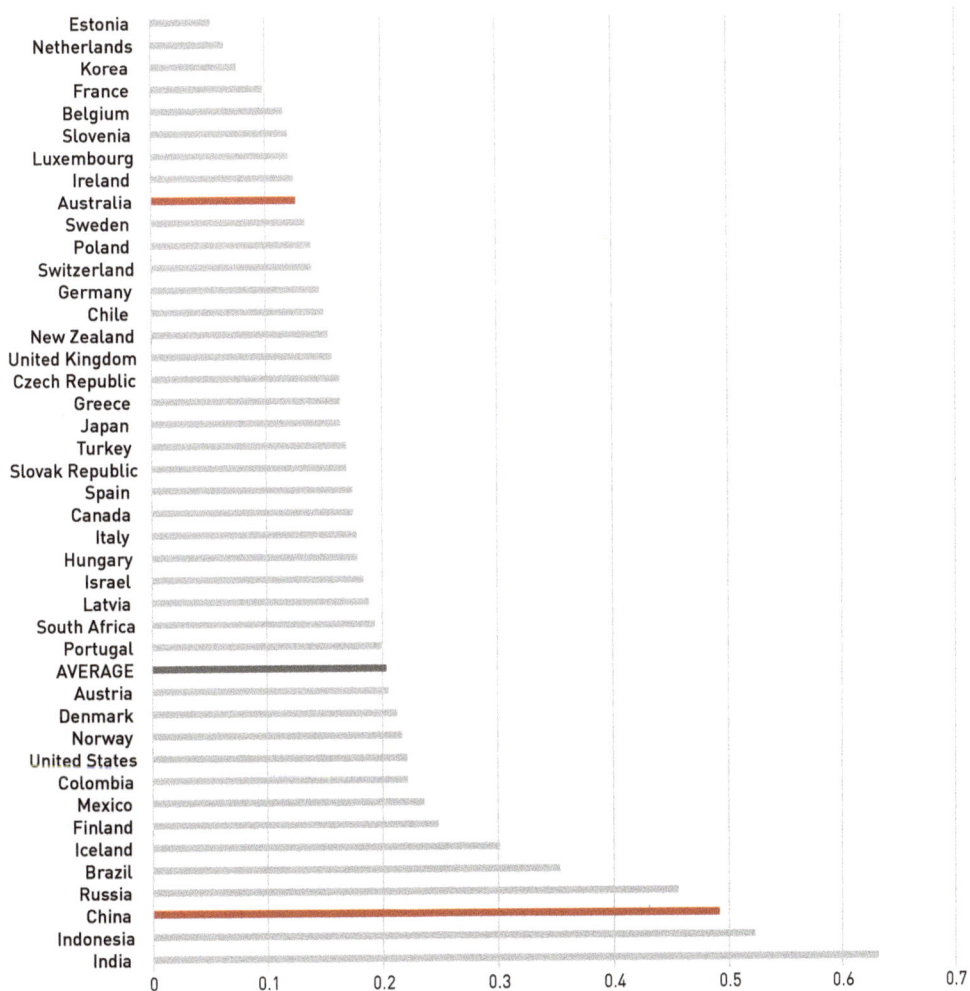

Source: OECD 2015.

The banking market in China is large and dominant, accounting for most financial intermediation in the financial system. Pension and wealth services are a nascent industry and insurance is only beginning to penetrate the Chinese market. Further progress will allow the financial services sector to properly intermediate funds between households and firms, and across the economy. Over time, this will support domestic interest rate liberalisation that will, in turn, improve the efficiency of capital allocation, enable transparent pricing, allow for smoother savings–consumption patterns and enable improved risk mitigation strategies. All of these are necessary developments for China to continue its economic rebalancing, and to move from a middle-income to a high-income economy.

China's domestic markets are already large by global standards. Even without an open capital account, China already accounts for 6 per cent of global cross-border financial transactions (Finsia 2014). China's domestic bank credit stock is larger than any other in the region, including Japan's (Auster and Foo 2015). Its equity and fixed income markets are now among the largest in the world, although they play a relatively smaller role in the operation of the economy. China's equity market has grown substantially to a peak valuation of over US$10 trillion. While recent volatility has significantly reduced stock market values, these reductions need to be considered in the context of long run growth in China's equity markets. From June 2014 to June 2015, the Shanghai Composite Index increased by 154 per cent. But this increase was unsustainable and not based on fundamentals. Despite recent volatility that saw a 45 per cent reduction in the index from June 2015 to the end of May 2016, the index is nevertheless 40 per cent higher than it was in June 2014 (Bloomberg 2016a).

Through initial public offering (IPO) listings activity was suspended from July to November 2015, China's exchanges nonetheless led the world in terms of IPOs in 2015. There were 89 IPOs valued at US$17.6 billion in 2015 in Shanghai alone — an increase of 107 per cent on the previous year. Mainland exchanges reopened in November 2015 to a pipeline of 690 companies ready to go public (EY 2015). However this, in part, reflects a distortion in China's financial markets, as IPOs require an approach to the China Securities Regulatory Commission (CSRC), which can cause a backlog.

China's fund management and insurance sectors have also grown substantially. The fund management industry first emerged in the early 1990s and has experienced tremendous advances in scale and sophistication. By the end of 1998, there were fewer than 10 fund management companies managing less than RMB500 billion. By May 2014, there were 91 fund management companies, with 48 foreign joint ventures and 43 domestic Chinese companies managing total assets of RMB5.13 trillion. RMB3.73 trillion was managed by mutual funds and RMB1.04 trillion by private funds (Austrade 2014).

The Chinese insurance industry's total assets were RMB8.3 trillion in 2013, while net assets were RMB847.5 billion (Austrade 2014). The launch of the Shanghai–Hong Kong Stock Connect program (Stock Connect) in November 2014 and the announcement of mutual recognition of funds (MRF) between mainland China and Hong Kong on 22 May 2015 marked significant developments in a series of moves which relax China's tight control of cross-border capital flows (King and Wood Mallesons 2015).

Launched in November 2014, Stock Connect is a joint initiative of the CSRC and Hong Kong's Securities and Futures Commission. It allows mutual stock market access between the Shanghai Stock Exchange and the Hong Kong Stock Exchange. Stock Connect is now complemented by a similar link for mutual funds. The organisations signed a Memorandum of Regulatory Cooperation concerning Mutual Recognition of Funds between the Mainland and Hong Kong in 2015, which allows retail public funds initially offered in the Mainland or Hong Kong to be sold to retail investors across the border (King and Wood Mallesons 2015).

China also has a burgeoning FinTech sector (an area also referred to as 'internet finance') that now supports a number of large firms supplying financial services and products. Companies such as AliPay and WeChat demonstrate the rising demand for sophisticated financial products and services in China.

China's reform agenda

Financial reform is at the centre of the new reform agenda. This includes developing efficient credit markets to better intermediate savings to productive investment at the lowest possible cost, improving the financial system's ability and efficiency in allocating risk, and ensuring appropriate regulatory and institutional settings are in place to sustain macro-financial stability.

A related but separate aspect of financial reform is financial integration. This means increasing China's integration with regional and global markets so that savings, investment and risk can be mediated globally, expanding the frontiers of production, investment and consumption. For China, financial integration will be achieved through two related processes: increased trade in financial services with overseas trading partners, and opening of the capital account to allow for increased cross-border investment.

China maintains a restrictive posture in relation to trade in financial services (Auster and Foo 2015). Unlike trade in goods, the restrictiveness of trade in financial services cannot be measured through tariffs. A primary mode of delivery for trade in financial products and services is the provision of these services through the branches or subsidiaries of foreign firms operating in the country. Restrictions on the opening or the operations of branches or subsidiaries represent a significant behind-the-border restriction to trade in financial services. The restrictions may limit a foreign firm's ability to generate a profit in the country, or may make the cost of operating in that country more expensive than would otherwise be the case. Examples of such restrictions include: limitations on the number or size of branches or subsidiaries of foreign companies; limited licenses to offer products or services in-country; requirements to hire a certain number of domestic staff per office or to set up a minimum number of offices in order to receive regulatory approvals; requirements to contribute a minimum amount of capital in the country; or limitations on the profits that can be remitted from the branch or subsidiary back to the home country. These types of restrictions are typical of what has been in place in China during the last three decades of reform.

Capital account liberalisation — that is, easing restrictions on capital flows across a country's borders — will be key to China accessing foreign markets, increasing returns on its savings, and using foreign financing to build its capital stock and grow the economy into the future. The internationalisation of the RMB is part of the opening of China's capital account, and will enable the interest rate and exchange rate flexibility that will help the economy to manage any shocks arising from sudden shifts in capital flows. To date, there has been an increasing openness to some types of cross-border investment in China, with flows of both foreign direct investment and bank lending rising significantly over the past two decades (Roberts et al 2016). In contrast, cross-border portfolio investment remains highly restricted and a binding constraint in the capital account. RMB liberalisation and its increasing use offshore does not guarantee capital account opening — it is connected, but not synonymous. RMB internationalisation is both a catalyst and an outcome of a liberalised capital account, and is key to China's future capacity for sustainable growth and ability to play a larger role in the global economy.

Financial reform, capital account liberalisation and internationalisation of the RMB are interdependent reform processes that must be sequenced carefully. In particular, capital account opening has to be sequenced carefully with reforms to strengthen the financial system, maintain macro-financial stability and allow for exchange rate flexibility. The most important difficulty in the sequencing of capital market liberalisation is the danger of precipitously removing restrictions on capital account transactions before the domestic financial system is able to manage volatility in the exchange rate and cross-border capital flows.

Financial reform in China

China has quickened the pace of domestic financial market deregulation, after periods in which the accelerating development of domestic financial infrastructure and rising banking sector fragility in the mid-1990s and early 2000s led to more gradualism in reform during the late 2000s. China's financial reforms have been part of the gradual and closely managed transition from a centrally controlled economy towards a market-based economy. The rapid expansion of domestic financial infrastructure in the 1980s and 1990s resulted from the substantial growth in the agricultural sector and the emergence of small- and medium-sized enterprises after the initiation of the reform and opening policy in 1978.

China has made substantial progress on interest rate deregulation. It has moved from a situation where both deposit rates and lending rates were centrally controlled, to one where deposit rate ceilings and lending rate floors are now being removed from official control. China has partially shifted away from a reliance on published benchmark interest rates. Over the reform period, the Chinese government has cautiously proceeded with increasing the flexibility of retail interest rates around benchmark rates through pilot programs and experiments, with the objective of protecting the profitability of enterprises.

Interest rate liberalisation also has important implications for making the transmission mechanism of monetary policy more effective. China is in the middle of transforming its monetary policy framework from one based on a quantity rule to one based on a price rule. The old quantity rule based system, which relied on direct control of credit and lending through state-owned banks, and interfered with the market allocating scarce capital to its most productive use, has become increasingly ineffective. The new price rule based system is now being put in place, although the PBoC is yet to indicate which interest rate it will target or what the timing of the change will be.

These reforms will also require a significant strengthening of Chinese institutions to ensure that regulatory and institutional settings are properly calibrated to sustain macro-financial stability. Among the problems in this area are:

- ensuring adequate accounting, auditing and disclosure practices in the financial and corporate sectors that strengthen market discipline within a robust corporate governance framework;

- avoiding implicit government guarantees that lead to the misallocation of capital; and

- ensuring adequate prudential supervision and regulation of domestic financial institutions and markets, which may help defeat corruption, connected lending and gambling for redemption (the pursuit of high-return but low-probability investments by institutions with low or negative net worth) (Eichengreen and Mussa 1998).

Of course, these reforms are not just narrow technical challenges. They will require a much more open and transparent set of institutional arrangements that push at the envelope of political reform. These challenges are embedded deep in China's political economy. They have a political dimension that will cut deeply into the close relationship between SOEs and the state. The political economy implications of reform should not be underestimated.

The success of China's domestic financial reforms will be particularly important for Australia. When completed, they will enhance regional stability and the depth of regional markets by laying the groundwork for a liberalised capital account and an internationalised RMB. Importantly, the reforms also provide significant opportunities to Australian financial firms in supplying financial services and products into Chinese markets. Australia, as a leading regional financial hub, has the potential to benefit significantly from this. Australia also has significant experience in financial liberalisation, which, through stronger engagement of ministers, officials and financial firms, could be an asset to China.

Capital account liberalisation in China

China's capital account has undergone significant liberalisation since the 1990s, with the exception of portfolio investment, which is still under strict control, although significant progress has been made through investment schemes such as RQFII and RQDII (Ballantyne et al 2014). Figure 5.4 shows the reduction in the index of controls on the capital account and current account from 1999 to 2013. In 1996, the current account achieved full convertibility, while the capital account remained largely controlled by the government. Capital account liberalisation was slowed by banking sector fragility that emerged in the wake of the Asian financial crisis of the late 1990s. Only recently has this process resumed.

Capital account liberalisation will provide significant opportunities for China. It is likely to result in a higher degree of financial integration with the global economy through rising volumes of capital inflows and outflows. Greater offshore integration complements interest rate liberalisation and ensures a more efficient allocation of capital across markets, diversification of risk and inter-temporal trade. The exchange rate liberalisation that accompanies the opening of the capital account also allows for a smoother path of adjustment for exogenous shocks.

Figure 5.4: Index of controls on China's capital account (ka) and current account (ca) over recent years

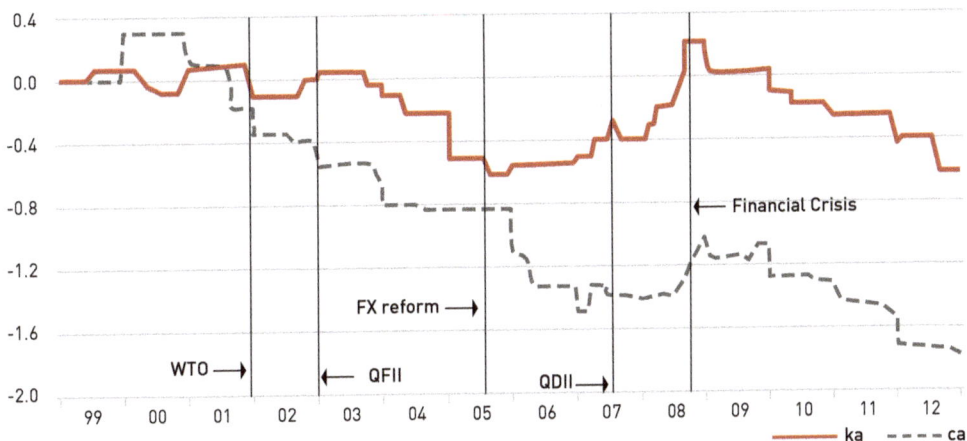

Source: Chen and Qian 2015.

For Australia, the incremental liberalisation of the Chinese capital account will increase China's role in international commerce and finance, including the prevalence of the RMB as a global currency. It will potentially have important implications in rebalancing the global economy in the future as demand for goods and services increases in China relative to advanced deficit economies. Over time, the integration of China's financial system into the global market via an open capital account will also fundamentally change the regional financial landscape and the nature of financial market linkages in the Asia Pacific.

As one of the region's key financial centres, and as a net importer of capital, Australia stands to benefit from increased flows of capital at potentially lower cost. This, in turn, helps fund investment, build the Australian capital stock and grow the economy. The big four banks in China have already increased their presence in Australia, which will help facilitate this increased flow of capital (Box 5.1). Liberalisation can, however, cause fluctuations in asset prices and international trade flows. In the short to medium term, capital flows may become more volatile in the region as China's capital account is further liberalised, and capital movements into and out of China could affect Australia.

There is a lot of uncertainty as to what the size and direction of capital flows would initially be if China were to liberalise further. Recent research by the Hong Kong Monetary Authority (HKMA) and the IMF on the likely implications of full capital account liberalisation in China generally suggest that gross portfolio outflows are likely to be substantial, although these papers disagree on the net impact. The rise in regional capital flows will also test Australia's capacity to absorb these flows, although Australia's floating exchange rate and strong institutional settings suggest that it is well placed to do so.

In February 2016, the PBoC took an important step in liberalising China's capital account by opening its interbank bond market to foreign investors (PBoC 2016). This builds on the development of the onshore ('panda') and offshore ('dim sum') primary issuances. The interbank bond market accounts for the bulk of China's fixed income market. Previously, foreign investors wanting to access China's domestic bond market had to use the QFII discussed above or similar programs, which placed a number of restrictions on investors (PBoC 2016). The PBoC has stated that access to the market will be restricted to medium and long term investors. AllianceBernstein estimate that this reform will cause an inflow of around US$3 trillion into China's bond market (Grigg and Murray 2016). The Chinese government has valued its total bond market at around US$10.4 trillion in size, but analysts project that this will increase significantly in coming years as the Chinese government runs larger deficits (Grigg and Murray 2016). However, as with any economy, a rise in China's debt-to-GDP ratio also carries with it certain risks that investors will need to assess carefully in deciding their level of exposure. As outlined recently by the IMF, bad loans have since been piling up on banks' books. The overall debt-to-GDP ratio in China is estimated to be 237 per cent, while the IMF estimates corporate debt-to-GDP at 145 per cent and raises concerns about Chinese financial fragility (Donnan and Mitchell 2016).

These bond market reforms should benefit the Chinese economy in a number of ways. Increased demand for the existing stock of bonds would reduce bond yields, all else being equal. This would reduce the fiscal burden of these debt instruments on the Chinese government and reduce the cost of funding across the economy. To the extent that increased flows also contribute to improved market liquidity, offshore participation may also improve market functioning and enable the fixed income market to represent a channel of transmission for monetary policy. This highlights the important stabilisation role that capital flows can play in international currency markets (McKibbin et al 1999).

BOX 5.1: CHINA'S 'BIG FOUR' BANKS IN AUSTRALIA

Although Chinese banking has a relatively long history in Australia, the number of Chinese banks, branches and the services they provide have increased significantly over the last 10 years. These banks have played a key role across a number of financial markets and have helped finance many substantial projects in Australia.

Industrial and Commercial Bank of China (ICBC) is the world's largest bank by market capitalisation. It opened a branch in Sydney in 2008 and was approved by the Australian Prudential and Regulation Authority (APRA) as a foreign authorised deposit taking institution. The successful establishment of the Sydney branch was regarded as a significant breakthrough in the bank's progress towards greater internationalisation, improving its international management standards and providing a comprehensive range of banking services to the Australian and New Zealand markets, which ICBC identifies as one of the most prosperous regions in the Southern hemisphere (ICBC 2016). ICBC has since expanded its network to Perth, Melbourne and Brisbane, offering banking services in trade finance, project finance, syndicated loans, corporate loans, deposits, foreign exchange, derivatives, remittances, settlement and clearing services. A third of its Sydney branch's corporate clients include Australian companies such as Westfield and Qantas, and it has provided capital for the State of Victoria's desalination plant, the Royal Adelaide Hospital renovation, and coal loaders in Newcastle and near Gladstone in Queensland (Industry NSW 2015).

Bank of China first established operations in Sydney in 1942 and now has nine branches in Australia, the most of any Chinese bank — five in Sydney, two in Melbourne, one in Perth and one in Brisbane. The financial services offered by Bank of China focus on trade finance, express remittance, local and foreign currency deposits, residential mortgages, commercial, construction and syndicated loans, overdraft facilities, foreign exchange margin trading and Australian dollar clearing and settlement services (Bank of China 2016). The *Australian Financial Review* recently noted the important role that Bank of China and other Chinese-owned banks are playing in filling the gaps left in the area of foreign lending by the big four Australian banks (Tan 2016).

China Construction Bank (CCB) is the second-largest bank in the world by market capitalisation. CCB opened a representative office in Sydney in 2007 and in August 2010, APRA approved CCB as a foreign authorised deposit taking institution, authorising it to carry on banking business in Australia. CCB's Sydney Branch is CCB's first branch in Australasia. It conducts wholesale banking business in Australia, including corporate lending and deposit, international settlement, trade finance and Australian dollar clearing and settlement services. CCB has noted that 'the establishment of CCB Sydney Branch will enable CCB to expand its global network and enhance customer service capability to facilitate the economic and trade cooperation between Australia and China' (CCB 2016).

The Agricultural Bank of China (ABC) was China's first commercial bank. It has the largest network of branches in China and the largest customer base, with 350 million customers and assets of US$2 trillion (Industry NSW 2015). The ABC Sydney Branch obtained the authority to carry on banking business from APRA in March 2014. It consists of seven departments including corporate banking, treasury, trade finance, operations, risk management and compliance, finance and accounting, and administration. ABC provides its clients with banking products including corporate lending, trade finance, multi-currency settlements, remittances and other services. The Sydney Branch conducts business activities with multinational enterprises, Chinese inbound investors in Australia, Australian companies and other financial institutions (ABC 2016).

Internationalisation of the RMB and the development of an offshore RMB market

The internationalisation of the RMB and the development of offshore RMB markets are two important government-supported policy initiatives that have progressed significantly since being launched many years ago. There has been increased use of the RMB as a transactional currency over the last few years. By the end of 2014, RMB-denominated current account transactions accounted for about one-fifth of China's total current account transactions. RMB-denominated investment has also increased in recent years, but remains small relative to the value of RMB-denominated trade settlements.

The RMB has gradually moved towards a more flexible exchange rate regime over the same period (see Figure 5.5). In 1994, the official and market-determined exchange rates were unified, leading to a large RMB depreciation. The exchange rate was pegged to the US dollar from during the Asian financial crisis to 2005 to reduce the volatility of the currency. From 2005 to 2010, the official pegging target of the RMB was switched from the US dollar to a basket of currencies and the pegging was managed within a trading band of 0.3 per cent (later 0.5 per cent). From 2012 to 2014, the PBoC widened the daily trading band of the RMB against the US dollar from 0.5 per cent to eventually 2 per cent. In August 2015, the PBoC devalued the RMB by almost 2 per cent. Despite a 2 per cent devaluation being small by the standards of most currencies, this move caused one of the largest central parity shifts in the RMB's history (second only to that following the cessation of the US dollar peg). More importantly, while the RMB's fixing rate was previously persistently higher than the spot rate, in August 2015 the PBoC depreciated the fixing rate and moved to a system where the fixing rate reflects the previous day's spot close and overnight developments. This change indicates an increasingly market-driven approach to currency reform from the PBoC and also acts to close the gap between onshore (CNY) and offshore (CNH) markets (Bloomberg 2015).

The internationalisation of the RMB has an important meaning for China's global economic status. Capital account liberalisation is essential to making the RMB a truly global currency and increasing China's role in international finance. This includes the RMB's recent inclusion in the IMF's Special Drawing Rights basket. This inclusion and internationalisation of the RMB brings benefits from reducing currency risks for Chinese exporters and importers as capital account liberalisation and exchange rate regime reform proceeds. In the longer term, this also has potentially significant implications for the structure of financial and commodity markets globally as transactions and contracts may become increasingly denominated in RMB.

Figure 5.5: Nominal and nominal effective exchange rates — the RMB against the US dollar

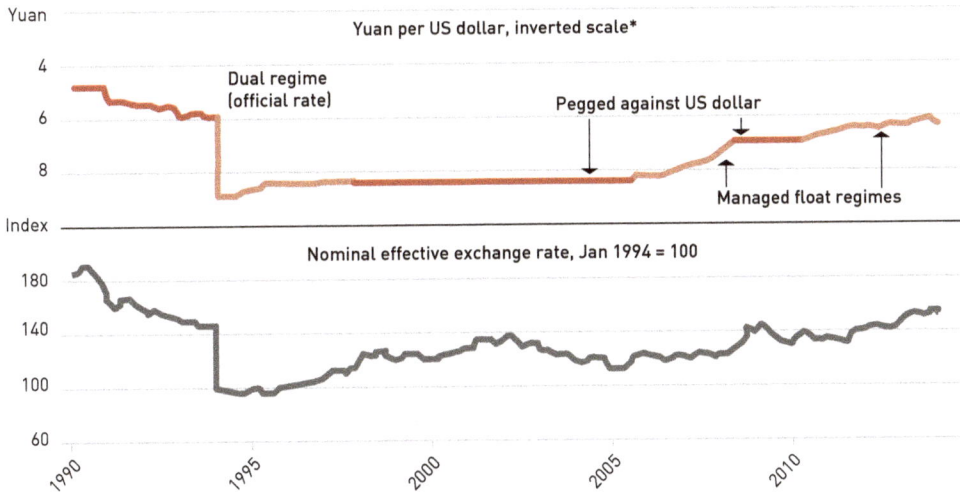

Sources: *Bank of International Settlements 2016; Bloomberg 2016b; RBA 2016.*

The opportunities for financial service providers in China

Australia can seek to engage actively in the process of China's financial reform, building off the close and established economic and trade linkages between China and Australia, and the growing potential for further financial integration. Australia must adapt and position itself strategically if it is to benefit from these reforms. One way to do this would be to increase the volume and value of trade in financial services between the two economies.

At first glance, trade in financial services does not appear to be an important part of Australian trade, or of the Australian economy. According to the ABS, total exports of 'financial services' and 'insurance and pension services' stood at A$3.9 billion in 2014, or just 6.4 per cent of Australia's services exports and slightly over 1 per cent of overall exports. Financial services account for A$3.3 billion (86.4 per cent of the total), and insurance and pension services account for the remaining A$539 million (13.9 per cent) of financial sector exports (ABS 2015b).

These ABS figures omit financial services that are provided onshore in China by branches or subsidiaries of Australian firms — the offshore operations of Australian companies. Technically these are called 'foreign affiliate sales'. If foreign affiliate sales are included, financial services are possibly Australia's largest single services export category, with a value that is likely over A$50 billion annually (Auster and Foo 2015). When foreign affiliate sales are included, China is a much smaller financial services trade partner for Australia when compared with the United States, the United Kingdom and New Zealand — but also Singapore, Thailand, Indonesia and Japan (Figures 5.6, 5.7 and 5.8). High barriers to financial services trade and cross-border investment in China may be inhibiting Australian firms and investors from growing their connections with the country. According to the OECD, China has highly restrictive regulatory and legal regimes in both commercial banking and insurance compared to OECD nations. Australia is among the most open economies in the Asia Pacific region, with a degree of openness that exceeds the OECD average.

Doing business in China's financial services industry remains very challenging. There are strong government regulations and vastly different business cultures and market environments. But the potential rewards for companies that are successful are significant. Although China is perceived as a challenging market for foreign insurers, Australian financial services companies have entered and many have established local representative offices (Box 5.2) or joint ventures in numerous areas (Box 5.3). Recent research from Munich Re predicts that China's ranking in global insurance premium volumes will climb from 10th in 2006 to third in 2020, behind only the United States and Japan (Austrade 2014).

Figure 5.6: Australia's exports of financial services to the Asia Pacific region

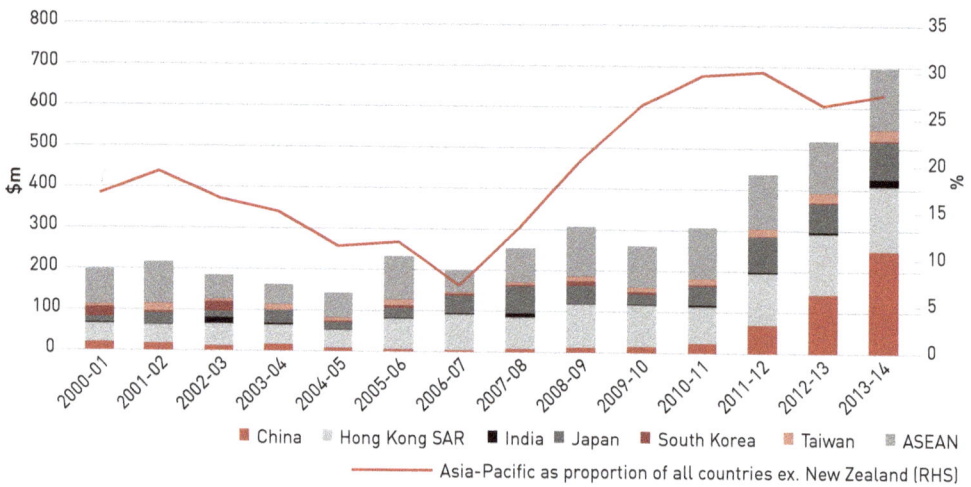

Source: Auster and Foo 2015.

Figure 5.7: Australia's exports of insurance and pension services to the Asia Pacific region

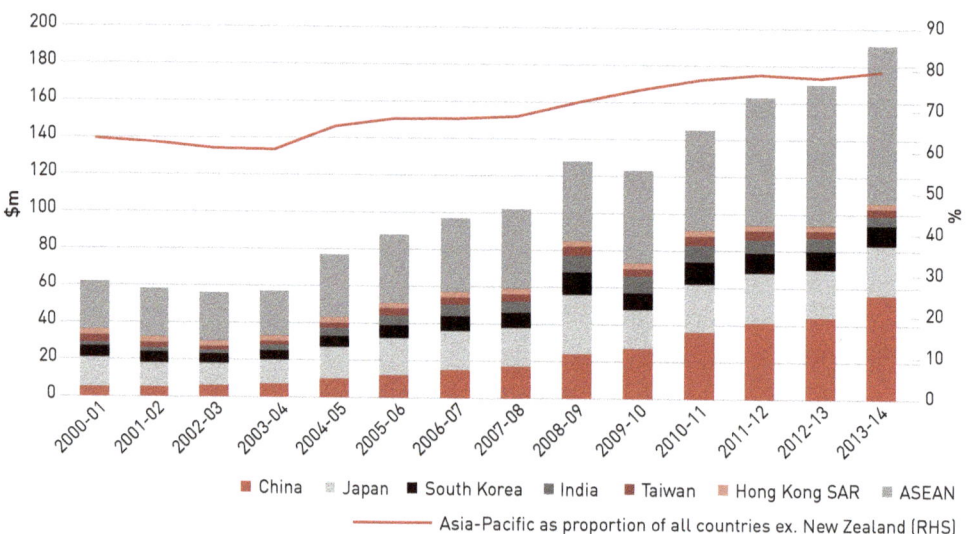

Source: Auster and Foo 2015.

Figure 5.8: Total sales of financial services and insurance and pension services by Australia by mode of supply, 2009–2010

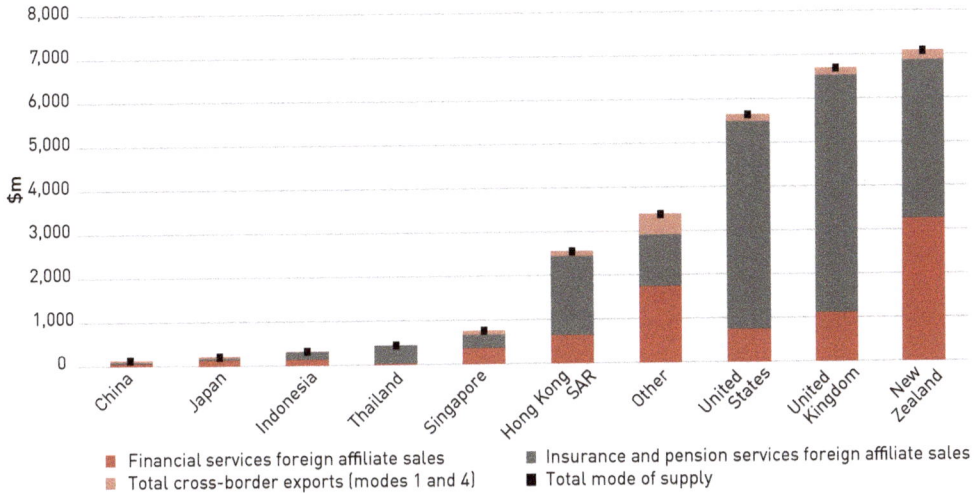

Note: Caution should be exercised in interpreting this chart as the ABS does not allocate Financial Intermediation Services Indirectly Measured (FISIM) to individual countries for mode 3, but does for modes 1, 2 and 4.
Source: Auster and Foo 2015; from ABS Cat. No. 5485.0, Table 4a, 2011.

BOX 5.2: AUSTRALIA'S 'BIG FOUR' BANKS IN CHINA

Australia and New Zealand Banking Group (ANZ) has been in China since 1986 and today it has seven branches and four sub-branches as well as an operations hub in Chengdu. Over the past three decades, ANZ has continued to expand its footprint and remains one of Australia's largest investors in China with successful partnerships with the Bank of Tianjin and the Shanghai Rural Commercial Bank. In 2010, the Australia and New Zealand Bank (China) Company Limited (ANZ China) was established, making ANZ the first Australian bank to be locally incorporated in China. ANZ is the only Australian bank with both local and foreign currency capabilities in retail and corporate banking in mainland China. ANZ China has around 500 employees as of April 2016.

Commonwealth Bank (CBA), Australia's largest bank, has been operating in China for over two decades. It has been granted a RMB licence for its Shanghai Branch by the China Banking Regulatory Commission (CBA 2015). The RMB licence enables CBA to broaden its institutional offerings to incorporate all aspects of trade and investment for clients doing business in the fast growing and deep trade corridor between Australia and China (CBA 2015). CBA has a branch in Shanghai, a branch in Beijing, a presence in the recently expanded Shanghai Free Trade Zone, a network of 15 branches across Henan and Hebei provinces, a life insurance joint venture with the Bank of Communications and two other key joint ventures (Finsia 2014). These are:

- Jinan City Commercial Bank (Qilu Bank) in Shandong province, northern China, of which CBA owns a 20 per cent stake purchased in 2004. This is the 10th-largest city commercial bank by assets in China, and CBA's partnership aims to introduce new financial products and technical skills, speed up compliance with international standards and improve the bank's competitiveness.

- Bank of Hangzhou: CBA has owned 19.9 per cent of this bank since 2005, with A$100 million invested.

National Australia Bank (NAB) provides a range of corporate, institutional, trade and selected personal banking services from a branch location in Shanghai and a newly established branch in Beijing. These branches support Australian and New Zealand businesses looking to trade with or invest in China and the rest of Asia. NAB's stated purpose is also 'to support institutional and corporate customers from China and Asia looking to trade with or invest in Australia and New Zealand, particularly in the bank's areas of expertise: the energy, utilities, natural resources, food and agribusiness sectors' (NAB 2015).

NAB first opened an office in China in 1982, and currently has a representative office located in the China World Tower in Beijing. NAB has partnerships and relationships with national bankcard association China UnionPay and banks including China Development Bank, Agricultural Development Bank of China, Shanghai Pudong Development Bank and Industrial Bank. It also works with wealth management institutions China International Industrial Trust and China Huarong Asset Management Corporation (Finsia 2014). In addition to the new Beijing branch, NAB's recent approval from the China Banking Regulatory Commission for a RMB license for its Shanghai branch will also help customers explore wider business opportunities, better manage foreign exchange risks and enhance business efficiencies in China (NAB 2015).

Westpac first opened an office in China in 1982, and since then has established offices in Hong Kong, Beijing, Shanghai and a Shanghai Free Trade Zone sub-branch with specialist teams focused on trade, structured commodity and asset finance, debt capital markets, derivatives, foreign exchange and natural resources (Finsia 2014; Westpac 2016). It has recently deepened its offerings to support increasing domestic and international RMB flows, and in 2013 was awarded a RMB-dollar market makers licence to trade the currency pairs in mainland China, followed by a derivatives licence. Westpac established an Asia Advisory Board in November 2013 to strengthen its connectivity across Asia.

In April 2012, Insurance Australia Group purchased a 20 per cent stake (since diluted to a 16.9 per cent stake) in Chinese general insurer Bohai Property Insurance Company Ltd to form a strategic partnership and increase its footprint in China. Similarly, in January 2010, CBA and China's Bank of Communications formed a 51:49 per cent life insurance joint venture (Austrade 2014).

These acquisitions, combined with organic growth strategies among some firms, suggest that the Australian financial sector can be one of the largest direct investors into China. Recently there has been a slowing in this process as some Australian financial services providers reduce their investments in China. ANZ, for example, recently reduced its stake in China's Bank of Tianjin, reportedly because of onerous capital requirements and restrictions it faced in operating in China. These issues are discussed in detail in the sections below.

BOX 5.3: AMP CAPITAL AND CHINA LIFE

In April 2006, Australian financial services company AMP Capital secured Australia's first QFII licence. Platinum Investment Company and Macquarie Bank followed in 2008 and 2012 respectively (China XBR 2016). The QFII program allows selected international investors to access RMB-denominated capital markets such as the 'A-shares' traded on the Shanghai and Shenzhen stock exchanges.

Though AMP Capital has had a presence in China since 1997, its engagement and cooperation with the Chinese financial sector expanded substantially following its QFII approval. The partnership between AMP and China Life, China's largest life insurance company, began in 2006. After three years of collaboration on QFII investments, the two companies entered a MoU to explore potential partnerships in pensions and fund management in late 2009 (Somasundaram 2013).

In June 2013, regulations came into effect that allowed insurance companies in China to establish fund management companies offering public mutual funds to retail and institutional investors (AMP 2013). AMP went into a partnership later that year with the China Life Asset Management Company (a China Life subsidiary), establishing the China Life AMP Asset Management Company. By January 2014, the new company had raised RMB11.9 billion (A$2.2 billion) on initial public offering for its first public mutual fund (AMP 2014). According to the Asset Management Association of China, China's managed funds market was worth US$2.5 trillion in 2015, up from US$100 billion 10 years earlier (Smith 2015).

In 2014, AMP announced its acquisition of a 19.99 per cent stake in China Life Pension Company, the largest pension company in China. The acquisition, worth A$240 million, meant that AMP was the first foreign company in the world to purchase a stake in a Chinese pension company with full licenses allowing end-to-end services throughout China (Austrade 2014).

Not all of AMP Capital's ventures have been as stable as its collaboration with China Life. The company's China Growth Fund increasingly came under fire from activist investors due to its discounted trading value, before investors voted to wind it up in July 2016 (Robertson 2016). The AMP Capital Asia Quant Fund, a long-short equity-focused fund, closed operations in February 2016 (Wille and Waite 2016). On balance, however, AMP's initiatives in China have continually been one of the company's most significant engines of profit, withstanding the volatile equity market periods in the second half of 2015 and January 2016.

Overall, AMP and China Life's partnerships have been a success story of ongoing bilateral cooperation. The China Life AMP Asset Management venture's exceptional growth was a major force behind AMP's record profits in 2015 (Letts 2016). Flow-on gains from the partnership have run both ways. AMP's property funds have benefited substantially from Chinese capital support, while the Australian company is initiating a pilot program for China Life insurance agents to gain financial advisory skills (Smith 2015).

The success, according to former AMP Capital CEO Stephen Dunne, is due to the closeness of the partnership. 'We could have partnered with a securities company or a regional bank but we took a strong view that China Life was a good partner because we share a lot of similarities and we like their distribution reach,' Dunne told the Australian Financial Review in 2015. 'We can't really put numbers around the opportunity that exists for us in China', said Dunne (Smith 2015).

A formal engagement program on financial integration

Australia has a strong comparative advantage in financial services in the region. It offers China the opportunity of a testing ground for reforms that will support China's continued opening and integration, globally and regionally. The current reform processes in China offer Australia a once-in-a-generation opportunity to establish the links necessary to supply the financial products and services that China needs and to strengthen Australia's position in global markets.

This outcome will not happen of its own accord. It requires the Australian and Chinese governments and private sectors to strategically position themselves and create the bilateral architecture necessary for collaboration to occur. This architecture should be centred on a formal engagement program on financial services and reform. This would complement the Australia–China SED, including the Australia-China Investment Cooperation Framework (Box 5.4), and engage ministers, officials and firms in a work program to deepen bilateral financial integration. The engagement program would have five key areas of focus (each is discussed in turn):

- piloting the select release of regulatory and licensing restrictions on Australian firms in China as a phase-in for regional liberalisation, expanding the financial services components of ChAFTA.

- developing a regular dialogue and a mutual recognition framework between financial regulators, and supporting the development of RMB-denominated assets and securities listings in Australia.

- reviewing regulatory restrictions, including those relating to taxation and to macroprudential regulations and dividend imputation schemes to ensure that Australian and Chinese entities are better able to invest and work together in the region.

- exploring the bilateral and regional opportunities arising from FinTech and digital finance to promote financial inclusion.

- commissioning research between Australian and Chinese institutions on financial services trade and cross-border investment.

Australia has experienced the benefits and the costs of economic liberalisation, having opened its economy and developed its financial infrastructure, institutions, regulatory settings and macro-financial frameworks over the last three decades. These reforms have been difficult, complex and time-consuming. They have required years of commitment from successive governments and have, at times, resulted in significant financial and economic volatility. Australia's experience in undertaking these difficult reforms is an asset for China as it undertakes the difficult processes of financial reform, capital account liberalisation and RMB internationalisation.

There is significant scope for Australian ministers and politicians, government officials, corporate regulators and private-sector financial firms to collaborate with the Chinese government and Chinese businesses on financial reform. There is great interest within Australia to share this experience with China.

BOX 5.4: THE AUSTRALIA–CHINA INVESTMENT COOPERATION FRAMEWORK

As discussed in detail in Chapter 4, the elevation of the Comprehensive Strategic Partnership into a Comprehensive Strategic Partnership for Change will be important to deepening the Australia–China relationship. This will add momentum over the next decade for moving to put in place a treaty-level commitment covering both countries' mutual interests in open markets, resource and energy security, sustainable agricultural development and food security, and reliable access for foreign investment in both countries. The Australia–China Strategic Economic Dialogue provides an opportunity for Australia and China to explore opportunities for closer economic ties and to discuss issues within the global economic environment. The inaugural SED was held in 2014 in Beijing and was attended by then treasurer Joe Hockey, then minister for trade and investment Andrew Robb and the Chairman of China's National Development and Reform Commission, Xu Shaoshi.

At the inaugural meeting, Australia and China established an Investment Cooperation Framework. The Framework goes beyond ChAFTA and creates new pathways for promoting the export of financial services, for realising two-way investment in new sectors, and for identifying roadblocks for investors from both countries. This allows significant opportunity to deepen the relationship at a number of levels including expanding services exports from Australia to China and improving investment opportunities.

'The investment cooperation framework goes beyond the free trade agreement', Australian Treasurer Joe Hockey said. 'The focus is to deepen the everyday engagement between China and Australia with some identifiable projects, and this is as much about investment in Australia as it is about Australia investing in China'. (see Chapter 4.)

Piloting the select release of regulatory and licensing restrictions

Australia's sophisticated, globally competitive and well-regulated financial markets can act as an effective stepping-stone for China's continued opening to the region. Australia can support China across many of the reforms it is undertaking, by piloting the select release of regulatory and licensing restrictions for Australian firms in China as a phase-in for non-preferential regional and global liberalisation.

There are multiple reform priorities that have been outlined by the Chinese government, and which Australia can assist. These are discussed in more detail in the sections that follow, but include:

- lowering barriers to entry — for example, by fast-tracking licensing for Australian firms and removing restrictions on branch locations, the number of branches, opening hours and other restrictions on foreign financial institutions.

- reforming policy institutions — by deepening official engagement between Australian and Chinese financial regulators and developing a mutual recognition framework between them.

- raising the proportion of direct financial intermediation — by piloting the select release of regulatory and licensing restrictions on Australian financial intermediaries operating in China.

- expanding access to insurance and reducing precautionary savings — by easing restrictions on Australian insurance firms and reforming macroprudential regulations to facilitate joint-partnerships, such as that between AMP and China Life.

- promoting inclusive finance — by sharing information on financial inclusion and financial resilience programs in Australia and by developing a private sector funded grant program on programs to promote financial literacy.

- promoting financial innovation through new markets and products — by exploring the bilateral and regional opportunities arising from FinTech and digital finance to promote financial inclusion and intermediation.

- liberalising interest rates, exchange rates and government bonds — by sharing Australia's experience in undertaking such reforms through the program of formal engagement on financial services and reform.

- achieving internationalisation of the RMB — by supporting the development of RMB-denominated assets and securities listings in Australia, including for bonds but possibly also extending to commodities contracts in gold, coal and iron ore.

- strengthening financial regulation and prudential regulation — through the above-mentioned mutual recognition framework and by undertaking mutual reforms to allow better engagement between Australian and Chinese firms.

- developing the deposit insurance system and resolution mechanisms — by easing restrictions on Australian insurance firms.

- developing financial infrastructure — by collaborating to give the OBOR initiative and the AIIB a focus on regional financial infrastructure investment (see below).

ChAFTA can serve as a bridgehead for the expansion of bilateral financial services trade. ChAFTA, and the institutional mechanisms that underpin it and can be built around it, offer significant opportunities to both countries in designing effective and efficient financial linkages through a gradual and pragmatic process. ChAFTA secures a range of financial services commitments between China and Australia. These commitments represent the most substantial market access commitments that China has agreed to with any FTA partner, and could create new commercial opportunities for Australian banks, insurers and securities firms. They facilitate deeper participation by Australian financial institutions in China, strengthen financial services trade and investment in both directions, and enable future growth in the broader bilateral economic relationship (DFAT 2014a).

Under ChAFTA, China agreed to comprehensive treaty-level commitments on financial services, including agreement to provisions on transparency, regulatory decision-making and streamlining of financial services licence applications. A financial services committee will be established under ChAFTA providing for deep engagement between Chinese and Australian financial regulators on issues of mutual interest, allowing issues to be addressed quickly and efficiently (DFAT 2014a). The work of this committee needs to be supported by the formal engagement program on financial integration through the Australia–China SED, to ensure that it advances reform priorities and deals with the regulatory challenges outlined above. Importantly, Australian and Chinese officials should engage more comprehensively with business and industry representatives prior to these bilateral negotiations so as to provide a mechanism for their input to be considered as commitments are developed.

Both sides have identified a range of areas for further cooperation to reduce barriers in the supply of financial services, which cover many of the issues listed above. These include Australia's foreign investment regime, as well as a range of barriers that Australian and other foreign firms face in China, such as limitations on bank branch openings, minimum capital contributions, maximum offshore funding from within the same institution, required onshore presence, domestic hiring requirements, domestic housing of data, and limited or long wait times for licenses to take RMB deposits. Issues around these restrictions have been raised by many of the financial institutions consulted for this Report.

Strengthening dialogue and mutual recognition between governments and private sectors

Australian and Chinese policy leaders, ministers and senior officials have a greater range of opportunities for engagement now than ever before. The bilateral relationship is officially a Comprehensive Strategic Partnership, which includes the annual Australia–China SED.

But despite the significant implications of China's reform processes, and the significant opportunities for financial service providers, there is no designated bilateral framework through which a specific focus on these issues can take place between policymakers in both Australia and China. By comparison, in other areas such as tourism, Australia and China have a MoU on strengthening cooperation.

The formal engagement program on financial services described above needs to be a proactive, strategically-led process, with a framework for bilateral policy development set out through the annual visits of finance and trade ministers (supported by other relevant ministers for financial services) followed through by taskforces of officials from three key areas: finance ministries, central banks and financial regulators.

There is also scope for expanding bilateral engagement between the central banks of Australia and China. This would complement existing multilateral engagement through institutions and forums such as the G20, and would build on bilateral initiatives such as the local currency swap line agreed between Australia and China. A stronger bilateral dialogue will be increasingly important as China deepens its reform process and achieves greater financial integration with Australia and the region. A routine dialogue can be particularly important in times of financial volatility and crisis when safety net arrangements, including bilateral swap lines, regional arrangements (such as the Chiang Mai Initiative Multilateralization, which does not include Australia) and multilateral arrangements (such as the IMF), may need to be accessed and coordinated.

In recent years the Australian government has developed mutual recognition frameworks with other countries. Mutual recognition means that the regulators in one country recognise the regulations of other countries so that businesses are not required to satisfy two parallel sets of regulations when they are working across borders. Mutual recognition frameworks improve the ease of doing cross-border business by reducing inefficiencies, decreasing compliance costs and saving time.

Mutual recognition frameworks can cover a range of different regulatory settings, including securities market regulations, fund management, collective investment schemes and licensing requirements for financial advisors, accountants, fund managers and lawyers. The general approach of the Australian government to recognising foreign regulation of financial markets and financial services providers has been based on unilateral recognition of the foreign jurisdiction.

In June 2008, Australia undertook its first mutual recognition agreement on securities offerings with New Zealand. Issuers of securities can now use one prospectus to offer shares, debentures or managed or collective investment schemes to investors on both sides of the Tasman Sea, subject to certain requirements.

Following this, Australia and Hong Kong extended mutual recognition to authorised collective investment schemes, which will facilitate the sale of retail funds in each other's market. The APEC Asia Region Funds Passport (discussed below) is similarly a form a mutual recognition that Australia is leading in APEC.

In August 2008, Australian authorities signed a third mutual recognition arrangement, with the United States Securities and Exchange Commission (SEC). The mutual recognition arrangement provides a framework for the SEC, the Australian government and ASIC to consider regulatory exemptions that would permit US and eligible Australian stock exchanges and broker-dealers to operate in both jurisdictions, without certain need for these entities to be separately regulated in both countries. It reduces the barriers that US and Australian investors face in investing in each other's markets.

As China's reform processes deepen, a goal should be the development of a mutual recognition framework between Australia and China. One of the pre-conditions of mutual recognition is that the regulatory framework of each jurisdiction must be substantially equivalent, thus ensuring investor protection and market integrity irrespective of the location of the investor. For this reason, a mutual recognition framework between Australia and China is not a goal that will be achieved in the near term, but is a goal that should be part of the broader future engagement program between the two countries. Importantly, this engagement program and greater collaboration between Australian and Chinese regulators will itself facilitate the move towards a mutual recognition framework.

In the private sector, there has been ongoing, albeit informal, collaboration on economic and financial reform. Given the opportunities for increasing the financial connections between Australia and China — and the vital role of the private sector in making this happen — a more formal approach to private sector engagement is necessary. Furthering this collaboration through the formal engagement program on financial services should therefore be a key priority. Australian financial firms have hosted dozens of delegations from China over the years — from policymaking and regulatory bodies as well as from financial services firms — to share knowledge about Australia's financial system and reform history. Within China, several of Australia's largest financial institutions have significant joint venture partnerships through which the transfer of technical and managerial knowledge and expertise has been taking place. Chinese financial services firms that have established operations within Australia have engaged proactively with the Australian financial services sector, including through groups such as the Australia–China Business Council.

A more formal mode of engagement by the private sector in China's financial sector reform has recently developed — the Sydney for RMB Committee. Formed in 2013, the Committee now comprises 30 senior financial sector professionals representing organisations that have a deep interest in developing greater financial connectedness between Australia and China. It is led by the private sector but has the support of the NSW and federal governments. The Committee has written several white papers and supported RMB offshore development by identifying the key blockages to increased take-up of RMB among Australian firms and by promoting Sydney as an important hub for RMB trade, finance and investment transactions in the Asia Pacific region.

Mutual regulatory reforms to increase engagement

Along with the mutual recognition framework discussed above, there is scope for other reforms in regards to professional services, regulatory restrictions around taxation and macroprudential regulations, which should also be explored to increase financial integration between Australia and China.

According to the Australian Chamber of Commerce in Beijing, the trained talent pool in China's financial services sector is limited, particularly when taking account of foreign language skills and depth of experience. For some specialist roles, it is increasingly difficult to recruit and retain staff (AustCham 2016).

Australian and Chinese academic institutions have an important role to play in supplying the next generation of financial services advisors. There is scope for joint ventures between Chinese universities and Australian financial institutions, which would result in a specialist talent pool that is trained on current international industry practices. A longer-term talent management plan needs to include an education push to enhance professional skills within the financial services sector.

The Chinese and Australian governments could also improve the attractiveness of their financial services sectors as career destinations for international talent. The Chinese government could give consideration to providing tax incentives comparable to Hong Kong or Singapore for employees, as well as for employers to invest in experienced foreign trainers who can educate local talent. The Australian and Chinese governments could partner with private firms from both countries to provide training and policy support in the development of the Chinese financial system through programs that encourage collaboration between Australian and Chinese financial firms.

While much of this chapter has considered reform processes in China, there are domestic regulatory settings that the industry suggests inhibit Australian firms from expanding into China and the Asia Pacific. Regulatory settings, including capital reserve requirements set by the Australian Prudential Regulation Authority, need to be carefully calibrated to ensure there are no unnecessary barriers to Australian firms' take-up of opportunities provided by free trade agreements that raise the maximum threshold of foreign equity in a joint venture financial services firm in Asia (Auster and Foo 2015).

The 2014 Financial System Inquiry recommended reviewing the state of competition in the financial sector, including identifying barriers to the cross-border provision of financial services. The Australian government endorsed this recommendation and committed to task the Productivity Commission to undertake this review by the end of 2017. It noted that 'deeper cross-border linkages promise enormous opportunities, if properly harnessed' and that 'our policy settings must facilitate entry of these disrupters rather than acting as a blockage' (Government of Australia 2015c). It is important that this review goes beyond Australia's traditional investment partners and looks specifically at the barriers to investing in China and other countries in the Asia Pacific region.

The Australian Financial Centre Forum's 2010 report on 'Australia as a financial centre' (Johnson Report 2010) also raised a number of tax issues where Australian regulations currently raise the costs of offshore capital borrowing and restrict Australian banks from accessing offshore retail and wholesale deposits (Finsia 2014). These issues should be examined as part of the Australian government's focus on tax reform.

Australia's Productivity Commission (2015) notes that strong competition and the growing levels of wealth in Asia mean that barriers to financial service exports from Australia will be increasingly costly. It notes there are regulatory barriers constraining the growth of exports from the managed fund sector in Australia (in particular, from managed investment schemes) as well as through taxation arrangements for international investment in managed funds.

Bilateral and regional opportunities arising from FinTech

Financial technology — or FinTech — is transforming financial systems and potentially entire economies. Globally, FinTech investment reached an estimated US$20 billion in 2015, a jump of around seven-fold over the last three years (Australian Treasury 2016). The FinTech industry has great potential to not only help drive expansion and growth in financial services and exports, but will also deliver benefits through new services that create value or bring new efficiencies. For these reasons, the engagement program on financial services should have a special focus on the opportunities arising from this sector.

China has a burgeoning FinTech sector that supports a number of large firms supplying financial services and products. Companies such as AliPay and WeChat demonstrate the rising demand for sophisticated financial products and services in China. This highlights the crucial importance of a free and open internet. The OECD recently warned that worldwide efforts to clamp down on cybercrime and terrorism, in particular, are putting the economic benefits of the free and open internet at risk. The OECD highlights the important link between innovation and internet freedom (OECD 2016) Australia and China must ensure a free and open internet if they are to capture the benefits of increasing economic activity in FinTech and other innovative sectors that are crucial to future prosperity. It is estimated that the uptake of information and communications technologies in Australia in the 1990s added upwards of 0.2 percentage points of multifactor productivity growth to Australia's annual economic growth (Gretton 2003). The absence of domestic and international impediments to internet access is essential to capturing the productivity-enhancing benefits of these technologies. The positive productivity-enhancing effects of openness to FinTech innovation are likely to be increasingly important as the industry matures.

During a FinTech roundtable organised by the Chinese government in Shanghai in February 2016, Lufax, the second-largest peer-to-peer lender in China, spoke about real-time personalised insurance options such as car insurance that could account for the places you might be driving through or to on a particular day, including weather and traffic conditions. During another FinTech roundtable in Shanghai, Chinese internet services giant Baidu, explained their 'Internet Plus' strategy was not about becoming a FinTech operator, but to enable them to act as an aggregator. They are focused on bringing together the partners needed to realise a new product or service to fill the gaps and to satisfy consumer demands by leveraging their digital distribution networks, data and insights (Australian Treasury 2016).

FinTech is about stimulating technological innovation so that financial markets and systems can become more efficient and consumer-focused. This can help drive improvements in traditional financial services and, perhaps more importantly, promote disruption through innovative new products and services, which can offer benefits to consumers and other sectors of the economy. FinTech is also reducing information asymmetry in the marketplace and thereby helping to mitigate risk and promote the efficient allocation of scarce resources (Australian Treasury 2016).

FinTech solutions hold enormous potential benefits to all business, especially new and existing small businesses. Small- and medium-sized enterprises (SMEs) are crucial for economic growth and jobs but some can face difficulty in securing the financing they need to survive and prosper. FinTech can offer solutions that are efficient and effective at lower scale, which will benefit small businesses and provide them with increased access to more diverse funding options. Innovative FinTech products can be better tailored to the needs of small businesses. These include marketplace (peer-to-peer) lending, merchant and e-commerce finance, invoice finance, online supply chain finance and online trade finance (Australian Treasury 2016).

In addition to financing and access to capital, FinTech can help all businesses through improved payment systems, customer relationship management and invoicing and collections. FinTech solutions include e-invoice management portals and supply chain finance solutions.

The Australian government outlined in a recent report (Australian Treasury 2016) that it is committed to working with the FinTech industry, regulators and other stakeholders, on the key issues that underpin this continued innovation in financial services. The government has publicly supported the industry's objective of making Australia the leading market for FinTech innovation and investment in Asia by 2017. Australia's fledgling but flourishing FinTech industry is attracting talent, promoting innovation in Australia's financial services industry and exporting talent abroad, such as:

- incubators (Stone and Chalk, and Tyro);

- venture capital funds with a focus on FinTech (H2 and Reinventure);

- personal and business finance (SocietyOne, Prospa, Ratesetter, Spotcap and Moula);

- capital market technology (OzForex and Pepperstone);

- payments providers (Tyro Payments and PromisePay);

- wealth management providers (Stockspot, Simply Wall Street and PocketBook);

- business-enabling technologies and data analytics (Avoka, Metamako, and Quantium); and

- crowdfunding platforms (Equitise, TMeffect and CrowdFundUp).

Research on financial services trade and cross-border investment

The Australian Centre for Financial Studies (Auster and Foo 2015) identifies a lack of research and data as an impediment to financial services integration in the Asia Pacific region. It argues that many of the enablers and impediments to greater integration, or their potential impact, are not well researched or understood and that policymakers, regulators and practitioners lack a strong evidentiary base from which to make well-informed decisions on matters of significance to the Australian and Chinese economies.

Australian and Chinese organisations should commission and encourage collaborative research programs to be carried out by Australian and Chinese institutions, to better understand and assess the impact of financial integration in the Asia Pacific. The research should look specifically at the drivers and mechanisms of financial integration, the impact of global regulatory reforms such as those resulting from Basel III and the Financial Stability Board, the institutional mechanisms that drive reforms, and Asia's voice in these mechanisms.

This research could have a specific focus on 'behind the border' barriers and the broader impacts of China's reform processes for Australia and the region. There is little substantive research that analyses the impacts of the opening of China's capital account on the Australian economy from a whole-of-economy perspective. Some industry studies predict increased investment or commercial flows in particular sectors, but no studies have looked at the Australian economy as a whole, or the impact on relevant sectors within financial services. Further, there is significant data development still to do on measuring and reporting China's financial data, including cross-border capital and investment flows.

Regional collaboration on financial services and flows

As the Chinese financial system opens to the region, there is a significant opportunity for these flows to finance productive investment, build capital stocks and increase economic growth in the region. For Australia, as a capital importing country, there is a great opportunity to import Chinese capital to finance investment and reduce the cost of capital to Australian firms and households. For China, these reforms offer the opportunity to increase the returns on the capital of firms and households, which is key to improving living standards and addressing challenges related to the ageing population. This section identifies a number of initiatives to help facilitate regional integration in financial services and flows.

One Belt, One Road

As the 'top and tail' of the region identified by the OBOR vision, collaboration between Australia and China on financial sector reform and developing financial infrastructure across the region will be an important source of stability to help ensure economic prosperity for future generations. As discussed in detail in Chapter 4, the partnership between Australia and China must be enabled on both sides by the provision of supporting financial infrastructure (including access to each other's financial services markets), the ability to make investments that support further trade and service delivery, and continued and easier flows of people between the two countries.

The OBOR initiative involves building a host of new infrastructure connections between China, Asia, Africa, the Middle East and Europe. A complementary series of ports and other infrastructure projects across the Indian Ocean and surrounding seas called the Maritime Silk Route adds a maritime leg to land-based connections including the China–Pakistan Economic Corridor (CPEC) and the proposed Bangladesh–China–India–Myanmar Economic Corridor (BCIM).

China has already established major financing bodies, including the AIIB and the Silk Road Fund, to help fund an estimated US$250 billion worth of OBOR projects (Australia–China OBOR Initiative 2016; Brewster 2015). OBOR represents an opportunity to further strengthen financial integration by complementing its trade networks and physical infrastructure investments with greater investment in financial infrastructure.

Along with infrastructure investment in Northern Australia, this represents another key way in which Australia and China can collaborate on OBOR. Investment in financial infrastructure such as financial institutions, financial intermediaries, payment systems, credit information bureaus and collateral registries should be seen as critical complements to the broader OBOR objectives of deepening trade and commercial links, and thus should receive the same level of attention and financial support.

APEC's Asia Region Funds Passport

Under the auspices of APEC, the Asia Region Funds Passport (ARFP) will, once implemented, provide a multilaterally agreed upon framework to facilitate the cross-border marketing of managed funds across participating economies in the Asia Pacific. The view is that a mutual recognition approach may be more realistic than pursuing regulatory harmonisation; in funds management, the ARFP is the preferred regional vehicle for cross-border marketing of managed funds. In the longer term, the ARFP could also facilitate funds from the Asia Pacific region being marketed in Europe through an Asian/European mutual recognition agreement.

The Australian Financial Markets Association states that the Passport provides a 'practical template for cooperation in the Asian region'. The Financial Services Council (FSC) says that the ARFP is its 'preferred mechanism for cross border trade in funds management, alongside bilateral and multilateral free trade agreements'. The FSC also notes that taxation regimes, both in Australia and overseas, are complex and that 'Australia will not be a successful participant in [the ARFP] unless accompanying domestic reforms are undertaken' (Productivity Commission 2015).

The ARFP is a region-wide initiative that was initiated by Australia, New Zealand, South Korea and Singapore. In September 2013, these four countries signed a Statement of Intent to jointly develop the ARFP to facilitate cross-border offers of funds in the APEC region. In April 2014, the signatories, together with the Philippines and Thailand, issued a joint consultation paper on the proposed rules and arrangements for the ARFP. Japan signalled its interest in participating in 2015. These seven 'pilot' economies have been working towards the launch of the ARFP. Five other APEC members not currently signed up to the ARFP — China, Hong Kong, Indonesia, Malaysia and Vietnam — have nevertheless joined parallel discussions on the ARFP rules (APEC 2015).

On 28 April 2016, a Memorandum of Cooperation (MoC) was signed by Australia, Japan, South Korea and New Zealand. The MoC comes into effect on 30 June 2016. The ARFP initiative is open to any APEC economy that signs on, and participating economies have up to 18 months from 30 June 2016 to implement domestic arrangements. Activation of the ARFP will occur as soon as any two participating economies implement the arrangements under the MoC.

The Australian government intends to legislate to give effect to the ARFP in the second half of 2016 (Productivity Commission 2015). The government should continue to progress the ARFP and, through work in international forums, encourage other jurisdictions to participate. China has been involved in discussions around the rules of the ARFP and could consider signing up formally to the initiative as a key way of attracting talent and expertise into its finance sector (APEC 2014b).

RCEP negotiations

There is significant scope to use RCEP negotiations to strengthen the supply of financial services throughout the Asian region. In the financial services sector, many types of services can be performed across borders, without sacrificing appropriate prudential supervision. These services include buying and selling financial products, participating in and structuring transactions, and providing investment advice. RCEP should consider permitting firms to provide cross-border services to clients and qualified investors without establishing an in-country commercial presence or being subject to the separate licensing and approval requirements that generally apply to firms commercially present in a market (see Chapter 7; and see discussion in Australian Services Roundtable 2013).

Managing risks

The liberalisation and opening of the Chinese financial system brings with it great opportunities for both China and Australia, but, as with Australia's reform experience, carries with it a number of risks (see Chapter 6). These include greater exposure to negative external shocks and contagion, challenges in relation to cross-border supervision and enforcement, and adverse effects from potentially higher volatility in capital flows — which can cause rapid changes in domestic asset prices for equities, bonds, commodities, foreign exchange and derivatives.

Increasingly correlated prices between different countries and asset classes reduce the benefits of portfolio diversification, while also potentially creating channels for contagion. The global financial crisis highlighted the fact that large capital flows can increase vulnerabilities at the macroeconomic level and exacerbate systemic risks in financial systems. The liberalisation and opening of China's financial system will fundamentally change the nature of financial linkages in the Asia Pacific region, with implications not just for finance but also for flows of trade, capital and people.

The flexibility of Australia's economy, particularly its floating exchange rate and inflation-targeting monetary policy, helps it weather volatility from international markets. As it has done in the past, this will play a fundamental role in Australia managing any future volatility resulting from China's reforms and regional integration more broadly. Financial reforms of past decades and the integration of Australia's capital markets into the global system have delivered the basis for sounder macroeconomic policy, more diversified portfolios for Australian investors and the development of tools for hedging risk. The Australian financial system proved resilient throughout the global financial crisis while others did not.

For China, risk management should be based on ensuring that reforms are properly sequenced in their implementation and undertaken at the appropriate pace. The Australian experience supports the notion that strong institutions and regulatory practices can go a long way toward mitigating the risks of deep financial reform.

Both Australia and China have a strong incentive to ensure that there is a well-resourced and flexible financial safety net in the region. On 4 February 2016, IMF Managing Director Christine Lagarde warned that the global financial safety net has become too fragmented, particularly in Asia, and needs to be reformed and strengthened. Reforming the safety net would benefit China, Australia and the Asia Pacific region (Lagarde 2016). This crucial task is discussed in more detail in Chapter 8.

Australia and China must focus their efforts in the G20 and in the IMF on ensuring that there is a holistic approach to addressing the root causes of safety net fragmentation in the Asia Pacific. This requires a focus on increased and more permanent funding for the IMF (although there are real constraints on this), better-tailored financing facilities to meet the needs of Asian economies, a new phase of IMF reforms that give Asian economies a greater voice, and better cooperation between the IMF and regional financing arrangements. These are perspectives that Australia and China should advocate for in the IMF and in the G20 (see Chapter 8).

Regional and bilateral arrangements, such as the use of currency swap lines and arrangements like the Chiang Mai Initiative Multilateralization, should not be discounted. They play an important and complementary role to the IMF. The IMF needs to look at how it can better cooperate with these arrangements by setting up guidelines before a crisis erupts in order to help guide how that cooperation would take place during a crisis. This is critical to the safety net's ability to respond quickly, flexibly and consistently to crises and is key to promoting market confidence in the safety net.

While many of these measures are politically difficult, China's G20 host year has seen incremental and pragmatic first steps, through the IMF's report to G20 finance ministers in April 2016, to bolster the adequacy of the safety net. The G20 must seize this opportunity to begin a conversation on these issues (see Chapter 8).

Finally, there is an increasing risk that slowing growth in China, as well as slowing growth regionally and globally, could dampen the motivation and drive for undertaking the reforms outlined in this chapter. Losing the momentum for reform would have significant consequences. It would not only risk the gains achieved thus far but could lead to increased volatility from a negative market response. The Australian and Chinese governments should emphasise the importance of these supply-side reforms in creating growth and boosting job creation in a sustainable and balanced way into the future. A weak global economy, combined with the decreasing effectiveness of macroeconomic policies in many countries, means achieving structural reforms and reducing barriers to international trade are now more important than ever.

The future of bilateral financial cooperation

China has achieved significant progress regarding the liberalisation of its domestic financial system, retail lending and deposit rates, usage of its currency in global trade settlements and offshore RMB markets, flexibility in its exchange rate regime, and openness of capital flows into and out of China. These developments have important implications for China's institutional and economic structure through reducing distortions in factor and financial markets and allowing a larger role for the market in the economy, while still maintaining an active state control of the process and increasing China's position in the global financial system.

However they turn out, the reform processes underway in China will profoundly shape the future of the Australia–China economic relationship. They will have implications across economic, political and social dimensions. The central argument of this chapter is that, if the governments and private sectors of Australia and China position themselves strategically, these reform processes offer a once-in-a-generation opportunity to deepen the relationship in financial services and financial flows which, at present, is nascent compared to the relationship in merchandise trade. This will be a long process, but this chapter has outlined a number of steps through which it can be achieved.

Most importantly, this chapter proposes that the Australian and Chinese governments develop a program of formal engagement on financial services and reform. The program would complement the Strategic Economic Dialogue and engage ministers, officials, regulators and firms in a work program to deepen bilateral financial integration. It is recommended that a key focus of this program be on piloting the select release of regulatory and licensing restrictions on Australian firms in China as a phase-in or 'testing ground' for regional liberalisation.

The chapter also recommends measures, which should be driven by bilateral commercial need, to improve the dialogue between Australian and Chinese central banks and regulators. The aim should be to develop a mutual recognition framework to improve the ease of doing business, progress the development of RMB-denominated assets and securities listings in Australia, review regulatory restrictions including in regard to taxation and macroprudential regulations, promote the bilateral and regional opportunities arising from FinTech and digital finance, and commission research between Australian and Chinese institutions on financial services trade and cross-border investment.

The chapter also recommends that these bilateral initiatives be complemented by a focus on regional financial cooperation. This includes building a bilateral financial infrastructure focus in regional initiatives such as OBOR and the AIIB to improve payment systems, credit information bureaus, collateral registries and financial intermediaries and institutions throughout the Asia Pacific. China should also sign on to, and Australia implement, APEC's Asia Region Funds Passport and both countries should advocate its greater use in the region.

This combination of a strengthened bilateral architecture and regional initiatives aimed specifically at financial services and financial integration will be key to catalysing greater financial integration. This is the vital next step in strengthening the relationship between Australia and China.

CHAPTER 6
Framework for capturing opportunities and managing risks

KEY MESSAGES

Australia and China should aspire to a bilateral relationship of the high level and scope that they established during the foundational period of economic ties in the 1980s, when they agreed on a 'model relationship' for cooperation between countries with different political and social systems and at different stages of economic development. The enormous transformation to new economic models that Australia and China are currently undergoing calls for the elevation and direction of their partnership in a similar way.

There are significant untapped opportunities to increase two-way bilateral trade, investment, finance and cooperation on regional and global issues. Realising these opportunities will be important for the long-term economic performance and security of both countries.

There are three major types of risk in the bilateral relationship: commercial risks; macroeconomic risks; and system difference risks. Commercial and macroeconomic risks require the adoption of normal business strategies and policy capabilities to avoid or ameliorate their cost. System difference risks are structural and subject to change over time. They are more complex to mitigate, requiring political as well as business leadership in order to frame strategic arrangements for the conduct of the relationship.

The opportunities are best realised and the risks best mitigated through political leadership on both sides that mobilises bi-national work programs to advance priority interests and work through issues in the relationship. This provides impetus and a uniting vision that is key to commanding the attention and focusing the resources of official and private actors.

- Australia and China should upgrade their bilateral relationship from a 'Comprehensive Strategic Partnership' to a 'Comprehensive Strategic Partnership for Change'. This unique categorisation of the Australia–China relationship would signal bilateral commitment to staying ahead of the reform curve in implementing needed economic policy initiatives and strategies, and provide an exceptional opportunity for China to work with the smaller-scale yet more developed Australian economy as a testing ground for change.

- Australia and China should work over the coming years to develop their new partnership into a comprehensive bilateral Basic Treaty of Cooperation that embeds frequent high-level political dialogue; institutionalises official bilateral exchanges and technical cooperation programs between ministries and branches of the military; pools approaches between federal–state governments in Australia and central–provincial governments in China; and provides for the comprehensive setting of strategic bilateral objectives and forward work agendas every five years.

- The Comprehensive Strategic Partnership for Change should encourage investment in national centres of research excellence to support understanding of the forces that will shape the development of the economic relationship between Australia and China in its regional and global settings. That will ensure the relationship has the necessary intellectual underpinnings to thrive.

- Australia and China should establish a bi-national Australia–China (Ao–Zhong) Commission to dramatically boost the level and range of scientific, official, business and community exchanges between the two countries and drive the accumulation of human capital and networks needed to take Australia–China economic relations to the next level. It will promote an ambitious bilateral program of 'literacy' capacity building, multi-level scholarly exchange, bureaucratic network building, political interactions and sustained high-level business dialogue, and develop a forward work agenda for improving economic policymaking coordination.

This is a time of great change in China, Australia, the region and the world. There are enormous opportunities still to be grasped on both sides. This chapter will review key opportunities in the relationship, identify the major risks in realising those opportunities and propose a framework for managing these risks and getting the most out of the relationship.

As both countries adapt to China's transition to a new economic model, this Report proposes that they upgrade their relationship from a Comprehensive Strategic Partnership to a new and unique level as a 'Comprehensive Strategic Partnership for Change'. This would signal the determination of both countries to focus the relationship on achieving their goals for economic and social change. The task of such a partnership would be to energise and deepen the current bilateral institutional arrangements, build trust around common economic and political interests, manage the uncertainties of change, and develop the close commercial and business engagement needed as the structure of the economic relationship shifts towards services and consumers (see Chapter 1).

Opportunities

The opportunities in the Australia–China relationship derive from the growth of China's wealth and its importance in the world economy, the strongly complementary relationship of Australia to China's trade and industrial transformation because of Australia's competitiveness in international resource and energy markets, Australia's ability to meet many of China's new demands, their relative geographic proximity and their close political engagement since China's reform and opening began in the late 1970s.

Foundations

The foundation of the interaction between Australia and China is their deeply complementary economic partnership, which continues as the bridgehead of bilateral engagement. The natural complementarity between their economies has deepened the relationship since Australia committed to engagement in China's reform and opening process. Australia's abundant, stable and low-cost supplies of resources are critical to China's continuing growth, investment and urbanisation. China's demand for these resources has sustained strong trade and economic growth in Australia — direct trade with China is calculated by the Australia–China Business Council (ACBC 2015) to have contributed over 5.5 per cent of Australian GDP between 1995 and 2011. This is the biggest contribution of any country and twice as large as that of agriculture, forestry and fishing.

The foundations of the bilateral relationship also encompass the assets that have been built through the success of the relationship, symbolised in the present Comprehensive Strategic Partnership.

New economic model

While the resource trade remains a central element in the bilateral trade relationship, the end of the commodities boom and the emerging transformation of China's economy from an investment-export model to consumption and services-led growth opens new opportunities in the trade relationship. The opportunities for growth in the relationship now lie in energy, agriculture, high-value manufactures and especially in services. China will continue to export manufactures and be a strong net source of migration to Australia while capital exports will grow and diversify. The upgrading of China's industrial economy will push growth in its trade with Australia into new markets for machinery, high value-added manufactures and equipment, and capital into all sectors of the Australian economy.

Major flows of Chinese tourists, students, investors and migrants into Australia and more Australians students, tourists and investors spending time in China will equip more Australians and Chinese with interests and capabilities in improving business, cultural and political relations.

Investment and financial opening

Two-way flows on investment, particularly FDI, will be critical to new trade and commercial growth between the two countries. Chinese investment can help Australia to address its significant infrastructure gap, while Australian investment is injecting developed-market expertise into emerging sectors of the Chinese economy. FDI in each other's economies will endow businesspeople in both Australia and China with a long-term commitment to managing not only commercial but also public issues that have to be navigated in the relationship as it changes to one that involves closer engagement in business in each country.

The financial integration that will flow from China's ongoing process of financial market and capital account liberalisation is an area of particular opportunity and importance. Liberalisation will release massive volumes of Chinese savings searching for higher returns, creating a major investment pool as Australia seeks to upgrade its infrastructure, internationalise its supply chains and invest in innovation. Reducing barriers to trade in financial services is part of the step-by-step process involved in these reforms and Australia can work with China in pioneering change in these markets. Liberal financial markets, fully convertible currencies, and open current and capital accounts will diversify and stabilise the interaction between Chinese and international capital markets, but this goal will take time to achieve. Meanwhile, steady experimentation and sharing of policy experience can help along the way.

The Comprehensive Strategic Partnership for Change would encourage and support new commercial partnerships between Australia and China that make use of both countries' innovation agendas to harness technology to improve bilateral trade and commercial ties.

Partnerships make commercial sense in building business only where local, up-close engagement delivers returns. Getting close to the customer requires knowing the customer well. Partnerships are an effective vehicle for bringing suppliers and customers in China or Australia closer together, expanding markets, improving efficiency and delivering competitive products and service.

Common regional and global assets

Australia and China have a strong interest in a peaceful and prosperous regional and international system. Crucial parts of this order are well established in the post-Bretton Woods institutions and the United Nations framework, but there are gaps and the order needs to evolve to meet new challenges. Some of the priorities are dealt with in Chapters 7 and 8. Here the focus is on the principles and approaches that will help create the consensus that is needed to make progress where significant deficiencies remain.

Australia and China have the chance to build bilateral partnerships that are ahead of the economic reform curve in both countries and that set the benchmarks for broader regional and global economic collaboration (Box 6.1). China is facing a decade of challenging yet crucial domestic and international economic policy reforms, and Australia provides a proving ground for China to test the pathways through many of these reforms on the way to higher-income advanced economy status. Australian and Chinese policymakers can use their partnership to help push through domestic economic reforms and to strengthen the structure of regional economic architecture.

China's standing in the Australian and Asia Pacific economies is bound to rise if it succeeds with its continued program of economic and social reform. In the international arena, China is becoming an increasingly global power and naturally seeks to secure commensurate representation in global governance and to play a more important role in international affairs. Australia can play a constructive role in supporting these developments.

The economic changes underway will also impact on political relations. Both countries share interests in developing arrangements that strengthen regional and global political security.

BOX 6.1: AUSTRALIA, CHINA AND REGIONAL INFRASTRUCTURE INVESTMENT

The Northern Australian economy is heavily dependent on the mining sector and is now seeking economic diversification. While resources, including energy, will continue to dominate Northern Australian industry, the Australian government is anticipating that growth sectors for its future include: food and agribusiness; tourism and hospitality; international education; and healthcare, medical research and aged care. Northern Australia has a sizeable deficit in the infrastructure that is needed to realise this growth potential. The Australian government has set up an A$5 billion concessional loan mechanism, the Northern Australia Infrastructure Facility (NAIF). Businesses from any country are potentially able to access these loans, but it is clear that still much more capital will be needed to develop the region (Government of Australia 2015b).

The North is already very open to foreign investment. Much of the capital used to finance the resource sector is already foreign-owned. There is a strong link between foreign investment and local wages and community development. The North's sparse population also makes finding the space for large developments easier than in many other areas of Australia. Most importantly, Australia simply does not have the domestic savings necessary to build and upgrade ports, pipelines, logistics networks and transportation facilities. Australia has persistently run large current account deficits, averaging above 3 per cent of GDP between 1960 and 2015. Any overall expansion in investment — whether in the North or anywhere else in the country — will likely come from foreign savings.

There are other reasons why Chinese investment in the North may be favourable to both China and Australia. China has developed a world-class infrastructure industry, while the North needs large-scale infrastructure development. Northern infrastructure can service and integrate with transport and communication networks elsewhere in the region, potentially achieving economies of scale and scope. Australia's demand for infrastructure investment in the North and across the country matches China's appetite for both infrastructure investment and for its firms to be involved in large-scale infrastructure projects. Investment in Northern Australia will facilitate regional trade, increasing Australia's regional integration with Southeast Asia and providing the region with better access to its land, resources and knowledge. With capacity to deliver abroad, China's strategy is to invest outwards to address the US$8 trillion regional infrastructure gap via initiatives such as OBOR.

OBOR consists of the New Silk Road Economic Belt and the 21st Century Maritime Silk Road. The Belt and Road are envisioned as extensive networks of Chinese commerce, investment and infrastructure projects extending along the country's key strategic trade routes west and south. China has committed US$40 billion to a Silk Road Fund and created the multinational US$100 billion AIIB, which could help finance OBOR projects. In his speech to a joint sitting of the Australian parliament on 17 November 2014, Chinese President Xi Jinping declared that Oceania was a 'natural extension' of the Maritime Silk Road, and he invited Australia to participate in OBOR (Thomas 2015).

The wheels are already in motion. The 2015 round of the Australia–China Strategic Economic Dialogue focused on regional infrastructure investment, and formed working groups to explore opportunities in Northern Australia and the region, including the potential role of the NAIF and AIIB (Treasurer of Australia 2015c). Representatives from major Chinese investors participated in the Northern Australia Investment Forum that was hosted by the then Minister for Trade and Investment Andrew Robb in Darwin in November 2015. Australia should seek to support the AIIB funding projects that are a part of OBOR, such as by using the AIIB to source capital for world class infrastructure.

OBOR and the AIIB also have the potential to facilitate partnerships between Australia and China on infrastructure projects in third countries. For example, a Chinese state-owned asset management company could provide the capital, a Chinese construction company could provide the materials and labour, and an Australian consultancy could provide the project planning, financial forecasting, risk and talent management, and contracting out specialised technical inputs for a major infrastructure facility project in a country like Myanmar or Indonesia (Lumsden et al 2015). A joint approach to regional infrastructure can be further enhanced through the Global Infrastructure Hub in Sydney.

Under the Comprehensive Strategic Partnership for Change, the Australian and Chinese governments should upgrade their cooperation on OBOR through appointing a dedicated high-level joint working group to deepen and extend the work already being undertaken by the SEC Investment Working Group to explore the practicalities of how the two countries can better work together to enhance domestic and regional infrastructure.

Risks

In all big economic and political relationships, such as that between Australia and China, there are uncertainties and unpredictable occurrences that create risks that have to be managed. In partnerships that are relatively new and growing rapidly, especially where the scale and activities of one partner changes rapidly, as has been the case with China, associated uncertainties and heightened chances of unpredictable events exaggerate perceptions of risk. Between countries that have different histories and political cultures, system differences add another dimension to risk in managing relationships. Learning and experience will reduce these risks. But private and public effort is important to the understanding of the risks born of change and the differences that will remain — and finding ways to work around them to achieve economically and socially productive outcomes from exchange. This Report sets out a taxonomy of risks that confront the Australia–China relationship: commercial risks, macroeconomic risks, and system difference risks. The goal of the Comprehensive Strategic Partnership for Change should be to forge a bilateral relationship that goes beyond that which is basic between two countries and that can withstand and thrive around unexpected changes in either country.

Commercial risks

There are firm- and industry-level commercial risks across all markets. These include issues of due diligence, market access, regulatory enforcement and local operations in other countries that impact upon specific actors in the bilateral economic relationship.

Commercial risks are a normal part of the decision calculus of a company seeking to expand its trade, investment or operations in another country. Companies that assume these risks in search of higher returns need to have a strong grasp of local markets, regulations and business practices. Still, such risks are amplified in new markets where companies have no prior experience and little background. This has been the case for some firms in Australia and China who, attracted by the excitement of new possibilities for profitable investment in the other country, were drawn into ventures that underestimated or otherwise miscalculated commercial risks. While the first-mover advantage is real, it needs to be adequately balanced by normal business considerations.

It is not the role of the Australian or Chinese governments to conduct due diligence on behalf of companies and cover their failures. But both leaderships have an important messaging role to play: in fostering bilateral business sentiment that is realistic about opportunities, while encouraging investment projects where there are the capabilities and relationships to forge sustainable commercial partnerships; in upgrading market awareness (through Austrade in Australia and MOFCOM in China); and in building competencies for both Australian and Chinese firms (Box 6.2).

BOX 6.2: EXPERIENCE WITH COMMERCIAL RISKS

Two early Australian movers into the enormous and potentially lucrative Chinese market were its major brewing companies, Lion Nathan (now Lion) and Foster's (Gettler 2004; Slocum et al 2006; Chung 2011). Lion Nathan spent over A$350 million building breweries and buying into joint ventures in the Chinese market from the mid-1990s, but eventually sold off its businesses for only A$220 million in 2004. Lion's strategy in China was similar to its approach in Australia, which was to invest heavily in volume-building and competitive pricing. However, confronted by high distribution costs and intense competition from local brands in the low-end of the market, it had to withdraw. For a foreign company in China's fragmented and still maturing beer market, other areas such as branding, marketing and the logistics of distribution should have been more important considerations. These areas required sophisticated market engagement and high-level knowledge of local operations that comprehended Chinese market realities and employed bicultural human resources. Foster's Group limped out of China in 2006 after experiencing similar challenges. The challenges faced by Lion Nathan and Foster's show the necessity of advanced market and regulatory knowledge, sustained on-the-ground engagement and the prudent assessment of logistical risks.

The Sino Iron project in Western Australia is 'famous in China as the single most disastrous outbound investment deal in Chinese history' (Garnaut 2014; Australian Centre on China in the World 2015). In 2006, Chinese state-owned holding company CITIC Pacific signed a A$5 billion 25-year deal with Australian miner Mineralogy to mine magnetite iron ore in Western Australia's Pilbara region — the largest-ever Chinese investment in Australia. When CITIC bought into the Sino Iron project it lacked experience in both the iron ore industry and in the Australian market, but was attracted by getting a slice of the lucrative Australian iron ore trade. The Sino Iron project suffered massive cost blowouts from a range of predictable risks — transportation bottlenecks, weather events, rising labour and capital costs, and a strengthening Australian dollar. A highly publicised dispute between Mineralogy's owner Clive Palmer and CITIC over royalty payments, among other issues, exacerbated the project's commercial problems.

But at the heart of Sino Iron's problems was the lack of a clear assessment of local conditions and regulatory processes (CITIC 2012; Duffy 2012). Differences in Chinese and Australian commissioning requirements, such as the certification of safety documents by licensed engineers, were not adequately considered. CITIC's budget and timeframe were stretched further by a shortage of the qualified electricians required by Australian regulations to commission control systems. Personnel movement posed problems as the processing of hundreds of equipment service providers' visas far exceeded the expected timeframe. A planned investment of A$3.46 billion ballooned to expenditures of over A$10 billion. When magnetite exports commenced in December 2013, the project was four years behind schedule. This delay cost CITIC dearly, as iron ore prices had started plummeting in 2013, leading CITIC to write-down Sino Iron by billions of dollars.

Macroeconomic risks

There are country-level macroeconomic risks around uncertainties about the economic and political stability and growth potential of another country's economy as well as the prospects for expanding bilateral trade, investment and flows of people and ideas.

China's economy faces a number of difficult, but inevitable, transitions. These transitions will benefit China and Australia significantly in the medium to long run (see Chapter 5). But in the short term, they have brought, and will likely continue to bring, adjustment costs as well as commercial opportunities for partners like Australia, and be the source of international economic shocks.

What are the potential impacts of shocks in the Chinese economy on Australia? There are two broad mechanisms between the Australian and Chinese economies through which shocks can be transmitted: trade and finance. Movement of people could be a third.

For trade, Australia will be negatively impacted by shocks in China that see a significant reduction in demand for Australia's major exports. It is instructive how relatively comfortably Australia has weathered a 60 per cent drop in the price of iron ore since the commodity boom burst.

Yet analysis from the IMF finds that Australia would be one of the worst hit advanced economy from slowing Chinese investment growth — only Iran, Kazakhstan, Saudi Arabia, Zambia and Chile could suffer bigger effects on their economies (Box 6.3).

Reducing reliance on investment and export-led growth is a key aspect of China's economic rebalancing and directly affects Australia. The IMF analysis suggests that for each percentage point decline in Chinese investment growth, Australia's potential GDP falls by 0.2 percentage points (Greber 2015). These estimates are built on the Chinese government's expectation that investment will fall steadily across the world's second-largest economy from 46 per cent of GDP to around 35 per cent over the next five to 10 years. This implies Australia's GDP could be 2 per cent below the levels that would occur if China's investment-led growth were to continue.

The projection is conditional on declining demand for Australia's mining and resources exports — other commodity exporting countries are also hit by this change in the Chinese economy. The analysis does not take into account the potential increase in Australian exports in other sectors, including services sector adjustments in the non-trade and import-competing sectors, nor associated responses in the Australian economy that can be achieved from improved engagement with China. It is an exercise that simply measures the immediate impact of a major shock to existing trade. Australian engagement and policy settings are therefore crucial to the final effect on the economy. If the exchange rate falls with reduced demand for established exports, there will be a fillip to expansion of other sectors. Crucially this will be assisted by more proactive re-positioning by Australia bilaterally, regionally and multilaterally to take full advantage of these opportunities. As shown in Chapter 5, Australia's economic flexibility allows these shocks to be absorbed without loss of the gains from trade.

For finance, direct investment and financial linkages through equity, bond, currency and property markets represent the key transmission mechanisms for shocks from the Chinese economies. Financial reform, capital account liberalisation and internationalisation of the renminbi will have a range of implications for Australia. They will bring deeper financial markets to the region, increased capital flows, a reduction in the cost of capital, and greater opportunities to supply financial services into these markets. However, they will also be a source of shocks to investment in Australia, Australian financial markets and Australia's macroeconomic situation.

BOX 6.3: AUSTRALIA'S REACTION TO SHOCKS FROM SHIFTS IN CHINESE MARKET SENTIMENT

Recent volatility in Chinese stock markets illustrates the way in which shocks can be transmitted through financial markets. China's stock market is still very underdeveloped and it plays a very small role in the economy. The stock market is about a third of GDP, compared with more than 100 per cent in developed economies. Less than 15 per cent of household financial assets are invested in the stock market. These shocks are, however, transmitted to Australia, causing volatility in Australian equity and currency markets and potentially hurting growth through wealth effects.

The ASX200, along with other indices globally and in the region, followed the downward trend in the Shanghai Composite through 2015. Commonwealth Bank China and Asia economist Wei Li asserts 'that China's financial market is becoming more integrated in global investor sentiment' (quoted in Desloires and Cauchi 2016). Analysis by Rodriguez and Ren (2015) finds that the Australian dollar is especially susceptible to volatility in Chinese financial markets. They find a 20-day correlation of 0.38 between the Australian dollar and the Shanghai Shenzhen 300, the largest correlation for any currency, including the Japanese yen.

A more significant financial risk is if there is a general loss of confidence by investors in China, potentially triggered by a broader loss of confidence in the emerging market economies given the challenges facing Brazil and Russia, in particular. Using an inter-temporal multi-sectoral DSGE (Dynamic Stochastic General Equilibrium) model called G-Cubed — the theoretical structure is outlined by McKibbin and Wilcoxen (1999) — the consequences of a 200 basis point increase in the risk premium of holding assets in emerging market economies could be significant for Australia.

The Australian economy is also in a period of transition. Capital, labour and other economic resources are moving from the mining and resources sectors towards other sectors of the economy. It is in Australia's interest to ensure that this reallocation of resources is carefully managed. The impact of a 200 basis point risk premium shock through a loss of investor confidence in China would be to speed up this change significantly. The earnings from Australia's mining and resources exports are already low compared to the mining boom period, and much of this demand comes from the emerging market economies. Reduced growth in these economies would see further contractions in demand for Australia's exports. Investment falls by 10 per cent in Australia's mining sector and 5 per cent in its energy sector (Greber 2015).

But on the financial side, capital flowing out of the emerging market economies flows into the advanced economies, including Australia. This appreciates the exchange rate by 3 per cent, which further exacerbates declining demand for Australian exports and weakens the trade balance. The capital flowing into the Australian economy favours the non-trade exposed sectors, which actually boosts investment in those sectors. Overall the shock has the effect of speeding up the economic transition in Australia through substantial reduction in investment and economic activity in Australia's trade-exposed sectors and increased investment elsewhere. Although, counter-intuitively, the net effect is marginally positive for Australian GDP (around 0.6 per cent), this shock tests the flexibility of the Australian economy and its ability to relocate capital and labour at a rapid pace.

The key policy message for Australia in considering how to deal with Chinese economic shocks is to underline the importance of having an open and flexible economy so as to manage these shocks and facilitate the smooth transition of the Australian economy. Australia's floating exchange rate, strong institutions and robust macroeconomic frameworks are critical. These need to be complemented with reforms to strengthen the flexibility of labour markets (particularly through improving workplace regulation and the education, training and re-skilling of workers) and product markets through microeconomic reforms to boost competition and reduce barriers to entry and exit.

System difference risks

There are system difference risks that create, among other things, uncertainties in sovereign behaviour towards private entities in other countries that are connected to policy frameworks and their stability (see Chapter 1). These uncertainties give rise to risks that are important to managing relationships in which the partners are undergoing rapid economic and social change. Within the bilateral relationship, these risks result from institutional and political differences as well as interest divergences between governments, and are embedded in the institutions and political and social behaviour of each country.

System difference risks and uncertainties derive from different histories, and from the economic and institutional transformations that both systems are undergoing. Even as the process of economic reform is further advanced, fundamental differences will remain between Australia and China in relation to political and legal institutions. The right of China and of Australia to determine and maintain their own political institutions, and defend their national sovereignty, is a premise in their bilateral relationship.

The Australian and Chinese governments recognise that they 'have different histories, societies and political systems, as well as differences of view on some important issues', but both countries 'are committed to constructively managing differences if and when they arise' (DFAT 2016a).

Australia is a multi-party liberal democracy. China is governed as a one-party state. Australia has a freewheeling media. China has a more controlled media environment. The Australian people provide input to their political system through regular representative elections. The Chinese people provide input to their political system through consultative mechanisms. The Chinese political and institutional system continues to change, with long-term goals for political reform, but there is uncertainty about when and how these goals will be delivered.

Australia is a federation, under a national Constitution of the Commonwealth. The federal government and state governments are separate political entities, whose parliaments are elected to be representative of the people in a system of multi-party democracy. Around 100,000 Australians are members of political parties. The Commonwealth Parliament has the power to pass laws subject to the Constitution in areas where it is competent. The prime minister and other ministers of state are drawn from the parliament and are subject to its laws. The government appoints judges, but the law is interpreted independently according to common law traditions. States have their own areas of jurisdiction. The economy is largely private. Whether a dispute is with another private company, a state or the federal government, it is settled according to this well-established legal framework.

China has a unitary political system under the leadership of the Chinese Communist Party. More than 80 million Chinese are members of the Chinese Communist Party. Since 2002, it has welcomed businesspeople as members. It guides the work of Chinese leading institutions, including the National People's Congress, and consults the people more broadly through the Chinese People's Political Consultative Conference (CPPCC). The general secretary of the Party is also the president of the People's Republic of China. The state and Party operate with respective formal constitutions. China is strengthening its system of laws and regulations at national and local levels. While a very large and dynamic private-sector economy has emerged (see Chapter 2), public ownership remains the foundation of key sectors of the state economy. Chinese company law requires companies to provide necessary conditions for Party establishments; however, only in SOEs does a company's Party committee play a formal leadership role in company affairs.

BOX 6.4: LANDBRIDGE GROUP AND THE PORT OF DARWIN

Under the relevant legal definitions governing Australian foreign investment, the Landbridge Group is a private company. Nevertheless, after the company was awarded a lease over the Port of Darwin in the Northern Territory, some security commentators raised alarms in the media about Landbridge's supposed connections to the Chinese government — in particular that the company has a Party Committee, and that its chairman is an advisor to and may be a member of the Chinese Communist Party.

But 1.63 million private companies in China have Communist Party committees — more than half of all Chinese private businesses — and millions of Party members work in China's private sector (Xinhua 2014). This is a natural result of China's political system, not evidence that companies are acting as agents of the state.

The Northern Territory government received A$390 million from the proceeds of the A$506 million lease awarded to Landbridge, and Landbridge has committed to spend a further A$35 million on the port within five years and to invest A$200 million over a 25-year period.

The structure of the sale of the Port of Darwin meant that only foreign government investors required FIRB approval. This was due to an exemption under the *Foreign Acquisitions and Takeovers Act (Cth) 1975* for asset sales by state and territory governments. Private foreign investors, including the Chinese private investor Landbridge, did not require approval.

To address any national interest concerns regarding the privatisation of the Port, the Department of Defence renegotiated a Deed of Licence with the Northern Territory government for defence access to the Port for the next 15 years with an option to extend to 25 years. The main naval defence base in Darwin, HMAS Coonawarra, was also excluded from the transaction.

On 18 March 2016, the Treasurer announced an amendment to the *Foreign Acquisitions and Takeovers Regulation 2015*, removing the exemption for private foreign investors acquiring an interest in critical infrastructure assets purchased directly from state and territory governments. From 31 March 2016, FIRB will formally review all critical infrastructure assets sold by state and territory governments.

These system differences can sometimes give rise to misunderstandings as well as be a cause of fundamental difference, but they need not be an obstacle to deeper trade or economic engagement. Chinese businesses investing or operating in Australia need to understand the political separation between different layers of government, and also be aware that in the context of representative government, the support of political representatives interacts with community attitudes and perceptions rather than dominating them. In addition, the support of elected representatives cannot be expected to facilitate the resolution of disputes or the conduct of business — that is determined by independent regulators and the courts.

In Australia, where fundamental political questions are resolved by legal interpretation, there is a tendency to categorise Chinese companies as 'state-owned' or 'private' based on black-letter provisions relating to equity-ownership. The boundary between Chinese political institutions, SOEs and private businesspeople is not always well defined or understood. Some Chinese companies, which are clearly private according to Australian legal definitions, are portrayed as being state-influenced because of family connections or historical links to the Party, the state or the military (Box 6.4).

Australia and China could further develop their legal frameworks to help clarify these issues over time. The legal framework of modern market economies, such as Australia, could provide useful assistance to China's own reform commitment to improving rule of law. This could help reduce uncertainty for foreign investors coming into China, seeking partnerships with local businesses and negotiating the local regulatory environments (Box 6.5). It is imperative that businesses operating in either country are able to make commercial decisions that rely on a robust rule of law rather than requiring non-legal recourse to political connections and other irregular channels should any business or regulatory issues arise. It is also important that both countries allow for open access to resources that are shared by all nations, such as sea-lanes, the internet and space.

The development of corporate governance and transparency in the operation of Chinese companies, including SOEs, can also help inform their dealings in a foreign setting. Australia would miss an opportunity for positive engagement with China if its formal policy settings discriminated against SOEs as a matter of principle. And it could misinterpret China's private sector were it to endorse a view that any company with links to the government was in some way commercially controlled by the state. Similarly, China will miss an opportunity if it widely and unnecessarily discriminates against foreign investment.

BOX 6.5: SINO GAS IN CHINA

Sino Gas and Energy Holdings (Sino Gas) is an Australian stock exchange listed company that explores for and produces natural gas into the Chinese market. Its competitive advantage is its skilled labour force and technological ability to drill and extract gas using advanced techniques at very low cost. Sino Gas has been operating in China since 2006 and is now Australia's largest energy investor in China and one of only a small number of foreign exploration and production companies producing gas commercially into the Chinese market. Gas production commenced from its Sanjiaobei and Linxing Production Sharing Contracts (PSCs) in China's Shanxi province in 2014. A total of approximately US$310 million has been invested in the two projects by Sino Gas and its partners since inception. Production from its Linxing central gathering station commenced in September

2015, after being slightly delayed due to a central government directive requiring safety reviews of all gas operations country-wide following the media sensation over a deadly explosion in Tianjin.

A total of US$10.1 million was received by Sino Gas' 49 per cent joint venture for gas sold from the Linxing PSC from December 2014 through to late February 2016. Proceeds for pilot gas sales from the Sanjiaobei PSC of approximately US$2 million have been made to its PSC partner, PetroChina CBM. However, production at the Sanjiaobei Central Gathering station remains suspended while negotiations are underway on the final allocation of pilot production proceeds to Sino Gas' joint venture. This is expected to be resolved shortly.

The anti-corruption campaign in China has created some uncertainty, and slowed dealings between Chinese authorities, SOEs and foreign companies. In the Chinese system, regulatory milestones can sometimes require a matrix of approvals from different departments at the local, provincial and national levels. These are issues that would naturally be taken up in a new investment agreement between Australia and China and might build confidence in the investment environment. In the current environment, many of these approvals have taken slightly longer than in the past due to the increased scrutiny of decisions made by regulatory authorities and SOEs. Delays on the receipt of sales proceeds and regulatory approvals has impacted Sino Gas' share price, though ongoing technology transfer as well as the high-level support of the Australian government are hoped to insulate Sino Gas from excessive project delays in China. Notwithstanding, Sino Gas has been one of the better performing ASX listed exploration and production stocks over the past two years. The China energy sector remains an attractive value proposition for foreign firms and operators given the favourable fiscal and regulatory regime.

Sino Gas is an Australian success story and the longer-term prospects for the company are very bright because the Chinese central government is looking to double the gas contribution to its energy mix by the end of the next Five Year Plan in 2020. Full production from the company's assets is expected to commence in 2017, and by 2021 Sino Gas' assets will produce approximately 3 per cent of China's total domestic natural gas production, making it a significant contributor to the energy objectives of the country.

Across-the-board policies that discriminate against foreign companies in general, or state-owned companies in particular, run the risk of confounding strategic intent with what is the unremarkable and unthreatening product of basic differences in each country's political institutions. Where either Australia or China does adopt policies to protect their core sovereign interests, whether in critical infrastructure, telecommunications or media (as they both properly do), these policies should be targeted to mitigate the actual risks identified, regardless of whether the threat comes from foreign or domestic actors, and whether they are legally private or state-owned. This is why institutions that foster mutual understanding, transparency and common interests are critical to allowing the full flourishing of the potential economic relationship between Australia and China.

Enhancing mutual trust and understanding is a key objective of the proposed Comprehensive Strategic Partnership for Change. The Partnership will help achieve these enhancements and mitigate system difference risks through: increasing public and commercial capacities to understand how the systems of the other country work; more focused and more useful strategic official dialogues, for instance on regulatory cooperation, risk management and reform; and close high-level ties between political leaders who can 'pick up the phone' to reduce misunderstandings.

Reducing risks

Most of the risks facing actors within the Australia–China economic relationship are normal commercial risks, and the Australian and Chinese governments should properly entrust the management of these risks to market mechanisms, given the legal frameworks of their respective systems. The risks of commercial failures and macroeconomic uncertainty should be accepted and occasional business failures are to be expected and learned from. Some of these risks are bilateral system difference risks, which are structural in nature and can be mitigated through political dialogue, public institutions and bilateral cooperation. They occur because of: differences in interests among Australian and Chinese firms in their operations in the other country; the entrenched interests of regulatory actors and domestic firms in the other country, which may be motivated to limit foreign competition and preserve markets share; and the way institutional systems and social behaviour affect business outcomes.

High-level political leadership, building on structured advice from key official and private stakeholders, can use bilateral and international pressure to make progress against these vested interests opposing domestic reform (Box 6.6). As it is an advanced economy, Australia is a valuable partner able to work at the frontier of opening Chinese markets to new actors and creating partnerships to share expertise on managing change.

In a globalised world economy, domestic reform can be incentivised and reinforced by international commitments to growth-promoting economic liberalisation. This strategy preserves the sovereignty of economic policy, while helping to overcome resistance from entrenched domestic interests who might otherwise stymie reform.

Through the Comprehensive Strategic Partnership for Change, both Australia and China can take advantage of this strategy to advance their respective economic transformations. This could be achieved through Australia serving as a possible testing-ground for gradual liberalisations of Chinese services trade, investment and capital account flows. Australia and China are a suitable match because Australia is too small an economy to have a significant effect upon global activity but it is large enough and well developed enough to provide a reliable feedback mechanism.

A prime example of success with this strategy is China's accession to the WTO and Australia's approach to it. One of the key drivers of global growth since the 1970s has been the integration of the global trading system. Conventional notions of three distinct economic systems — the capitalist 'first world', the socialist 'second world' and the developing 'third world' — gave way in the 1990s to the idea of a single global economic system, guided within a common set of institutions based around the WTO, the IMF, the multilateral banks and other entities that derived from the postwar Bretton Woods system. Economies that opened themselves to the global economy grew faster — not only because their producers gained access to overseas markets, but also because international competition places pressure on governments to reform domestic economies.

China was a latecomer to this global trading system. While a key plank of China's economic reforms after 1978 was opening up to the outside world, making it an exemplar of 'export-led growth' in the 1980s, there was still great progress yet to be made in the mid-1990s. But China had been interested in joining the global trading regime since it first requested observer status at the WTO's predecessor — the General Agreement on Tariffs and Trade (GATT) secretariat — in 1980. China joined the multi-fibre agreement that regulated global trade in textiles in 1984, and in July 1986 China requested full status as a GATT contracting party.

China's GATT application was an early example of close practical cooperation between China and Australia in support of both countries' economic transformations. Australia had been encouraging China to join GATT from late 1985, and provided an advisor to China's Ministry of Foreign Economic Relations and Trade from 1986 to 1987 to assist in preparing the application. A GATT working party considered China's application from 1987 to 1996, and was concerned about many Chinese policies that remained as a legacy of the planned economy. These included then-high tariff barriers (averaging above 35 per cent), lack of transparency or uniformity in customs requirements, the absence of opening up of China's financial sector to foreign competition, subsidies for SOEs, as well as a lack of currency convertibility, labour standards and intellectual property rights enforcement.

BOX 6.6: CHINA'S ACCESSION TO THE WTO

At the Osaka APEC Summit in 1995, China committed unilaterally to one of the largest single trade liberalisations, as bona fides of its intention on the way to WTO accession. The Chinese premier visited the United States for negotiations in April 1999, and the presidents of both countries met at the Auckland APEC summit in September that year. Final bilateral negotiations between the premier and the American ambassador in Beijing resulted in a 250-page agreement that paved the way for China's full accession. All the while, Australian advisers worked closely with Chinese officials on the substance and tactics of achieving WTO membership (Garnaut 2005).

China's accession to full membership of the WTO in 2001 reduced the tariff barriers facing Chinese exporters, fuelling a boom in what had already been a fast growing sector. In 1980, China's share of global manufacturing exports was just 0.8 per cent. By 2001 it was already 5.2 per cent. Following WTO accession, China's share of global manufacturing exports grew by 1 percentage point per year, making China the source of 18 per cent of world manufacturing exports by 2014. This was not only beneficial for consumers of low-cost Chinese manufacturing products worldwide, but also a boon for raw materials suppliers such as Australia (Anderson et al 2014).

Just as significant as the growing market for Chinese exports was the external anchor that China's accession protocol provided for China's own domestic reforms. Commitments to phase out government subsidies for loss-making SOEs hardened the budget constraint in the state sector, improving SOE efficiency and therefore generating significant welfare gains over and above the trade policy effects. Commitments on transparency, intellectual property, finance and environmental protection also supported China's development (Bajona and Chu 2015).

Accepting WTO disciplines did not mean going against China's national policy interests. SOE reform, for example, was already well under way, with thousands of small and inefficient SOEs being closed well before WTO entry (Zhang and Freestone 2013). Nevertheless, by working towards and committing to standards in an international agreement, the WTO provided China's leaders with an external anchor with which to consolidate existing gains and to push for future reforms.

International commitments, from this perspective, are not 'concessions' that a country gives up in order to secure benefits elsewhere, but rather serve to secure the benefits that are delivered at home from win–win cooperation with international partners and institutions through which all countries can thrive (Sachs et al 1995). This is the philosophy that underpins a joint Australian and Chinese economic transformation.

While developing countries were allowed some leeway in meeting full GATT obligations before joining, the United States was reluctant to allow China to join either the GATT or the WTO until all these concerns had been addressed. Indeed, the protocols of China's accession to the WTO (for example on export controls) were in some respects stricter than those applying to existing members (Box 6.6). Rather than change policies suddenly and risk immense social disruption, China continued its policy of gradual and pragmatic liberalisation. Economic leaders in China saw the opportunity to prosecute China's domestic reform agenda by using WTO requirements to force change in sectors that resisted opening to competition, and so pledged reforms in these areas in exchange for US agreement.

Managing risk

All the risks that business and countries face in other markets are susceptible to amelioration by a range of strategies. Commercial risk, associated with uncertainty about future prices or incomes, can be managed by contracting and exchange hedging strategies, and importantly by investment in the acquisition of market knowledge (Box 6.7). Through international agreement or treaty, governments can provide protection against capricious policy behaviour that increases economic risks.

The Australia–China relationship has been built around enshrining market principles in the two countries' bilateral and global approach to trade, investment and finance, and working to remove impediments to the operation of market forces so as to improve the efficiency of commercial exchange and therefore enhance growth prospects.

Yet business relies on access to information about, and analysis of, the events and trends that influence the formation of efficient market outcomes, and nowhere is this more the case than in the discovery and development of new and prospective markets. Governments are one source of information and analysis, but building reliable and independent centres of analysis in universities and think tanks, which can inform firms of trends and developments likely to affect market outcomes, provides another important source. The Comprehensive Strategic Partnership for Change should encourage investment in national centres of excellence in analysis to support understanding of the forces that will shape the development of the economic relationship between Australia and China in its regional and global settings. That will ensure it has the necessary intellectual underpinnings to thrive.

In Australia, the ANU houses one of the strongest concentrations of research expertise on the Chinese economy outside of China. Each year its China Economy Program (CEP) publishes a peer-reviewed edited volume of international research on the Chinese economy — the China Update series — and hosts a major conference that brings together Chinese, Australian and international academics and policymakers to discuss its findings. Yet even the CEP would need to be significantly strengthened into a truly national endeavour — through cooperation and research collaboration with official agencies in Australia and China as well as through routine links with other centres of research in Australia and internationally — if it were to play a lead role in implementing a strategic research agenda that connects its bi-national economic scholarship directly to the practical advancement of the economic transformation occurring between the two countries.

The important role that independent academic interlocutors can play in reinforcing the validity of market approaches on both sides is revealed in the communication breakdowns, institutional confusion and resultant mistrust that characterised the explosion of the price boom in iron ore exports from Australia to China from around 2007 to 2012.

The CEP in Australia could appropriately serve as a foundation for a network of research capacity, due to its existing work and its deep connections to equivalent Chinese centres such as the National School of Development at Peking University, Renmin University's National Academy of Development and Strategy, the Chinese Academy of Social Sciences and the Center for China and Globalization. Processes such as those set in motion by this collaboration between CCIEE and EABER can add momentum and direction to these efforts.

BOX 6.7: DELIVERING PROSPERITY AND SECURITY THROUGH THE MARKET

In the early 2000s, the global market for iron ore had to adjust to a large positive demand shock from China, which required enormous amounts of iron ore to build the housing and infrastructure needed to sustain rapidly expanding urbanisation and industrialisation. As international supply struggled to keep up with soaring Chinese demand, and high-cost marginal producers in China and other countries entered the market to fill the supply gap, the price of iron ore was pushed up to record-high levels by 2011.

The magnitude of the increase in iron ore prices, led some to suspect that the 'Big Three' major intra-marginal iron ore suppliers — Rio Tinto and BHP Billiton in Australia and Vale in Brazil — were taking advantage of China's iron ore shortage by engaging in strategic supplier oligopolistic behaviour to extract super-normal profits. Natural constraints on the expansion of iron ore production caused a short-run supply gap following the surge in China's iron ore demand, combined with pre-existing market conditions and delayed price signalling.

The iron ore market adjusted to the demand shock in a competitive way in the longer run. Up until 2009, the global iron ore price was set by a benchmark pricing system, which involved direct negotiations between contract holders — for example Australian suppliers and Chinese buyers — and delivered internationally competitive pricing outcomes. In 2009, the state China Iron and Steel Association (CISA) intervened in annual iron ore price negotiations by threatening to boycott Big Three iron ore imports unless a below-market price was agreed. This intervention failed because Chinese importers were dependent on Big Three supplies, the intervention was therefore not supported by the central government or by the steel business, and the threat could not be enforced because of the competitive nature of the domestic industry and the international market.

This episode created unnecessary tensions in the bilateral economic and political relationships. It also led to the collapse of the benchmark pricing system, which was replaced by a spot market pricing system. This change altered how bilateral quasi-rents from geographic closeness were distributed between Chinese and Australian iron ore traders. In the first 21 months after the switch to the spot market price mechanism, Australian exporters received, on average, a gain of around US$288.3 million per month, as compared to what they would have received under the 2008 pricing system. The division of bilateral quasi-rents is a zero-sum scenario, meaning Australia's US$288.3 million average gain per month meant that China's iron ore importers from Australia lost US$288.3 million per month. For context, during this period, China's steel industry made an average profit of US$1.1 billion per month (Hurst 2016).

The Australian and Chinese systems would have profited during this earlier phase of economic transformation from having direct policy access to an independent centre of economic research excellence that was dedicated to furthering bilateral relations based on market principles.

Policy uncertainty and its impact on businesses and whole economies is never absent, even between countries that have the most familiar and institutionally similar market structures, and even when governments have a range of macroeconomic instruments and policy settings to cushion against unexpected shocks from other economies while preserving the gains from exchange. These macroeconomic instruments notably include flexible exchange rates, sound macroeconomic policy strategies, and access to reserves and international support from the IMF or major economic partners.

High volatility on the Chinese stock market and the slowing headline growth figures are sources of uncertainty. Also, some of the public reactions to economic news from China is noise and could affect short-term decision-making. But reasoned commentary that is informed by close working relationships at the official level and serious independent analysis — for example, of the role of key developments in each country such as stock market variability or market developments — are essential to balanced and measured responses to events that prevent market and policy stakeholders in each country from being diverted by non-significant signals and misreading underlying trends.

A new and rapidly expanding partnership requires private and public investment in developing knowledge, literacy and understanding both to maximise opportunities and to protect against risks.

An Australia–China Comprehensive Strategic Partnership for Change

When the Australian prime minister visited China in April 2013, the two countries announced that they had established a 'Strategic Partnership'. They agreed to have regular meetings between the Chinese president and the Australian prime minister and to hold three high-level annual bilateral dialogues: a Leaders' Meeting between the Australian prime minister and the Chinese premier; a Strategic Economic Dialogue between the Australian treasurer and trade minister and the chairman of the NDRC; and a Foreign and Strategic Dialogue between the Australian and Chinese foreign ministers. In November 2014, when China's president visited Australia and met with the Australian prime minister, bilateral ties were upgraded to a 'Comprehensive Strategic Partnership'.

This diplomatic nomenclature is not unique to Australia, but is part of the 'partnership diplomacy' that is the foundation of China's 'non-alignment policy' in international affairs. To be a 'partner' of China requires a level of mutual trust, an absence of fundamental differences on the major issues of territorial sovereignty such as Tibet, Xinjiang and Taiwan, and an importance to China in strategic, security or economic issues. Of the more than 170 countries that have diplomatic relations with China, less than 60 are 'partners'. Unlike alliance relationships, China's partnership relations are announced in joint statements rather than enshrined in treaties.

China's partnerships mostly fall into four categories, which in order of ascending importance are: cooperative partnerships; comprehensive cooperative partnerships; strategic partnerships; and comprehensive strategic partnerships. The term 'comprehensive' indicates that a country collaborates with China across a broad range of spheres, including politics, economics, culture and military affairs. The term 'strategic' signifies that a country works with China at a high level on issues of common interest that have a global dimension and which impact the overall blueprint of each country's international policymaking. Strategic partners are considered to be reliable colleagues and to share similar strategic objectives in transnational arenas. Countries tend to start at lower levels and work their way up over a period of many years.

In this ranking, China already recognises the strategic importance of relations with Australia. Yet China has 'comprehensive strategic partnerships' with over 20 other countries, including countries that are seemingly of far less economic, political and strategic consequence to China, such as Algeria and Peru. Indeed, certain countries of special importance for China have their own unique classification within China's partnership diplomacy. Russia is a 'comprehensive strategic coordination partner'. Pakistan is an 'all-weather strategic cooperative partner'. The Indo-China Peninsula states of Vietnam, Laos, Cambodia, Myanmar and Thailand are 'comprehensive strategic cooperative partners'. Germany is an 'all-around strategic partner'. The United Kingdom and China recently declared a unique 'global comprehensive strategic partnership for the 21st century'. For various reasons, neither the United States nor Japan is part of China's formal 'partnership' system.

Given the developments in the relationship and its prospects, Australia and China should now contemplate upgrading their partnership to a unique 'Comprehensive Strategic Partnership for Change'. This would send an important high-level message that Australia and China extend trust to each other as partners in a working relationship that aims for substantial change towards significant mutually agreed goals and objectives. Already, only much larger countries such as the United States, the United Kingdom, Russia and Germany have an equal or greater level of regular interaction with the Chinese political leadership. Australia's placing in China's partnership system shows that both the Australian and Chinese polities recognise how important the other country is to the other. Now is the time to convert this bilateral understanding and existing bilateral dialogues into closer economic and political cooperation.

Bilateral political meetings are part of a process of developing understanding and trust, improving policy coordination and creating norms of consultation between Australia and China. These are crucial both to capitalising on bilateral policy arrangements such as ChAFTA, and to establishing confidence in being able to communicate during situations where there are difficulties in the relationship or crises to be managed. Importantly, as partners for change, both Australia and China will work across a range of priority areas on a common language for framing and advancing bilateral relations, and entrenched procedures for notifying the other side about upcoming policy announcements and developments that affect mutual interests. This ensures, as far as possible, that there are 'no surprises'. Frequent high-level political leadership meetings, frequent senior bureaucratic meetings, and deep levels of working relationships characterised the rapid development of bilateral relations in the 1980s, and they are the key to success in the relationship in all its dimensions in the decade ahead.

The revitalising visit by the Chinese vice-premier to Australia in October 2009 set the tone for the future relationship. That visit followed two difficult years in the bilateral relationship (Australian Centre on China in the World 2015): Australia's then prime minister referenced human rights problems in Tibet during a speech at Peking University; Australia's 2009 Defence White Paper ignited controversy by concluding that China's military modernisation could be 'cause for concern' and was 'beyond the scope of what would be required for a conflict over Taiwan'; Chinalco's bid for an increased stake in Rio Tinto fell through; a Rio employee was arrested in China on bribery charges; and a Uighur leader visited Australia. Yet Australia and China agreed on a 'blueprint for the further development of China–Australia relations' and this visit is widely credited with laying a new foundation for stable bilateral ties and improved political relations. It led to an 'Australia–China Joint Statement', in which both sides agreed that 'stronger practical cooperation for mutually beneficial outcomes serves the fundamental interests of the two countries', and committed to 'sustain and enhance their dialogue, engagement and cooperation at all levels, including the senior leadership level' (Australian Embassy China 2009). This outcome is an exemplar for the future of the bilateral relationship.

A new partnership for change between Australia and China that supports the economic transformation in both countries can only work if institutions and arrangements are jointly put in place to sustain regular engagement and targeted policy initiatives that are ahead of the curve of reform. These institutions can aim at entrenching a culture of cooperation within the relationship, both from the top-down through political leadership and from the bottom-up through official and private initiatives, and through combinations of both.

As the Australian prime minister said in 2013, 'new architecture will not do the work for us or make hard problems in our relationship easy', but 'what it will do is elevate our existing habits of dialogue and cooperation' (Kenny 2013). Australia and China can give substance to their Comprehensive Strategic Partnership and signal commitment by raising it to a new and unique level.

A purely transactional approach to bilateral relations is in neither Australia nor China's interests. This is because, from its modern beginnings, the Australia–China relationship has been premised on both countries' ambitions for reform and change. From the opening of diplomatic relations to the prospects we have laid out for the decades ahead, managing change on a huge scale has been, and will continue to be, the premise of the success of the relationship. As this Report makes clear, this requires long-term commitments and institutions that help to frame common principles and reference points for progress in the relationship that help with the project of managing change, around all the uncertainties and risks that are its inevitable by-product. This change will bring prosperity and security not only to Australia and China but also to our region and the world.

In building new diplomatic architecture for the Australia–China relationship, it is instructive to examine the history of Australia–China cooperation, and particularly its high watermark in the 1980s (Garnaut 2005). Following the establishment of diplomatic relations in 1972, bilateral ties flourished, and with the launch of China's opening and reform phase from 1978 the level of political engagement and economic collaboration between the two countries reached a peak during the 1980s.

During the 1980s, East Asia was central to the international dimension of Australia's own economic reform; at the same time, China was opening up to the world through its first round of market reform. Australian political leaders and their advisers directed efforts to linking Australia's domestic reform process to that occurring in China. The foundations laid by high-level political visits, government visits, policy discussions, exchanges and joint working groups encouraged greater engagement by private business, state enterprise and other economic actors.

In the early 1980s, the Australian government recognised the enormous potential for bilateral economic benefits if China could grow its domestic economy rapidly and create transitional institutions that secured for foreign actors rules-based access to the Chinese market. This was seen as an important way to ensure that China exercised its growing future power through constructive multilateral dialogue.

The bedrock of the relationship during the 1980s was the personal interest of and exceptional access between top leaders. This closeness was due to the initiative of previous Australian prime ministers and sustained official commitment. In Beijing in February 1984, the Chinese premier suggested, and the Australian prime minister accepted, that the two countries should aim to create a 'model relationship', one where Australia–China relations became a model for how countries with different political and social systems and at different levels of economic development could interact.

During this time, China needed to open up to the world, and Australia wanted the credibility that could come from showing that it was acting consistently with its prescriptions for China. So while the 'model relationship' included the important qualifier that there would be no special privileges — just equal rights, treatment and access — both sides committed to implementing all promises and commitments made under the model relationship.

Economic relations were central to this model relationship. A strategic China Action Plan was developed following discussions between the Australian prime minister and the Chinese premier in 1983, and was agreed in Beijing in February 1984. It committed to advancing trade and investment in both directions. In Australia, the Plan set an objective of doubling the value of Australian exports to China within five years, and took into account China's desire to expand imports to Australia. The Plan's target was reached in only two years.

Under the Plan, Australia decided to maximise its impact in China by focusing engagement and government follow-through on a small number of industry sectors and Chinese provinces. The four key export sectors for Australia were: iron and steel, non-ferrous minerals and metals, wool and grain. In February 1984, Australia and China established a Joint Working

Group on Iron and Steel. Similar groups were formed for non-ferrous minerals and metals, and for wool, and China agreed to soften its grain self-sufficiency targets. China made its first two major overseas investments in Australia — a brownfield investment in the Portland aluminium smelter in Victoria and a riskier greenfield investment in the Mt Channar iron ore mine in Western Australia.

The Plan significantly reduced commercial risks for Australian enterprises dealing with China by providing high-level political support for major projects, establishing working relationships and conducting regular visits with key officials in target areas, obtaining information regarding the project and reform priorities of provincial and local governments, and making introductions between firms and relevant officials.

Australia invested considerable effort in creating business and public sector capacity for analysing the trade, investment and other opportunities in the China relationship. Australian diplomatic officials strived to understand complex decision-making structures and built effective relationships with the large number of Chinese policymakers with effective veto power over reforms. The Australian Embassy was able to help obtain authoritative responses to major Australian business proposals. Australia and China worked together closely on cultural exchanges, immigration normalisation and regional nuclear non-proliferation.

Although it was recognised towards the end of the decade that, as China became more powerful and its ties with the major industrial countries expanded, it would be increasingly difficult for Australia to sustain the structure of its relationship with China, the Australia–China relationship continued to have a special if diminished place in both countries' diplomacy. Competition increased as other countries sought to participate in China's economy. Inflationary booms and growth corrections in both countries in the late 1980s shifted attention from international to domestic markets, and several major players shelved their bilateral investment plans. The reform pace of the Chinese economy slowed for a variety of reasons, creating uncertainty for business.

Three decades later, looking back at the foundations of the Australia–China economic relationship gives insight into what is needed for future success in the relationship. High-level political commitment is essential, as is high-level bureaucratic support. Bi-national collaboration on reform and change is critical. Strategic frameworks, such as the Comprehensive Strategic Partnership for Change, will be vital to setting the pathway forward.

Both Australia and China aspire to be leaders in economic reform and can support each other in this common objective. An upgraded and unique bilateral architecture aligns both with the Australian government's commitment to an 'Ideas Boom' under its National Innovation and Science Agenda and with the Chinese government's prioritisation of innovation in its 13th Five Year Plan.

The next phase of the two countries' relationship needs to build on established trust around shared and common interests in their economic and political relationships, manage the uncertainties and risks from change, and develop deeper, up-close commercial and business engagement as the structure of the economic relationship shifts towards services and consumers. It will flourish all the more if both countries succeed in continuing to nurture in their societies a culture of cosmopolitan human capital that is literate in the business, society and discourse of the other country.

Dialogues

Top-level political leadership meetings signal, and ideally improve, the overall tenor of the Australia–China relationship. They normally occur only once each year, although there is scope for significant additional contact on the margins of the many international leaders and key ministers meetings that now exist.

Since 2014, Australia and China have held two iterations of an annual 1.5-track dialogue known as the Australia–China High-Level Dialogue (HLD), which is a recasting of the 1.5-track Australia–China Forum held annually from 2011 to 2013. Representatives of government, business, academia, think tanks and non-profit organisations attend from both sides to 'consider the future shape and direction of the relationship' and 'how to deepen our ties across the breadth of our common interest and priorities' (Bishop 2015). Engaging a diversity of bilateral stakeholders in semi-official dialogue mechanisms is useful, but the HLD is broad and its focus diffuse, so it does not lead to concrete outcomes or conceptual advancements in bilateral relations. This is in keeping with the aim of the HLD to enhance mutual understanding and provide a platform for developing ideas for the relationship, but real progress requires sustained high-level attention married to intensive joint working arrangements between the relevant agencies associated with specific policy issues.

The government assists specific industries in bilateral engagement through the coordination of support across related government departments. For example, the Department of Agriculture and Water Resources administers an Australia–China Agricultural Cooperation Agreement (ACACA) for target groups in the agriculture, fisheries and forestry sectors that are looking to enhance cooperation and develop linkages with China. This agreement offers opportunities for Australian businesspeople to visit locations within China and to make business contacts that might otherwise not be possible. To enhance the value of the program for Australia, delegates are required to share key lessons and contacts from their visit with their broader industry.

The Australia–China Council (ACC), established by the Australian government in 1978 with the Secretariat located within DFAT, plays an important role in fostering bilateral cooperation and people-to-people relations by activities including funding Australia–China initiatives that broaden and strengthen Australia's engagement with China, Hong Kong, Macau and Taiwan in the ACC's priority areas of economic diplomacy, education, and arts and culture. The ACC has been at the forefront of establishing private sector linkages to support Australian studies through the creation of the Foundation for Australian Studies in China (FASIC), which supports the BHP Billiton Chair in Australian Studies at Peking University, along with a network of over 30 Australian Studies Centres in China.

The youth sphere is another area in which both sides, often with official support, have progressed the development of valuable bilateral dialogues and community organisations that help to connect young Australians and Chinese across disciplines and across linguistic divides. The Australia–China Youth Association (ACYA) is a volunteer organisation which promotes bilateral youth engagement and provides community, careers and education opportunities for over 5000 Australia and Chinese students and young professionals across more than 20 chapters in both Australia and Greater China. The Australia–China Youth Dialogue (ACYD) is a marquee annual event that brings together emerging Australia and Chinese leaders from different fields to forge ongoing professional networks and collaborations. The Australia–China Young Professionals Initiative (ACYPI) is the premier platform for young professionals in Australia and China to engage with the most significant issues of the bilateral relationship. The Australian government has invested in all of these initiatives, and their long-term benefit to the bilateral relationships will become more apparent as their alumni become the next generation of leaders in Australia and China.

The Australia–China business dialogue is primarily driven through the Australia China Business Council in China and the Australian Chambers of Commerce in China. These organisations are committed to advancing business and trade between Australia and China and do so through lobbying governments to remove barriers to bilateral commerce, providing business introductions and networks for members in both countries, and maintaining research programs that feed into events, advocacy and publications. The Australian government also runs a biennial Australia Week in China (AWIC) that coincides with state visits to China by the Australian prime minister. The AWIC involves a federal- and state-leader headed delegation of several hundred Australian businesses that participate in sector-specific programs of seminars, site visits, product showcases and networking events with Chinese firms and officials. These initiatives form a good basis for cooperation, but they would be improved through more bilateral involvement that commits senior Chinese business leaders to ongoing strategic cooperation.

BOX 6.8: MODELS OF BILATERAL COLLABORATION

Some models of productive bilateral collaboration in other areas that could be emulated in business and commercial affairs include:

The Australian Open: In 2015, the Australian Open tennis tournament, which has long positioned itself strategically as the 'Grand Slam of the Asia Pacific', signed a 'friendship agreement' with the Shanghai Rolex Masters to share resources and engage in joint promotional activities. China is a growing market for tennis participation, spectating and sponsorship, and there is already significant Chinese interest, attendance and marketing at the Australian Open. ANZ and Rolex are major sponsors of both tournaments, and the friendship agreement will enable staff exchange and combine the two events' platforms to promote bilateral tennis tourism. The 2016 Australian Open was 'launched' in Shanghai in October 2015. Additionally, the Australian Open has launched a WeChat account, opened an office in Hong Kong, signed agreements with 12 Asia Pacific broadcasters, and engaged China's only Australian Open champion, 2014 women's singles winner Li Na, as a brand ambassador.

The National Library of Australia (NLA): The NLA partnered with the National Library of China (NLC) to compile and curate the 'Celestial Empire: Life in China, 1644–1911' exhibition that showed exclusively at the NLA in Canberra from January to May 2016. The exhibition featured precious artefacts from China's last imperial dynasty that were displayed outside of China for the first time, as well as rarely seen treasures from the NLA's own Chinese collections. To complement the exhibition, the NLA also hosted a series of academic lectures and community educational activities to increase public interest in and understanding of China. The exhibition was also expected to boost tourism to the Australian Capital Territory (ACT). The NLA received promotional support from the ACT government, building on previous partnerships between the two entities, on the 15-year sister-city relationship between Canberra and Beijing, and on an NLA–NLC MoU agreed in 2012. The NLA also received support from the Australia-China Council and from a number of corporates, which were either building relationships with China or of Chinese origin and seeking to build their profile in Australia.

The Sydney Symphony Orchestra (SSO): Billing itself as 'the leading cultural ambassador for Australia', the SSO signed a MoU with the Shanghai Symphony Orchestra and the Shanghai Orchestra Academy in April 2015. The MoU formalises the commitment of each party to their ongoing relationships and will see regular performance tours between the two cities. The SSO will also provide mentoring and performance opportunities to Chinese students in Sydney in Shanghai. The SSO already has MoUs with China's National Centre for the Performing Arts, Guangzhou's Xinghai Conservatory of Music and the Guangzhou Opera House.

The business relationship does have a dedicated high-level dialogue mechanism in the Australia–China CEO Roundtable, which held its first meeting in 2010. The Roundtable meets on the side of leader-level state visits and discusses possibilities for deepening bilateral trade and investment. It is a worthy initiative but it might be of greater service to business engagement if there was effective inter-sessional pursuit of targeted agendas for enhancing business relationships and if there were a secretariat that could sustain a cooperation agenda and program of forward work. The Australia-China Senior Business Leaders' Forum, which is a purely business-to-business dialogue also provides another forum for corporate leaders to advance discussion and policy recommendations on bilateral challenges and opportunities on the occasion of Australia-China state visits.

The essence of a bilateral strategy should be to work together to achieve common objectives rather than having meetings for their own sake, and so the positive sentiment and resources behind the HLD might helpfully be deployed in more targeted ways. This could be achieved by holding a range of HLDs, each focused around bringing together bilateral counterparts in a particular area to deliver specific outcomes. A good model could be the Australia–Japan Public–Private Policy Dialogue (AJPPPD), an initiative of the Australia–Japan Business Cooperation Committee (AJBCC), which focuses specifically on promoting Australia–Japan infrastructure cooperation and has led to successful investments by Japanese firms in Australians infrastructure projects. The Australian–American Leadership Dialogue (AALD) also organises several events each year that focus on defined themes.

A number of successful official dialogues exist between Australia and China that could be a template for the many sub-components of an Australia–China Comprehensive Strategic Partnership for Change. The Australia–China Human Rights Dialogue, which was initiated in 1997, institutionalises official discussion of sensitive political issues in a structured, systematic and productive fashion. It provides a mechanism for raising specific and difficult issues in a quietly productive atmosphere, and seeks to resolve rather than draw attention to problems. In addition to supporting existing commitments, the Dialogue can be used to inform parties about future reform. The Dialogue also interacts with and complements the work and resolutions of multilateral human rights organisations, such as the UN, and works with NGOs. The Dialogue strengthens multilateral commitments while allowing Australia and China to discuss human rights in a collaborative setting and display a commitment to action in domestic medias. It also houses other relationship-building initiatives. The Human Rights

Technical Cooperation Program, which operates under the Dialogue, facilitates collaboration between the Australian Human Rights Commission and partner organisations in China, such as the All-China Women's Association and the Beijing Legal Aid Organisation.

Such Australia–China collaboration is an example of targeted cooperation that delivers specific objectives that have a broad appeal across the Australian and Chinese communities, and will therefore create a multiplier effect on broader bilateral ties. More strategically focused planning of official dialogues, and support for non-official dialogues, will form well-calibrated partnerships between Australians and Chinese at the forefront of economic transformations and social exchange that can better advance bilateral goals set at the political partnership level.

As well as the direct differences in cultural, institutional and political systems, there are additional questions of how governance systems impact on commercial exchange and what protocols and arrangements can be developed to help build understanding and trust between both countries.

Australia and China have a wide range of bilateral mechanisms including regular ministerial meetings, political exchanges, taxation agreements, disaster relief cooperation and cultural exchange programs. Increasingly targeted, strategic bilateral engagement in priority areas of economic transformation will increase trust, share knowledge of reform processes and implement practical collaborations that facilitate greater trade, investment and financial linkages in line with the direction of each country's transformation. Bilateral business councils, professional associations and forums build relationships between business leaders while providing a platform for sharing in-country expertise. High-level meetings in government and business encourage flows of people and ideas, and collaboration on policy outcomes.

Bilateral policy institutions such as the Australia–China SED bring together top ministerial-level policymakers to address a strategic agenda. The inaugural SED dialogue, held in 2014, focused on closer financial cooperation, advancing offshore renminbi market development, and highlighting areas of potential collaboration during the two countries' G20 and APEC host years. The following year, the dialogue specifically addressed investment opportunities in Northern Australia, including discussion of the prospective role of the AIIB.

Yet the most productive bilateral interaction is likely to be maintained within treaty frameworks because these regularise dialogue and objectives. For instance, there has not been a meeting of the Australia–China Human Rights Dialogue — which is not embedded in a treaty — in over two years, since the 15th meeting in February 2014.

The most important bilateral treaty currently in effect between Australia and China is ChAFTA. It locks in bilateral commitments to market opening and sets a definitive timetable for future consultations to further these reform commitments, thereby creating incentives for continuing dialogue and for finding cooperative solutions to opening up each other's economies.

The next step for Australia and China is to expand this closer relationship beyond just the economic realm through embedding the Comprehensive Strategic Partnership for Change.

Ironically, when China was a more closed economy and society, political system differences were clearer and engagement through trade and investment (involving directly state-owned entities) may seem to have been conducted in a more certain environment, albeit one that vastly limited the possibilities for exchange and investment. As China has become a more open and complex society, there appear to be more uncertainties and attendant risks. This is a 'quality' problem associated with greatly elevated openness and opportunities for business around the successful accretion of China's economic power. This circumstance requires engagement, not retreat, in order to take advantage of the new opportunities presented by China's increased opening on many fronts.

Bridging the distance

Political and institutional system differences can make it difficult for countries to develop the certainty and confidence necessary to commit to long-term policy endeavours and investment projects. In Australia, different systems of governance, perceptions of human rights, cultural values and regional security issues increase feelings of distance from China. In China, misreading the hostile attitudes of some in Australia to investment projects, lack of knowledge about how democratic systems work and doubts about regional security strategies similarly creates distance.

Australia and China have very different social traditions, systems of government and business cultures. Consequently, a most important aspect of improved bilateral relations and the successful realisation of a Comprehensive Strategic Partnership for Change is developing deeper relationships between Australian and Chinese people — whether they be political leaders, departmental officials, corporate employees, or communities of migrants, tourists, students and citizens. Initiating and consolidating these relationships requires mutual trust and a deep understanding of how the other country works. Improving this stock of human, social and cultural capital should be the goal of 'China literacy' for the Australian system and the goal of 'Australia literacy' for the Chinese system. It is critical to be able to understand another country on its own terms — 'seeing out from the inside' as well as 'looking in from the outside' (Loubere 2016).

It is only through knowledge of the political institutions, economic system and sociocultural circumstances of the other country that a bilateral strategic partnership can fulfil its potential. This means that more people on both sides must be able to speak the other country's language, understand the other country's thinking and contemporary debates, and be able to contribute to the national life of the other country. This will require significant investment in education, realignment of bureaucratic, corporate and non-profit career paths, and the deepening of interactions between the peoples of Australia and China.

Presently, Australia's assets for understanding China are less well developed than they will need to be. While Australia may have been highly adept at exporting resources to China, building a commensurate relationship in manufactures and services will depend on greater China capabilities. While resources trade relies on the 'hardware' of extraction technology and transportation infrastructure, manufacturing and services trade is dependent on the 'software' of sales, marketing and design. Without knowledge of the tastes, preferences, hopes and fears of another society, businesses are unable to effectively position themselves to take advantage of that market or efficiently use marketing and promotional resources.

This highlights the crux of the major problem that Australia faces: while it can provide more Chinese people with high-quality, English-language education, it cannot simply assume a linear rate of progress in other areas of Australia's services industries without addressing Australia's capacity to develop services expertise. There have been constant calls from within the business, policy, academic and education sectors for Australia to increase its 'China literacy' — a concept typically described as the knowledge and skills necessary to 'understand' China and navigate cross-cultural social and professional interactions.

The *Australia in the Asian Century White Paper* (2012) and bodies as diverse as Asialink, the Australian Industry Group, the Australian Public Service Commission and the Business Council of Australia have argued that there is an 'absence or underdevelopment of critical individual and organisational capabilities' on Asia. More Australian students are studying Chinese today than ever before, but most are of Chinese heritage. Authoritative reports tell us that Chinese classes are 'overwhelmingly a matter of Chinese teaching Chinese to Chinese' (Asia Education Foundation 2008). Excluding first language and heritage speakers, more Year 12 students study Latin than Chinese as a second language. A recent report estimates that there are less than 150 Australians of non-Chinese heritage who can speak Chinese fluently (Orton 2016). It would be sensible to resurrect and properly fund the recommendation of the Asian Century White Paper to provide Australian school students with continuous access to priority Asian languages throughout their education.

It is difficult to imagine how Australia can fully grasp China opportunities in the services sector without either encouraging the targeted immigration of skilled Chinese, without speaking Chinese, without understanding Chinese society and without knowing the Chinese regulatory environment. And the need of services firms for China (and Asia) literacy will only grow (BCG 2012). Logistics company Linfox notes that it 'faces the challenges of running a large, complex organisation in multiple geographies and cultures ... 12,000 of Linfox's 19,200 employees are now in Asia (only 13 are expatriates) and 20 different languages are spoken across the firm' (BCG 2012). All Australian firms need the services capacity to face challenges similar to those of Linfox.

One, often underexplored part of this problem, comes down to business. If business wants a workforce with China skills (or 'China literacy'), business needs to create a market for this workforce. It is estimated that, the resources sector aside, Australia could lift its economic performance with Asia by up to A$275 billion over the next 10 years by improving Asia capabilities (Asialink 2012). The Australian Department of Industry, Innovation and Science has mandated Asialink Business as Australia's National Centre for Asia Capability, to support Australian organisations to develop the knowledge and networks needed to engage with Asian markets, including China. It has made progress towards cultivating a more China capable workforce through initiatives such as the China Country Starter Pack to fill the gap in China information available to Australian businesses and training over 5000 professionals across the country annually.

Even today, very few managers in Australia have developed the time-consuming specialist language, cultural and analytical skills that are necessary to be China-literate. Another shift has to come in how graduates are recruited at the entry-level of business and public service. Very few jobs ask for specialist China-literate skills, focusing instead on 'generalist' skills. But the higher the proportion of China-literate senior leaders, the more likely businesses (or policy agencies) will perform above expectations. With this in mind, Australia needs to think about how to best use the China skills that it already possesses. For example, a starting point would be to provide young Australians in industry, government and other professional careers with pathways that allow them to maintain and improve their China skills.

China literacy is not determined either solely or even necessarily at all by one's level of Chinese-language proficiency. Perhaps even more importantly within the ranks of corporate leadership is an understanding of how to do business in China, where personal networks and influence is key to building trust with potential partners. A former Australian ambassador to China has opined that the most important aspect of China-literacy for Australian businesses is investing high-level time and effort in maintaining relationships with commercial partners and government officials through visiting China and through inviting Chinese partners to spend time in Australia, as well as putting serious resources into training and retaining appropriate bicultural talent (Raby 2011).

It is true, of course, that Australian and Chinese firms operate a market for China literacy, and this can be assumed to be working — these businesses will structure their hiring and management practices as needed to attract the necessary talent. But the ambitions of Australian and Chinese companies in this area are constrained by the supply of bicultural and bilingual workers that emerge from each education system. It is in relation to public institutions such as schools that governments have a role to play in investment in China-literacy and Australia-literacy as a public good.

An asset that appears underutilised is the language and cultural skills of many people of Chinese descent living in Australia. Of 22 million Australians counted in the 2011 Census, close to one million had some form of Chinese ancestry. Australians with Chinese heritage comprise 4 per cent of the total population and 44 per cent of the Asian Australian population, with Sydney and Melbourne the major centres of concentration of Chinese Australians. Since 2011, mainland China has been the largest source of permanent migrants to Australia, and there are now 319,000 Australian residents who were born in mainland China — the third-largest foreign-born ethnic group — as well as 75,000 born in Hong Kong, 25,000 born in Taiwan and 2000 born in Macau. Mandarin Chinese is the second-most-spoken language in Australia after English. Yet Chinese and other Asian Australians are underrepresented in professional and leadership positions — Australians of Asian ancestry comprise only 1.7 per cent of parliamentarians, 3 per cent of company executives and 3.8 per cent of public service leaders. The analysis at this point suggests there might be a 'bamboo ceiling' that needs to be broken if Australia is to call itself Asia-literate (Soutphommasane 2014).

There is also underdeveloped 'Australia-literacy' in China. Australia has its own institutional, legal, political, social and cultural system that has to be understood in order to be navigated by foreign commercial entities. While China's foreign linguistic capabilities and international trade integration are more extensive than Australia's, many Chinese entities are unfamiliar with how to do business in relation to Australia's democratic political system, regulatory, labour, environmental and economic policies, as well as its social norms and practices. This means that there are great opportunities for Australian financial, legal and business service-providers to work productively with Chinese enterprises trading and investing in Australia. Chinese business and government also need to recognise the benefit of investing at all levels in understanding unique Australian characteristics. For example, Australians' discomfort with the idea of a larger Chinese economic presence in Australia will be ameliorated by the efforts of Chinese investors that are Australia- and community-literate.

While individuals and even groups may invest in serious bicultural literacy, Australia and China cannot be expected to become productively literate in each other's society without high-level political advocacy and encouragement. The Comprehensive Strategic Partnership for Change should create a properly resourced bi-national commission that would, among its larger goals, assist in promoting institutional exchanges across schooling, university, business and government that are linked to a strategic agenda for incentivising improvements to bicultural literacy and business capabilities.

These perceptions are revealed in various measures of distance between the countries and in polling data that suggest how close countries feel towards each other. These data reveal variations over time, but they show that Australians have a high degree of respect for China's achievements and status, and that Chinese have a warm regard for Australia's openness and role in the region. Despite system differences, Australia and China have a history of high-level, strategic cooperation and outstanding achievement in policy cooperation, from the early opening of the resource trade through to China's accession to the WTO, the recent negotiation of ChAFTA and their close cooperation in G20 affairs.

BOX 6.9: REGIONAL SECURITY AND THE AUSTRALIA–CHINA RELATIONSHIP

Both countries have a core interest in a secure region that provides a stable foundation for advancing international commerce and increasing prosperity. Both countries recognise the need for the regional order to continue to adapt and evolve to ensure this, in a way that respects and upholds the security and influence of all countries in the region.

Australia has relied on the United States for its defence since the wartime agreements of 1942 and has maintained a formal military alliance with the United States since the Australia, New Zealand and United States Security Treaty (ANZUS) was signed in 1951. The military alliance between Australia and the United States includes a mutual security commitment. It also includes intelligence sharing arrangements. There has been a longstanding, bipartisan commitment in Australian politics to this arrangement, it has wide public support and it is unlikely to change. This alliance relationship does not preclude cooperation with China in areas of shared interest.

While political and security relations can sometimes cut across economic interests, the foundation of a Comprehensive Strategic Partnership for Change is the long-term national interests of both countries. A current security issue of prominence in the region is conflicting territorial claims made in the South China Sea and the East China Sea. This Report has no role in weighing up these claims or their resolution, but it is in the shared economic interests of all parties to see the settlement of any disputes amicably and to ensure that the region remains open to trade.

In tandem with the technical advances and development of China's economy, its People's Liberation Army (PLA) has invested in a program of military development and modernisation. Recent investments in aircraft carriers, submarines, long-range missiles and an emerging 'blue water' navy have increased China's capabilities and ability to influence the region and beyond. Even in the context of a 'peaceful rise', it is to be expected that China will take steps to protect its own access to global trade, and to contribute to the security of its citizens and investments abroad.

China's emergence as a regional military power creates a potential strategic rival for the United States in the region. Under certain contingencies involving military conflict, Australia's alliance commitments might be invoked. Australia has already increased the number of

US forces rotating through Australia as part of the American 'Rebalance to Asia' strategy. The Australian government believes that 'any disruption to key regional sea-lanes and to Australia's ability to trade would have a fundamental impact on our nation' (Hurley 2014).

But Australia's alliance with the United States does not preclude security cooperation with China. Australia has the closest defence relationship with China of any of the United States' English-speaking allies. In December 2015, Australia hosted the 18th round of the official Australia–China Defence Strategic Dialogue in Canberra. This remarkable record of dialogue on military matters is a key asset for navigating not only bilateral defence relations but also, potentially, the future of regional security.

Regular bilateral exchanges take place between the Australian Defence Force and the PLA, including high-level officer visits, naval ship visits, strategic policy forums, humanitarian relief drills, cultural exchanges and an overarching Australia–China Defence Engagement Plan. In July 2014, PLA Navy vessels operated under Australian command during US-led 'Rim of the Pacific' naval drills, and Australia hosts an annual US–China–Australia trilateral military exercise in Northern Australia called Exercise Kowari. The Australian government is committed to continuing the development of its defence relations with China. Australia and China could demonstrate their respective commitments to transparent regional security cooperation by strengthening bilateral integration of their global peacekeeping and disaster relief forces.

Australia and China can build on this foundation of cooperation by working with other regional countries in existing forums like the ASEAN Defence Ministers' Meeting Plus and the East Asian Summit as well as in new multilateral policy dialogues on regional security issues.

The Comprehensive Strategic Partnership for Change recognises that regional politics are undergoing enormous change. This change needs to occur in a peaceful and progressive manner where no one country dominates another, and all states, large and small, are able to express their views and contribute to common security objectives. Australia and China can play vital roles in leading regional dialogue and brokering security, with their partnership as a vehicle for promoting regional security initiatives (Australian Centre on China in the World 2015).

Managing uncertainties

Learning how to make the Australian and Chinese systems work together in the process of enormous change and reform is crucial to the vitality of the Australia–China relationship. The different natures of the Australian and Chinese systems impact on economic uncertainty and risk directly; they play into how the two countries conduct their political and diplomatic relations, and these affairs ultimately affect the depth of their economic relations (Box 6.9). The principles and understandings that both countries articulate, and are guided by, in managing these differences have been, and remain, central to the success of their relationship. That is why the development of their Comprehensive Strategic Partnership for Change is important as the overarching framework for the relationship.

Change in the political and global order highlights the special importance of clarity in each country's approach to regional security affairs. (This issue is discussed in detail in Chapter 7.) Australia's alliance relationship with the United States and China's understanding of that relationship provides a foundation for their own pursuit of closer bilateral security and military exchanges. Giving priority to the development of these ties across a wider range of traditional and non-traditional areas of security must be an active part of the agenda of the Comprehensive Strategic Partnership for Change and will serve indirectly to reduce economic risk.

More importantly, the foundations of trust (Box 6.10) that Australia and China already bring to their economic relationship, provides a base for them to work with their partners in the region, such as Japan, the ASEAN countries, South Korea and India to take initiatives towards addressing issues of common concern that have the potential to contribute significantly to enhancing regional economic and political security (see Chapter 7).

BOX 6.10: BUILDING POLICY TRUST

The elevation of the Australia–China bilateral relationship to a Comprehensive Strategic Partnership for Change requires a high level of trust between the two governments. The Partnership provides a base for expanding common ground for cooperation at the same time as managing risks, including policy and system difference risks. The foundations of a high level of trust reside with officials of both countries — in their professional capabilities, their in-depth knowledge of each other's systems and their being culturally savvy. These capabilities and familiarities are essential to good judgment about policy intention, confidence in engagement and avoiding inadvertently harmful actions.

Australia and China have already come a long way in laying the foundation for confident high-level government-to-government engagement, with many steps already taken by both governments and central economic agencies in establishing strong institutional and official-to-official links. One example is the relationship between the Australian Treasury and China's NDRC. Australia's was the first Treasury of a Western country to set up an office within their Beijing Embassy, in 1993. The Australian Treasurer and the NDRC Chairman signed a MoU in 2008, which provided the institutional framework to guide the development of the agency-to-agency relationship in following years. The NDRC Chairman and the Treasurer have since met annually at Macroeconomic Dialogues to discuss global developments as well as macroeconomic policies and reform challenges in each country. Officials of the two agencies have paid frequent visits and engaged on a range of macroeconomic and structural reform policy issues of direct relevance to the policy agendas in China and Australia. The Australian Treasury has organised an annual seminar series conducted by Treasury officials in China, directed to developing an understanding of Australia's economy and of Australian social and economic policy that is of relevance to China's reform policies.

Recognising the importance of China to Australia's prosperity as well as the complex and dynamic change taking place in the Australian economy, Australia's central economic agencies, including the Australian Treasury, the RBA, PM&C and DFAT, have invested in developing skills and capacity for better understanding the Chinese economy and developing a more effective policy engagement with China. A strong motivation for this endeavour is that improved China knowledge, skills and capacity will enhance China policy and the benefits from the relationship for both countries.

These beginnings provide the foundation for the engagement that will be needed to manage and develop a more sophisticated relationship over the coming decade. The proposed Australia–China (Ao–Zhong) Commission, through its promotion of high-level exchanges, can assist in this. Existing institutional links demonstrate, however, that central economic agencies in both countries can profitably expand their ties. This Report, which has enjoyed the blessing of both the Australian and Chinese governments, is an example of effective working cooperation at the highest level between the two countries. The commitment by the Australian Treasury to support a follow-up project, to enhance Australian understanding of China's economic policy and engagement with Chinese policymakers, is a further useful step in this direction.

Policy and institutional innovation

In all these areas, there is need for innovation in institutional mechanisms that will facilitate familiarity and understanding of motivations and intentions at the highest levels of policymaking, cooperation at the working level in policy development between governments, and investment in the human capital and collaborative policy infrastructure on both sides.

There is a broad and vast array of exchanges that occur within the Australia–China relationship. They span academia, the arts, business, culture, defence, economics, politics, science and security. Strengthening and encouraging these exchanges will be vital to success with the relationship in the coming decades.

The Comprehensive Strategic Partnership for Change can provide an overarching framework for long-term, high-level engagement that brings the countries closer by working together to advance articulated strategic objectives across all aspects of the relationship. It would enable the Australia–China relationship to become a model of how countries with different political and social systems and at different levels of development can collaborate to enhance collective welfare. Progress with deepening the Comprehensive Strategic Partnership for Change would build stronger holistic networks between the Australian and Chinese systems, rather than only disparate sectors, and this will in turn forge bilateral partnerships directed at realising particular opportunities and managing specific risks.

The future of the Australia–China relationship is best guaranteed through strong institutional arrangements and through an entrenched culture of cooperation between the two countries. The Australian and Chinese leaderships can encourage and promote a range of official, political, business and community initiatives in both countries to define and fulfil the potential of an enhanced Comprehensive Strategic Partnership for Change.

The Australia–China Comprehensive Strategic Partnership for Change would:

- underline both countries' commitment to mutual trust;
- institutionalise their dialogues on strategic objectives and work programs on economic reforms and policy change;
- build bi-national capacity to support the new economic engagement; and
- lay the basis for deeper political cooperation.

The Partnership will entrench deeper and broader dialogues and cooperation across the relevant ministries and departments. It will be served by joint working groups on reform drawn from the national government, state and provincial officials, business, the military, research leaders, academia and the broader community. It will foster joint training and the development of long-term working associations in key areas between the officials of both countries. It will develop joint protocols for working together on bilateral, regional and global concerns.

Australia–China (Ao–Zhong) Commission

Beyond high-level official and semi-official exchanges, a major bi-national effort to upgrade the breadth and depth of exchanges is needed to support the development of the Comprehensive Strategic Partnership for Change. This effort needs to match the character and depth of exchanges that Australia has with other major partners, such as the United States. A model, on which Australia and China could build and extend, is the Australian–American Fulbright Commission, which is a non-profit organisation that was founded by a treaty between Australia and the United States. Core funding of a new Australia–China (Ao–Zhong) Commission should come from both national governments equally. But the Commission should also be open to approving and managing programs sponsored by state government agencies, business, academic institutions and personal bequests, as well as by both national governments. The Commission would be independently governed by persons of standing in both communities and protect the development of exchanges against particular influence or favour (Drysdale and Zhang 2016).

The Fulbright Commission coordinates educational partnerships and funds academic scholarships with a focus on developing 'long-lasting, productive bilateral relations, partnerships and connections between Australia and the US' (Australian–American Fulbright Commission 2016). However, a truly comprehensive and strategic Australia–China collaboration framework would extend beyond educational cooperation by also advancing and finding synergies between political, official, subnational, business and cultural exchanges and partnerships.

The Commission would further mutual understanding through educational and cultural exchange between the two countries. A crucial part of this program will be the development of deep networks between Australian and Chinese people across all areas of the relationship through the pooling of significant private resources into a public framework. Its importance could be symbolised by the two heads of government serving as dual honourary patrons. It would have three main purposes.

First, the Commission would foster high-quality research and academic exchange. The goal of this cooperation would be to increase the bi-national human capital across Australian and Chinese society, which will create deeper pools of talent from which to drive the bilateral relationship. Apart from scientific and research exchange, the Commission could support leadership in creating collaborative excellence in language and cultural education in primary, secondary and tertiary education systems through improved funding models, curriculum design, teacher training and attitudinal change. This would build into a version of the Australian–American Fulbright Commissions' model of public and privately sponsored postgraduate, postdoctoral, early-career researcher and senior academic exchanges, with a focus on building long-term partnerships for research, mentorship, scientific innovation and entrepreneurial commercialisation. The Commission would also leverage existing official initiatives such as Australia's New Colombo Plan and the Chinese Government Scholarships, and private initiatives such as the BHP Billiton Australia–China Scholarships and the Westpac Asian Exchange Scholarships.

Second, the Commission would foster policy exchanges. The goal of this cooperation would be to produce a cadre of political and government leaders in both countries who are familiar with the policymaking dynamics of the other country and have deep personal networks with their bilateral counterparts. There is positive experience with this through the programs that currently facilitate exchanges with China's Organisation Department through the Australia and New Zealand School of Government, and through the ANU's exchanges with the Central Party School. The deeper policy linkages that would result will sustain greater dialogue and more productive bilateral initiatives. The Commission can build on existing programs such as the National Parliamentary Fellowships Program and the National Government Fellowships to facilitate an extensive program of professional secondments and research fellowships for Australian and Chinese public servants and policymakers to either receive training in the regulatory workings of the other system or to work on targeted bilateral priority issues within the elite policy-shaping institutions and with the policy thought leaders of the other country. This would form a bilateral bridgehead between policymaking institutions and intellectual communities.

Third, the Commission would foster business and economic exchange. The goal of this cooperation would be to propel strategic collaboration on economic reform priorities that will help Australia and China to manage their respective transformations. This will be supported by the forward work agenda of this Report to undertake a comprehensive analysis of Australia and China's economic policymaking structures across all sectors and investigate how Australia and China should therefore best relate to each other across business, government and society. This project will be collaborative and serve to underpin Australian and Chinese economic engagement for the next decade. This research will become the platform for establishing the Commission and collaboration on similar institutions in different countries.

Across all of these sectors, the Commission would serve as an overarching framework that allows public and private actors in Australia and China to invest their resources in creating large-scale national programs of exchange for building talent in the pursuit of specific or general bi-national outcomes.

The Commission and the overall Comprehensive Strategic Partnership for Change are initiatives on which joint work can begin immediately for timely implementation by both sides. The process of planning, negotiating, launching and administering these arrangements, and the productive bilateral engagements and changes that they achieve, will lay the groundwork for Australia and China to upgrade their 'model' relationship over the longer-term into a bilateral treaty framework. This framework will cement political commitment to the relationship, institutionalise bilateral cooperation and perpetuate economic reform partnerships.

The common theme of bilateral collaboration across all sectors should be working together on joint initiatives with specific objectives and purposes towards outcomes that are a priority to both sides. Mobilised through the joint commitment of both governments, an expanding network of collaboration will constitute a truly strategic partnership for change. This partnership needs to be founded on deeper policy collaboration at all levels in developing the new bilateral relationship, defining joint interests in the regional economy, and strengthening the global economic system on the basis of inclusion and consensus.

CHAPTER 7
Australia and China in regional economic diplomacy

KEY MESSAGES

Australia and China face new challenges in Asia and the Pacific as a result of the changing structure of regional and global economic power. The economic and political rise of China is changing the regional as well as the global order. Regional economic interdependence now includes a wider group of economies, including India, and a wider range of issue areas. The established regional institutions and arrangements in East Asia and across the Pacific do not encompass all economies and were not set up to deal with the interaction between economic and political-security affairs, and there are gaps in coverage within the architecture for economic and political-security cooperation. These challenges require Australia and China to play an active role in forging a new consensus around the principles that will guide future regional cooperation. Over the past three decades, Australia's and China's economic integration into the regional and global economy has occurred within a framework that has been inclusive, has avoided arrangements that weaken the global system and has led political cooperation. The two countries can now direct their bilateral relationship toward these common regional and global objectives.

Australia and China should work with other partners in Asia and the Pacific to:

- Connect and extend existing regional arrangements, such as APEC and the EAS, so they can provide a platform to address the new priorities in regional cooperation.

- Initiate high-level political dialogue on cross-cutting issues that require close cooperation, including the environment, energy transformation and regional infrastructure investment.

- Mobilise a coalition to define the path forward in forging the TPP and RCEP into a Free Trade Area of the Asia Pacific (FTAAP) that strengthens the WTO and the global economic system. Consolidation of the TPP and RCEP may not be a practical objective in the medium term but finding ways to make both the TPP and RCEP inclusive and complementary is.

- Seek to establish a common framework for infrastructure investment and funding in the region. Currently many players are acting independently and at cross-purposes. Ministers and senior officials can meet to discuss priorities, strategies and mutual interests in infrastructure delivery to further regional connectivity. Such a regional forum might involve the AIIB, ADB, World Bank, country-specific institutions and recipient regional groupings such as ASEAN.

- Use ambitious bilateral initiatives to progress regional and global arrangements. China could use the investment chapter in ChAFTA to push for a higher quality investment chapter in RCEP and set the benchmark for other bilateral investment treaties. Australia and China can pioneer services sector opening, capitalising on Australia's potential role as a testing ground for wider domestic and regional liberalisation.

- Initiate a dialogue on the articulation of a common, plurilateral set of principles to govern foreign investment — both for facilitating investment before it is made and the treatment of investment once it has been implemented.

- Leverage the bilateral relationship to build cooperation in third countries in areas such as aid and development and infrastructure and connectivity.

- Further enhance bilateral security ties as an important step in creating effective working relationships on security issues among all countries in the region, thereby strengthening the foundation for political confidence and regional economic prosperity.

China and Australia are both integrated into the regional and global economy, and their bilateral relationship is nested in a highly integrated East Asian region. China is the centre of regional supply chains and its trade and investment expansion have been the driving forces of its rapid development and industrialisation. Going forward, regional trade and investment liberalisation and integration will continue to be key drivers of China's future economic development and reform. The share of East Asia in Australia's trade is one of the highest of any country in the world, with 66 per cent of Australia's trade taking place within East Asia (Figure 7.1). Moreover, Australia is a stable and secure supplier of energy and raw materials to China and the rest of Northeast Asia.

East Asia is one of the most economically integrated regions in the world — on par with Europe by a number of important measures. Economic cooperation has led political cooperation, and regional economic integration has been market-led rather than institution-led. As Asian economies have liberalised and opened up to regional and global trade, institutions have been created to help manage and secure these thickening and deepening economic relationships. Asian countries opened their economies to international competition within the global institutional frameworks and did so because they had growing confidence in the global trading system and the global economic order created after World War II around the Bretton Woods institutions.

Australia and China have also actively engaged in regional cooperation and institution-building as a way to promote economic development and reform at home, and to foster closer political cooperation in the wider Asian region. The relationship between Australia and China has developed in the context of deepening regional economic integration, and strengthening the bilateral relationship serves to foster broader regional cooperation. For both countries, economic cooperation has underpinned regional economic diplomacy and institution-building processes in Asia. Regional political and security cooperation, on the other hand, has been piecemeal and less comprehensive, but includes notable achievements, such as cooperative efforts on the Cambodian peace settlement and the United Nations Transitional Administration in East Timor.

The diversity within the Asia Pacific region — with countries having different economic and political systems, and being at different stages of development — demands a collaborative approach to regionalism. Regional cooperation has occurred on a voluntary basis where agreements were based on forging consensus and ordered around positive-sum economic interests. Importantly, the political and security relationships have been underpinned by the US alliance framework created after World War II, and US rapprochement with China since 1972.

The institutions that have furthered regional cooperation in Asia and the Pacific, including APEC, ASEAN and its Plus Three and Plus Six processes (including the subsidiary Chiang Mai Initiative), have done so largely on the basis of non-binding commitments and without the cession of sovereignty to any supranational regional authority. The establishment of these institutions was characterised by evolution, flexibility, consensus and voluntary participation, because of the differences in political and institutional systems in the economies around which they have been built. They have served to build political trust and cooperation among countries across a region in which previously there had been a substantial deficit in mechanisms through which that could be done. This model of cooperation constitutes an important institutional innovation that has proved valuable in other theatres, such as in the global G20 forum, which has a similar modus operandi.

Asian regionalism has therefore not proceeded at the expense of, or in a manner that undermines, global institutions. On the contrary, it has sought to complement and reinforce global institutions. That remains an overarching objective for both Australia and China in their approach to regional cooperation. The principle of open regionalism — that is, regional cooperation and integration that is open to the rest of the world and which reduces barriers to all states in a non-discriminatory fashion — on which Asia Pacific economic cooperation was built, has ensured that regional cooperation has strengthened, rather than detracted from, global cooperation.

But things are changing. The rapid pace of economic growth and integration in Asia is bringing about a more complex and multipolar order, and throwing up new economic and political-security challenges. A new regional consensus is needed to ensure that the principles upon which Asia's economic cooperation was built — open regionalism, consensus-driven cooperation and stable relations between the great powers — are not eroded. Australia and China are well placed to work together to forge this new consensus because they have successfully worked together in the past to foster regional economic cooperation on these same principles.

This chapter describes Australia and China's joint interests in regional economic diplomacy and some of the principles that have served their past cooperation well. It reviews the changes to the structure of the regional and global economy that have already occurred as a consequence of the rise of China and the rest of Asia, and outlines some future trends. The chapter then examines whether current institutional arrangements are adequate under circumstances in which the structure of regional and global economic weight has changed significantly, and discusses the areas that are most in need of change. The chapter concludes by identifying common interests and goals for China and Australia in regional economic diplomacy.

Australia and China's joint interests in regional economic diplomacy

Australia and China share a number of common interests in their pursuit of regional economic diplomacy:

- using regional economic frameworks to strengthen and reform their domestic economies;

- promoting an open trading environment in Asia that supports the global economic order; and

- using regional economic institutions to build stronger frameworks for political and security cooperation in Asia.

These interests have underpinned Australia's and China's approach to regional economic diplomacy over the past three decades. Australia and China have a successful record of working together in building the foundations for Asia's regional economic cooperation.

Following World War II, Australia built steadily its engagement with Asia and reduced its economic dependence on Britain. Australia's Menzies government signed a momentous bilateral trade agreement with Japan in 1957, and renegotiated its traditional preferential ties with the United Kingdom as the formation of the European Common Market loomed. This steady diplomatic shift was accelerated with the reforms of the 1980s, which reoriented Australia's economic and foreign diplomacy towards Asia. Australia sought to capitalise on the large-scale economic growth and structural changes taking place in Asia and their potential economic benefits to Australia. There was recognition that unless Australia removed its protectionist trade barriers and undertook major domestic economic reform, it would not enjoy the benefits of Asia's economic ascendancy and risked being left behind by rising Asian powers. Trade liberalisation thus became a key policy strategy and was viewed not only as a way to unleash Australia's domestic economic potential, but also as a way to underpin Australia's engagement with Asia.

In 1989, the Australian government proposed a new mechanism —APEC — to promote regional objectives in the GATT Uruguay Round and to foster long run economic development cooperation. APEC was designed to foster trade liberalisation and economic reform in Asia and to bolster the global trade liberalisation agenda of the Uruguay Round. But, importantly, APEC also served Australia's goal of pulling together the two halves of Asia and the Pacific — East Asia and North America — in a cooperative endeavour. This goal was driven by the alignment of Australian and East Asian interests in improving access for labour-intensive and other manufactures in North American and other international markets, and improving Australia's own direct engagement with the East Asian economies. APEC was therefore explicitly designed to link the countries of the Western Pacific (including Australia and New Zealand) and East Asia with those of North America, via common multilateral economic opening strategies.

Crucially, this period of reform coincided with China's own efforts to reform and open its economy and to deepen its economic and diplomatic engagement with Asia. After three decades of limited trade and other economic interdependence, the introduction of Deng Xiaoping's 'reform and opening' policies in 1978 paved the way for greater Chinese engagement with regional economies. Australia sought to harness these changes taking place in China by involving the Chinese leadership in the development of ideas about Asia Pacific economic cooperation. Economist and former secretary of the Australian Department of Trade, Sir John Crawford, led a mission to China in 1980 to talk about China's participation in informal processes of regional cooperation. In 1986, China, Chinese Taipei and Hong Kong were, at Australia's initiative, invited to join the tripartite Pacific Economic Cooperation Council (at its Vancouver meeting of that year). Australia also attempted to engage China in the first foreign and economic ministers' meeting in Canberra in 1989, although the Tiananmen Incident earlier that year made this politically impossible. In 1991, China joined the APEC meeting in Seoul, and in 1993, China's then president Jiang Zemin attended the first APEC Leaders' Summit in Seattle.

APEC provides China with an important channel for participating in the process of international economic governance and regional economic integration, as well as promoting its own domestic policy agenda (China APEC Development Council 2009). Like Australia before it, the Chinese government used participation in APEC and the regional trade liberalisation agenda to push politically sensitive tariff reduction and economic reforms at home. At APEC's Osaka summit in 1995, China announced reductions in tariffs on 4900 items, and within a year the simple average tariff rate was reduced from 36 per cent to 23 per cent. By October 1997, China had reduced its simple average tariff rate even further, to 17 per cent. APEC's agenda closely coincided with the global agenda, and it was in this context that China undertook the liberalisation and economic reforms necessary for its accession to the GATT/WTO. But China's unilateral trade liberalisation efforts and active participation also helped to bring momentum to APEC, and brought economic gains to China and its trading partners, such as Australia.

After laying the foundations for regional economic cooperation in the 1980s, the 1997–1998 Asian financial crisis revealed the benefits but also the limitations of existing regional economic frameworks. Australia's economic system and institutions allowed it to benefit from economic integration with Asia while protecting against much of the potential financial volatility. The floating exchange rate, for example, was key to Australia avoiding recession or any severe downturn during the Asian financial crisis. The exchange rate acted as a shock absorber as exchange rate movements protected against volatility in the domestic economy. In China's case, the Asian financial crisis deepened its understanding of the benefits of regional economic cooperation. The contagion-like spread of the financial crisis around the region demonstrated that regional economies were now deeply interconnected, and that in this era of globalisation, states could not act alone in trying to protect against economic vulnerability. China received international accolades for resisting pressure to devalue its currency — thus avoiding beggar-thy-neighbour exchange rate competition — and for providing aid packages and low-interest loans to its crisis-affected neighbours. The Asian financial crisis increased China's confidence in its ability to play a constructive leadership role in the region, but also demonstrated the limitations of existing regional and global economic mechanisms such as APEC, the World Bank and the IMF.

The Asian financial crisis therefore spurred greater regional efforts to develop new East Asian economic arrangements, such as ASEAN Plus Three (including China, Japan and South Korea) and the Chiang Mai Initiative (CMI). At a time when global financial arrangements were perceived to have failed the region, these new East Asian arrangements sought to strengthen and deepen East Asian regional economic and financial cooperation as well as regional regulatory capacity. Bolstered by its leadership role during the Asian financial crisis, China played an important role in this regional cooperation process, joining the ASEAN Plus Three group and subsequent East Asian economic arrangements with enthusiasm. China unilaterally liberalised many of its key sectors, including agriculture, thereby opening its markets to Southeast Asian exports. In 2002, China initiated a framework agreement for the China–ASEAN Free Trade Agreement. China's commitment to further opening up, and its willingness to sign up to the rules and norms of the global trading system through accession to the WTO in 2001, gave trading partners confidence in the direction of Chinese reforms. Unilateral trade liberalisation also created significant goodwill between China and its smaller Southeast Asian neighbours. Even in Northeast Asia, where political and security relationships waxed and waned, trade and economic exchange grew rapidly.

Beyond economic benefits, Australia and China have also viewed regional economic diplomacy as a way of building stronger political and security cooperation in Asia. The legacy of colonialism, Cold War division, and unresolved historical tensions between Japan and its neighbours had stymied institution-building processes in Asia since the end of World War II. Although ASEAN had been established in Southeast Asia in 1967, the wider Asia Pacific region remained institutionally underdeveloped. The region was comprised of states with very different political systems, as well as many newly independent states that were fiercely protective of any perceived threats to their sovereignty. Indeed, these factors had led ASEAN, the region's most significant existing institution, to develop particular practices of consensus, flexibility, non-interference in internal affairs and non-binding resolutions, as a way of reassuring postcolonial states' anxieties about international institution-building.

Given these obstacles, the Australian and Chinese governments have both observed the value of economic cooperation as a non-threatening way for regional states to develop habits of dialogue and cooperation, and the ASEAN approach to institution-building as a way to foster trust and ultimately political cooperation in the region. In addition, participating in APEC provided a valuable way for Beijing to reassure regional neighbours of its peaceful rise, and to help build a stable regional environment that would be conducive to China's future economic growth (Zhang 2014; Zhong et al 2014). China was encouraged by the way in which Australia, Japan and the Southeast Asian states used regional economic institutions as a way to enmesh China into a regional web of relationships, and to demonstrate the benefits of regional cooperation. China publicly acknowledged these benefits in 1997 when its 15th Party Congress officially declared that 'multilateralism' was a guiding Chinese policy principle (Harris 2000).

Asia's economic integration

China, Australia and the wider Asia Pacific region have benefited greatly from the stunning levels of regional economic integration that have been achieved since the late 1980s. Despite the comparatively lower density of its multilateral economic institutions, as compared with Europe for example, Asia now enjoys high levels of trade interdependence in resources and intermediate goods, and high levels of exports of final goods. By many measures, East Asia is the most economically integrated region in the world, led by its extensive production networks (Armstrong and Drysdale 2011).

The ongoing success of Asia's economic integration is critically important to Australia and China's prosperity. Trade with East Asia accounts for 66 per cent of Australia's total trade (Figure 7.1). This makes Australia the most East Asian-oriented trading nation in the world. Just under 46 per cent of Australia's trade is with Northeast Asia (ASEAN's 'Plus Three' countries), higher than any other major East Asian country. Australia also has the highest trade dependence with ASEAN, at 15 per cent, of the other non-ASEAN economies in the ASEAN Plus Six arrangement (New Zealand, India, China, Japan and South Korea). Indonesia and Malaysia also have over 60 per cent of their total trade within the ASEAN Plus Six grouping, with over a quarter of their trade within the ASEAN grouping. In China's case, just under 27 per cent of China's trade is with the rest of East Asia. The China–ASEAN free trade area is now the world's largest free trade area comprised solely of developing countries, with trade of US$480 billion in 2014 and total mutual investment reaching more than US$150 billion. By 2020, China–ASEAN trade is expected to reach US$1 trillion (Zhong 2015).

Figure 7.1: Asia Pacific economies' share of trade with East Asia, 2014

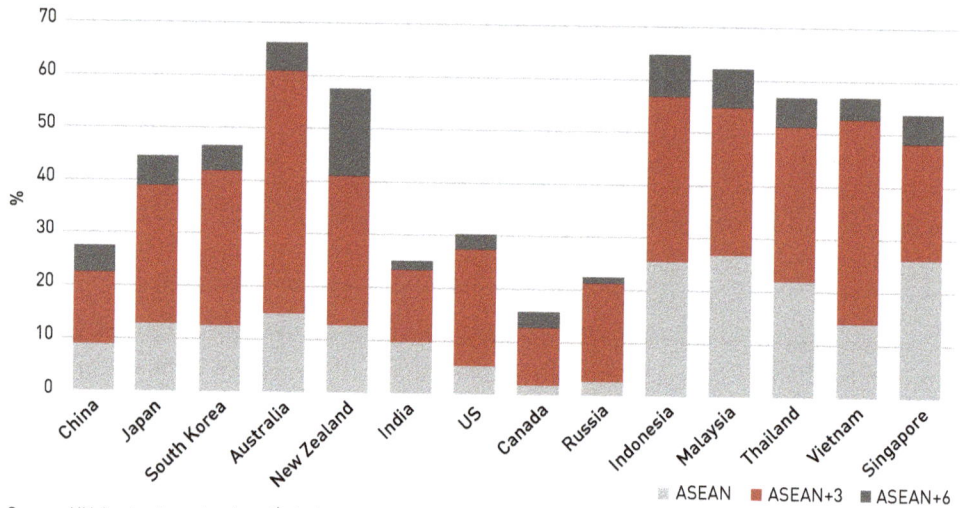

Source: UN Comtrade and authors' calculations.

China is at the centre of regional supply chains and has been a hub for East Asian trade with the rest of the world. In the past it played a major role in the assembly of manufactured goods that would be exported to North America and Europe, but the value-added in China during the production process has already started to increase rapidly and China is becoming a much larger consumer of those final goods (see Chapter 2). China is now focused on further liberalising regional trade and investment as well as strengthening regional connectivity and integration as a way to enhance the international competitiveness of the Chinese economy, and to gradually build a global, high-standards free trade area. China is also the largest trading nation globally and its vast trade relationships with North America, Europe and the rest of the world mean that it is a key global trader.

Shared principles

The success of Asia's regional economic diplomacy and the achievement of deep economic integration has been underpinned by three core principles: open regionalism in support of global frameworks; consensus-driven cooperation; and stable relations between Asia's great powers.

Open regionalism in support of global frameworks

Regional economic integration has been open and has developed in support of global frameworks. Asia's economic successes outlined above have been achieved because Asia's economic arrangements have generally been outward-looking rather than inward-looking. That is, they have worked to strengthen rather than substitute global economic arrangements such as the GATT and WTO. As trading nations, Asia Pacific regional economies have learned that their own economic prosperity relies on open engagement with North America, Europe and other parts of the globe.

Open regionalism — regional economic integration that is not at the expense of economies outside of the region and is supportive of the global trading system — can be seen most prominently in APEC and ASEAN. At the APEC summit in Bogor, Indonesia in 1994 member economies agreed to the 'Bogor goals'. These were a set of ambitious targets that aimed to achieve free and open trade and investment in the Asia Pacific, by 2010 for industrialised economies and by 2020 for developing economies. The Bogor goals encouraged member economies to undertake unilateral liberalisation — that is, not preferential or between members only — and therefore promoted free and open trade with the rest of the world, rather than just among APEC members.

Much of Asia's regional cooperation — economically and geopolitically — is ordered around the ASEAN grouping, which has also pursued open regionalism. This is because most of ASEAN's major economic partners have always been outside of Southeast Asia — including China, Japan, Australia, the United States and the European Union. For ASEAN to have pursued inward-looking arrangements — that is, liberalisation at the expense of these major economic partners — would not have been politically or economically sensible. This approach is recognised in the design of the ASEAN Free Trade Area (AFTA), which was launched in 1992. AFTA initially pursued preferential liberalisation by only removing border barriers to goods traded within the ASEAN zone. However, from the outset there was an agreement that these preferences would be extended to all external trading partners as well, and thus multilateralised, when it became politically feasible to do so in each domestic polity.

More recently the ASEAN region has been pursuing an ambitious ASEAN Economic Community (AEC), which was established in November 2015. The aim of the AEC is to 'transform ASEAN into a single market and production base, a highly competitive economic region, a region of equitable economic development, and a region fully integrated into the global economy' by 2020 (ASEAN 2008). The AEC would allow the free flow of goods, services, investment and skilled labour, and the freer movement of capital across the region. Because integration into the global economy is one of the four pillars of the AEC, integration in the ASEAN region will not divert trade or commerce away from non-members towards the ASEAN grouping. The goal is ambitious but would help move ASEAN towards a single market and production base that furthers the opportunities and economic engagement of China, Australia and other neighbours in the Asia Pacific.

Consensus-driven cooperation

Consensual processes have driven Asia's economic integration. Consensus has been critical for achieving cooperation among a group of states with diverse political systems and levels of economic development. Consensus has also encouraged the cooperation of Asia's many postcolonial states, which had little or no prior experience of multilateralism before World War II, and which have therefore always been strongly attached to the protection of state sovereignty. But this approach to regional and international diplomacy has enduring value. Consensus-forming strategies reassure small powers that large powers will take their views into consideration in adopting policy positions and that they will not dominate institutions; they also reassure large powers that smaller countries will not band together against them. This consensus-building approach has encouraged Asia's diverse mix of states to participate in regional institutions, even at times when they have been uncomfortable with the membership, structure, approaches or the issue-focus of a particular institution.

Though often criticised for being process-driven (rather than outcome-driven) 'talk shops', the Track 1.5 and Track 2 dialogues, meetings and other processes that have accompanied the creation of institutions such as APEC and the ASEAN Plus processes have been crucial in shaping shared regional understandings about the importance of trade and investment liberalisation, economic reform and multilateral economic cooperation. In particular, Asia's regional institutions have acted as forums for building critical consensus on three issues: first, that opening up to trade and investment benefits one's own economy; second, that these benefits are compounded if opening up occurs in concert with other countries; and third, that opening up without discriminating between trading partners is the best mode of strengthening economic relationships. Achieving consensus on these issues underpinned Asia's rapid expansion in trade and investment in the 1990s, lifted the incomes of Asia Pacific economies, and ensured that economic relationships deepened even in the absence of strong political relationships. That Asia has been able to achieve these levels of regional cooperation and economic integration is because institutional arrangements have evolved through consensual processes, have protected state sovereignty, have been voluntary and have allowed a diverse group of states to make non-binding commitments that are appropriate to their levels of economic development.

BOX 7.1: ASIA PACIFIC REGIONAL INITIATIVES AND THE GLOBAL SYSTEM

When APEC was created in 1989, disadvantage to non-member economies would have been inconsistent with the importance of economic links between member economies and those outside the grouping. APEC cooperation was founded on the principle of aligning Asia Pacific trade standards with global standards, and resulted in extending and strengthening the global GATT process. APEC has taken initiatives to the global level.

In 1996, APEC initiated negotiations on an Information Technology Agreement (ITA) in the WTO, and the agreement was concluded in December that year. The ITA prevented countries from introducing trade barriers for what were then relatively new forms of trade in information and communications technology (ICT) goods and services. By requiring countries to apply zero tariffs and other barriers to newly emerging ICT goods and services, the ITA encouraged rapid expansion in the trade of these new technologies. This in turn made possible the proliferation of supply chains in the electronics industry, which have fundamentally changed the way in which countries' international business is integrated, and which have deepened economic interdependence across Asia. Supply chains rely on logistics driven by rapid communications and technology, and the proliferation of supply chains has been critical in transforming China into the 'factory of the world'. Without the ITA's agreement on zero tariffs for newly emerging ICT trade, supply chains would not have developed so readily as they did.

More recently, the ITA 'model' has been emulated for trade in environmental goods. In 2012, APEC negotiated the Environmental Goods Agreement (EGA), which removes tariffs on trade on goods such as equipment for air pollution control and wastewater management. The global market for these new environmental goods and technologies is expected to expand to around US$3 trillion by 2020 (DFAT 2015a). Building on APEC's regional agreement, negotiations on an EGA were subsequently launched on a plurilateral basis (that is, with many but not all members participating) in the WTO in 2014.

The CMI, which was created in 2000 in the wake of the Asian financial crisis, represents another case in which regional cooperation has sought to strengthen — not divert from — global financial arrangements such as the IMF. The CMI endorses global, market-based principles of financial cooperation, and only permits a small percentage of its funds to be released to ailing economies without IMF approval.

Not all regional arrangements, processes or institutional innovations have been the product of consensus, but those that have had success, buy-in and ownership by countries in the region have done so through a process of building consensus. For example, the formation of APEC was an initiative taken by Australia and Japan, but the idea of APEC required much socialisation among other Asia Pacific economies before it could be introduced and accepted. APEC has subsequently evolved and has been shaped over time by its members. The ADB (Box 7.2) is another example of the way in which consensus has underpinned Asia's approach to regional economic cooperation and institution-building. Ultimately, examples like APEC and the ADB demonstrate that economic institutions and other regional arrangements have had to evolve and develop through consensual processes. It is often assumed that a static 'rules-based order' was created in 1945 and has remained unchanged since that time. That is not the case. As new economic issues and demands have arisen in the region, new institutions, norms, rules and regional arrangements have evolved through processes of consensus, communication and socialisation.

BOX 7.2: CONSENSUS AND THE CREATION OF THE ASIAN DEVELOPMENT BANK

The principle of consensus has been a critical element underpinning the evolution of rules and norms in Asia. One key example is the ADB, which was created in 1966. The ADB was created on the back of Japan's rising economic power. Japan was dissatisfied with its lack of representation in global institutions such as the World Bank and International Bank for Reconstruction and Development (IBRD), which were dominated by the interests of countries in Europe and North America. Japan also viewed the ADB as a way of achieving greater international political power, and of maintaining its export-led economic growth strategy. Though fellow Asian states supported Japan's developmental agenda, they were also fearful that the ADB would become a platform for Japanese regional dominance. At the same time, the United States was wary of Japan's development-state approach to economic development.

Thus, although Japan has always contributed the largest share of capital to the ADB, and holds the largest number of official positions — including that of Bank president — Japan has not dominated the ADB. Instead, since the 1980s in particular, the almost equal voting shares held by the United States and Europe have balanced Japan's voting share. This has required member states to engage in a consensus-building process to determine the Bank's principles on procurement, lending practices and issue focus. For example, the United States' preference for private capital and market-based economic development has always been balanced by Japanese and East Asian preferences for more state-activist approaches to economic development. Since its creation, the ADB has continued to evolve as a multilateral development financing institution.

Stable relations between Asia's great powers

The achievement of deep economic integration in Asia has been underpinned by stable, peaceful relations among Asia's great powers. The most important of these relationships is that between the United States and China. US–China rapprochement in 1972 transformed the relationship between these two countries in ways that were of great benefit not only to the United States and China but also to the wider region. Since 1972, China and the United

States have developed deep diplomatic ties and high levels of economic engagement, and have recognised that stable bilateral relations are the only way to ensure a peaceful Asian region. Moreover, the leadership role played by the United States has been of great value to both Australia and China. The United States has played a leading role in creating and underwriting the global economic and financial system, and has strongly encouraged China's integration within that system. The United States' diplomatic and military presence in Asia has also served as an important 'backstop', which has encouraged regional states — many of whom have adversarial political and security relationships — to feel secure enough to pursue economic cooperation and institution-building. These arrangements have been helpful in a number of ways to Asian nations in the past, including those that are not United States alliance partners, such as China.

Alongside bilateral cooperation between the region's great powers, Asia's economic and other institutions have also served as important venues for trust-building, dialogue and socialisation around regional norms of behaviour. This is due, in part, to the 'ASEAN-way' principles of consensus, non-intervention, sovereignty and non-binding resolutions on which they are built. These principles have been critically important in enmeshing great powers such as the United States and China into regional multilateral processes. These institutions have never replaced the need for direct negotiations between the great powers themselves. But these institutions have provided important occasions for bringing the great powers together in frameworks respectful of wider interests. They have also provided opportunities for great powers to hold off-the-record, informal meetings on the sidelines of public summits, and have impelled the great powers to listen to the concerns of smaller states in the region.

Changing structure of regional and global economic power

For the past three decades, Asia has been a remarkably peaceful and prosperous region. Asia's peace and economic vibrancy has been underpinned by: the United States-led economic, political and security order created at the end of World War II, China's acceptance of that order since 1972, and by the efforts of China, Australia and others to foster regional economic cooperation since the 1980s. But this existing order is now under strain — partly because of its success and the dramatic economic rise of China and other regional states.

The latter half of the 20th century saw the rapid industrialisation and rise of the Japanese economy in the 1960s through to the 1980s, with the newly industrialised economies (NIEs) of Singapore, South Korea, Taiwan and Hong Kong following in the 1980s and 1990s. The major force of growth in the global economy since the turn of the century has been China, with an average growth rate of 10 per cent per year over the 30 years since reform and opening in 1978 (Figure 7.2). The growth rates of the economies of Japan, China and the NIEs have slowed as they have become larger and more mature economies with higher per capita incomes. India's economic development and the rise of other Southeast Asian economies such as Vietnam, Myanmar and Indonesia are already showing promise as the next driving force of growth in Asia and the global economy.

China's economy has already grown to be as large as that of the United States in purchasing power parity (PPP) terms (see Chapter 1, Figure 1.6). Forward projections on current trends with conservative assumptions will see China overtake the United States as the largest economy in the world in nominal market exchange rate terms by the end of the 2020s, with many projecting this to happen earlier in that decade.

The growth of China's importance in the world economy has occurred very rapidly. This swift change is creating some uncertainty about how to manage the new responsibilities and challenges posed by the rise of China and other regional economies (Zhang 2015). There is a risk that some of the responses to these quick changes could unravel the shared principles that have underpinned Asia's economic achievements to date.

Threats to open regionalism

First, there are growing challenges to maintaining the primacy of open regionalism in Asia. In the past, Asia's deep economic integration was built on the basis of the Most Favoured Nation (MFN) principle, which extends trade and other economic benefits to all states, regardless of whether they are members of the agreement or not. Now, we are witnessing the proliferation of exclusive, preferential trade agreements (PTAs) in Asia, which serve only to deepen economic ties between PTA member countries. Some of the proposed multinational preferential agreements — such as the Trans-Pacific Partnership (TPP) agreement and Regional Comprehensive Economic Partnership (RCEP) — are particularly large and comprehensive. While these large and comprehensive preferential agreements offer more benefits to their members than narrower bilateral agreements, they also have the potential to impose more adverse effects on non-member economies. This can be avoided. Agreements and arrangements that are preferential and exclusive can be made more inclusive over time, just as the AFTA was, and creative ways can be found to extend benefits to non-members. How to negate some of the adverse consequences of new regional agreements such as the TPP and RCEP is discussed later in the chapter.

Figure 7.2: Waves of regional and global economic growth

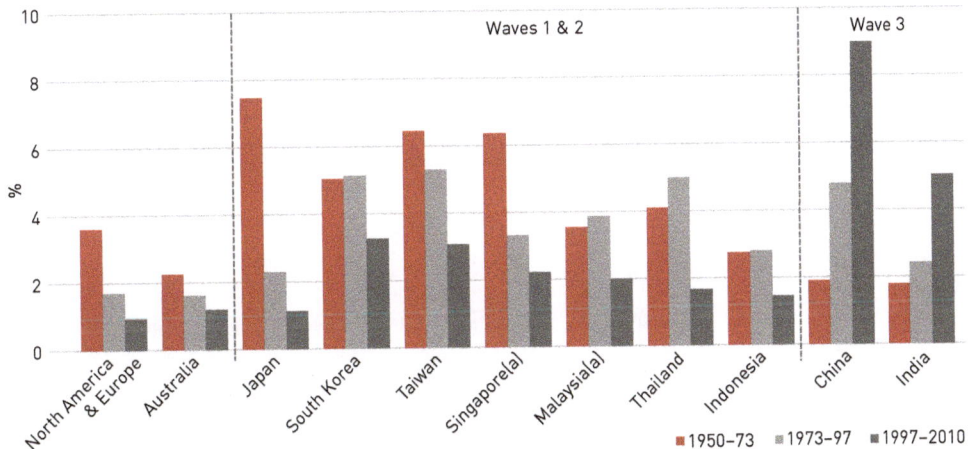

Source: Australia in the Asian Century White Paper 2012 and authors' calculations.

Threats to consensus-driven cooperation

Second, there are growing threats to Asia's consensus-based approach to regional cooperation. As cross-border economic issues have become increasingly complex, and have begun to affect a wider range of interests and countries, it has become more and more difficult to achieve consensus-based regional cooperation among larger groups of countries. At times, the principle of consensus has also been used and abused as a way for countries to avoid making progress on reform. In these circumstances, smaller 'coalitions of the willing' have been formed to achieve faster progress on issues including trade and investment liberalisation. For example, with the Doha Round of trade liberalisation stalled, some countries have resorted to bilateral or plurilateral agreements in order to open up market access. Similarly, in areas such as investment liberalisation, where there is no existing global or regional regime, small groups of countries have begun working together to progress bilateral deals or regional agreements. There is nothing inherently wrong with smaller groups of countries working together to introduce new arrangements. Indeed, the presence of coalitions of the willing is a well-established practice in Asia. APEC, for example, has historically used the approach of 'pathfinder initiatives' to achieve progress; these allow some member economies to work together in establishing new cooperative arrangements, which are then communicated to other APEC members who are encouraged to participate when they are ready. In order for these initiatives to succeed in gaining acceptance by non-participants, however, it is important that they be communicated transparently to other countries so as to avoid surprises, and to be developed in a manner that does not disadvantage other countries.

Threats to stable relations between the great powers

Finally, the existing economic, political and security order in Asia is under strain because of the economic rise of China and others in the region. The transition to a more multipolar order is inevitable, but the challenge facing the region is how to manage that order transition peacefully. China's vast trade, financial, demographic, environmental and military footprint gives it a growing and legitimate interest in playing a larger regional and global role. At the same time, while major shifts in the regional distribution of wealth and power make comparable shifts in the regional strategic order inevitable, Australia and other regional states very much prefer that the United States retains a strong and stabilising role in whatever new order emerges. The goal must be to reconfigure a new regional order that enables a leading role for both the United States and China. This new regional order must also allow space for other established powers such as Japan, and for rising powers such as India and Indonesia. Any new regional order must ensure that smaller and middle powers, such as Australia, South Korea and Southeast Asian countries, continue to feel secure and able to participate with independent voices.

Managing this order transition will not be easy. And it will largely be a job for the great powers themselves. Nevertheless, Asia's middle powers still have a vital role to play. They should continue to use Asia Pacific institutions to help manage the orderly transition, playing a positive role in promoting cooperative regional initiatives and moderating great power rivalry. There is a need to ensure that current regional institutions and arrangements are suitable for managing economic integration, structural change and political cooperation as Asia's order changes. Frequent dialogue between the United States and China is critically important, and it is imperative that this dialogue takes place routinely and within frameworks that involve interests and issues beyond the US–China bilateral relationship. There are two regular meetings a year between the president of China and the president of the United States within a framework that includes other countries: the APEC summit and the G20 summit. While there are other occasions for bilateral meetings, including state visits and meetings of the UN General Assembly, for example, the APEC and G20 summits allow for US–China cooperation in the context of broader regional and global cooperation. Those occasions should be made as productive as possible for building consensus towards effecting gradual and peaceful order transition.

Australia and China should seek to enhance their bilateral security ties as an important element that contributes to building effective working relationships on security issues among all countries in the region. Closer bilateral security ties will help to strengthen the foundations of political confidence on which regional economic prosperity can continue to grow. Australia is committed to its longstanding alliance with the United States, but this does not preclude security cooperation with China. The development of closer bilateral security cooperation on a range of traditional and non-traditional security issues will be an important element in elevating the Australia–China relationship to a Comprehensive Strategic Partnership for Change and in deepening strategic trust between the two countries. The changing regional order makes it increasingly important for China and Australia to clearly understand each other's approach to regional political and security affairs. A particular area in which there is scope for expanding dialogue that will contribute to this understanding is related to China's evolving thinking about its maritime economy, in which both countries have direct mutual interests.

Moving forward with common interests

The economic and political rise of China and other regional economies is changing the Asian order and bringing about new economic and political-security challenges. Based on their successful history in jointly building regional economic cooperation, Australia and China are well placed to work together to forge a new consensus around the principles that will guide future regional cooperation.

Australia and China can direct their bilateral relationship toward common regional interests in a number of practical ways. Joint cooperation with third countries can benefit from complementary comparative advantages and can advance broader regional cooperation. There is scope for working together — given Australia's expertise, regional interests and connections to the United States — on Chinese global governance initiatives such as the AIIB. There are already areas, such as in development cooperation in the Pacific, where Australia and China actively work together. These cooperative endeavours should be extended so that progress in development cooperation, infrastructure investment and other initiatives can help to deepen progress at the regional level.

As China's economy undertakes its huge structural transformation, many opportunities will be opened up in labour-intensive manufacturing and the sectors that China transitions out of. India, the rest of South Asia and much of Southeast Asia can emulate China and Northeast Asia's economic success, realise their comparative advantage and transition into low-cost manufacturing. Realising these opportunities in South and Southeast Asia will assist in China's own transition. And China's regional infrastructure and connectivity initiatives can play a major role alongside exporting China's over-capacity, surplus savings and expertise.

The largest opportunity lies in India. India can realise its 'Make in India' economic reform agenda through liberalising labour laws, improving infrastructure investment and financing, opening to foreign investment, and pursuing regional economic integration. Regional cooperation that facilitates a more open and dynamic external environment will help India and other economies undertake such difficult reforms. Successful reforms in India will leverage its abundant and growing low-cost labour resources to exploit a comparative advantage in labour-intensive manufactures and services. Australia and China have a strong interest, and can play an active role, in supporting India's economic growth ambitions.

Strengthening and connecting existing institutions

Asia is now home to a complex web, or 'variable geometry', of regional economic, political and security institutions with diverse memberships and functions. Economic interdependence in Asia and across the Pacific includes a wider group of economies, such as India. In reality there is no single regional institution that currently addresses all of the region's economic, political and security issues.

The established regional institutions, arrangements and groupings in East Asia and across the Pacific do not encompass all economies and were not set up to deal with the interaction between economic and political affairs, and there are gaps in coverage within the architecture for economic and political cooperation (Figure 7.3).

APEC remains the region's primary venue for discussion of economic issues, and has a particular focus on trade and investment liberalisation. It is the primary institution for US engagement on regional economic affairs, and the APEC Summit has proved to be an important venue for leaders to discuss win-win economic issues and promote economic cooperation initiatives. The routine work done among countries at the official level of APEC has also served to bridge understanding between members, to deepen cooperation and to lead to outcomes that have benefited members and non-members alike (Box 7.1). The network of officials, the work program, and the leaders' meeting has meant that member economies feel ownership of the process and the institution. Yet there are major gaps in APEC's membership. As Figure 7.3 shows, while APEC's membership is broad, there are a number of regional economies — including India, Cambodia, Laos and Myanmar — who are not APEC members. APEC's diverse membership of economies, rather than states, makes it an inappropriate platform for discussing East Asia's political and security challenges. While informal meetings on political and security issues take place between leaders on the sidelines of APEC, these issues are not on the main agenda.

Figure 7.3: ASEAN, APEC, EAS and ARF membership compared

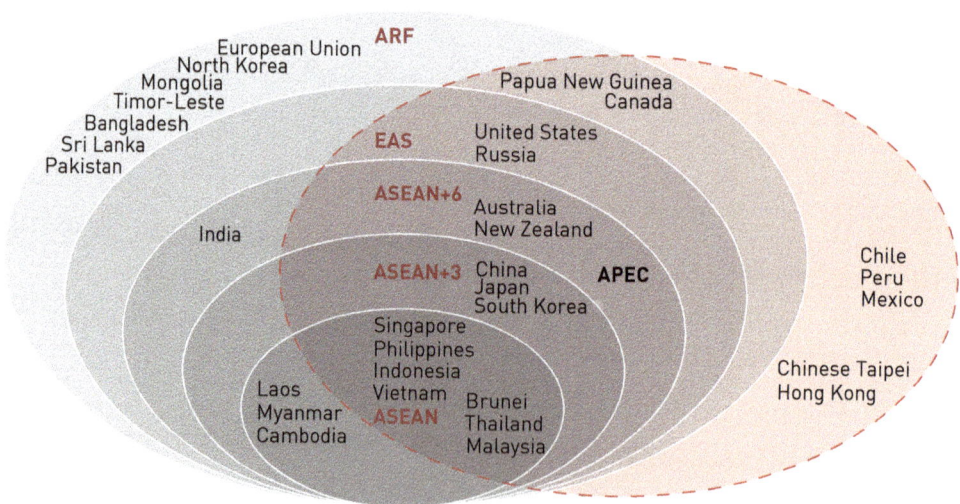

Source: Authors' schema.

The ASEAN Regional Forum (ARF), created in 1994, has focused more on regional security issues. It is a large and diverse organisation, involving 27 participants, including the EU. Though it has been a useful platform for regional states to get to know one another, and to participate in confidence-building measures, the ARF's size and the diverse character of its participants has made it very difficult to achieve substantial progress on regional security disputes.

The East Asia Summit (EAS) was created in 2005 and is another ASEAN-led institution. The EAS emerged out of proposals, in the early 1990s, to create an East Asian Economic Caucus. The Asian financial crisis then prompted ASEAN countries to work with their 'Plus Three' Northeast Asian neighbours — China, Japan and South Korea — to build an East Asian economic community. With Japan eager to broaden its membership, India, Australia and New Zealand subsequently became founding members of the EAS in 2005. In 2011, membership of the EAS was further expanded to include Russia and the United States. This expansion in membership has also changed the character of the EAS from being an organisation predominantly focused on economic issues, to one where political and security issues have come to dominate the agenda. In comparison with APEC, the EAS has never enjoyed the same dense network of institutionalised official activity among its members. Given its shift away from economic issues in recent years, there is a risk that much of the EAS agenda will become dominated by countries' political declarations rather than institutionalised cooperation. EAS' main asset is that its agenda does encompass security issues, and that its membership includes all of the major powers in Asia and the Pacific, including India.

These institutions and arrangements have served the region well to this point, but in quite different ways. As relative economic and political power shifts in the Asia Pacific and globally, there is a pressing need to connect and extend existing regional arrangements so that there is a ready platform to address new priorities in regional cooperation. Regional cooperation has to build on and move beyond the core economic agenda. The web of economic, political and security institutions in Asia must now be better linked to address the gaps in membership and function. The flexibility of Asian regional arrangements allows opportunities to connect existing arrangements in ways that allow them to address these new challenges and opportunities.

At the regional level, one option would be to strengthen the connection between the annual APEC Economic Leaders' Meeting and the East Asia Summit. These two meetings are now held back-to-back in November in order to allow the US president to travel to Asia once a year. Currently, leaders move from one host country to the other and discuss different agendas with different memberships. This means that there is a distinct contrast in the nature of the discussions at APEC and the EAS. The Chinese head of state does not currently attend EAS meetings. The APEC host and ASEAN Chair (which hosts the EAS) could work together to ensure that APEC's economic cooperation agenda feeds into the EAS' political and security agenda, without diluting the issue focus of each. This could be facilitated via joint meetings between the APEC and EAS 'troikas' (that is, the previous, current and future APEC hosts and ASEAN Chairs) in advance of the annual Leaders' Meeting and Summit.

Another way of strengthening the connection between regional institutional arrangements might be to reach out to invite India and other ASEAN states to join the APEC process — not necessarily as formal members initially but rather as participants. The APEC host has the right to invite government leaders from non-APEC member economies to attend the annual Leaders' Meeting. Building on the initiative taken by China when it hosted APEC in 2014, future APEC hosts could invite India, Cambodia, Laos and Myanmar — that is, those countries who are members of the EAS but not APEC — to attend the APEC Leaders' Meeting. The APEC

Economic Leaders' Meeting will next be held in East Asia in 2017 when Vietnam hosts APEC. In 2017, therefore, there is an important opportunity for Vietnam to invite India, Cambodia, Laos and Myanmar to attend APEC. Leaders could then travel to the Philippines (which will be the ASEAN Chair in 2017) for the East Asia Summit. Finding creative solutions to have all ASEAN members join APEC meetings will make it easier to more effectively connect these regional processes. East Asia and the trans-Pacific relationships have benefited greatly from ASEAN centrality and there is good reason to preserve and strengthen ASEAN as the fulcrum of regional cooperation. Australia, China and the rest of the region have a stake in the success of the ASEAN Economic Community and a unified and integrated ASEAN makes broader Asian cooperation easier.

Important, cross-cutting issues that require close cooperation such as energy and environmental transformation should be the focus of high-level policy dialogue led by a coalition of interested powers in the region and carried across different forums. These issues cut across energy security, climate change, and political and economic cooperation. These are issues that affect all states in the region, and can be advanced by leader-level agreement among all of the major regional players. The energy transition from fossil fuels to renewables will bring new opportunities and challenges that have large transnational spillovers. Focusing on an issue such as energy transformation could lift the level of cooperation between countries, give regional arrangements new impetus and provide a framework for closer political cooperation. This is an issue that affects China and Australia acutely, but also affects Japan, the United States, India, Indonesia and every other country in the region, whether they are energy producers, consumers or both. There is currently no regional forum or theatre in which energy issues are prominently on the agenda, but a small coalition of countries including Australia and China could initiate a dialogue in one or more of the established regional platforms and carry policy development forward across all these forums.

At the global level, Australia and China have a shared interest in feeding regional interests and initiatives into global arrangements. The Asian members of the G20 — Australia, China, Japan, India, Indonesia and South Korea — and the Pacific members of the G20 — Canada, Mexico and the United States — are all leaders in the various Asia Pacific regional forums. A better connection between the regional forums and the G20 at the global level will help to shape the G20 agenda, to implement G20 outcomes through regional institutions and to build confidence among countries that are not members of the G20 in its inclusiveness and credibility. The Asian G20 members are the most important economies in the region, and individually and collectively they represent important voices in global affairs. They already exercise a measure of influence globally, and can represent the interests and views that are expressed in regional forums that operate through a process of consensus.

Regional institutions such as the Chiang Mai Initiative Mulilateralization (CMIM) and the ASEAN Plus Three Macroeconomic Research Office (AMRO) surveillance unit can act to strengthen and reinforce the global financial safety net and global surveillance. Although the currency swaps in CMIM have yet to be drawn on — even during the global financial crisis — CMIM and AMRO can build trust and capacity and play an important role as part of the broader global financial safety net in the event of a future financial crisis (see Chapter 8). These new Asian arrangements mark a significant step forward in Asian financial and monetary cooperation. To be truly effective, they need to be coordinated with the IMF. Asia, left to its own devices, would find it difficult to mobilise the resources or impose the conditions on neighbouring countries needed to manage financial crises. A strengthened AMRO that coordinates with the IMF will help regional financial surveillance. Australia is not party to CMIM or AMRO because they emerged from ASEAN Plus Three, but Australia has an interest in helping to build AMRO's capacity and playing a supporting role within CMIM. More broadly, the Australia–China bilateral relationship should include dialogue and cooperation on issues that can feed into and shape those regional forums and arrangements in which only one country is a member, such as CMIM. There should be creative ways to have Australia become a de facto partner in AMRO. It is in Australia's interest to help strengthen the coordination between the IMF and regional financial arrangements (see Chapter 8).

The institutions and arrangements that have served China, Australia and Asia well in the past must evolve to reflect new regional realities and interests. There is little appetite in the region to create entirely new institutions, but existing institutions could be re-energised and their connections strengthened. And regional efforts should be concentrated on important cross-cutting issues such as energy transformation. Australia and China can work together with regional partners to reform and strengthen these existing institutions and arrangements.

Moving towards inclusive regional agreements

The Asia Pacific region has seen a plethora of bilateral and regional trade agreements signed since the early 2000s. But none of the regional or plurilateral agreements signed to date have been as consequential or large in membership as the TPP, RCEP or the Transatlantic Trade and Investment Partnership (TTIP). These regional economic agreements aim to make major progress on trade and investment liberalisation where the global system has stalled, and to further cross-border commerce and exchange in new areas of importance to business, in some cases by creating new international rules.

Regional agreements can deepen regional and global economic integration and make progress where the WTO has been unable to, and in the process strengthen prospects for progress at the global level. Yet there are risks that these agreements can harm non-members, and that different agreements with different memberships can become avenues for competitive rule-making, thus fragmenting regional and global economic integration. There is strong interest in avoiding or ameliorating these adverse consequences in order to build an inclusive, global economic system.

The 12-member TPP includes Australia, the United States, Japan, Canada, Mexico, Vietnam, Brunei, Singapore, Malaysia, New Zealand, Chile and Peru. Large Asian economies such as China, Indonesia and India are yet to join. Given the standards that the TPP applies and the fact that new members will be required to negotiate bilateral agreements with all other members and be ratified by US Congress, it is unlikely that China will be able to join the TPP in the near future. However, the TPP does provide some country-specific carve-outs and special and differential treatment for developing members regarding their transition periods.

Compared to the TPP, RCEP covers a broader range of countries with more varied levels of economic development. ASEAN's aim is for RCEP to consolidate and harmonise the existing ASEAN Plus One FTAs with China, South Korea, Japan, India and Australia–New Zealand. These FTAs vary considerably in terms of their scope, comprehensiveness and market access commitments. RCEP is expected to be characterised by a set of common rules, but with flexibility for developing countries to commit to certain standards in reasonable timeframes, and market access commitments by individual countries that take account of their level of economic development.

Figure 7.4: ASEAN, RCEP, TPP and possible FTAAP membership

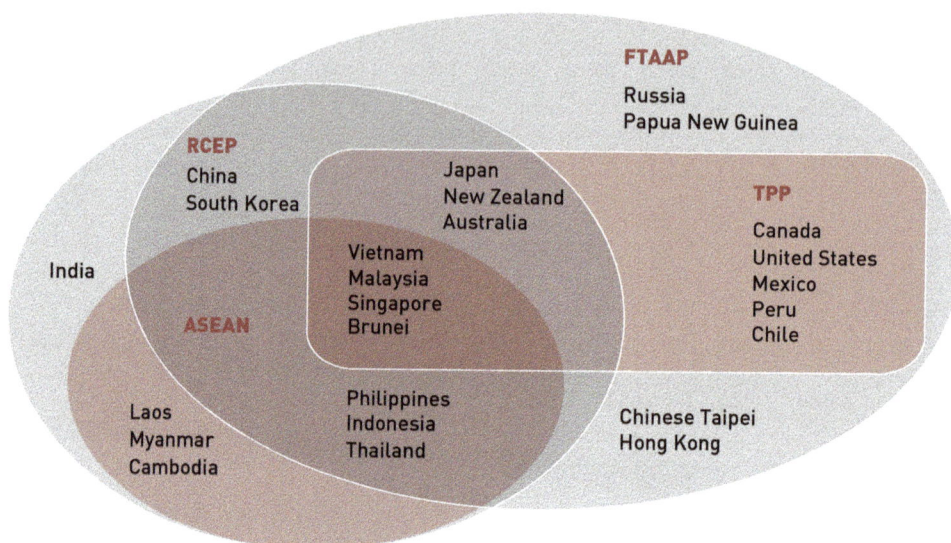

Source: Authors' schema.

Australia is party to both the TPP and RCEP and has a role to play with other partners, such as Japan, in dialogue, capacity building and experience sharing to bridge the gap between members and non-members. This bridge-building role is vital because Australia, Japan and others have a number of important trading partners that are not members of both the TPP and RCEP. The TPP and RCEP agreements should be used to deepen market-based economic interdependence and any barriers against non-members should be watered down. The agreements need to be 'living' agreements that change with circumstances and give all members a voice. The criteria for accession to these agreements will also be particularly important if the benefits of these agreements are to be expanded beyond the original signatories.

The TPP and RCEP should not become competing blocs but instead need to be made complementary. RCEP does not include the United States and the TPP does not include China. These arrangements should be directed to enhance economic integration in Asia without fragmenting economic linkages within the region or between the region and the rest of the world.

The TPP and RCEP will serve their purpose only if they are used to foster domestic economic reform agendas. China has been highly successful in its strategy of using membership of external organisations like the WTO to leverage and entrench major domestic reforms. China now has an opportunity to pursue a new round of reforms via external engagement, including financial sector and investment reform, reform of SOEs, locking in improved environmental and labour standards, and further modernising its economy. But the prospect of achieving any of these reforms via the TPP will be long term rather than short term, particularly because China is not a member of the TPP and there will be many hurdles for new members to joining the TPP, and it is not clear when accession might become possible for China. More importantly, those reforms and commitments that China will have to make in order to join the TPP will have to be structured in a way that is consistent with China's domestic reform goals. The major challenge for China, but more broadly for the TPP, will be whether the TPP is able to create an external environment for China and other non-members that is conducive to their pursuit of domestic reforms. An exclusive set of arrangements in the region that makes the external environment more difficult for further opening up of economies and implementing of domestic economic reforms needs to be avoided.

The RCEP process, on the other hand, shows much more immediate promise through China's participation in negotiating the opening up of borders to trade and investment. China's WTO accession experience demonstrates how interests can align to create win–win commitments via negotiation. It is harder to negotiate domestic reform externally. Reform is more sustainable if it is implemented with external support in the form of agreeing to mutually beneficial goals, capacity building and experience sharing, and by giving countries space to find the best reform path for their own circumstances and institutions. So rather than externally mandating reforms, international agreements can work to provide external impetus for ongoing domestic economic and regulatory reform processes.

The RCEP agreement has the potential to create an environment for both members and non-members that is conducive to opening up of markets and the prosecution of domestic reforms. There is the opportunity to create an agreement that extends the principles and modes of cooperation of ASEAN, especially the AEC, to a broader grouping that includes major-economy neighbours such as China, Japan and India, as well as advanced-economy neighbours such as Australia, South Korea and New Zealand. By RCEP's setting binding goals and allowing some countries to reach those goals in the most suitable way for them over time, with capacity building and experience sharing along the way, the broader East Asian region will move closer to a single market and production base.

Much broader and deeper integration would occur with the East Asian economies through RCEP adopting the four pillars of the AEC — a single market and production base, a competitive economic region, equitable economic development and integration into the global economy — and committing to major liberalisation. This will involve commitments to comprehensive freeing of trade in goods, services and investment and with a framework for economic cooperation. Recognising that a successful agreement will require an ongoing process, members should commit to ambitious binding goals for delivery by 2025, with built-in institutions such as working groups for ongoing implementation.

RCEP has real potential to avoid overly prescriptive outcomes, by providing country-specific market access commitments and setting some agreed rules and directions for future work. As with the experience of ASEAN, multilateralising preferences — so that benefits are extended to non-members — over time will be important to avoid an exclusive membership that truncates economic integration across the Pacific or with the rest of the world. Whether RCEP ultimately results in open regionalism depends on the mode of cooperation, the end goals and how those are pursued.

RCEP countries already account for a larger share of the global economy than do the TPP countries and its members also include a faster growing group of countries, led by India and China. RCEP is diverse, with some of the least developed countries in the region such as Cambodia, Laos and Myanmar, which are not APEC or TPP members. The GDP of the RCEP grouping — on conservative projections — could be close to double the TPP's size in 15 years (Figure 7.5).

Pursuing an ambitious RCEP agreement alongside the TPP will be important for furthering economic integration, and Australia and China have a role to play in setting high standards in this process. In doing so, Australia and China can use the best features of ChAFTA —

including the liberalisation of services and investment access — to set the benchmarks for RCEP. Strong initial liberalisation and commitments for phased liberalisation in investment by China and others would help to develop competitive liberalisation between RCEP and the TPP. It would also ensure that a future US–China BIT could incorporate the best features of both the TPP and RCEP, taking account of the interests of the whole region rather than just bilateral interests. This approach would help to achieve convergence between the two regional agreements, thereby addressing the biggest problem they currently face: namely, that the United States and China are not party to both agreements.

Early consolidation of the TPP and RCEP is an unrealistic objective. The track record of consolidating smaller bilateral agreements has not been good and has tended to lead to the creation of additional layers rather than consolidation. The longer-term convergence of the TPP and RCEP, however, can be pursued. A practical way forward would be to mobilise a coalition of the willing to work together in defining the path forward in linking these two regional agreements. Australia, as a member of both agreements, has a crucial role to play, but China and others that are party only to one agreement are also important for finding creative ways to bridge the gaps between the TPP and RCEP.

Figure 7.5: GDP projections of RCEP and TPP groups, 1980–2050, at purchasing power parity

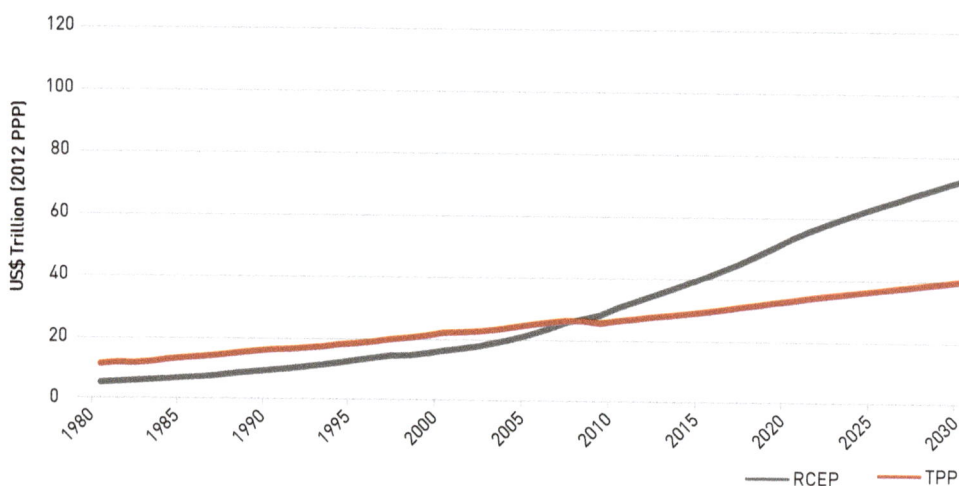

Note: IMF projections to 2020 followed by projections based on an estimate of potential labour productivity for countries currently in transition given institutional quality measured by the World Economic Forum's Global Competitiveness Index. Source: Hubbard and Sharma 2016.

A related initiative is the effort to develop the Free Trade Area of the Asia Pacific (FTAAP), which was put back on the regional agenda in 2014 when China hosted APEC (APEC 2014a). The FTAAP builds on the ongoing regional undertakings of the ASEAN Plus Three, TPP and RCEP and aims to further APEC's regional economic integration agenda. Consistent with the principles of economic cooperation that have served the region so well until now, APEC leaders have agreed that the FTAAP should support and complement the multilateral trading system, work to help achieve the Bogor goals, and be pursued with a step-by-step, consensus-based approach. It would also need to be a high-quality, 'next generation' agreement and run in parallel to — not as part of — the APEC process so that non-binding voluntary cooperation can be preserved in APEC.

The principles that have served East Asia and its trans-Pacific cooperation so well in the past should guide the formation and architecture of the FTAAP so that it strengthens the WTO and the global economic system. Recognition of the importance of ASEAN centrality and extending the best features of the AEC will be important in achieving a high-quality agreement that moves the region towards a single market in the Asia Pacific. Building on the shared principles that have underpinned Asia's economic integration to date, it is also important to ensure where possible that regional agreements do not undermine the global multilateral system by adversely affecting non-members.

BOX 7.3: BUILDING A MULTILATERAL REGIME FOR GOVERNING FOREIGN DIRECT INVESTMENT

The global trading system has been integral for China's integration into the global economy and regional arrangements such as APEC have helped in this. As investment flows have become more important in the region, the lack of a regional or global investment regime is emerging as a significant gap in the multilateral architecture. Chinese outward direct investment is already large and will only become more important regionally and globally. Australia is a major recipient of Chinese investment, and both countries have a role to play in developing arrangements at the regional and global levels that help with the management of foreign investment and further regional economic integration.

Currently, the lack of a regional or global regime for investment has led to a mix of both unilateral policies (mostly on the part of recipient countries) and bilateral policies, using investment treaties and economic agreements that have varying provisions and protections. Australia and China have an interest in initiating dialogue around the articulation of a common set of principles to govern foreign investment — both for facilitating pre-establishment foreign investment (before it enters a country) and the national treatment of post-establishment foreign investment. This might begin with the implementation of ChAFTA (see Chapter 4). Australia and China can also carry their work on an investment agreement under the aegis of ChAFTA into the RCEP negotiations. Without regional guiding principles, there is a risk that agreements between large countries — such as the United States–China Bilateral Investment Treaty (BIT) — will become the default template for those between all states in the region. It is important that the interests of smaller countries are represented in these discussions so that outcomes are in the interests of all investors and recipients.

Promoting infrastructure investment as multilateral regional goods

Promoting infrastructure funding and investment is a particular priority in Asia and the Pacific. The World Bank has estimated that each additional 10 per cent of global investment in infrastructure increases global GDP growth by one percentage point. Given the modest and uneven growth in the global economy, increasing infrastructure investment is important for many countries. In particular, there is great demand for infrastructure investment within the region. The ADB has estimated that Asia will need US$8 trillion in national infrastructure and US$290 billion in infrastructure connecting economies by 2020 (ADB 2009). Meeting that US$8 trillion deficit in regional infrastructure demand by 2020 is critical to the continuing growth and development of regional economies. Yet, as is widely recognised, there are currently a number of constraints on infrastructure investment. The scale of funding through the multilateral development banks such as the World Bank and the ADB, which are small relative to the size of demand, has shrunk in recent years. Indeed, since the 1990s, some of the existing multilateral banks, such as the World Bank, have increasingly focused on funding 'social' projects in areas such as education, health, environment and urban development, rather than funding investment in roads, railways, ports and other infrastructure projects. Moreover, the APEC Connectivity Blueprint (2015–2025) released at the 2014 APEC Summit recognises that the quality and distribution of infrastructure in the region remains uneven, and that many countries lack financial support for infrastructure funding. There is clear scope for intermediating Asian savings and facilitating greater private sector financing to cope with the huge shortfall in regional infrastructure investment.

China's launch of the AIIB is an important moment in the emergence of China as a contributor to regional and global public goods (Lin 2015). China already has a number of existing avenues through which it finances infrastructure projects in Asia, including the China Development Bank, its new OBOR initiative, the Silk Road Fund and traditional bilateral financing. Through these avenues, China seeks to strengthen Asian connectivity and economic integration through investment in road, rail, shipping, aviation, telecommunications, power and energy pipeline infrastructure. But the AIIB represents something new. In developing the AIIB, China has voluntarily committed its resources to a multilateral body with formal governance structures and with external oversight. While this multilateral approach necessarily limits China's freedom of action, it offers many advantages to China and the wider region.

First, multilateralising financing decisions can insulate China from bilateral political tensions. With competition among recipients for large infrastructure investment projects, investment deployed through multilateral processes are less likely to become politicised. When commercial decisions take place on a unilateral or bilateral basis, they run the risk of being second-guessed, or being viewed as connected to unrelated disputes or disagreements.

Second, it is in China's direct interest to ensure that the AIIB meets all the standards of a multilateral institution. The AIIB is under intense scrutiny and the international tolerance for missteps will be low. While China originally formed the concept of the AIIB, its governance arrangements have been shaped by its many founding members, and should ensure that the AIIB meets all the accountability and transparency standards of other multilateral development banks and has an appropriately skilled international workforce. The downside of building in those processes and procedures is that it may take longer than China and recipient countries may wish for the AIIB to become a significant player in the region. But China will benefit significantly because there is no question that the AIIB truly is a multilateral institution and not one controlled by China. This does not mean that the AIIB needs to mirror all of the procedures of the existing multilateral development banks. On the contrary, the AIIB should seek to be more effective and efficient than the other multilateral development banks. In doing so, this demonstrates that China can make an effective contribution to providing global public goods and actively lead a multilateral organisation. Moreover, the areas of the AIIB's operations where time and care should be taken — such as rigorous credit assessments, careful project selection, careful attention to environmental and social issues and strong accounting and transparency arrangements — are ones where China can learn from the experience of others. As such, there are a number of indirect benefits that China can gain from the careful establishment of the AIIB.

The OBOR initiative aims to connect Asia, the Middle East, Europe and Africa. It is a bold plan by China that could greatly facilitate infrastructure connectivity and economic integration within and across regions and sub-regions (State Council of the People's Republic of China 2015). China's surplus savings and infrastructure development expertise can be mobilised for the benefit of the development of other countries that lack capital and infrastructure development expertise. It can also ease some of the overcapacity issues in China while expanding trade and commerce for Chinese and other companies. As the success of this Chinese initiative requires active involvement of other countries based on their own interests, the OBOR initiative can also provide a platform for cooperation between developed and developing economies (Zhang 2016b). Australia is actively developing the Northern Australia region and has strong interest in being part of the OBOR initiative. Beyond the bilateral interest in AIIB and OBOR, both Australia and China have an interest in regional infrastructure building and connectivity that would be made more effective through bilateral and regional cooperation.

Ultimately, China's contributions via the AIIB and OBOR form an important plank in Asia's wider connectivity agenda. China's neighbourhood in Southeast Asia has a well-developed ASEAN Master Plan for Connectivity (AMPC). The AMPC is a regional plan for transport and institutional connectivity designed to bring countries closer to one another, and to facilitate better access to trade, investment, tourism and people-to-people exchanges. The AIIB and the AMPC share similar goals. China's capital and expertise in building infrastructure is already highly sought after in Southeast Asia and elsewhere — Chinese-developed ports, high-speed rail and major infrastructure projects such as the Trans-Asian Railway Network and Asian Highway Network have earned China an impressive reputation. Working alongside the AMPC will help China to prioritise investment and embed cooperation among recipient countries. For instance, roads and rail networks will connect countries with shared borders, while a system of short sea shipping will link maritime Southeast Asia with ports for roll-on roll-off vessels.

The AIIB represents an important step in China's provision of regional and global public goods. A successful AIIB will mean Chinese funds, expertise and leadership can be leveraged to support demand for infrastructure investment in Asia and beyond. It is in the interests of Australia and the wider region to see the AIIB succeed.

But the AIIB is not the only important infrastructure investment institution operating in Asia. The ADB, World Bank, and unilateral lenders and donors are all important for infrastructure development in Asia. A positive development is that in its initial operations, the AIIB is focusing on co-financing arrangements with the ADB and the World Bank. However, there is a danger that some of the players may act independently and at times at cross-purposes. It would be productive to ensure a common understanding and coherence to the infrastructure investment network in the region. There would be value in ministers and senior officials from the countries in the region regularly discussing priorities, strategies and mutual interests in infrastructure delivery to further regional connectivity. Regional infrastructure funding and investment is clearly a cross-cutting issue that would be best served by high-level political dialogue. While ASEAN has the AMPC for advancing connectivity among its members, Australia and China could initiate a broader dialogue involving regional countries, regional and multilateral development banks, international financial institutions and recipient regional groupings such as ASEAN. Moving towards establishing a common framework for infrastructure investment and funding in the region would be a major contribution. Existing arrangements should be used creatively and non-exclusively to foster an important dialogue of this kind.

Australia, China and the next decade of regional cooperation

Australia and China have enjoyed growing prosperity as a direct result of the domestic economic reforms and regional economic integration initiatives they have jointly pursued over the past three decades. But large changes are now underway in Asia due to the changing structure of regional and global economic power. Close cooperation and communication is required in order to avoid misunderstandings and disputes, to narrow differences, and to maintain and build trust among countries in the region. The shift towards a more complex and multipolar order has already created new tensions and has begun to erode some of the region's shared principles. The major challenges now facing Asia's regional economy require innovative solutions.

Australia and China share a common interest in forging a new consensus on the shared principles of cooperation that can bring further economic interdependence, build political cooperation and maintain stable relations between the region's great powers.

The regional and global economic systems are changed as a result of what large economies do by themselves to manage their interactions with other economies and polities. But if we are to achieve a peaceful transition to a more multipolar world, these changes must take place through collective consensus among all the countries that are affected. This chapter has identified a number of areas in which collaboration between China, Australia and their partners in regional economic diplomacy will be of special importance in the coming decades.

Practical progress can be made in strengthening, extending and better connecting the established regional economic cooperation arrangements, such as APEC, the ASEAN Plus frameworks and the EAS, and in securing a framework for political confidence and security within which economic prosperity can be attained. A starting point will be to better connect the cooperation and dialogue on economic issues that takes place in APEC and the ASEAN Plus processes with the cooperation and dialogue on political-security issues discussed within the EAS. Important, cross-cutting issues that require close cooperation, such as energy and environmental transformation as well as regional infrastructure funding and investment, should be the focus of dialogue led by the major powers in the region and carried across different forums.

Australia and China have a strong, shared interest in mobilising a coalition for defining the path forward in forging the TTP and RCEP together towards a FTAAP that strengthens the WTO and the global economic system. The ChAFTA agreement can set benchmarks that will help with ambitious and high-quality outcomes in the RCEP agreement, especially in the investment chapter. Australia and China can pioneer services sector opening, capitalising on Australia's potential role as a good testing ground for liberalisation. China can use ChAFTA as a testing ground for a high quality US–China BIT.

Asia's future economic growth and integration is increasingly dependent on investment in critical infrastructure. Australia and China will both benefit if the region is better connected through sea, road and rail networks and other connectivity projects. The AIIB is an important new channel to funding Asia's infrastructure needs. Starting a high-level dialogue among all the actors in the region — both funders and recipients — aimed towards establishing a common framework for infrastructure funding and investment would reduce costs, bring better understanding and help improve connectivity.

CHAPTER 8
Collaboration in the global system

KEY MESSAGES

Australia and China both benefit from strong global institutions that are inclusive, rules-based and promote open and efficient international markets. An effective global governance framework will be critical to the success of China's economic transition and the resilience of the global economy. But many of these institutions were created decades ago and do not reflect current realities of the global economy. Australia, China and other partners can effect incremental change in reforming global governance.

Australia and China have powerful interests in entrenching the G20 as the preeminent forum for global economic governance. Without the G20, Australia may be excluded from a smaller alternative grouping (such as a 'G10') which, dominated by developed rather than emerging economies, would also see China with less voice in global rule-setting. Australia and China should actively use the G20, ensure its agenda is inclusive and targeted, ensure continuity by prioritising its multi-year 'two-in-five' growth agenda, and deepen its work on global governance reform. Most importantly, deficiencies in the global financial safety net create systemic risks that threaten the trading, financial and production networks that are integral to the Australian and Chinese economies.

- Australia and China collaborate within the G20 on global financial safety net issues on four key fronts: the next stage of IMF reform, implementing arrangements to make the IMF and regional financing arrangements more cohesive, renegotiating bilateral loans and strengthening domestic macroeconomic frameworks.

- In the near term, China should work to build-up the analytical capacity of the ASEAN Plus Three Macroeconomic Research Office and strengthen institutional collaboration between regional initiatives and the IMF. In the longer term, Australia and China should encourage G20 discussions on the next stage of IMF quota reform, assume a leading role in renegotiating bilateral loans between G20 countries and the IMF, and focus the G20 growth agenda on improving macro-financial resilience of all countries.

Australia and China benefit more from multilateral trade liberalisation than from plurilateral or bilateral initiatives. But increased fragmentation is swelling business costs, reducing trade flows and weakening production networks.

- Australia and China should lead a greater G20 focus on the multilateral trading system and initiate a pragmatic, incremental process on WTO reform and define a pathway for RCEP and other arrangements like the TPP to raise the standard of regional agreements and strengthen the WTO. They should also encourage the use of the G20 growth strategies to achieve ambitious commitments under the Trade Facilitation Agreement.

Australia and China can take other important steps to progress collaboration.

- Australia and China should initiate a step-by-step process towards a multilateral framework for investment, as well as increasing and streamlining multilateral funding for investment in infrastructure. Australia and China should collaborate in the G20 towards instituting more structured cooperation between the AIIB, the BRICS New Development Bank and existing multilateral development banks.

- Both countries should work within the G20 to promote global energy governance reform that addresses the substantial gaps in existing frameworks and institutions like the International Energy Agency.

- Australia and China should develop their partnership within the global response to climate change. This cooperation can draw on a variety of existing forums for dialogue at the official and political levels, including ministerial-level consultations and academic collaborations.

The global economic system has many dimensions: trade, finance, energy, development, security, climate and many more. Ensuring that markets are open, inclusive and governed by a predictable and stable set of rules and norms is critical to their successful functioning. Australia and China will both be active beneficiaries of good outcomes in all of these dimensions.

The system of rules, norms and institutions that govern the interactions between countries, in all of these dimensions, is collectively referred to as the 'architecture of global economic governance'. This architecture is becoming more fragmented. In the aftermath of World War II, the global governance system consisted of large multilateral institutions like the United Nations, IMF and World Bank. Today, it is more diversified across multilateral, regional and bilateral layers. This fragmentation has challenged the ability of global policymakers to respond adequately to the needs of the international community.

The architecture of global economic governance is now in need of reform. The changing structure of the global economy and the rise of emerging market economies, particularly China, have presented immense opportunities for the world but have also presented challenges for global governance. Global institutions that have served the international community well have not kept up with these transitions. They are in need of reform and the gaps that have emerged in global economic governance need to be filled.

The G20 is now the world's primary vehicle for such a reform of global economic governance. It is vital that the G20's status as the 'global steering committee' is entrenched. The G20 is the only forum in which it is possible to determine, and remake, the priorities of the institutions, forums and organisations that together make up the architecture of global economic governance. In addition, the G20 is the only forum in which advanced and emerging economies can cooperate in this governance reform on an equal footing.

Making sure that this happens is something that is particularly important for both Australia and China. The decline of the G20 would represent a substantial risk for Australia, given that Australia is much more likely to be excluded from the smaller ad-hoc groupings of great powers which would likely then emerge. As for China, these smaller ad-hoc groupings might well be dominated by advanced economies, and China's input in them would be afforded less weight. As a consequence, there would be less international balance in the global process of economic rule-setting.

Australia and China are in a position to cooperate, in important ways, in ensuring that this objective is achieved. Acting together, Australia and China should ensure that the G20 agenda remains inclusive and that its members work collaboratively on global economic issues in a way that resonates across the full membership of the G20 and beyond. In particular, Australia and China can promote the G20 by actively using it as a forum in which major global issues are raised and negotiated, instead of that being done in an ad-hoc way in other global or regional bodies.

There are five key areas of global policymaking in which Australia and China share an interest in strengthening the G20's leadership.

The first priority area for Australia and China is to ensure continuity in the G20 agenda by maintaining its core focus on growth and strengthening the recovery from the global financial crisis of 2007–2008. It is nearly a decade since this crisis struck, and yet the global recovery is still not complete. The G20 is in a position to make a difference to the strength of this recovery: the 'two-in-five' agenda that Australia initiated when it held the G20 presidency in 2014 has put it in a position to do just this. This agenda, agreed at the G20 Leaders' Summit in Brisbane in November 2014, is a process in which G20 members undertook to carry out policies which — when taken together — would ensure that global GDP is 2 per cent higher by the year 2018 than it would otherwise have been. This agreement was a significant achievement, but the follow-through since Brisbane then has been patchy. China can strengthen this follow-through by reinvigorating the G20 Mutual Assessment Process (G20MAP). The two-in-five process could also play an important part in a resurrection of the G20's leadership role in international cooperation on macroeconomic policies. This was a role that the G20 held in 2008–2009 during the global financial crisis; it is important that it takes this role again. The G20's ability to take a lead in strengthening the global recovery will also be helped by its ability to promote infrastructure investment worldwide. This agenda item is discussed in more detail below.

The second priority area for Australia and China is to ensure the adequacy of the global financial safety net. There are big gaps. It is too small and too fragmented. This reduces its coverage, consistency and responsiveness. Australia and China have a common interest in a strong, inclusive and responsive global financial safety net, centred on a representative IMF and with strong cooperation among the major economies. Australia and China should use their influence in the G20, IMF and regional arrangements to focus on five key issues: the next stage of IMF quota reform; the necessity, at both global and regional levels, of countries being able to obtain liquidity financing as necessary, including the urgent need for China to gain access to the group of countries that are able to obtain very large currency swaps; the implementation of arrangements to make the IMF and regional financing arrangements, such as the Chiang Mai Initiative Multilateralization (CMIM), more cohesive; renegotiating bilateral loans between G20 countries and the IMF; and using the G20 growth strategies and peer review process to boost efforts on strengthening domestic macroeconomic frameworks to improve resilience.

The third priority area is trade. Australia and China benefit most from trade liberalisation when it is multilateral rather than bilateral or plurilateral. Australia and China should work to support the cohesiveness of the global trading system by encouraging the G20 to refocus on the multilateral trading system rather than on regional or bilateral alternatives. This should include a focus on what incremental and pragmatic steps could be taken on WTO reform. Australia and China should use regional arrangements, such as RCEP, to raise the standard for cohesive regional agreements, pushing for better collaboration between the WTO and regional agreements and by delivering ambitious commitments under the Trade Facilitation Agreement by giving the structural reforms under the G20 growth strategies a stronger trade focus.

The fourth priority area is investment. There is scope for Australia and China to support the G20 in consolidating the work of the WTO, G20, OECD, UNCTAD and others on a process towards a multilateral framework for investment. There is also specific scope for greater multilateral cooperation on infrastructure investment. Australia and China should promote infrastructure investment in the G20 as a cross-cutting theme to bring G20 countries together to take action on multiple fronts, including growth, macroeconomic management, development, trade, energy and climate change. There is scope for better cooperation and synergies between the AIIB, the BRICS New Development Bank and existing multilateral development banks. The G20 should continue to support development banks in optimising their resources by leveraging private-sector finance. Success in this area will clearly be helpful in taking forward the G20's agenda of promoting a sustained worldwide recovery from the global financial crisis.

The fifth and final key area for collaboration between Australia and China concerns energy transformation and climate change. The global energy governance architecture has failed to keep up with significant changes in global energy markets and the global economy, and needs to be reformed. Australia and China should support the positive momentum in the G20 on global energy governance reform in building and adapting existing organisations and ensuring that they work together effectively. Closely related to the need for energy collaboration is the fact that Australia and China both have a vital interest in supporting a strong global response to climate change. China's economic and climate change strategy is increasingly geared towards low-carbon growth. Australia has the potential to become an exporter of low-carbon energy, which could supply China. Australia and China should work together on both climate change and energy strategies. This should involve government, industry and the research community. An existing research-based collaboration model could be scaled up to an international initiative.

Australia and China within the global system

The foundations of the economic partnership between Australia and China are multilateral and global in character. There are many areas in which collaboration between China, Australia and their partners in global affairs will become increasingly important because China's role in the global economy is growing. Although participation in some global or regional institutions is unique to just one of the two countries, Australia and China have more in common than not given the nature of their economic ties and their location in the world.

Australian and Chinese leaders, ministers and senior officials have a greater range of opportunities for regular engagement now than ever before. Figure 8.1 gives a snapshot of how Australia and China engage in global governance — the institutions they have in common and those they do not.

Figure 8.1 provides several important insights. First, it shows the scale of multilateral cooperation between Australia and China. The leaders of both countries come together at least four times a year at the G20, APEC, East Asia Summit and United Nations. The finance ministers of both countries meet around five times a year just for the G20, as well as separate regular meetings for APEC, ASEAN, the IMF and the World Bank. Central bank governors meet regularly at the Bank for International Settlements, G20 and APEC. For each of these institutions and forums, hundreds of Australian and Chinese officials are engaging on an almost continual basis in support of their ministers and leaders.

Second, Figure 8.1 illustrates the breadth of issues on which Australia and China cooperate through multilateral institutions and forums. Today, almost every domestic policy issue has an international dimension, and most international issues can have significant domestic consequences. As a result, the agendas of international institutions and forums have increased exponentially over time, covering a broad range of issues from trade, finance, development, tax, financial regulation and macroeconomic policies to issues like security, human rights, climate change, the environment and reforming the global governance architecture itself.

Third, Australia and China have more in common in these affairs than not. The institutions in which Australia and China cooperate are more influential and systemically important than the institutions unique to just one of the countries. These processes have helped develop extensive personal networks of leaders, ministers and officials, as well as representatives from business, labour, academia and civil society.

Finally, Figure 8.1 highlights the large number of regional institutions in which Australia and China cooperate, some of which compete directly or indirectly with existing global institutions. The only major global institutions in which Australia and China do not both participate are the United Nations Security Council (which excludes Australia), and the OECD and related International Energy Agency (which exclude China, although China participates in both institutions through an associate status).

Figure 8.1: Australia and China in the global governance architecture

China only	Australia only	Both China and Australia
• UN Security Council	• Trans-Pacific Partnership	• G20
• New Development Bank (formerly the BRICS Development Bank)	• Asian Development Bank	• ASEAN+6
	• International Energy Agency	• UN General Assembly
• Chiang Mai	• Pacific Islands Forum	• East Asia Summit
• Brazil-Russia-India-China-South Africa	• OECD	• APEC
• One Belt, One Road Initiative	• ANZUS treaty	• IMF
	• Commonwealth Heads of Government Meeting	• WTO
		• World Bank
		• Regional Comprehensive Economic Partnership
		• International Energy Forum
		• Asian Infrastructure Investment Bank
		• Bank of International Settlements

Source: Authors' schema.

The Australia–China relationship and sustaining international cooperation

The Australia-China relationship is of geopolitical significance, both for economic reasons and for reasons of political economy. This is despite the disparity between China and Australia in terms of economic and political weight. It is this fact that makes Australia–China cooperation particularly important, both in relation to strengthening the G20's role in global economic governance and in relation to the five key areas of global policymaking discussed above.

The geopolitical significance of the Australia–China economic relationship stems from Australia's role as a major supplier of primary commodity inputs to the Chinese industrial system, and the emerging future of bilateral services trade, direct investment and economic partnership. Prosperity in the two economies goes together. Such prosperity is vital for the world economy.

While its economy is closely linked to China, and to Asia more generally, Australia's strategic and political alliance with the United States has been confirmed as paramount by successive Australian governments. Australia has a strong incentive to avoid conflict between its economic partners and its US alliance. Australia's ability to steer such a middle path is greatly helped by its long history of engagement with global economic institutions such as the IMF, World Bank, WTO and UN agencies. For many years Australia has played an important role both in the governance of these institutions and in the determination of their policy stances. Australia's ability to keep the Australia–China relationship within such a broad multilateral framework, while at the same time building on the bilateral relationship, gives Australia the ability to make a significant contribution to the task of addressing global challenges and disputes. Such a contribution by Australia might help the world to avoid the counterproductive and unnecessary fragmentation of relationships, something that will hurt both countries.

On many issues, the most effective way for Australia and China to engage bilaterally will be to work together within multilateral frameworks and to develop coalitions of like-minded countries that can attract broader support for action. Collaboration between Australia and China is itself symbolic of the sort of global coalitions that need to be built — those that form across the divides of advanced and emerging economies. The focus of coalition-building efforts should be on both process and content.

On process, Australia and China have a common interest in ensuring that the global and regional rules, norms and institutions that govern interactions between countries are effective, inclusive and comprehensive. This Report has already argued that the G20 is the primary vehicle for achieving this. This chapter will illustrate some of the challenges facing global governance mechanisms, and will identify the common interests which Australia and China have in working with their partners in the G20 in addressing these challenges.

On content, Australia and China should work within these global frameworks to promote the common global interests that the two countries share in relation to particular areas. This Report has already mentioned five of these on which this chapter will focus: fostering global macroeconomic policy cooperation; strengthening the global financial safety net; strengthening the multilateral trading system; fostering better global coordination of infrastructure investment; and addressing global energy policy and climate change.

Strains on the global governance architecture

At the end of World War II, countries set about building a new global order to govern the interactions between countries and promote peace, stability and growth. This global architecture has served the global community well. It has provided a framework within which Australia and China have been able to pursue their national economic and political goals. Its core design remains important to serving those objectives consistently with the interests of other countries. Although it has been relatively resilient up to this point, a number of related forces are now straining this architecture and it will need to be reformed if it is to be as effective in the future as it has been in the past.

One such force is globalisation. Emerging economies now constitute a large share of the global economy (Figure 8.2). Economies are more connected and integrated than ever before. Figures 8.3 and 8.4 illustrate this through two key and related transmission mechanisms: trade and capital flows. From 1980 to 2015, global trade flows have increased six-fold. Similarly, there has been a significant increase in the size of gross capital flows. Global gross capital flows increased from less than 5 per cent of global GDP during 1980 to a peak of around 20 per cent by 2007.

This increased interconnectedness means countries are more susceptible to the policies and events in each other's economies. It also means that the global institutions and forums developed to govern the interactions between countries have a much larger task on their hands, requiring increased resources and a broader focus.

Figure 8.2: Share of global GDP (ppp)

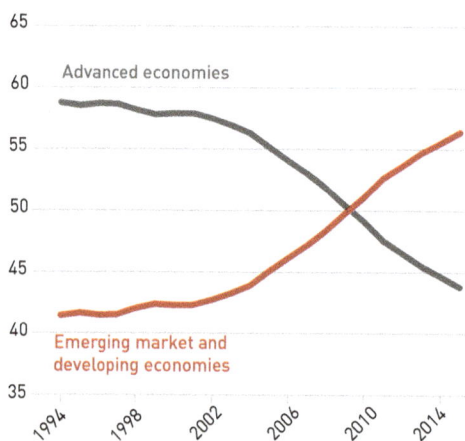

Figure 8.3: Global trade volumne of goods and services (1980=100)

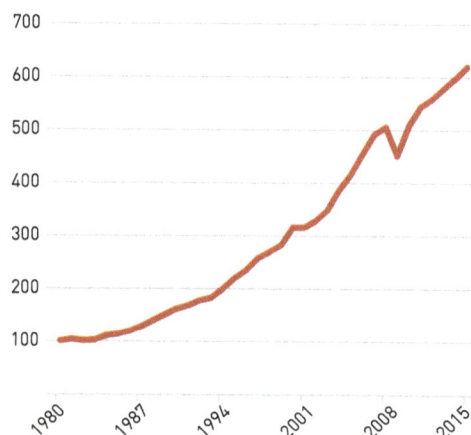

Source: IMF WEO 2015.

Figure 8.4: Global capital flows since 1980

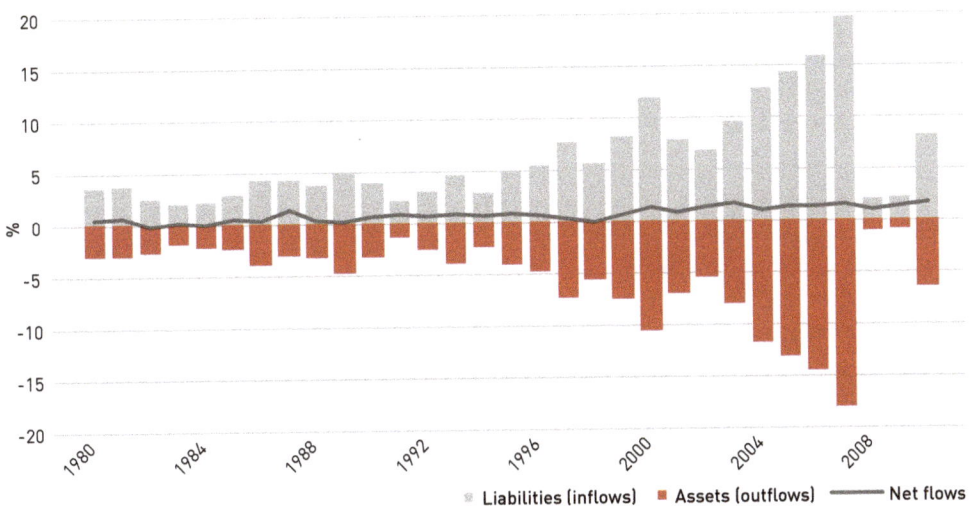

Source: Hawkins et al 2014.

While the size of the global economy has increased, countries' relative shares of global GDP have changed. Figure 8.2 shows the change in the composition of global GDP from 1994 to 2015. Emerging market and developing economies now contribute a greater share of global GDP (purchasing power parity) than advanced economies. As the composition of the global economy changes, so too must the composition of the international institutions and forums that govern it. Failure to do this not only means that these institutions' decisions will appear less legitimate, but it would also impair their effectiveness, due to the reduction in the funding and coverage of their activities.

Innovation and advances in technology also act to strain the existing global governance architecture. New technologies alter the ways in which countries interact, potentially requiring new governance structures to deal with emerging issues. Advances in technology and transportation, for example, have changed the way in which countries trade, from imports and exports of final products to global and regional production networks. Financial innovation has similarly posed challenges that have required new regulatory frameworks through the creation of the Financial Stability Board and Basel III.

Retaining the G20 as the preeminent forum for global economic governance

For many years, the G20 remained below the radar, working quietly but effectively at the level of finance ministers and central bank governors (Hulst 2015). This changed in 2008 when, faced with the global financial crisis, the need for significant macroeconomic policy cooperation led to the evolution of the G20 as a forum for national leaders. Leaders identified 'inconsistent and insufficiently coordinated macroeconomic policies' as a root cause of the crisis, and responded with the largest coordinated policy response in history, consisting of liquidity support to stabilise markets, the use of conventional monetary policies to support demand and fiscal stimulus packages coordinated across almost all G20 countries.

In 2009, under the presidency of the United States, G20 leaders declared it as 'the premier forum for international economic cooperation'. Its attention gradually shifted from fighting the crisis to implementing the longer-term policies, both macroeconomic and structural, that were necessary to promote strong, sustainable and balanced growth. Although the legitimacy of the G20 as a 'self-appointed club' is questioned, the G20 is today established as the only global economic forum where advanced and emerging economies cooperate on an equal footing (Hulst 2015).

Since 2008, the G20's agenda has expanded significantly. It now includes specific agenda items devoted to growth, employment, trade, anti-corruption, financial regulation, tax, infrastructure, investment, development, climate change, energy, food security, remittances and, at times, pandemics and terrorism. A consistent and cross-cutting theme of the G20 has been global governance reform. The G20 has emerged as the world's primary vehicle for reforming the global governance architecture and in helping steer the priorities of the institutions, forums and organisations that underpin it. The G20 is often referred to as the 'global steering committee', with a focus on rules-based and market-oriented approaches. This is an area in which the G20 has a clear comparative advantage given the composition of its membership, reflecting, in particular, the growing dynamism of the Asia Pacific region and the global influence of emerging economies.

G20 decisions, which take the form of policy proposals rather than enforceable policy strategies, must in most cases be brought before the governance organs of treaty-based institutions, such as the IMF, and be adopted by them on behalf of the global community. The G20 cannot decide for others, although the voting power that G20 members have in most international institutions means that their proposals are likely to become decisions (Drysdale and Dervið 2014).

The importance of the G20 to Australia and China

Unlike the G7, the G8 or the former G10, the G20 includes Australia and China. There are no guarantees the G20 will be a permanent fixture, let alone remain as a global steering committee. Leaders have a variety of multilateral, regional and bilateral institutions and forums available to them, as well as the ability to create new ones if they see fit. If the G20 stops being effective in the eyes of leaders, then the G20 may quickly find itself replaced.

Losing the G20 would represent a particular risk for Australia given Australia is much more likely to be excluded from alternative, smaller groupings than is China, as Australia is less important to the global economy. But China faces risks too. Should the G20 fall into disuse, a new smaller grouping may be dominated by advanced economies, which may not share China's perspectives, concerns and challenges as an emerging economy. There is a worse danger, still, that competing non-cooperative centres of global power are established — such as a BRICS versus G7 dichotomy — although these are to be avoided within a forum like the G20 too.

The G20 is the best avenue for Australia and China in influencing the rules, norms and institutions of global governance and the delivery of global public goods. Working within this framework is one of the most effective ways for Australia to engage with the international system. Australia has a strong incentive to have a seat at the table and influence how this framework develops. As a key beneficiary of global governance reform, China also has a strong incentive to play an active role in these discussions. As global governance evolves to reflect economic realities, China will find itself playing an increasing role in global institutions as well as in shaping the rules and norms that underpin them.

Increased Chinese leadership in global governance will be of significant importance into the future, particularly within the G20. Vines (2015) has argued that two things are required for effective Chinese leadership. The first is domestic competence. This requires transforming China's model of economic development from export-led growth to consumption-led growth, supported by a resilient financial system (see Chapters 1 and 2). The second is global leadership. This means developing an understanding of how to act on the world stage and an understanding of how the actions of different countries might be brought together. Most importantly, this requires China, and all countries, to nurture a forum in which information is exchanged, preferences articulated, discussions take place and compromises reached. The G20 is the ideal forum for this to take place. As such, maintaining the relevance and effectiveness of the G20 should be a top priority for China.

The G20 is not just a means for Australia and China to influence global outcomes. It is also a means for influencing outcomes and priorities domestically. When used strategically, the G20 can be an effective way of providing political cover to help undertake tough domestic reforms. This was on display, in particular, in how countries responded to the global financial crisis. Coordinated stimulus gave political cover to governments in implementing their own fiscal measures. Showing that other countries were undertaking similar actions not only gave these policies credibility, it also helped alleviate concerns that other countries might free-ride on the fiscal leakages from one country to another. The coordinated loosening of monetary policy similarly helped reduce the risk of a loss of confidence or currency attack (Vines 2015).

Maintaining the relevance and effectiveness of the G20

There are practical things Australia and China can do both individually and jointly to help maintain the relevance and effectiveness of the G20. Australia and China must ensure its agenda is inclusive. They should work collaboratively not only on issues that are \ important to the global economy, but also on issues that both countries can exhibit strong leadership on to help motivate others. Importantly, Australia and China must ensure there is continuity in the G20's agenda.

The two-in-five agenda has put the G20 in a position to ensure continuity and support for the global economic recovery. In 2014, countries put forward over 1000 reforms with the goal of ensuring that the G20 GDP in 2018 is 2 per cent higher than it would otherwise have been. Countries have since implemented, revised and added to these reforms in 2015 and 2016 through a comprehensive peer review process. This process should play an important part in the resurrection of the G20's leadership role in international cooperation on macroeconomic policies. The two-in-five agenda can help overcome the 'growth versus austerity' debate within the G20 by providing an acceptable means for countries committed to austerity to undertake public investment while all countries simultaneously undertake supply-side reforms to boost potential output. This, in turn, helps boost global aggregate demand and takes some pressure off monetary policy.

A strategy of investing more in infrastructure and carrying out supply-side reforms will stimulate global demand. This would lead to the creation of capital assets, which increase the supply-side potential of the economy, and would also increase demand during the investment period. While public–private partnerships can help optimise public resources, infrastructure investment will also enable a moderation of austerity in advanced countries that have fiscal space for public investment. The justification would be that investment in infrastructure leads to the creation of assets that can be used as collateral to the additional public sector debt incurred. Policymakers may be more willing to moderate austerity in the knowledge that additional infrastructure investment will not lead to a worsening in the public sector balance sheet.

In terms of the G20 agenda, another option for achieving continuity would be to create a permanent G20 secretariat. G20 countries would continue to take turns hosting the G20 Summit, but the secretariat would help manage the expanding agenda and ensure continuity from one year to the next. The cost of having a permanent secretariat, however, is that the G20 loses its status as an informal forum; it makes the G20 less country-owned as the secretariat will become its own political entity which must then be negotiated with, slowing down reform processes. Past experience with other international forums that created permanent secretariats would also suggest that this does little in improving continuity and that, instead, it is the political will of countries that determines whether any particular summit is successful or not. Given the G20 has routinely rejected the notion of a permanent secretariat, emphasising the G20's long-run growth agenda is likely a better option for promoting continuity.

Australia and China can also promote the G20 by actively using it to raise and negotiate global issues, instead of using other regional or global alternatives. This includes having leaders and ministers use the G20 for key announcements that are of global significance, as well as using the G20 as the platform for important negotiations. Australia and China can also promote the G20 by being ambitious in the commitments they make and in encouraging other countries to do the same.

Ensuring the G20 remains an effective forum requires Australia and China to actively avoid G20 gridlock by not supporting or participating in the formation of damaging strategic blocs. In particular, this means avoiding a G7 versus BRICS scenario where countries agree to pre-align their positions within the G20. China and Australia should deliberately and publicly approach the G20 on an issue-by-issue basis and seek to build coalitions on individual issues across advanced, emerging and developing divides, as well as geographically across Europe, Asia, the Americas, Africa and the Middle East.

Supporting a stronger global financial safety net

The global financial safety net consists of the international financial resources and institutional arrangements to help countries experiencing a financial or economic crisis and preventing its contagion. It is of fundamental importance to the Australian and Chinese economies through the stability it provides to the global financial system by ensuring countries can access liquidity financing as necessary. It supports stability by acting as a financial backstop, providing emergency financing where a country is unable to meet external payments and cannot access markets (Sterland 2013). The safety net also acts as a form of insurance (Shafik 2015). Countries contribute resources to the safety net and, knowing they will receive assistance if they experience problems with their external payments, are more willing to open their economies. Both Australia and China have played key roles in strengthening the safety net in the past. This includes through their quota and bilateral contributions to the IMF, their support for G20-led initiatives around IMF reform and, for China, through its leadership in regional initiatives and establishing currency swap lines to bolster the safety net in the Asia Pacific.

It is therefore important to ensure the adequacy and effectiveness of the global financial safety net as part of the reform of the international monetary system that the IMF should advance. As PBoC Governor Zhou Xiaochuan stated on behalf of China to the recent International Monetary and Financial Committee (Zhou 2016), this requires enhancing the role of the IMF, improving its lending facilities, allowing regional financial arrangements to play a better supplementary role, and further improving the sovereign debt restructuring mechanism, with better coordination among creditors and debtors and wider use of its enhanced contractual clauses.

Given the strong institutions, macroeconomic policy framework and flexibility of the Australian economy, it is unlikely that Australia will require any direct support from the IMF in the future. This is similarly the case for China given the significant domestic buffers and policy space available to Chinese authorities — and also because, in the event that China did require external assistance, the sheer size of its economy would mean the amount of support required would utterly dwarf the capabilities of the IMF and all regional institutions combined. External support would instead come from countries in the region and the reserve-asset countries, particularly the United States and the European Union. Big player cooperation has to be the anchor for an IMF-based financial safety net. The relevance of the global financial safety net to Australia and China is in the fundamental role it plays in stabilising the global financial system given its proven ability to transmit shocks into the Australian and Chinese economies through trade and investment channels.

Australia is an open economy that is dependent on foreign savings to finance investment, particularly for its mining and resources sectors, and on international trade for maintaining its high standard of living. Australian authorities hold limited domestic reserves, relying instead on the economic flexibility that has been developed in the Australian economy over many decades. Although the flexibility of Australia's economy, particularly its floating exchange and inflation-targeting monetary policy, helps it weather volatility from international markets, the Australian economy is nevertheless susceptible to global and regional shocks through trade and investment channels. Australia significantly benefits from the stability derived from the safety net and from having strong mechanisms and institutions underpinning it. Australia also benefits from ensuring the IMF remains central to the global financial safety net because, unlike China, Australia does not yet participate in any regional financing arrangements such as the CMIM or the European Stability Mechanism (ESM).

While China does participate in regional initiatives and has significant domestic reserves, the Chinese economy has shown itself to be increasingly susceptible to international shocks. The Asian financial crisis, the global financial crisis and more recently the so-called Taper Tantrum in 2013 have highlighted the susceptibility of the Chinese economy to global shocks through financial channels. These shocks, particularly the European debt crisis, have also highlighted the susceptibility of the Chinese economy to reduced global demand through trade channels. China is a key beneficiary from global efforts to have the IMF, and global governance more generally, better reflect the economic realities of the 21st century. These reforms will be key to facilitating China's economic transition and having it play a more active role in the global financial system of the future, as well as in having input into how global rules, norms and institutions develop over time.

Ensuring that countries can access liquidity financing, both regionally and globally, in times of difficulty is of critical importance. The response to the global financial crisis, particularly through the currency swap lines established between central banks, showed both the importance of ensuring adequate access to liquidity but also the ad hoc and unpredictable nature in which this is currently supplied. The global financial safety net is particularly important for Australia and China. Emerging market economies are more systemically important to the global economy than ever before and many of them are facing difficult transitions and significant risks in the short to medium term that threaten to reduce the confidence of investors in holding assets in these economies. Capital outflows from emerging markets have surged toward US$1 trillion over 2014–2015. That is approximately double the amount that exited emerging markets during the global financial crisis (NN Investment Partners 2015). According to the Bank for International Settlements, investors are increasingly focused on growing vulnerabilities in the emerging market economies as they reassess the global growth outlook (BIS 2015).

Figure 8.5 shows that economic activity in these economies is now projected to slow for the fifth successive year (IMF 2015a). These downgrades reflect common as well as country-specific factors. Common factors include weaker demand from advanced economies, weaker growth in oil exports, adjustments in the aftermath of credit and investment booms, a weaker outlook for exporters of other commodities (including in Latin America), as well as more difficult external financing conditions. Should downside risks increase or materialise for the emerging market economies, the global financial safety net will have a critical role to play in preventing contagion and buffering its effects on the Australian and Chinese economies. But, as the following section explains, the safety net, at present, is too small, too unresponsive and too fragmented to play this role.

Figure 8.5: IMF GDP forecasts for emerging market and developing economies

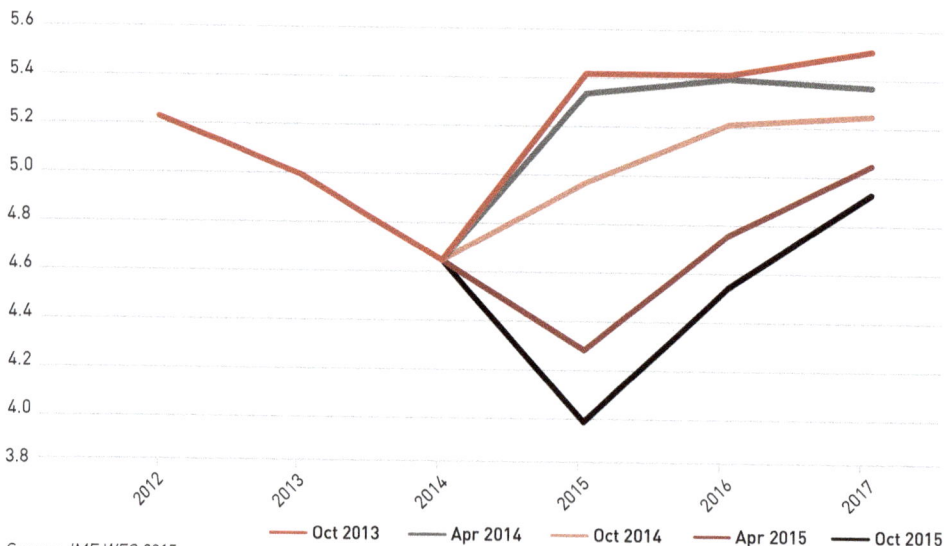

Source: IMF WEO 2015.

The evolution of the global financial safety net

In 2003, the safety net consisted predominantly of the IMF and the US$365 billion it held to fight crises (Australian Treasury 2014). Since then, the safety net has significantly increased in size but has fragmented in composition. There are several reasons for this fragmentation. The most significant is the slow pace in reforming the IMF so as to boost its permanent funding and make its governance structure more representative of the contemporary global economy.

The slow pace of IMF reform has made the IMF more reliant on secondary sources of funding, such as bilateral loan commitments, and has made the global economy more reliant on regional and bilateral alternatives outside of the IMF. In 2010, the euro area created the European Financial and Stability Fund, which later became the European Stability Mechanism, to respond to the European debt crisis. Similarly in 2010, BRICS countries created the US$100 billion BRICS currency reserve pool and the 13 ASEAN Plus Three countries created what is now the CMIM — a pool of foreign exchange reserves that expanded to US$240 billion in 2012 (Kawai 2015).

For the emerging market economies, these initiatives occurred because of insufficient IMF resources as well as dissatisfaction with the IMF's response to the Asian financial crisis and the slow pace of IMF reform. This has also seen countries increase domestic and bilateral buffers through foreign exchange reserves and bilateral swap lines, respectively. Foreign exchange reserves have increased from less than US$2 trillion in 1990 to over US$11 trillion in 2016 while the value of currency swaps utilised during the global financial crisis was over US$600 billion (Australian Treasury 2014).

These challenges are more apparent in Asia than anywhere else. While Asia is large compared to other regions, the safety net in Asia is highly fragmented and patchy in its coverage. As of 2016, it consists of the IMF, CMIM, BRICS currency reserve pool, bilateral currency swap lines, domestic foreign exchange reserves and, potentially, the World Bank and the ADB — which provided liquidity support during the Asian financial crisis.

Of course, this 'fragmentation' is not necessarily new. Historically, most crises have required some form of a coordinated, ad hoc response between different institutions, organisations and countries, whether it be Mexico in 1994 (requiring a coordinated response from the US administration, US Federal Reserve, the IMF and Bank for International Settlements) or Asia in 1997 (with resources from the IMF, World Bank, ADB, the United States, Japan and others). But the size of the current designated safety net is too small to assist even those economies that are relatively small and not necessarily systemically significant.

Quantifying the size and adequacy of the safety net

Quantifying the size of the safety net means adding together its multilateral, regional and bilateral components (Figure 8.6). The global component consists predominantly of the IMF. As of June 2015, the IMF has total resources of US$1.3 trillion, which includes its quota resources, resources from the IMF's New Arrangements to Borrow and General Arrangements to Borrow, and bilateral loans with the IMF. The regional component totals around US$840 billion if the resources available in the major regional arrangements are added together — the European Stability Mechanism, the CMIM and the BRICS currency reserve pool. Finally, a good proxy for the size of swap lines during a time of crisis is to use the peak value of the dollar swap lines during the global financial crisis. These peaked at around

US$600 billion, although it should be noted that many of these swap lines no longer exist (the United States still has unlimited swap lines with the United Kingdom, European Union, Switzerland and Japan) and additional swap lines have been created since then, particularly by China.

Adding these components together, the overall safety net is around US$2.7 trillion: about 50 per cent comes from the IMF, 20 per cent from swap lines, 20 per cent from the European Stability Mechanism and 10 per cent from BRICS and the CMIM. The IMF (2016) estimates the safety net to be around US$3.7 trillion. This larger number appears because the IMF includes additional, albeit smaller, regional financing arrangements. If we were to include even more regional arrangements, including regional development banks, which have historically played a role in crisis response, the size of the safety net is even larger still, calculated in this Report at around US$4.6 trillion. However as the analysis below shows, the adequacy of the safety net's size is questionable even using these larger estimates.

While domestic foreign exchange reserves could be added as a fourth component, these reserves are generally a country's first line of defence. Although important (as discussed below), it can be argued that they are no more part of the global financial safety net than domestic macroeconomic policy.

The adequacy of the safety net relates to its size and composition, which, in turn, influences its coverage, consistency and speed in responding to a crisis (IMF 2016). Countries are now more exposed to financial contagion than ever before, so a larger safety net makes sense. But the US$2.7 trillion figure represented above, or the IMF's US$3.7 trillion figure, overstate the safety net that is actually available.

First, Figure 8.7 shows that, if we exclude resources that are not immediately available, the size of the safety net drops to around US$1.75 trillion. For the IMF, much of its resources are tied up in existing programs or come from borrowing commitments that have not been paid-in. As a result, its resources drop from US$1.3 trillion to US$421 billion. Similarly, the forward commitment capacity of the ESM drops from US$500 billion to US$369 billion. It should also be noted that the dollar swap lines from the US Federal Reserve may not necessarily be of the same size or extended to the same countries. How the US Federal Reserve chose these countries also remains unclear.

Second, whether a safety net of US$1.75 trillion is adequate or not depends on the size of the crisis that it is responding to. The IMF (2016) notes that the size of the safety net, and particularly the IMF's resources, have not kept pace with the 25-fold increase in global capital flows since 1980 (Lagarde 2016). It has also failed to keep pace with the increasing stock of debt among troubled economies. Greece, for example, represents just 0.25 per cent of global GDP (PPP; IMF 2016). But if the IMF were required to shoulder the burden of the Greek bailout on its own (approximately US$279 billion since 2010), this would absorb almost 70 per cent of the IMF's capacity. A worse scenario would be bailing out a larger economy, such as Spain. Spain represents 1.5 per cent of global GDP (PPP; IMF 2016) and has US$669.5 billion of debt to refinance in the five years from 2015 to 2020 (Gilbert 2014). This would exhaust the IMF's capacity and most of the ESM.

Figure 8.6: The components of the global financial safety net

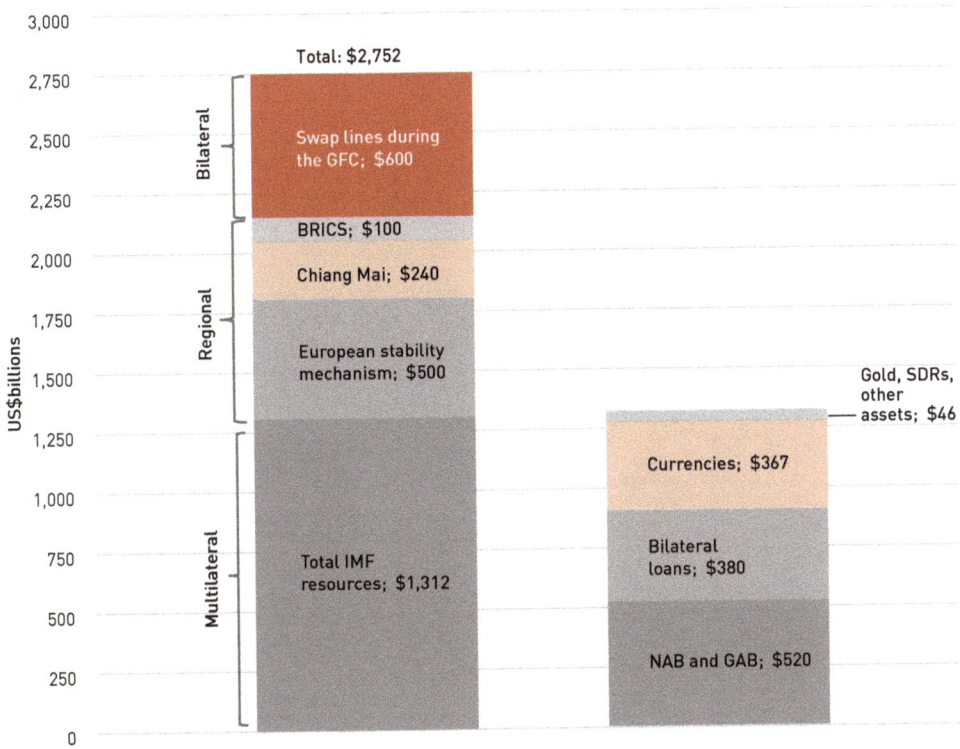

Source: Authors' calculations.

Third, the adequacy of the global safety net depends on what is meant by the term 'global'. The actual size of the safety net depends on the country in question. For Australia, the safety net consists entirely of the IMF and its swap line with China, since Australia does not participate in any relevant regional initiatives. Similarly, swap lines are only available to those who can negotiate them, and it is worth noting that emerging markets and developing economies were excluded from the US Federal Reserve swap lines in the global financial crisis. The IMF (2016) acknowledges that the safety net's coverage is increasingly patchy, which is a particular risk for non-developed countries.

Fourth, market confidence is reduced when investors are unable to see a designated war chest and necessary institutional arrangements to respond to a crisis. Assuming that only ad hoc international cooperation will be forthcoming during a time of crisis is not conducive to market confidence. It also erodes the implicit insurance policy, which encourages countries to open their economies in the first place (Shafik 2015). Having a strong safety net can help encourage cross-border investment and increase consumption through reduced precautionary savings.

Fifth, increased fragmentation means greater dependence on the ability of different institutions and arrangements to coordinate with one another at a time of crisis. This can mean a slower and less consistent response from one crisis to the next (IMF 2016). The G20 identified these concerns as reasons for developing principles to guide cooperation between the IMF and regional funding arrangements (RFAs) (G20 2011). The IMF (2016) has also found that most countries would need to use several elements of the safety net to fully cover their financing needs, the coordination of which the IMF calls 'a strong assumption'.

Figure 8.7: Total resources compared to available resources

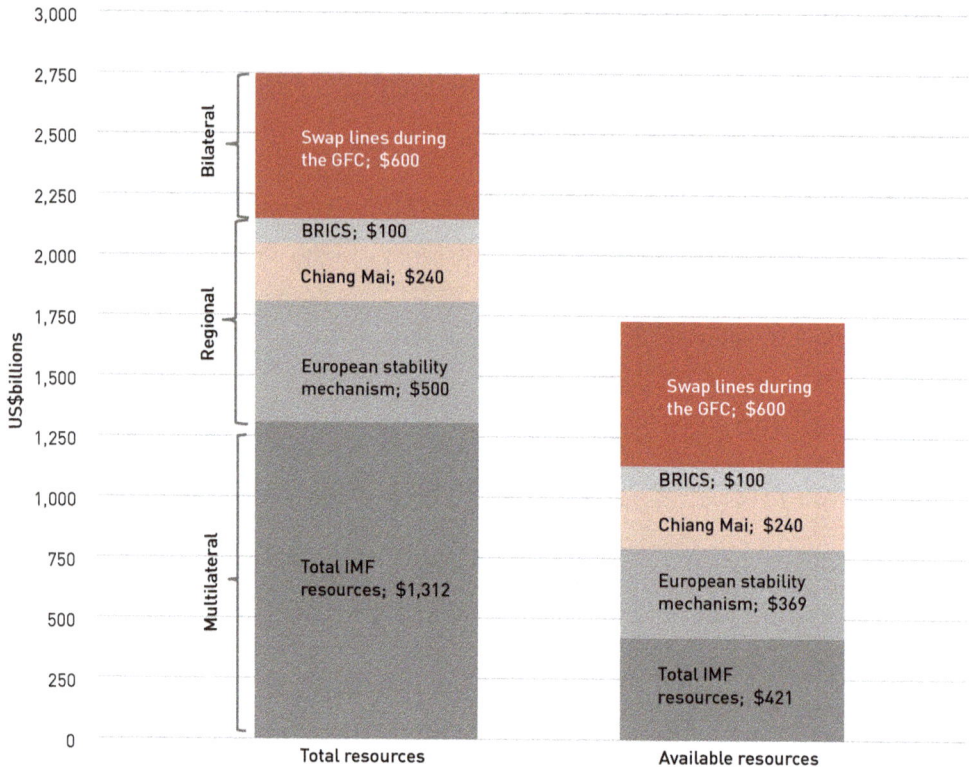

Source: Authors' calculations

Finally, these regional financing arrangements are weak substitutes for the IMF. The closeness of countries that participate in regional arrangements means that imposing potentially painful but necessary conditionality can be difficult and uncomfortable. The narrower base of resources means they are less reliable, less diversified and more risky for contributing countries. Surveillance activities also tend to be partial as the global picture is not as obvious.

For these reasons, the IMF should remain at the centre of the global financial safety net. Its diverse membership and long history provides the IMF with several unique features that are irreplaceable at a regional or bilateral level. The IMF has the greatest capacity to raise resources in times of need and to ensure that credit risk is diversified globally to the greatest extent possible. As such, it provides the most effective and low cost insurance against crises.

Avenues for collaboration between Australia and China in the G20

Reforming the safety net would benefit the Asian region if the IMF takes a holistic approach that addresses the root causes of its fragmentation. This requires a focus on increased and more permanent funding for the IMF, better tailored financing facilities to meet the needs of Asian economies, a new phase of reforms to give Asian economies a greater voice in the IMF, and better cooperation between the IMF and RFAs.

The global financial safety net is a policy challenge that G20 finance ministers and central bankers have been at the frontier of for close to 15 years. It is an issue uniquely suited to the G20 as all countries benefit from the positive externalities that flow from an effective global financial safety net that takes in global, regional, bilateral and national arrangements.

The G20 is uniquely suited to address the inadequacies of the current safety net. One-third of the IMF's funding from bilateral loans will start to expire over 2016 and 2017, and the G20 will need to discuss the next stage of IMF reform following the recent ratification of the 2010 quota reforms by the United States Congress. The G20's history has shown, however, that efforts to achieve sweeping changes to global governance, so-called 'grand bargains', have been unsuccessful, except perhaps in the context of an emergency on the scale of the global financial crisis. The focus of the G20 under the French presidency in 2011, for example, was to take a holistic look at the international monetary system with a focus on radical reforms. The outcomes achieved from this process, however, were significantly less than the amount of political capital that was expended.

Instead, the G20 should focus on what pragmatic steps it can take in supporting an incremental process to strengthen the safety net. To this extent, Australia and China should support G20 efforts on the issue of the global safety net from four key perspectives: the next stage of IMF reform, implementing arrangements to make the IMF and RFAs more cohesive, renegotiating bilateral loans, and strengthening domestic macroeconomic frameworks.

IMF reform

IMF reform is the linchpin for addressing the challenges facing the global financial safety net. China's G20 presidency in 2016 presents an awkward contradiction where the country chairing the global steering committee remains grossly underrepresented in many of the world's most important institutions. While the ratification of the 2010 IMF reforms helped address this, there is still much to be done. Australia and China should encourage the G20 to start a conversation on the next stage of IMF quota reform. This will be an incremental process over many years, and it is reasonable to expect hesitation from some members, notably the United States, in wanting to advance a new round of reforms so quickly after the ratification of the last round. However, momentum from the recent success of the 2010 reforms should not be lost.

There are a number of other aspects of IMF reform that similarly still need to take place. This includes bringing forward the 15th General Review of Quotas and implementing the agreement reached in 2010 whereby advanced European countries would free up an IMF board chair for an emerging market economy. There is also additional work to do in reviewing the IMF's quota formula, although resolution on this issue will require a political solution and will not be solved through technical reviews. Finally, there is a longer-term opportunity for Australia and China to begin planting the seeds for having a representative from an emerging market economy appointed as the head of the IMF at the end of Lagarde's term.

Reforms to the IMF could also focus on its financing facilities to ensure they are meeting the needs of its members. This could include a greater use of precautionary financing to make the safety net faster, more flexible and more responsive. The IMF took a significant step in this direction in developing the flexible credit line and the precautionary and liquidity line in 2010. These facilities are aimed at strongly performing economies hit by external shocks — the so-called 'innocent bystanders'. The IMF (2016) has found that without prompt liquidity provision, innocent bystanders can quickly become vulnerable during systemic crises. This is also a motivation for countries to stockpile foreign exchange reserves. Having a greater focus on precautionary financing could help better meet the needs of members, reduce fragmentation and improve the IMF's response to crises.

Composition of the SDR basket of currencies

On 13 November 2015, IMF staff recommended the renminbi (RMB) be included in the Special Drawing Rights (SDR) basket (IMF 2015c). China, of course, continues to have a key role to play in this regard. Liberalisation of China's capital account is pivotal not only to the RMB's inclusion in the SDR, but also for China to play an increasing role in the global economy more generally. Importantly, the RMB's inclusion can be used by China as a catalyst to help drive difficult financial reforms at home.

Strengthening collaboration between the IMF and RFAs

While reforming the IMF is the best way to address the challenges facing the safety net, there are other steps that can be taken to make the patchwork of global and regional initiatives more cohesive. Regional and bilateral initiatives can have an important role within the safety net, but they must be rigorous and structured so as to complement the IMF. At the Cannes Summit in 2011, leaders endorsed 'G20 Principles for Cooperation between the IMF and Regional Financing Arrangements' (G20 2011). This should be used as the basis for developing an overarching framework for better cooperation between the IMF and RFAs.

Such a framework could be gradually developed and strengthened through informal and formal methods. Informally, regular dialogues could be held between the IMF and RFAs to reach a better understanding on how to coordinate with each other, such as establishing procedures for information sharing and jointly conducting crisis scenario exercises. This suggestion was put forward by South Korea in 2012 and received broad support (G20 India Secretariat 2014). It has also been canvassed by the IMF (2013) as a practical step to fine-tune the current flexible approach to IMF–RFA cooperation.

More formally, the G20 could task a working group to develop detailed guidelines on IMF–RFA cooperation. Such an agreement could formalise the expectation that co-financing operations would be subject to certain principles and safeguards, similar to those stipulated under the IMF's lending framework. The detailed guidelines could provide concrete guidance on how these principles could be achieved. This proposal has also been canvassed by the IMF (2013) and should be considered by the G20.

Renewing bilateral funding of the IMF

The expiration of US$369 billion of IMF bilateral loan funding over 2016 and 2017 requires an urgent response under China's G20 presidency. This funding represents a third of the IMF's funding and its potential loss introduces an unacceptable amount of systemic risk into the global economy at a time when many economies are going through difficult transitions. These loans must be renewed.

However, Australia and China should not lose sight of the ultimate goal, which is long-term, adequate and sustainable funding for the IMF. While these bilateral loans are critical in filling a short-term gap, their renewal should form part of a broader discussion around the timetables for quota reform so that, ultimately, these bilateral loans can be folded into longer-term forms of IMF financing.

Strengthening domestic frameworks

Finally, the safety net also needs to be considered in a broader context. It is not a panacea. It is, and should remain, a last resort. There needs to be an equal focus on domestic reforms to build sound macroeconomic frameworks within countries to cushion against economic shocks and ensure flexible responses. Australia and China should ensure that the macroeconomic focus of the G20 growth strategies is not lost, and that these strategies and the G20 peer review process expressly consider how domestic frameworks could be strengthened, with analytical support from the IMF.

Supporting and promoting the global trading system

The global trading system refers to the rules, norms and institutions that govern international trade. Although it can be characterised in many ways, the system consists of multilateral, plurilateral and bilateral components. Bilaterally, it consists of hundreds of FTAs or other forms of trade agreement that have emerged over the last 20 years. Plurilaterally, the system consists of regional and cross-regional agreements such as the North American Free Trade Area (NAFTA), TPP, RCEP and TTIP. Multilaterally, the system consists of the WTO and the multilateral agreements it has produced.

Australia and China actively cooperate multilaterally through the WTO as well as bilaterally through ChAFTA, which has set new directions in trade policy strategy. Differences emerge, however, in regards to plurilateral arrangements. While Australia and China cooperate through RCEP under the auspices of ASEAN, Australia is a member of the TPP while China is not. Figure 8.8 gives a snapshot of how Australia and China fit within the increasingly complex global trading system.

All three of these components — multilateral, plurilateral and bilateral — are important and relevant to the Australia–China relationship. Australia and China are both trading nations. Both countries have benefited immensely from the global trading system through increased consumption, investment and higher productivity through the more efficient allocation of resources that trade liberalisation facilitates.

Exports represent about 21 per cent of Australian GDP and about 23 per cent of China's GDP. Compare this to the United States, where exports represent just 13 per cent of GDP, and it is clear that Australia and China have strong interests in the efficiency and effectiveness of the global trading system. Australia and China have a particular interest in ensuring the global trading system supports regional and global value chains by facilitating trade and investment flows across borders. This has been aided by improvements in physical infrastructure and logistics services, rapid developments of information and communication technology, and falls in trade barriers and trade costs, all of which have helped expand trade and foreign investment. The fact that the WTO has been locked in a decade-long preoccupation with 20th century trade issues (such as tariffs and agriculture) in the Doha Round has merely exacerbated this regionalisation effect (Baldwin 2013).

Australia and China gain the most from trade liberalisation when it is multilateral, rather than bilateral or plurilateral. In short, the GDP and, more importantly, consumption growth enjoyed by Australia and China will be bigger when liberalisation efforts are undertaken within larger, and preferably worldwide, groups (McKibbin 1998). The larger the group, the greater the potential for more efficient allocation of resources within these economies is. In larger groupings the stimulation of demand for exports and capital as trade barriers are also lowered. A larger grouping also helps prevent trade being diverted away from non-participating countries.

There are three priority areas for collaboration between Australia and China. First, given the benefits of multilateral trade liberalisation to both countries, Australia and China should refocus the G20's efforts on boosting the multilateral trading framework by promoting an incremental process through which the G20 can work towards WTO reform over the coming years. Second, Australia and China should focus their efforts in the G20, WTO and RCEP on taking practical steps to try to reduce fragmentation in the global trading system. Third, given the importance of investment to the effectiveness of the global and regional value chains Australia and China participate in, both countries should support the G20 on an incremental process that supports a multilateral framework for investment.

Figure 8.8: Australia and China within the global trading system

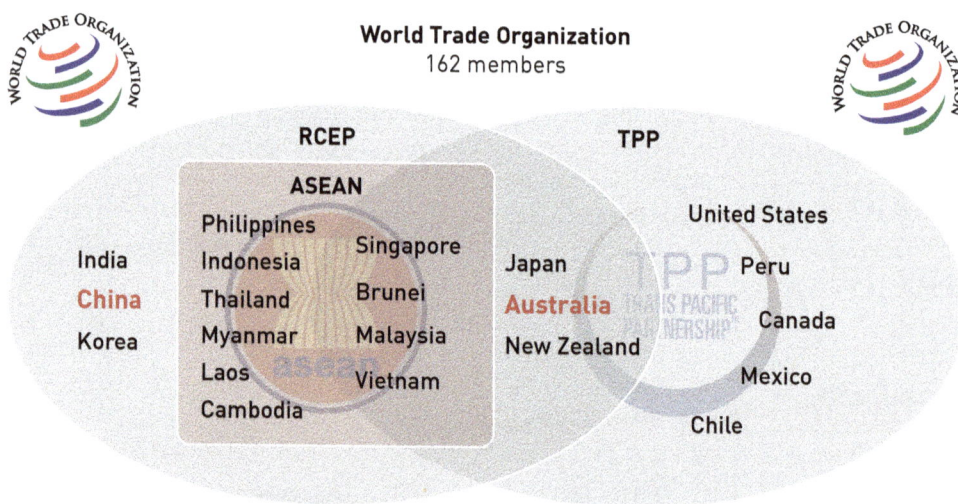

Source: Authors' schema.

Promoting multilateral liberalisation and WTO reform through the G20

The responsibility for global trade governance has rested with the WTO since its creation in 1995. Its membership has grown to 162 as of May 2016. The WTO's central function is to provide a forum for international trade negotiations, which results in WTO agreements. The WTO's other functions include administering WTO agreements, monitoring national trade policies, and providing technical assistance and training for developing countries (Baldwin 2013).

The WTO is the preferred vehicle for pursuing trade liberalisation and managing the global trading system for both the Australian and Chinese governments. It is the only organisation that can take a comprehensive view of the increasing complexities of the evolving economic engagements between countries. But WTO negotiations have now been stalled for two decades, largely over a divide on major issues such as agriculture subsidies, industrial tariffs and non-tariff barriers.

As a result, the WTO has not kept up with the evolution of the global trading system, particularly the development of global and regional value chains and the intertwining of trade, investment, intellectual property and services. While the WTO remained focused on tariffs and agriculture, more complex global and regional production networks were forming. Without WTO reform that allows entrenchment of the stronger regulatory and institutional arrangements necessary for more complex international commercial ties (in trade, services and investment), the global economy risks the steady decline in the relevance of one of its most valuable international institutions and the consequent loss of extraordinary opportunities to improve global living standards and creation of a permanently fragmented global economic system.

The difficulty in reforming the WTO is not in coming up with alternative rules or institutional frameworks but in achieving political agreement that reform is required and on what form it should take. The focus needs to be on developing an incremental, inclusive and robust process through which such issues can be discussed. The G20 presents the most effective forum given its global governance focus.

The G20's focus on trade has been moving in the wrong direction in recent years, giving greater emphasis to FTAs and regional agreements. Under Australia's G20 presidency, as under Turkey's, the focus was on domestic structural reforms in national growth strategies to reduce the cost of doing business, streamline customs procedures, reduce regulatory burdens and strengthen trade-enabling services. While these are important areas of focus, the G20's key area of comparative advantage is in tending to the multilateral system and shaping how bilateral, plurilateral and multilateral components fit together. Increasingly, communiqués depict the G20 as a forum for information sharing on trade issues rather as the driving force for instigating necessary global governance reform.

The G20 needs to refocus on the multilateral trading system and develop a process for moving forward on WTO reform. Pangestu and Nellor (2014) provide practical suggestions on how a G20 process could be developed, building on the creation of a designated G20 working group. They suggest that leaders announce the appointment of an Eminent Persons Group (EPG) comprised of highly regarded people in international governance, trade and other areas, tasked to make recommendations on the global trade regime and specifically on the principles to be observed by G20 members as they consider governance reform in regards to trade. The composition of the EPG should reflect the need to move trade discussions beyond the negotiation paradigm to reflect the broader economic 'wins' of a stronger, more modern regime.

Reforming the WTO and entrenching its authority is of central importance to Australia and China. Regional agreements are fragmenting the relationship and both countries benefit the most from trade liberalisation that is undertaken across the largest number of countries possible. WTO reform is also the linchpin for addressing fragmentation in the global system, which benefits neither Australia nor China given the increased cost of trade and investment it entails.

Integral to this will be giving the business community (represented through the Business 20, or 'B20') a greater voice within the G20. The B20 has a fundamental role to play in advising G20 leaders, ministers and officials on the practical steps the G20 can take to improve the ease of trading and doing business across borders, particularly by producing a more cohesive international trade architecture. The G20 needs to ensure it provides platforms for the B20 to make its recommendations to leaders, including significant engagement by leaders, ministers and officials with the B20 and its recommendations. Responsibility also falls to the B20 to ensure its recommendations are specific, targeted and firmly rooted in a robust evidence-base. The B20 can play a continued role in the implementation of those recommendations and should not concern itself only with the recommendations themselves.

A more cohesive and integrated global trading system

There are other practical steps Australia and China could support to help address fragmentation in the global trading system. Called the 'noodle bowl effect' in the context of Asia, trade fragmentation risks reducing trade and investment flows by increasing the cost and complexity of doing business across borders (Urata 2013). These costs include different and competing tariff schedules, exclusion lists, rules and standards. Since the coexistence of bilateral, plurilateral and multilateral agreements is unlikely to change any time soon, the focus should be on achieving greater coherence between these diverse agreements.

Preferential trade agreements have positive and negative effects. The positive effects come from the exposure of uncompetitive, sheltered home producers to competition from lower-cost partner country suppliers. The negative effects are that these agreements divert trade away from more efficient and competitive third country suppliers towards partner suppliers who only become competitive because of the preferential treatment they receive under the agreement (Armstrong 2015; see Chapter 7). Having a large number of intertwined preferential trade agreements not only risks trade diversion but also exacerbates these negative effects by increasing complexity and compliance costs. The 'noodle bowl' can make Asian firms — particularly small- and medium-sized enterprises, which disproportionately use FTA preferences — face costly business procedures and cumbersome requirements (Baldwin 2013). Ensuring coherence between these agreements helps eliminate these negative effects.

The goal for the TPP and RCEP must be to ensure they act as a stepping-stone towards multilateralisation. The TPP was signed in February 2016, although it still awaits approval in the US Congress and in other jurisdictions. There is a risk that these rules and standards have been negotiated bilaterally such that the TPP may have some of the characteristics of a series of bilateral arrangements rather than a genuinely common set of regional rules. This is far from ideal in terms of economic efficiency since it will protect suppliers within the arrangement against lower cost suppliers outside it, such as China, Indonesia or Europe for instance, diverting trade rather than creating it (Drysdale 2015).

The focus of Australia and China should now be on working with partners in RCEP to ensure it is not only complementary with the TPP but goes further on key issues so as to raise the standard for regional agreements. This requires a strong political commitment from leaders to better integrate the five ASEAN Plus One FTAs with China, Japan, South Korea, India and Australia–New Zealand. From a practical point of view, the ASEAN Plus Six countries should adopt a gradual approach, which has been shown to be effective in the establishment of the ASEAN Free Trade Area (AFTA), in tariff elimination, as well as a co-equal approach in the definition of rules of origin (Urata 2013).

There are other practical things that can be done to help ensure coherence between these agreements. These include encouraging rationalisation and flexibility of rules of origin, upgrading origin administration, improving business participation in FTA consultations and strengthening support systems for SMEs (Baldwin 2013). There are also important ways in which the WTO process can be used to assist with these regional integration efforts to help ensure they act as stepping-stones for multilateralisation. For example, the WTO and ASEAN could collaborate on judicial and monitoring functions to ensure greater coherence between global and regional rules (Oshikawa 2013).

Finally, implementation of the Trade Facilitation Agreement (TFA) offers opportunities for reducing the cost of trade. The 2015 OECD Trade Facilitation Indicators find that the implementation of the TFA could reduce worldwide trade costs by between 12.5 and 17.5 per cent. Countries that implement the TFA in full will reduce their trade costs by between 1.4 and 3.9 percentage points more than those that do only the minimum that the TFA requires (OECD 2015).

Australia and China should use their influence in the G20 to modify the G20 growth strategy process to require each country to include specific reforms to implement the TFA. Trade is already a component of the growth strategies; however, to date it has been one of the weakest areas. The TFA provides something tangible for countries to aspire to. The OECD's Trade Facilitation Indicators should be used to measure and report on the level of ambition being displayed by individual countries.

Multilateral cooperation on investment and infrastructure

While trade barriers have typically fallen over past decades, barriers to foreign direct investment remain high. Then Director General of the WTO, Pascal Lamy, calls this a gap in international cooperation:

> We see the absence of multilateral rules on investment as a gap in cooperation. Current bilateral arrangements are not a satisfactory substitute for a comprehensive international investment agreement (Lamy 2013).

Barriers to foreign investment are a significant issue for Australia and China. Foreign investment flows are fundamental to the spread of global production networks, from which Australia and China are significant beneficiaries.

As a capital-importing country that relies on foreign savings to finance investment in fundamental sectors of its economy such as mining, resources and agriculture, Australia has a strong interest in ensuring these channels remain open. For China, like many developing countries in Asia, much of its success in participating in global value chains has come from being able to attract the necessary investment to build production bases. Since 2008, East Asia, and China in particular, attracted the largest share of global foreign direct investment because of its high growth rate and large markets (Zhang and Wang 2014).

Globally, subdued investment remains a stubborn legacy of the global financial crisis. G20 leaders noted in 2014 that 'tackling global investment shortfalls is crucial to lifting growth, job creation and productivity' (G20 2014). Figure 8.9 shows total investment (public and private) as a percentage of GDP for advanced and emerging market economies. For advanced economies in particular, investment has struggled to rebound from its fall following the global financial crisis. While investment has been growing rapidly over time for emerging market economies, it has plateaued since 2009 and is now growing at a lower rate. Emerging market economies have also faced significant investment challenges in recent years as global capital flows respond to monetary policy changes in advanced economies. Improving domestic investment climates is a critical element in addressing this.

Addressing these global investment challenges has three components. The first is domestic. Improving domestic investment and financing climates is essential to ensuring the competitive, stable and predictable returns necessary for attracting private sector investment. Australia and China should support the G20 in the special focus it has given in recent years on reforms to improve domestic investment environments. These include increased public investment in infrastructure, regulatory and institutional reforms to leverage public–private partnerships, introducing tax incentives to raise investment and enhancing access to finance for SMEs.

The second component in addressing the global investment challenge is multilateral. There has been an unrelenting movement towards the adoption of a de facto investment agreement at the global level through a variety of multilateral, regional and bilateral initiatives (Dhar 2013). These include investment measures under GATT, the WTO Agreement on Trade-Related Investment Measures (TRIMs), the OECD's Declaration and Decisions on International Investment and Multilateral Enterprises, UNCTAD's Investment Policy Framework for Sustainable Development, the G20's Global Infrastructure Hub, and regional initiatives such as the European single market, NAFTA, the ASEAN Investment Area and the investment component of RCEP. These initiatives have developed good practice guidelines for foreign investment, but this is insufficient. A case emerges for an eventual multilateral agreement on investment covering transparency on investment rules and investor facilitation, ideally housed in the WTO (Baldwin 2013).

The G20 stands as the most effective forum for continuing this push. It has also taken important steps in regards to the need for collective, multilateral action on investment through its global infrastructure initiative and work on SME financing. The next step is for the G20 to consolidate the work done to date and begin a holistic discussion around developing a multilateral foreign investment framework. Importantly, the G20's work also needs to address increasing fragmentation between regional agreements and the investment mechanisms they embody, specifically on investor–protection. The investor–protection mechanisms embodied in a number of regional agreements, particularly the TPP, as well as the differences between these agreements, act to significantly fragment the existing system. Consolidating the existing work on a multilateral foreign investment framework needs to have a specific focus on achieving harmony across these mechanisms.

Figure 8.9: Investment as a percentage of GDP

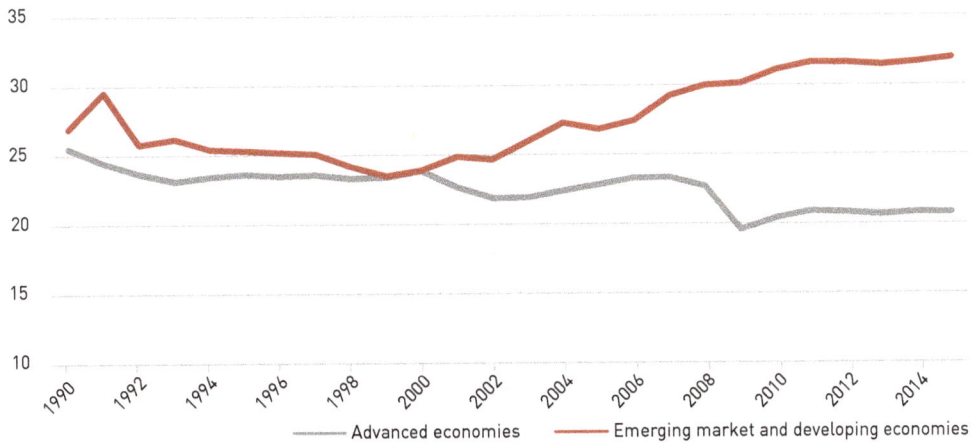

Source: IMF WEO 2015, Investment (public and private) as a percentage of GDP.

Despite all the shortcomings of the deadlocked Doha Round WTO negotiations, the best framework for such an initiative is still the WTO. Not only does it already contain general principles on MFN status, national treatment, general exceptions and the right to regulate, among other key elements, but it also has the most effective system under international law to settle disputes between states. The shape of such an agreement and what flexibilities would be available for specific countries are matters that have to be discussed and settled during the negotiations (Jara 2013).

Zhang and Wang (2014) have shown that a foreign investment framework could be obtained by consolidating the work done by the G20, UNCTAD and the OECD. But it should go further, to a higher-level arrangement that realises an integrated framework beyond TRIMs. It is important that a single agreement at the multilateral level be the ultimate goal. Basic components should include transparency on investment policies, rules and regulations, with a clear identification of agencies responsible for issuing relevant licenses, permits and approvals. Foreign investors should also be required to commit to transparency in their labour and environmental standards, and public scrutiny of their conformance.

The third component for addressing the global investment challenge relates specifically to infrastructure investment. According to the OECD, total global infrastructure investment requirements by 2030 for transport, electricity generation, transmission and distribution, water and telecommunications will come to US$71 trillion, or about 3.5 per cent of the annual global GDP from 2007 to 2030 (OECD 2012). However it is widely recognised that public investment, including that from the multilateral and national development banks, will be insufficient to meet the global shortfall in infrastructure investment. Greater private sector investment in infrastructure will be fundamental. Although investment opportunities are plentiful across developed and developing countries alike, investors are not fully seizing them — often due to gaps in the domestic investment environment (OECD 2012).

Infrastructure investment is a significant domestic priority for the governments of both Australia and China. There are a number of benefits to both countries from supporting a continued, and greater, international focus on this issue, both as participants in the global economy and for country-specific reasons.

The common interests between Australia and China on infrastructure investment should be capitalised on within international forums and institutions. The focus of the collaboration efforts between Australia and China should be on maintaining a strong focus through China's G20 presidency on infrastructure investment. As discussed earlier, this is a cross-cutting theme that is capable of assisting on multiple fronts — including growth, macroeconomic policy coordination, development, trade, energy and climate change. Infrastructure investment, particularly through the G20's two-in-five growth agenda, has the capacity to bridge the gap in the international community on the need for macroeconomic policy cooperation. It provides a much-needed framework for surplus economies to increase public investment and contribute to global aggregate demand while deficit economies undertake commensurate structural reform to boost the supply side of their economies.

China should build on the efforts of Australia and Turkey, utilising the G20 growth strategy and mutual assessment processes to deliver ambitious commitments from G20 members and, from Turkey's presidency, using the estimated 1 percentage point increase in the aggregate G20 investment-to-GDP ratio as a means for targeting G20 efforts. There is continued scope for greater public investment from many key G20 countries as well as increased efforts across the membership in improving domestic investment environments and identifying innovative ways of crowding in private finance.

Australia and China should use their influence in the G20 to achieve better cooperation and synergies between the AIIB and New Development Bank with existing multilateral development banks. China has already outlined this as a priority in the concept note for its G20 presidency. There should similarly be an increased focus on coordinating funding between these different institutions, centred on a concrete list of bankable projects that could be developed through G20 support. The G20 should continue to support and drive the efforts within development banks to optimise their resources with an eye on how best to leverage private-sector finance.

Supporting global energy governance reform and action on climate change

The existing architecture for global energy governance has been described as 'a mess, with many actors, many priorities, little coherence and limited effectiveness' (Florini 2012). There are countless multilateral, regional and bilateral initiatives relating to energy. Figure 8.10 gives a snapshot of just a few of them and shows how Australia and China fit in with this broad framework.

The need for global energy governance reform is well recognised, particularly by the G20, which has had a special focus on this issue in recent years. The global energy sector has undergone, and continues to undergo, significant transitions. World energy consumption and trade used to be dominated by the developed nations of the OECD, but now major developing nations like China, India and Brazil are amongst the largest players (Hirst 2012). Countries, like China, which just a few years ago were major energy exporters, have become energy importers. China is now the world's largest energy consumer and the world's largest oil importing country. The United States, which used to be the largest oil importer, has similarly made spectacular technical progress in oil and gas production and is now heading towards self-sufficiency.

Global energy governance has not kept up with these transitions (Hirst 2015). It is now widely recognised among policymakers and commentators alike that the global energy governance architecture needs to be reformed. At present, there is no genuinely global energy organisation that can bring the major energy consumer countries around to table to address the core energy challenges of security, equity, development and the environment (Hirst 2015).

Figure 8.10: Australia and China within the global energy governance architecture

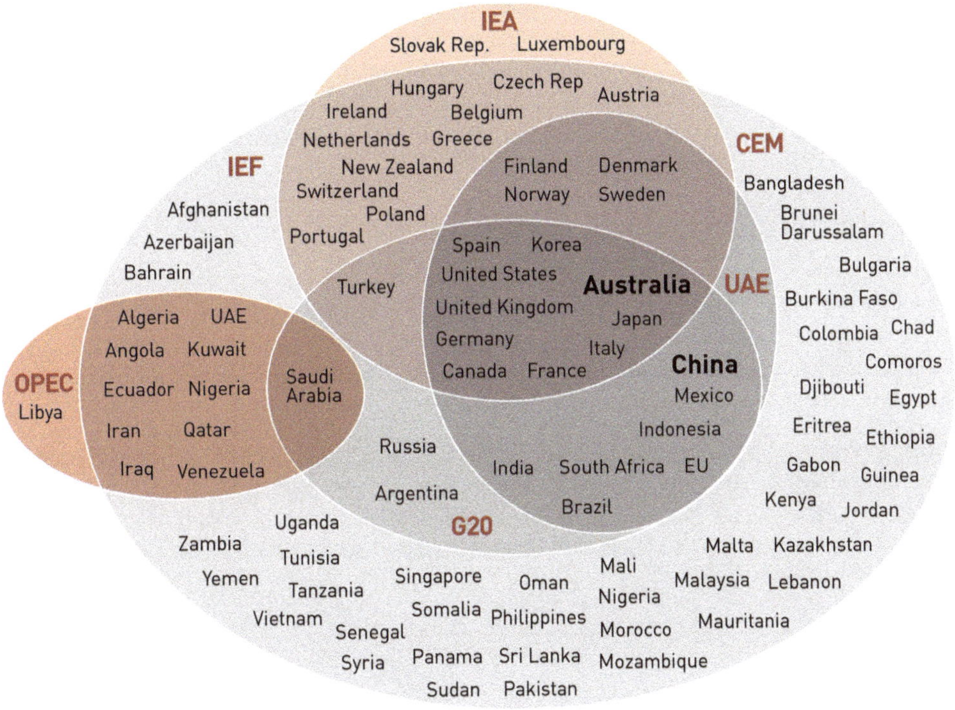

Acronyms: Organisation of Petroleum Exporting Countries (OPEC), International Energy Forum (IEF), International Energy Agency (IEA), Group of 20 (G20), Clean Energy Ministerial (CEM).
Source: Authors' schema

The fact that major emerging market and developing economies are underrepresented in the global energy governance architecture is a serious problem for several reasons. First, it limits the scope for global cooperation on energy policy, which is critical in addressing broader challenges around development, infrastructure, the environment and climate change.

Second, a major objective of international diplomacy more generally is in managing the inclusion of these new powers in global governance so that they make peaceful contributions to world leadership. This is especially true in the field of energy, which has historically been a source of conflict.

Third, the International Energy Agency's (IEA) limited membership undermines global energy security by weakening the IEA's emergency oil plans. These plans rely on IEA members holding strategic oil reserves equivalent to 90 days of imports. The more countries that are absent from these arrangements the weaker these reserves are. Hirst (2015) has similarly shown that the existing governance structure preserves the divide between developed and developing countries. The IEA's restricted membership results in it being insufficiently engaged on the energy challenges facing developing nations, particularly development and access to affordable energy. This leaves a big gap at the heart of its process.

Finally, the existing fragmented governance architecture has resulted in a serious lack of cooperation on specific areas of energy technology and policy. Technology collaboration has rightly been identified as a crucial dimension of climate change mitigation and, as described above, this has led to the creation of a number of new collaborations in the most important areas. Unfortunately, mainly due to the limited membership of the IEA (and notwithstanding the fact that the IEA's technology networks have been opened to non-members of the IEA), these collaborations have generally not been built on the IEA's networks but have, to some extent, duplicated them (Hirst 2012). There is an obvious need for better coordination of these bodies through broader governance reform.

The benefits of governance reform to Australia and China

The energy sector plays a vital role in both the Australian and Chinese economies. Given the significant extent to which this sector is shaped by global forces, Australia and China have a strong common interest in ensuring they are actively participating in global energy policymaking and in shaping the rules, norms and institutions that will govern this sector into the future.

The slowdown in global commodity prices and the deterioration in Australia's terms of trade in recent years have illustrated the extent to which global forces shape the Australian economy through its energy sector. Australia is the among the world's largest exporters of LNG, coal and uranium, and Australia's importance to global energy markets will continue to grow (Department of Industry 2014).

China is the world's largest energy consumer and has been the key driver of the increase in energy consumption globally over the last 10 years (EIA 2015). In 2009, it went from being a net exporter to a net importer of coal for the first time in 20 years. It is now the largest producer and consumer of coal in the world and accounts for almost half of the world's coal consumption. China is similarly the world's second-largest consumer and importer of oil and the fourth-largest consumer of natural gas.

Multiple Australian prime ministers have noted the deficiencies in the existing governance architecture and the need for reform. Prime Minister Turnbull in November 2015 said 'the reform of the International Energy Agency is very important … the IEA's membership should reflect the reality of the energy producers and consumers of 2015, not the 1970s' (Turnbull 2015). Similarly, for China, in a speech in Abu Dhabi in 2012, then premier Wen Jiabao highlighted the deficiencies in the existing architecture and proposed multilateral cooperation on energy 'within the framework of the G20' China has since been a strong supporter and advocate for the G20's work on reforming global energy governance (Hirst 2012).

Importantly, the United States and other key countries are also strong supporters of the G20's efforts to reform the global energy architecture. When Secretary of State, Hillary Clinton advocated for Chinese and Indian membership of the IEA (Hirst 2012), and Henry Kissinger, the founding father of the IEA, has called for the evolution of the institution, noting that it 'stands at a critical juncture' (Kissinger 2009). In their New Delhi summit communiqué, the BRICS nations have said that 'strengthening representation of emerging and developing countries in the institutions of global governance will enhance their effectiveness' (BRICS 2012).

Ensuring security and the role of strategic oil stockpiles are similarly important issues for both Australia and China, for different reasons. China has been building its oil stocks for some time now (Hirst 2012). Australia, on the other hand, does not stockpile oil reserves. As a result, Australia has been in breach of the IEA Treaty for some time. This gives Australia a strong incentive to work with the IEA and emerging economies, particularly China, in helping shape the rules and norms that will operate into the future.

Supporting the G20's progress in reforming global energy governance

While the G20 has made significant progress on the issue of global energy governance reform, there is still much work to be done. It is in the interests of Australia and China to support this incremental process and the Chinese G20 presidency provides a unique opportunity to do so.

Although there was some discussion of energy topics in 2012 and 2013, it was not until 2014, under the Australian presidency, that energy became a major part of the G20's remit. Hirst (2015) outlines three highly significant developments from the 2014 G20 summit: first, leaders agreed to work together to achieve nine 'G20 principles on energy collaboration', including having energy governance reflect economic reality; second, leaders had G20 energy ministers meet in 2015 and report on the way forward; and third, leaders consolidated the role of the G20 energy sustainability working group as a regular forum for G20 senior officials.

It is important now to build on this positive momentum. This should follow the pragmatic approach that has been adopted by the G20, which focuses on building and adapting existing organisations and ensuring that they work together effectively. Hirst suggests that a practical way to do this would be to have the G20's Energy Sustainability Working Group commission from the main international organisations their analyses of the roles they can play in delivering the principles agreed by the G20, including how they can cooperate with other organisations, the actions that they are planning and any gaps that they see.

G20 energy ministers could report to leaders on progress, offer their suggestions on how to improve cooperation between the organisations and fill gaps in the delivery of the principles. The IEA has a vital role to play, especially in how it responds to the G20's calls to 'make international energy institutions more representative and inclusive'. The IEA could consider further steps towards closer relations with the other partner countries in the Association initiative.

Climate change and energy transformation

China and Australia both have a vital interest in strong global action to limit future climate change. Both countries are particularly exposed to the expected future impacts from climate change, which would bring significant economic and social risks. The UN Paris Agreement on climate change provides a solid basis for nationally determined yet internationally agreed, and to some extent coordinated, action on climate change.

The Paris Agreement sets out a strong long-term global ambition of limiting global warming to less than two degrees, that was agreed to by all countries. It puts in place a system of nationally based pledges for emissions targets and actions, and a mechanism for regular review and ratcheting up of national pledges. Both China and Australia have been supporters of the agreement, and in their respective capacities contributed to the successful conclusions of the negotiation process. Both countries can position themselves to maximise gains from successful global action on climate change.

As part of this, there are opportunities for Australia and China to jointly develop new strategies for growth in both countries based on the low-carbon technologies of the future. Such strategies could entail Australia supplying resources and energy, as well as specialised knowledge services, and China utilising Australia's inputs to support its industries and then provide capital for investments in Australia. This pattern is similar to what is already starting to occur. However, the new waves of economic integration and growth would rely on different resources and new technologies.

China is strengthening its climate change policy portfolio with the aim of achieving a 60 to 65 per cent reduction in the emissions intensity of its economy (the ratio of carbon dioxide emissions to GDP) in 2030 compared to 2005, with a peak in carbon dioxide emissions by 2030 or earlier. The 2020 target is a 40 to 45 per cent reduction in emissions intensity relative to 2005 (Government of China 2015).

China is on track to achieve its 2020 target, and can achieve or outperform the 2030 target if the current policy effort is intensified. The targets require an average annual reduction in emissions intensity of around 4 per cent. China has achieved this on average over the last 10 years, largely by way of reducing the energy intensity of its economy (Figure 8.11). This was made possible through improvements in energy efficiency and structural change. China's slowing economic growth is now tending to make it more challenging to achieve the 4 per cent annual decarbonisation rate. However, if that rate continues to be achieved then a slowing economy means that the peak in emissions will be achieved earlier.

Figure 8.11: China's annual growth in GDP, CO2 emissions, energy and emissions and energy intensity, 2005–2014

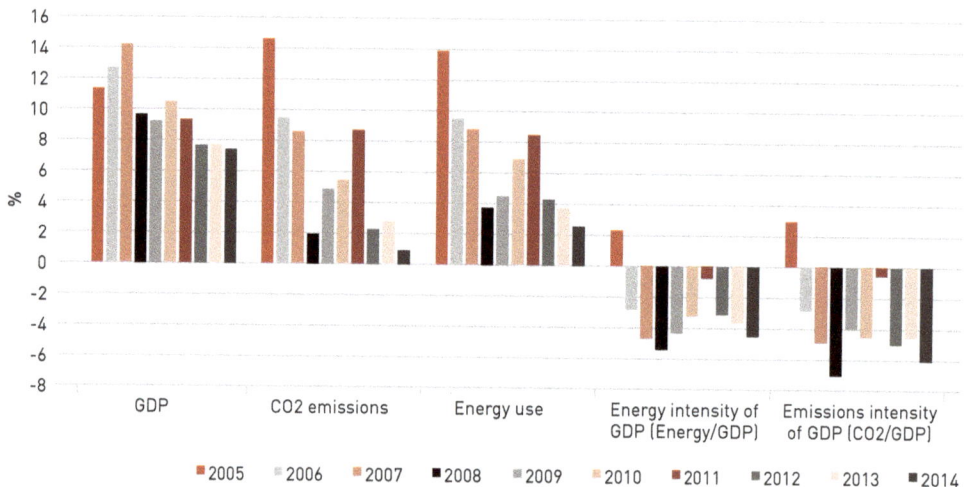

Source: BP 2015 (for total primary energy use and CO2); IMF 2015a (for GDP).

In future, limiting and then reducing emissions will require much greater structural change in China's economy towards higher value-added activities; continued improvements in the technical efficiency of power generation, industry, transport and housing; and a sustained shift away from coal as the mainstay of energy supply towards renewable energy, nuclear power and gas, with remaining coal use potentially equipped with carbon capture and storage technology (Deep Decarbonization Pathways Project 2015; Teng et al 2014). These changes are already underway and it is expected that they can be sustained at relatively high annual rates for decades to come (Jotzo and Teng 2014).

Australia's national emissions target is a reduction of 26 to 28 per cent in emissions levels at 2030 relative to 2005 (Department of the Environment 2015). Achieving this will require a turnaround in emissions trends. It is technologically possible to achieve this and more ambitious targets, including net zero emissions by mid-century (Denis et al 2014). The key is a sustained shift from coal towards renewable or other zero-carbon energy sources, accelerated improvement of energy efficiency and sequestering carbon emissions on the land, including through forest plantations.

A recent study of Australia's options for future sustainability and economic growth (Hatfield-Dodds et al 2015) found that Australia is 'free to choose' a trajectory that will result in better long-term environmental outcomes and sustained economic growth: the technical opportunities are there, but the new technologies and activities will become widely used only if there is deliberate and broad-based policy intervention.

Benefiting from low-carbon growth

China has recognised the opportunities from low-carbon growth and has begun to grasp them in a number of areas, as have some Western countries. Archetypal examples are renewable energy systems, which during the last decade have seen massive improvements in technology and costs, and the emerging wave of electric vehicles. For China to achieve the transition to an innovation-driven economy with an environmentally sustainable development trajectory, China will need to invest significantly in research and development and knowledge industries (Jin and Zhang 2016).

In Australia, policy development and business investment on the whole has been more defensive to date, with a relatively strong emphasis on traditional resource extracting industries. To quote Martin Parkinson (2015):

> This capacity for technological leap-frogging, combined with the need to address global and geographically specific environmental problems (i.e. climate change and air and water pollution), lies behind China's massive investments in low-emissions technologies. The US is also investing massively in these technologies. Australia is not.

Reducing carbon dioxide emissions goes hand in hand with other Chinese policy objectives, including improving air quality, improving energy security by shifting away from fossil fuels and the emergence of new manufacturing industries in the production of wind turbines and solar panels, for example (Teng and Jotzo 2014).

It is likely that China is already past the point of peak consumption of coal, as the production of commodities such as steel and cement is declining, the efficiency of coal use keeps improving and alternative energy sources are growing. China's coal imports have fallen and a three-year ban on approvals of new coalmines has recently been put in place. The rate of emissions growth has slowed dramatically in the past two years, and some observers believe that 'peak CO2' could occur sooner than is implied in China's emissions targets (Green and Stern 2015).

For Australia, the most significant effects are related to exports of energy and energy-intensive products. A low-carbon transition in China and globally poses near-term difficulties for some industries, but also longer-term opportunities — potentially of very large magnitudes — for others.

International moves towards lower-carbon energy systems mean less favourable conditions for the export-oriented fossil fuel industry, in particular for producers of thermal coal (as distinct from coking coal used for steel production). Global coal demand growth has been tailing off, and steam coal prices have fallen (by around 60 per cent over the last five years) (World Bank 2016).

Coal demand continues to rise in many developing countries including India, but this growth cannot last if the world is to achieve meaningful outcomes on climate change. Even if technology to use coal with carbon capture and storage became technologically mature, the longer-term outlook for global coal demand is weakening.

Demand in China and globally for natural gas, by contrast, is increasing and is projected to increase for some time given increasing climate action. Gas is much lower in carbon dioxide emissions than coal, and is a suitable bridge from coal to a zero-emissions energy system. It also burns much more cleanly than coal and is therefore attractive to China and many other countries in the bid to reduce air pollution. Australia's gas industry is benefiting from strong global demand. Demand for uranium, which Australia also exports, is set to increase as well.

In the longer term however, Australia's opportunities as an energy producer lie in entirely new industries. Australia has very large technical and economic potential to become an 'energy superpower' in a carbon-constrained world (Garnaut 2015).

Australia as a zero-carbon energy supplier to China

Achieving the global goal to keep temperature rises to well below two degrees would require a complete de-carbonisation of the world's energy system (IPCC 2014). The pace and depth of this transition largely determines how close the world can get to the goal set out in the Paris Agreement.

In scenarios run by the Deep Decarbonisation Pathways Project (DDPP 2015), a detailed nationally grounded technical study, under a two-degree compatible trajectory, electricity becomes nearly carbon-free by 2050, with average carbon intensity across 16 major countries reduced by a factor of 15 below its 2010 value. The Chinese DDPP study shows a scenario with dramatically reduced emissions by shifting electricity production to a mix of renewable sources and nuclear power and by equipping the majority of remaining fossil fuel power plants with carbon capture and storage by 2050.

Australia is in a favourable position as a large scale producer of renewable energy, on account of its practically unlimited access to a range of different renewable energy sources including high insolation rates, large amounts of available land, extensive technical expertise and business frameworks in energy industries, and a comparatively stable regulatory and investment environment. Australia is thus well placed to supply a large share of its domestic energy use from renewable energy sources.

A global low-carbon economy could bring new and large-scale comparative advantage for Australia. First, Australia could be a producer of energy-intensive commodities using zero-emissions electricity (Denis et al 2014). This could include, for example, aluminium, which requires large amounts of electricity to produce. Given that the majority of Australia's heavy industry installations are relatively old, this would mean building up a new stock of industrial infrastructure.

Second, Australia could be an exporter of renewable energy, producing fuels such as hydrogen or methanol in Australia using renewable energy and exporting these to the densely populated areas of East Asia (Drew 2015). Producing and shipping synthetic renewable fuels would draw on a broadly similar engineering base and industrial structures as existing industries such as natural gas production and processing.

The potential for Australia as a large producer of zero-carbon energy is obvious; however, the prospects for building export industries based on that potential require much further investigation. Research is needed into: the technological basis for producing exportable renewable energy and energy-intensive products using renewable energy; whether and to what extent Australia has a comparative economic advantage and cost advantage that would warrant production for export; to what extent such energy and energy-intensive products could fit in with China's future energy and industrial system; and what policy and regulatory frameworks would be needed to facilitate the development of these technologies and industries.

The potential benefits of a renewables-based energy export industry for Australia in a decarbonised world economy are very large, as are the potential benefits to China of having a secure source of such low-carbon energy and energy intensive products to supplement domestic production.

A new agenda for cooperation

Australia and China can benefit by broadening and extending the bilateral dialogue and collaboration on climate change measures and the transition of energy systems.

A first plank is to intensify government-to-government cooperation on climate change issues. The Paris Agreement has prepared the ground for a new phase of international collaborations on climate change. Australia and China's objectives on climate change are compatible and complementary. The two countries can build on a variety of forums for dialogue at the official and political level, including the ministerial-level consultations on climate change that have taken place on several occasions and the Australia–China Climate Change Forums held at the ANU and the UNSW in recent years.

Second, the two countries should strive to facilitate business and investment relationships in the areas of climate change and low-carbon energy. This may involve reducing remaining regulatory hurdles to investment in new energy technologies, especially for Chinese investment in Australia. The two countries can also strive to enhance knowledge exchange at the business level. There is also a critical opportunity to better involve the financial sector cooperatively across both countries through 'green finance'. As part of a broader focus of integrating financial services and financial flows between Australia and China (discussed in detail in Chapter 5) both countries should explore how cooperation on financial products and financial services can be tailored to improve access to finance for green projects, such as investment in renewable energy and low-carbon technologies.

Third, experience has shown that active support by governments for research in energy technology development can bring substantial benefits in accelerating technological change. China has provided substantial support in many different forms to the deployment of renewable as well as nuclear energy, and advanced energy-saving technologies. In Australia, there are new government institutions that have proved successful in supporting the development and deployment of clean energy, especially the Australian Renewable Energy Agency (ARENA) and the Clean Energy Finance Corporation (CEFC). These models may be attractive for China also. The model of co-financing commercial investments in cutting edge clean energy via a government-financed body like the CEFC may prove successful in stimulating investment in new energy options in the Asian region. Options to link this to operations of the AIIB may be worth investigating.

Finally, collaboration should be fostered between research organisations and universities in Australia and China, in the form of joint initiatives on scientific research and engineering as well as economic and regulatory frameworks. Promising models exist such as the Australia–China Research Program on Climate Policy, which has brought together researchers from several leading Australian and Chinese universities to work on specific joint research projects. The program has operated at relatively small scale, convened at the ANU and with particular support at Tsinghua University in China. It could be readily expanded to cover a broader range of issues and a wider range of research institutions, and scaled up to a national initiative in both countries.

CHAPTER 9
Conclusions

Conclusions

China and Australia are natural economic partners. China — already, on one measure, the largest national economy in the world — has relied on Australia for the raw materials it required to industrialise; Australia, a small open economy dependent on trade, has outperformed most of its advanced country peers thanks in no small part to its trade with China. As the next phase of Chinese development proceeds, there is every reason to believe that this relationship can become of even greater importance to China and to Australia. China and Australia also share a profound common interest in the evolution of institutions of regional and global governance and cooperation to reflect the realities of the 21st century. In this sense, the China–Australia relationship has, if stewarded with prudence and foresight by the public and private sectors, the potential to become a powerful force for stability and prosperity beyond the bilateral relationship.

There is no economic or geopolitical future for China, Australia or the world that would not be improved by China's sustained and balanced economic growth. And yet the future direction of Chinese growth will be very different from that over the past four decades. The forces of change that have already unleashed a wave of consumption growth are affecting the relationship with Australia profoundly. Economic reform and liberalisation can intensify the ongoing change in the structure of the Chinese economy and, while these changes imply a less heavy reliance in Australia on the resource sector for economic growth, there are opportunities for growth in agriculture, advanced manufacturing, investment, finance, healthcare, education, tourism and other services. But these opportunities will not materialise automatically; their benefits can only be brought to fruition through concerted reform and action on both sides. It will require substantial repositioning of policy and commercial strategies by both countries and the development of a still closer relationship between the two countries.

The recent history of the growing ties between the two countries shows that the determined pursuit of a deeper relationship yields tangible benefits. The institutions and policy frameworks that have emerged to provide structure for the relationship in recent years provide a strong starting point for the next phase of the China–Australia partnership.

Australia has embraced China's openness and reform as a critical factor in Asian prosperity and stability, and China has embraced the partnership with Australia as a strategic element in its foreign economic policy strategies. Both countries have invested heavily in their partnership. The path-breaking record of the Australia–China partnership in opening the resource trade, foreign investment, regional cooperation initiatives and China's accession to the WTO provides a legacy on which to build new international standards into their bilateral trade, investment and all other dealings. Their high-level Comprehensive Strategic Partnership and the China–Australia Free Trade Agreement (ChAFTA) are major institutional assets, embodying mutual trust and practical commitment, that can be deployed to manage change over the decades ahead. Still closer engagement and institutional arrangements are needed to capitalise on the opportunities that these foundations present.

ChAFTA is a blueprint for initial change, not an end-point in the bilateral relationship. A joint work plan for achieving change will not only define progress in the bilateral trade, investment and commercial relationship over the coming decade; it will also provide the foundation for Australia and China pushing liberalisation and reform in the Asian region and setting out the pathway towards reform and strengthening of the global trade and economic systems.

The scale and significance of developments that are now taking place — especially in China through its advance towards a high-income economy and deeper financial integration with the world — recommend deeper bilateral institutional arrangements between Australia and China. These arrangements would build on existing bilateral frameworks, including in the areas of investment, tourism, people movement, science and educational exchanges, with bold new bi-national initiatives. They will need to be directed at capturing the opportunities in the relationship, and managing the risks and processes that are an inevitable consequence of large-scale economic and social change.

Both countries have a deep intersection of interests in working together to strengthen the established regional economic cooperation arrangements (such as APEC, the ASEAN Plus frameworks and the East Asia Summit) and to secure the framework of political confidence and security within which economic prosperity can be attained. But there are gaps in regional policy strategies that Australia and China must now work more actively with regional partners to fill.

The Australia–China relationship is anchored in global institutional and political arrangements. Australia has a direct and important stake, in partnership with China, in working to ensure China's success in the assumption of its role of shared leadership in global economic affairs.

Australia and China should aspire to a bilateral relationship of the high level and scope that they established during the foundational period of economic ties in the 1980s, when they agreed on a 'model relationship' for cooperation between countries with different social systems and at different economic stages of development. The enormous transformation of China's economic model and the impact that this is having on the Australian economy calls for the elevation and calibration of their partnership to achieve these goals.

New model for the relationship

- The framework of a new model for economic collaboration requires the Australian and Chinese governments to elevate the Australia–China relationship to a unique, higher level, in a *Comprehensive Strategic Partnership for Change*. This partnership should promote change through the achievement of joint goals in the bilateral relationship and forge common priorities and initiatives on regional and global issues through the Strategic Economic Dialogue and parallel ministerial mechanisms.

- The Australian and Chinese governments should underpin their *Strategic Economic Dialogue* with joint policy taskforces and working groups on policy and institutional change that:

  - develop initiatives on issues flowing from the dialogues and other commitments;

  - work with state and provincial authorities in developing these initiatives;

  - encourage programs of research within and beyond government and higher educational institutions on longer-term aspects of the relationship;

  - engage with the business sectors in both countries in undertaking their work;

  - promote joint training and the development of long-term working associations in key areas among the officials of both countries; and

  - reflect upon community interests and concerns in both countries.

- Both governments should work, in the decade ahead, to develop their new partnership into a *comprehensive bilateral framework treaty* that embeds frequent high-level government dialogue; institutionalises and enfolds official bilateral exchanges and technical cooperation programs between economic and foreign affairs ministries, including branches of the military; pools approaches between federal–state governments in Australia and central–provincial governments in China; and provides for the comprehensive setting of strategic bilateral objectives in a forward agenda. There is precedent for moving towards a comprehensive bilateral treaty in the 1976 *Basic Treaty of Friendship and Cooperation between Australia and Japan*.

- The high-level capacities necessary to this engagement should be promoted through the establishment by both governments of an independent and well-resourced bi-national *Australia–China (Ao–Zhong) Commission* to boost the level and range of political, scientific, official, business and community exchanges between the two counties. Its nearest parallel in Australian experience would be the treaty arrangement between Australia and the United States that established the Australian–American Fulbright Commission. The Australian–American Fulbright Commission is an independent bi-national non-profit organisation, established by a treaty between the Australian and US governments, that promotes education and cultural exchange between Australia and the US through managing a bilateral exchange program students, researchers and scholars.

Partners for change

In the next decade, the Australia–China relationship will be re-shaped by the large-scale transformations now underway in each economy. In China, the economic structure is shifting towards the services sector and high-technology manufacturing, while consumer spending is becoming a larger part of the economy as household incomes rise.

China finds itself at a point in its economic trajectory that has in some other countries proved challenging. Some middle-income countries, especially in Latin America, have seen relatively weak growth rates and productivity stagnation. Other countries, like Japan and the 'Tiger' economies of East Asia, adapted their institutions and policies to the challenges of middle-income status and consequently 'graduated' to high-income status relatively quickly (Kharas and Gill 2016). China, Australia and the world at large would all gain immeasurably from China's rapid progression from middle-income to high-income status. But the path through middle-income status will need to be supported by reforms to lift China up the manufacturing value chain and increase productivity across the economy (Huang 2016). These productivity-enhancing reforms will support China's efforts to move from a model of growth centred on imitating ideas from advanced economies towards a model of growth based on domestic innovation.

To lift productivity, as foreshadowed under the 13th Five Year Plan, China must improve the efficiency of investment, in part through pushing ahead with financial market reforms. Greater private sector involvement in a number of industries still dominated by state-owned enterprises — such as banking, utilities and transport — could unlock productivity gains in these sectors. For Australia, the relative decline in its productivity performance over the past decade can be addressed through domestic-led initiatives, such as improving labour market regulation, strengthening and extending national competition policy, and facilitating the efficient allocation and management of investment in social and physical infrastructure.

China's transformation and deeper financial integration with the world will have a profound impact on the international economy, including Australia.

China's large and growing middle class will demand an increasingly broad range of goods and services, providing vast opportunities for exporters in areas from financial services to food, while a more open capital account could fundamentally reshape the global investment landscape. Chinese spending on education, medical services, cultural activities and tourism will grow steeply. Overall retail sales are expected to increase by two-thirds between now and 2020. While Australia benefited more than most from China's commodity-intensive growth of the last decade, Australia will need a renewed focus on productivity enhancing reforms to capture these emerging export markets and maintain prosperity. Particularly given these changes occurring in China, Australia must also adjust its policy strategies to help facilitate innovation and support the up-take of new production technologies and consumer services. Increasing competition in sheltered industries will be crucial in driving productivity and innovation, as will remaining open to foreign investment and skills.

- To support the economic transformation underway in each economy will require a continuing commitment to market reforms to those parts of the economy that remain sheltered from competition, overly-regulated or where the degree of public sector involvement is unwarranted. The Australia–China *Comprehensive Strategic Partnership for Change* should be shaped and evolve as a close working partnership that *advances the reform agendas in both countries to promote economic transformation.*

- The *innovation in bilateral architecture* that is proposed can be aligned under the Australian government's National Innovation and Science Agenda and with the Chinese government's prioritisation of innovation in its 13th Five Year Plan. This would see the prioritisation of bilateral cooperation in future opportunities such as research and development, capital sourcing, STEM collaboration, research commercialisation, tech landing pads, the digital economy, and people-to-people entrepreneurial exchanges.

Transforming trade and investment

Australia and China have a strong, established trade and investment relationship, built on the deep complementarity between their economies and their closeness, which is in part a legacy from the high-level commitment to the relationship on both sides. That relationship is based generally on the exchange of Australian raw materials for Chinese manufactured goods. Australia will continue to be a key and reliable source of raw materials to China, supplying more than half of China's iron ore needs and a major proportion of other minerals and energy products. Resource security is provided through the functioning of global commodity markets to which both countries are committed.

In less than three decades the geographical orientation of the Chinese economy has changed fundamentally, from being continentally self-contained to being the largest maritime economy in the world. Resource dependence has grown as commodity prices have fallen and high-cost domestic suppliers have become less attractive sources of industrial inputs. This development has naturally and steadily drawn China into the maritime economy, including the construction of huge sea freight capacities, interest in maritime safety, and concern about securing international supplies. As one of the world's largest maritime resource suppliers, Australia fully reciprocates these interests.

Thinking about the implications of China's maritime economy has lagged behind the pace of this change. The major effort now underway in China to redress this deficiency *would be assisted by collaboration between Australia and China regarding the implications of growing resource dependency for resource security; maritime resource development and protection; maritime scientific and weather research; and Australian participation in the Maritime Silk Road initiative.*

The shift towards consumption-led growth in China is now forging a new economic relationship between Australia and China that requires new strategies and institutional arrangements to support closer commercial engagement in a whole range of new merchandise and services trades as well as closer investment and financial market ties. Energy, agriculture and food products provide significant opportunities both to develop regional Australia and to meet new patterns of demand by middle-income Chinese consumers. Development goals in Australia provide new opportunities for upgrading China's trade structure and investment in Australia's economic future.

To support the continued economic adjustment in both economies, and to help both sides weather the changes taking place in the global economy, it is necessary to go beyond a merely trade-focused approach to a comprehensive economic partnership.

- This requires the elevation of the Australia–China Comprehensive Strategic Partnership into an Australia–China Comprehensive Strategic Partnership for Change (see above) and commitment over the next decade to put in place a *treaty-level commitment* covering both countries mutual interests in open markets, resource and energy security; sustainable agricultural development and food security; and reliable access for foreign investment in both countries. It should also acknowledge the global market context of the adjustments that are taking place in materials-based manufacturing (such as steel production) and commodity markets (such as iron ore).

- This Partnership can only be built on more extensive top-level exchanges between the two countries. Australia and China should conclude a *formal agreement to set up an Australia–China (Ao–Zhong) Commission* to promote deeper exchanges between the two countries as soon as is practicable.

- ChAFTA provides a foundation for advancing the opening of new markets and the transformation of the bilateral trade relationship. A *high-level joint working party* consisting of representatives from government and business can support the work of the Australia–China Strategic Economic Dialogue in advancing the implementation of ChAFTA and, beyond ChAFTA, the development of reliable investment arrangements and financial and service market opening initiatives.

- Delivering reliable trade in high-quality food products and internationally competitive tourism and education services requires a deep understanding of each country's consumers, and a tailored approach to trade and investment in country and market knowledge. Both countries should support *programs of public and commercial training and engagement* at the national and local levels that will contribute to the expansion of new market opportunities.

- Investment flows from China to Australia and from Australia to China will play a critical role in the development of the new economic relationship. *Both countries should commit to a 'negative list' approach to foreign investment*, in which foreign investment is welcomed except in specifically designated sectors of the economy. *A new bilateral investment agreement between Australia and China can be concluded* ahead of Chinese agreements with the European Union and the United States, and could serve as the nucleus of broader regional governance arrangements for bilateral investment flows.

- Australia should provide *reliable access* to Chinese investment through standardising the threshold for screening investments across all sources, including those from China, offering equal treatment to market-conforming state-owned enterprise investments, and moving from an 'application and review' to a 'notification and compliance' system under the Foreign Investment Review Board (FIRB). China should provide reliable access for Australian investors by establishing mechanisms to ensure that, after their establishment, Australian investments are subject to national treatment as well as consistent and equitable regulatory treatment in the Chinese market.

- The partnership must be enabled on both sides by the provision of *supporting financial infrastructure* (including access to each other's financial services markets), the ability to make investments that support further trade and service delivery, and continued and easier flow of people between the two countries.

- The *freer movement of people between the two countries* for commerce, business, education and tourism is important to development of the overall relationship. The two countries should establish a joint taskforce whose mandate is to establish most-favoured-nation treatment in visa and other matters affecting sojourn in each country, including the expansion of working holiday visas for young people both ways, and opportunities for Australians to access loans for study in top Chinese universities. This is a clear area of mutual benefit and could be an early reform success story in the new Australia–China partnership for change.

- *Cooperation between Australian states and Chinese provinces, sister cities and NGOs, and bilateral community organisations such as the Australia–China Youth Association (ACYA), should be incorporated into national policy development* through the expansion and formalisation of the role of the Australia–China State/Provincial Leaders' Forum into an Australia–China Leaders' Forum, to identify further practical areas for cooperation, as well as to build the understanding and trust that is the basis of a true partnership.

- *Peak business bodies* in both countries should be encouraged to make an ongoing input into the development of the relationship through the establishment of their own joint working parties and task forces as well as their participation in those established by both governments.

- Effective, independent research and analysis and the fostering of the capacities to undertake it are critical to effective understanding of longer-term developments in the economic relationship. The *China Economy Program* should be encouraged to fulfil its national responsibility in building economic research capacities with institutions across Australia and promoting research collaboration with Chinese think tanks so that there is effective independent advice on longer-term developments in the relationship available to both governments.

- *The collaboration established between the China Center for International Economic Exchanges (CCIEE) and the East Asian Bureau of Economic Research (EABER) at The Australian National University and their government and non-government partners in both countries through this study provides a natural foundation for continuing the implementation of the initiatives recommended here, especially the development of closer research and official relationships between both countries and the commitments to secondment of officials to an ongoing program of work over the coming years.*

Financial integration

China is at a critical point of its economic transition, committed to continued financial reform and capital account liberalisation while simultaneously managing associated domestic and external challenges. The extent to which China can successfully liberalise its financial sector to better channel capital to the most productive sectors of its economy will largely determine whether it will stagnate at middle levels of income per capita or whether it can, like its neighbours in Northeast Asia, rapidly attain high-income status. Australia, China and the world at large have every interest in the success of this endeavour. Similarly, capital account liberalisation in China will unlock a vast pool of savings and unleash financial flows that will profoundly change the financial structure of the regional and global economies. Handled intelligently and deftly, this change will constitute a powerful force for prosperity in the region.

The lessons of the past three decades of Asian financial history are that financial sector liberalisation and capital account opening must be managed with care by policymakers, with particular attention paid to the correct sequence of reforms. Chinese policymakers are aware of the need to proceed with prudence. Australia offers the possibility of a 'testing bed' for the opening up of Chinese finance to the outside world. Australia, meanwhile, must be careful not to squander the historic opportunities inherent in this fundamental reshaping of the financial geography of the region and the globe. Seizing the potential benefits will require active engagement on Australia's part with China on the latter's financial opening rather than reactive policymaking, or, worse, a turn towards protective economic nationalism.

These reform processes clearly have particular implications for the future of the Australia–China relationship across its economic, political and social dimensions. But if the governments and private sectors of Australia and China position themselves strategically, these reforms offer a once-in-a-lifetime opportunity to deepen the relationship in financial services and financial flows, which are still nascent compared to the relationship in merchandise trade.

Financial services are the largest single component of the Australian economy. With A$6.4 trillion in assets, the fourth-largest superannuation system in the world, a robust regulatory framework and one of the least restrictive industries in the region, Australia has a clear comparative advantage in exporting financial services into the region. Investing in deeper links and greater engagement with growing Chinese markets offers an immense opportunity to the Australian financial services industry. It is an investment in future growth that will be key to supporting the Australian economy's transition towards services following the mining boom.

For China, Australia offers the opportunity of a testing ground for reforms that will support China's continued opening and financial integration, both regionally and globally. Australia can support China across the many reforms it is undertaking, including expanding access to insurance, promoting inclusive finance, raising the proportion of direct financial intermediation, liberalising interest rates, promoting the internationalisation of the RMB, and helping strengthen financial and prudential regulation and the institutions that underpin it.

But building this relationship will not happen on its own. It is an ambition that will not be achieved quickly. It will require determination and commitment from the highest political levels and will be more challenging than was the case in building the relationship in merchandise trade. Australian and Chinese governments and private firms should strategically position themselves and build the infrastructure necessary to foster this relationship through the following measures:

- The Australian and Chinese governments should engage with the business sectors of both countries while *developing a formal program on financial services, development and reform*. It would complement the Strategic Economic Dialogue and engage ministers, officials, regulators and firms in a work program to deepen bilateral financial integration that would be focused on:

  - piloting *the select release of regulatory and licensing restrictions on Australian firms* in China as a phase-in for regional liberalisation, through expanding the financial services components of ChAFTA;

  - developing *a regular dialogue and a mutual recognition framework between financial regulators, and supporting the development of RMB-denominated assets and securities listings in Australia*;

  - pursuing mutual *reforms of macroprudential regulations and dividend imputation schemes* to ensure that Australian and Chinese entities are better able to engage with one-another in the region;

  - promoting *the bilateral and regional opportunities arising from fintech and digital finance*; and

  - commissioning *research between Australian and Chinese institutions on financial services trade and cross-border investment*.

There are also opportunities for partnership in regional financial cooperation:

- Both countries should work to build a bilateral financial infrastructure focus into regional initiatives such as One Belt, One Road, the Asian Infrastructure Investment Bank and the Asian Development Bank to improve payment systems, credit information bureaus, collateral registries and financial intermediaries and institutions throughout the Asia Pacific.

- China should sign on to, and Australia implement, APEC's Asia Region Funds Passport and both countries should advocate its greater use in the region.

Framework for capturing opportunities and managing risks

There are untapped opportunities in the Australia–China relationship to increase two-way bilateral trade, investment, finance and cooperation on regional and global issues. Success will be important for the long-term economic performance and security of both countries. There are three major types of risks that need to be managed in realising the opportunities:

commercial risks, macroeconomic risks and system difference risks. Commercial risks are the province of normal business strategies. Macroeconomic risks are common to all economic partnerships and can be avoided or their costs mitigated through appropriate policy settings, strategies and investing in policy capabilities. System difference risks — which are a consequence of sovereignty and are also normal in all major bilateral relationships, even between countries that have relatively similar institutional and political systems — are structural and therefore more complex in character. However, there are bilateral, regional and international institutional frameworks for dealing with the many dimensions of system difference risk that can be deployed to alleviating those risks particular to the relationship between Australia, China and the world.

The opportunities in the Australia–China relationship will be best achieved, and the risks best dealt with, through high-level political leadership and commitment to institutional arrangements that promote common understandings and norms of behaviour, and mobilise bi-national and plurilateral work programs to advance priority interests in the relationship.

Australia and China have a bilateral legacy from the 1980s of a 'model relationship' that was initiated between the two countries as an effective means to propel their respective domestic reform agendas. This history can be drawn upon in forging a new Strategic Comprehensive Partnership for Change that would both capture the new opportunities in the relationship and ameliorate the impact of system difference risks. This partnership requires entrenching a culture of cooperation within the relationship across government, business and both communities through regular working engagements, jointly targeted policy initiatives and through inculcating in China and Australia a deep understanding of the other country's society, culture and economy, as well as close personal connections. High-level political commitment and a uniting vision are key to commanding the attention and focusing official resources to address system risks, and key to providing the confidence and leadership that encourages private initiatives to flourish.

- The Australia–China Comprehensive Strategic Partnership for Change would provide *an overarching framework for long-term, high-level engagement that creates a culture of cooperation and trust between the two countries' different systems that advances their respective economic transformations.*

- The Australia–China relationship should be *a model of how countries with different social systems and at different levels of economic development can collaborate to enhance domestic as well as mutual bilateral, regional and multilateral objectives.*

- The essence of an upgraded partnership will be Australia and China's *working together in a strategic fashion within bilateral collaborations that deliver specific objectives of common priority and focus on shared ambitions for reform and change.*

- The top-level leaderships of both countries should establish a '*working group on bilateral reform*' that will structure the future bilateral political relationship to achieve: increased depth and scope of political dialogue; strategic forward agendas for leaders' meetings; joint working groups on reform between government agencies; and joint protocols for working together and managing differences.

- The new Australia–China (Ao–Zhong) Commission (see above) *should enable the two national governments to pool their resources with those from private and other sources to nurture the relationship through creating an independently governed public institution for programs of exchange and development sponsored by subnational governments, corporate businesses, academic institutions, cultural foundations, community organisations and individuals.* The heads of government of both countries will serve as dual patrons.

- The Commission will foster *high-quality research and academic exchange to increase the pool of Australia- and China-literate human capital across Australian and Chinese society.* This will include: scientific research; the promotion of language and cultural education at all levels; public and privately sponsored postgraduate, postdoctoral, early-career researcher and senior academic exchanges; and long-term partnerships for innovation and entrepreneurial commercialisation.

- The Commission can assist to *foster policy exchanges to produce future cohorts of political and government leaders in both countries who are familiar with the policymaking dynamics of the other country and have deep personal networks with their bilateral counterparts.* Deeper policy linkages will be achieved through an intensification of joint work on policy initiatives and agreed objectives, professional secondments, research fellowships, and training for Australian and Chinese officials in both countries. The Commission will leverage existing partnerships between the Australian Treasury and China's National Development and Reform Commission (NDRC), the Reserve Bank of Australia and the People's Bank of China, between the ANU and the Central Party School, and between ANZSOG and China's Organisation Department, as well as the National Parliamentary Fellowships Program proposed between the Australian Parliament and the National People's Congress.

- The Commission will foster *business and economic exchange to propel strategic collaboration on economic reform priorities* that will help Australia and China to manage their respective transformations. This will be supported by the forward work agenda from this Report on Australia and China's economic policymaking structures and how Australia and China can relate effectively to each other across government, business and society.

- The *Australia–China CEO Roundtable can be upgraded with a secretariat structure* that sustains effective collaborations on enhancing the business relationship, including through strategic engagement and the recommendation of future policy programs.

- *The process of planning, launching and implementing the Australia–China (Ao–Zhong) Commission and the Comprehensive Strategic Partnership for Change would lay the groundwork for Australia and China in the long-term to upgrade their 'model' relationship into a bilateral treaty framework.* This treaty framework would help enshrine the principles outlined in this Report and provide an umbrella for future bilateral agreements. Such a framework is a goal to be worked towards over a period of many years, but this process will cement political commitment to the relationship, institutionalise bilateral cooperation and perpetuate both countries' economic reform partnerships.

Regional initiatives

Australia and China have both enjoyed economic prosperity as a consequence of their domestic economic reforms and their integration into the international and regional economy. Openness, within the broader context of a more integrated regional economic order, has been an important dimension of their economic success. There are large changes underway in Asia due to the scale and pace of economic growth and Asia's growth has created a more complex and multipolar regional and global order. The existing regional institutions and arrangements in East Asia and across the Pacific were not designed to deal with all the challenges that have come with the changing structure of regional and global economic power, and there are gaps in their membership and issue coverage of economic and political cooperation institutions.

Neither Australia nor China would have prospered without the confidence and stability offered by the regional cooperation and governance frameworks that have underpinned Asian growth. Neither country would be benefited were these processes and institutions to fall into disrepair or irrelevance because they did not evolve to respond to the new challenges faced by the region.

- Australia and China share a common interest in working together to *forge a new consensus around the principles that will guide future Asian regional cooperation*. To that end, they should work with partners in Asia and the Pacific to strengthen and better connect existing regional institutions and arrangements, such as APEC, the ASEAN Plus Six arrangements and the East Asia Summit, and to initiate high-level political dialogue on important, cross-cutting issues such as energy and environmental transformation and regional infrastructural funding and investment.

- Australia and China should also *work to mobilise a coalition to help define the path forward in making the Trans-Pacific Partnership (TPP) and Regional Comprehensive Economic Partnership (RCEP) inclusive and complementary, and in transforming the TPP and RCEP into a Free Trade Area of the Asia Pacific that strengthens the WTO and the global economic system* (see Global Goals below).

- Asia's future economic growth and integration is increasingly dependent on investment in critical infrastructure, and Australia and China should seek to create *a common framework for regional infrastructure investment and funding that draws together key actors in the region including AIIB, the ADB, the World Bank, national development funding institutions, and recipient regional groupings such as ASEAN*. Australia and China can *use ambitious bilateral initiatives developed through ChAFTA as a model to advance progress in regional and global arrangements*, especially by driving regional investment and services sector liberalisation through RCEP.

Both countries should *continue to build their growing bilateral military-to-military relationship as an important step towards creating effective working relationships on security issues in the region*, and in strengthening the foundations of political confidence on which regional economic prosperity can continue to grow.

Global goals

The joint interests of Australia and China in regional cooperation, and the potential to use the bilateral relationship to prosecute these shared interests, is just as valid on the global level. Australia and China both benefit from strong global institutions, that are inclusive, rules-based, and promote open and efficient international markets. Many of the institutions that underpin the international economic system were created many decades ago and do not accurately reflect the relative size and importance of many countries within the global economy.

The G20 has emerged as the world's primary vehicle for reforming global governance and steering the priorities of the institutions, forums and organisations that underpin it. It is the only major forum where advanced and emerging economies, and the world's major borrowers and lenders, cooperate on an equal footing. Maintaining the G20's status as the 'global steering committee' and the preeminent forum for economic cooperation is in both Australia's and China's interests. Without the G20, there would be a particular risk for Australia given it is much more likely to be excluded from smaller groupings. But China would also be disadvantaged in a smaller forum dominated by advanced economies, with less influence over global rule setting.

Australia and China also need to ensure the adequacy of the global financial safety net. The needs of the region are not being met by global institutions, leading to greater reliance on more costly and less efficient regional and bilateral arrangements and the accumulation of foreign exchange reserves. The huge potential for Chinese financial sector reform and capital account liberalisation to transform the structure of the region's financial integration means that it is imperative that the global safety net is sufficient to respond to instability.

Australia and China benefit the most from trade liberalisation when it is multilateral rather than bilateral or plurilateral. Australia and China should work to support the cohesiveness of the global trading system by encouraging the G20 to refocus on the multilateral trading system rather than regional and bilateral alternatives.

The global governance architecture faces additional challenges in terms of its representativeness, effectiveness and legitimacy, and needs to be reformed. These challenges impact on Australia, China and the Asia Pacific region in particular. Australia, China and their partners can effect incremental change in addressing these issues, and the three areas set out above deserve special priority:

- Australia and China have powerful interests in *entrenching the G20 as the preeminent forum for global economic governance*. They should actively use and promote the G20, ensure its agenda is inclusive and targeted and ensure continuity across G20 presidencies by prioritising its multi-year growth agenda and deepening its agenda on global governance reform.

- In the near term, China should work to build up *the analytical capacity of the ASEAN Plus Three Macroeconomic Research Office and strengthen institutional collaboration and information and data sharing between the Chiang Mai Initiative Multilateralization, the BRICS currency reserve pool and regional development banks with the IMF.*

- With a view to the longer term, Australia and China should *encourage G20 discussions on the next stage of IMF quota reform, assume a leading role in renegotiating bilateral loans between G20 countries and the IMF, and focus the G20 growth agenda on strengthening domestic macroeconomic frameworks to improve financial resilience.*

- Australia and China should *lead a greater G20 focus on the multilateral trading system.* Australia and China should initiate a pragmatic, incremental process around WTO reform and *define a pathway for RCEP and regional arrangements like TPP to both raise the standard of regional agreements and strengthen the WTO.* They should encourage the use of the G20 growth strategies to achieve ambitious commitments under the Trade Facilitation Agreement and *encourage the G20 to consolidate existing work programs* to initiate a step-by-step process towards a multilateral framework for investment. Other important areas for collaboration are on *global energy governance and the reform of the membership and structure of the International Energy Agency, developing their partnership in the global response to climate change and promoting better coordination of global financing for infrastructure investment.* In each of these areas there is scope for Australia and China to collaborate and use their participation in global and regional forums to support and steer pragmatic, incremental steps in the interests of both countries.

References

ABARES 2014, *What China Wants: Analysis of China's Food Demand to 2050*, Conference paper 14.3, http://data.daff.gov.au/data/warehouse/9aat/2014/WhatChinaWants/AnalysisChinaFoodDemandTo2050_v.1.0.0.pdf

ABARES 2016, *Agricultural Commodities: March Quarter 2016*, Table 18 http://data.daff.gov.au/data/warehouse/agcomd9abcc004/agcomd9abcc20160301_cQe9T/AgCommodities201603_v1.0.0.pdf

ABC News 2014, 'China's Alibaba signs deal with Australia Post to attract shoppers', ABC Online, 30 May, http://www.abc.net.au/news/2014-05-28/alibaba-australia-post-deal/5484458

ABS 2002, *Year Book Australia*, cat. no. 1301.0, Australian Bureau of Statistics, Canberra, http://www.abs.gov.au/Ausstats/abs@.nsf/Lookup/B6362CCD5E7158FECA256B35007F93AC

ABS 2011, 'Census of Population and Housing', http://www.abs.gov.au/census

ABS 2015a, *Australian System of National Accounts*, 2014-15, Category 5204.0, http://www.abs.gov.au/ausstats/abs@.nsf/mf/5204.0

ABS 2015b, 'Feature Article: A Country Case Study, China', in *Balance of Payments and International Investment Position, Australia, Jun 2015* Cat No 5302.0 – http://www.abs.gov.au/AUSSTATS/abs@.nsf/featurearticlesbytitle/6273F9F94262C003CA257F680014A8BE?OpenDocument

ABS 2015c, *International Trade: Supplementary Information, Financial Year, 2014-15*, cat. no. 5368.0.55.003, Canberra, released 20 November, http://www.abs.gov.au/ausstats/abs@.nsf/mf/5368.0.55.003

ABS 2016a, *International Trade in Goods and Services*, Australia, cat. no. 5368.0, Canberra, released 3 February, http://www.abs.gov.au/ausstats/abs@.nsf/mf/5368.0.55.004

ABS 2016b, *Overseas Arrivals and Departures, Australia*, cat. no. 3401.0, Canberra, released 7 March, http://www.abs.gov.au/ausstats/abs@.nsf/mf/5368.0.55.004

ABS 2016c, *International Trade in Services by Country, by State and by Detailed Services Category, Calendar Year, 2014*, cat. no. 5368.0.55.004, Canberra, http://www.abs.gov.au/ausstats/abs@.nsf/mf/5368.0.55.004

ABS 2016c, *Overseas arrivals and departures*, cat. no. 3401.0, Canberra, http://www.abs.gov.au/AUSSTATS/abs@.nsf/DetailsPage/3401.0Mar%202016?OpenDocument

ABS 2016d, 'Overseas born Aussies highest in over a century', Press release, 30 March, http://www.abs.gov.au/ausstats/abs@.nsf/Latestproducts/3412.0Media%20Release12014-15

ABS 2016e, 'Australian National Accounts: National Income, Expenditure and Product', cat. no. 5206.0, Canberra, http://www.abs.gov.au/ausstats/abs@.nsf/mf/5206.0

ABS 2016f, 'International Investment Position, Australia: Supplementary Statistics', cat. no. 5352.0, Canberra, http://www.abs.gov.au/ausstats/abs@.nsf/mf/5352.0

ACBC 2015, 'The 2014 Australia-China Trade Report', http://acbc.com.au/admin/images/uploads/Copy2ACTradeReport_WEB_v4.pdf

ACCCI 2001, 'Position paper on sister state and sister city relations between Australia and China', 14 November, http://www.accci.com.au/sister.htm

ACRI 2016, 'Building Chinese language capacity in Australia', http://www.australiachinarelations.org/content/building-chinese-language-capacity-australia

ADB 2009, *Infrastructure for a Seamless Asia*, Asian Development Bank and Asian Development Bank Institute, Tokyo

Agricultural Bank of China 2016, 'Branch Profile: Sydney, Australia', accessed 6 June 2016, http://www.au.abchina.com/en/branch_profile/

AmCham China 2015, 2015 *American Business in China White Paper*, 17th edition, http://www.amchamchina.org/policy-advocacy/white-paper/2015-american-business-in-china-white-paper

AMP Capital 2013, 'AMP Capital enters China funds management with China Life JV', 2 September, http://www.ampcapital.com.au/article-detail?alias=/site-assets/articles/media-releases/2013/2013-09/amp-capital-enters-china-funds-management-with-chi

AMP Capital 2014, 'AMP Capital's joint venture with China Life raises A$2.2 billion for first mutual fund', 23 January, http://www.ampcapital.com/site-assets/articles/media-releases/2014/2014-01/amp-capital%E2%80%99s-joint-venture-with-china-life-raises

Anderson, TB, Barslund, M, Hansen, M, Hansen, CW, Harr, T & Sandholt PJ 2014. "How much did China's WTO accession increase economic growth in resource-rich countries?" *China Economic Review* vol. 30, pp 16-26.

Ang I, Tambiah Y & Mar, P 2015, 'Smart engagement with Asia: leveraging language, research and culture', Australian Council of Learned Academies, http://www.acola.org.au/PDF/SAF03/SAF03%20SMART%20ENGAGEMENT%20WITH%20ASIA%20-%20FINAL%20lo%20res.pdf

Anhui Foreign Affairs Office 2011, 'Northern Territory, Australia', 25 May, http://www.ahfao.gov.cn/English/NewsDetails.aspx?ClassId=10913&TypeId=10914&Id=3472

Anhui Foreign Affairs Office 2015, 'A List of Anhui's Sister Provinces', 16 September, http://www.ahfao.gov.cn/English/NewsDetails.aspx?ClassId=10913&TypeId=10914&Id=3520

Australian-American Fulbright Commission, viewed 5 July 2016, http://www.fulbright.com.au/index.php/about

Australia and New Zealand Banking Group Ltd 2016, 'ANZ in China', ANZ, January, https://www.anz.com/china/en/about-us/our-company/china/

Asia-Pacific Economic Cooperation 2014a, 'Annex A - The Beijing Roadmap for APEC's Contribution to the Realization of the FTAAP', APEC, http://www.apec.org/meeting-papers/leaders-declarations/2014/2014_aelm/2014_aelm_annexa.aspx

APEC 2014b, 'Asia Region Funds Passport: A Study of Potential Economic Benefits and Costs', APEC Policy Support Unit, July, Singapore, http://www.fsc.org.au/downloads/file/policyresearch/AsiaFundsPassport-AStudyofPotentialEconomicBenefitsandCosts.pdf

APEC 2015, 'Asia Region Funds Passport', November 2015, http://fundspassport.apec.org/about/

Armstrong, S & Drysdale, P 2011, 'The Influence of Economics and Politics on the Structure of World Trade and Investment Flows', in S Armstrong (ed.), *The Politics and the Economics of Integration in Asia and the Pacific*, Routledge, London.

Arnold, W 2014. 'China's global mining play is failing to pan out'. Wall Street Journal, 15 September. http://www.wsj.com/articles/chinas-global-mining-play-is-failing-to-pan-out-1410402598

Asia Education Foundation 2008, *The Current State of Chinese, Indonesian, Japanese and Korean Language Education in Australian Schools*, Language Report Series, Melbourne, http://www.asiaeducation.edu.au/research-and-policy/research-reports/aef/language-reports

Asialink 2012, *Developing an Asia Capable Workforce: A National Strategy*, http://asialink.unimelb.edu.au/__data/assets/pdf_file/0008/619793/Developing_an_Asia_Capable_Workforce.pdf

Association of Southeast Asian Nations 2008, 'ASEAN Economic Community Blueprint', ASEAN, ASEAN secretariat, Indonesia, http://www.asean.org/archive/5187-10.pdf

ATC 2014, 'Australia positions itself for traditional Chinese medicine market', 19 December, http://www.austrade.gov.au/International/Invest/Investor-Updates/2014/australia-positions-itself-for-traditional-chinese-medicine-market.

ATSE 2016, 'Australia-China Young Scientists Exchange Program', https://www.atse.org.au/content/international/australia-china-young-scientists-exchange-program.aspx

Au-Yeung, W, Keys, A & Ficher, P 2012, 'Australia-China: not just 40 years' Economic Roundup 4, http://www.treasury.gov.au/PublicationsAndMedia/Publications/2012/Economic-Roundup-Issue-4/HTML/article1

AustCham 2012, 'Australian Financial Services Business in China: 2012 White Paper', Australian Chamber of Commerce Beijing and Shanghai Financial Services Working Group, http://austcham.org/wp-content/uploads/2015/12/AustCham-White-Paper-ENlr.pdf

Auster, A & Foo, M 2015, 'Financial Integration in the Asia-Pacific: Fact and Fiction', Australian Centre for Financial Studies, June 2015, http://www.australiancentre.com.au/sites/default/files/ACFS%20Financial%20Integration%20website%20version_0.pdf

Austrade 2014, *Financial services to China*, Australian Trade Commission, 5 December, http://www.austrade.gov.au/Australian/Export/Export-markets/Countries/China/Industries/Financial-services

Austrade 2015a, 'The world's leading trading nations', *Economic Analysis*, http://www.austrade.gov.au/News/Economics-at-Austrade/the-worlds-leading-trading-nations

Austrade 2015b, 'How dependent are Australian exports on China?', *Trade and Investment Note*, http://www.austrade.gov.au/News/Economics-at-Austrade/how-dependent-are-australian-exports-on-china

Austrade 2016a, *Working With China*, http://www.austrade.gov.au/Australian/Tourism/working-with-china

Austrade 2016b, *Agribusiness to China: trends and opportunities*, http://www.austrade.gov.au/Australian/Export/Export-markets/Countries/China/Industries/agribusiness

Australia–China Business Council 2015, 'The 2014 Australia-China Trade report', http://acbc.com.au/admin/images/uploads/Copy2ACTradeReport_WEB_v4.pdf

Australia–China Youth Association, 2016. 'ACYA'. http://www.acya.org.au/australia-china-youth-association-group-acya-group/

Australian Centre on China in the World 2015, *The Australia–China Story Archive*, http://aus.thechinastory.org/archive/

Australian Embassy China 2009, *Australia-China joint statement*, 30 October 2009, viewed 5 July 2016, http://china.embassy.gov.au/bjng/statement.html

Australian Manufacturing 2014, 'Victoria and Jiangsu reaffirm relationship; commit to future partnership', 31 July, http://www.australianmanufacturing.com.au/20275/victoria-jiangsu-reaffirm-relationship-commit-future-partnership

Australian Minerals Council 2015, 'China, minerals and energy and the China-Australia Free Trade Agreement (ChAFTA)', Sydney, http://www.minerals.org.au/file_upload/files/publications/China_FTA_Policy_Paper_FINAL.pdf

Australian Services Roundtable 2013, 'Regional comprehensive economic partnership: Response by Australian Services Roundtable', 19 April, https://dfat.gov.au/trade/agreements/rcep/Documents/asr-submission-to-rcep.pdf

Australian Treasury 2007, 'Treasurer Signs Memorandum of Understanding with China's National Development and Reform Commission', 3 December, http://ministers.treasury.gov.au/DisplayDocs.aspx?doc=pressreleases/2008/114.htm&pageID=003&min=wms

Australian Treasury 2015, *Foreign Investment Review Board Annual Report 2013-2014*, https://firb.gov.au/files/2015/11/FIRB-AR-2013-14.pdf

Australian Treasury 2016, 'Backing Australian FinTech', http://FinTech.treasury.gov.au/files/2016/03/FinTech-March-2016-v3.pdf

Bajona, C & Chu, T 2010. "Reforming state owned enterprises in China: Effects of WTO accession." *Review of Economic Dynamics* vol. 13 no. 4, pp. 800-823.

Baldwin, R 2013, 'WTO 2.0: Thinking ahead on global trade', in Baldwin, R, Kawai, M & Wignaraja, G (eds.), *The future of the world trading system: Asian Perspectives*, Centre for Economic Policy Research.

Ballantyne, A et al 2014, 'Financial reform in Australia and China', Reserve Bank of Australia, http://www.rba.gov.au/publications/rdp/2014/pdf/rdp2014-10.pdf

Bank of China 2016, 'About Bank of China', accessed 6 June 2016, http://www.bankofchina.com/au/en/4-15.html

Bank of International Settlements, 2016. *Effective exchange rate indices*, 17 June, https://www.bis.org/statistics/eer.htm?m=6%7C187

Barratt, P 1992, 'Winning Asian markets in the eighties: A model for the nineties', Australian Quarterly, Summer.

Barton, D 2013, *The Rise of the Middle Class in China and Its Impact on the Chinese and World Economies*, McKinsey.

Battersby, L & Zhou, C 2015, 'Six tonnes of shopping flying from Swanston Street to China every week', *The Age*, 21 August, http://www.theage.com.au/victoria/six-tonnes-of-shopping-flying-from-swanston-street-to-china-every-week-20150818-gj1vxf.html

BP 2015, *Statistical Review of World Energy*, https://www.bp.com/content/dam/bp/pdf/energy-economics/statistical-review-2015/bp-statistical-review-of-world-energy-2015-full-report.pdf

BCA 2014, 'Discussion paper on foreign investment and state-owned enterprises', http://www.bca.com.au/docs/1bfca3a6-e06b-49a4-bd5a-a3d730772d9c/Disc_Paper_on_Foreign_Investment_WEB_FINAL_28.8.2014.pdf

Berkelmans, L & Wang, H 2012, 'Chinese urban residential construction', *Reserve Bank of Australia Bulletin*, September Quarter, http://www.rba.gov.au/publications/bulletin/2012/sep/pdf/bu-0912-3.pdf

BIS 2015. 'International banking and financial market developments', *BIS Quarterly Review*, September, Monetary and Economic Department, Bank for International Settlements, available at: https://www.bis.org/publ/qtrpdf/r_qt1509.pdf

Bishop, J 2015, *Australia-China High Level Dialogue*, media release, 27 November, viewed 5 July 2016, http://foreignminister.gov.au/releases/Pages/2015/jb_mr_151127.aspx

Bloomberg 2016, *Shanghai Composite Index*, 29 February, http://www.bloomberg.com/quote/SHCOMP:IND

Bloomberg 2016b, *Currencies*: RMB:USD, 25 June, http://www.bloomberg.com/markets/currencies

Boston Consulting Group 2012, *Imagining Australia in the Asian Century*, Sydney, www.bostonconsulting.com.au

Brown, K & van Nieuwenhuizen, S 2016, *Australia-China healthcare opportunities*, China Studies Centre, University of Sydney, https://sydney.edu.au/china_studies_centre/images/Business%20Forum/2015/reportchinesehealthcarereportfinal.pdf

Burbank, J 2014, *Consumers without borders: Chinese shoppers present a key growth market for the U.S. market this season.* Nielsen, 12 March, http://www.nielsen.com/us/en/insights/news/2014/consumers-without-borders--chinese-shoppers-present-a-key-growth.html

Callaghan, M 2013, 'Is the G20 agenda too big?', *The Interpreter*, Lowy Institute, 15 January, http://www.lowyinterpreter.org/post/2013/01/15/G20-agenda-too-big.aspx

CBA 2015, 'Commonwealth Bank widens Australia-China corridor', 1 June, https://www.commbank.com.au/about-us/news/media-releases/2015/commonwealth-bank-widens-australia-china-corridor.html

CCB 2016, 'China Construction Bank: About us', accessed 6 June 2016, http://au.ccb.com/sydney/en/gywm.html

CCTV 2016, 'China urbanization rate reached 56% in 2015', CCTV *English*, 30 January, http://english.cntv.cn/2016/01/30/VIDEf3nCcpAilTmx5J17brHD160130.shtml

Chen, X 2014, 'Talking in detail about China's foreign partnership relations: Strategic coordination is the highest level', *China Business News*, 24 November.

China APEC Development Council 2009, *China & APEC*, http://www.chinaapec.org/en/about_apec/content_5.shtml

China Daily 2006, 'Wal-Mart sees first Party branch', *China Daily*, 24 August, http://www.chinadaily.com.cn/china/2006-08/24/content_673263.htm

China Daily 2015, 'CPC has 87.79 million members: authority', *China Daily*, 1 July, http://www.chinadaily.com.cn/china/2015-07/01/content_21154422.htm

China General Administration of Customs 2016, retrieved from CEIC China Premium Database, https://www.ceicdata.com

China National Bureau of Statistics 2015, 'System of National Accounts', retrieved from CEIC China Premium Database, https://www.ceicdata.com

China XBR 2016, *QFII data*, http://china-xbr.com/xbr-quota-data/qfii/

Chinese Embassy Australia 2009, 'Chinese vice-premier, Australian prime minister meet on relations', press release, Canberra, 31 October, http://au.china-embassy.org/eng/zagx/zzgx/t623807.htm

Chung, M 2011, *Doing Business Successfully in China*, Chandos Publishing, Oxford.

CITIC Pacific Limited 2012, 'Announcement of Results for the Six Months Ended 30 June 2012', http://www.citictel.com/upload/announcement/792605927835.pdf

CMBA 2012, 'National regulation begins July 2012 for Chinese medicine practitioners', press release, 16 January, http://www.chinesemedicineboard.gov.au/News/Media-Releases.aspx

CNTA 2016, 'Tourism Statistics: Major source markets in December 2015', 15 January, http://en.cnta.gov.cn/Statistics/TourismStatistics/201601/t20160115_758275.shtml

CNTA 2016, 'Major Source Markets in December 2015', released 15 January 2016, http://en.cnta.gov.cn/Statistics/TourismStatistics/201601/t20160115_758275.shtml.

Conference Board 2015, 'Total Economy Database', https://www.conference-board.org/data/economydatabase/

CSIRO 2015, *Australian National Outlook 2015*, Canberra.

DAF 2016, *Jujubes in Western Australia*, https://agric.wa.gov.au/n/2373

Dee, M 2006, 'Friendship and cooperation: the 1976 Basic Treaty between Australia and Japan', Department of Foreign Affairs and Trade, Canberra, https://dfat.gov.au/about-us/publications/historical-documents/Documents/basic-treaty-between-australia-and-japan.pdf

Deep Decarbonization Pathways Project 2015, 'Pathways to deep decarbonisation', 2015 report, Sustainable Development Solutions Network and Institute for Sustainable Development and International Relations, Paris, http://deepdecarbonization.org/wp-content/uploads/2016/03/DDPP_2015_REPORT.pdf.

Denis, A, Jotzo, F & Ferraro, S 2014, 'Pathways to deep decarbonisation in 2050: how Australia can prosper in a low carbon world', ClimateWorks Australia and ANU.

Department of Education and Training 2015, 'Export income to Australia from international education activity in 2014-15', https://internationaleducation.gov.au/research/Research-Snapshots/Documents/Export%20Income%20FY2014-5.pdf

Department of Industry 2015a, *Energy White Paper*, Department of Industry and Science, April 2015, http://www.industry.gov.au/EnergyWhitePaperApril2015/index.html

Department of Industry 2015b, *Resources and Energy Quarterly: September Quarter 2015*, Canberra, http://www.industry.gov.au/Office-of-the-Chief-Economist/Publications/Documents/req/Resource-and-Energy-Quarterly-September-2015.pdf

Desloires, V & Cauchi, S 2015, 'China panic feeds into Australian sharemarket', Sydney Morning Herald, 9 July, viewed 5 July 2016, http://www.smh.com.au/business/markets/china-panic-feeds-into-australian-sharemarket-20150708-gi7nyk.html

DFAT 2009, 'Australia-China Joint Statement', 30 October, http://dfat.gov.au/geo/china/pages/australia-china-joint-statement.aspx

DFAT 2011, *Australia's exports to China, 2001-2011*, https://dfat.gov.au/about-us/publications/Documents/australias-exports-to-china-2001-2011.pdf

DFAT 2012, *Feeding the Future: a joint Australia–China study on strengthening agricultural investment and technological cooperation to enhance food security*, Canberra, https://dfat.gov.au/about-us/publications/trade-investment/feeding-future/Documents/feeding-the-future.pdf

DFAT 2014a, 'Fact Sheet: Financial Services, China-Australia Free-Trade Agreement', accessed January 2016, http://dfat.gov.au/trade/agreements/chafta/fact-sheets/Documents/fact-sheet-financial-services.pdf

DFAT 2014b, 'Fact Sheet: Agriculture and Processed Food, China-Australia Free-Trade Agreement', accessed January 2016, http://dfat.gov.au/trade/agreements/chafta/fact-sheets/Documents/fact-sheet-financial-services.pdf

DFAT 2015a, 'Environmental Goods Agreement', http://dfat.gov.au/trade/agreements/environmental-goods-agreement/Pages/environmental-goods-agreement.aspx

DFAT 2015b, 'Australia's trade in goods and services', http://dfat.gov.au/about-us/publications/trade-investment/australias-trade-in-goods-and-services/Pages/australias-trade-in-goods-and-services-2015.aspx

DFAT 2015c, *Composition of Trade Australia* 2014, http://dfat.gov.au/about-us/publications/Pages/composition-of-trade.aspx

DFAT 2016a, 'China Country Brief', http://dfat.gov.au/geo/china/pages/china-country-brief.aspx

DFAT 2016b, 'Record numbers of international students choose Australia', press release, 29 February, http://dfat.gov.au/news/news/Pages/record-numbers-of-international-students-choose-australia.aspx

DFAT 2016c, 'Trade statistical pivot tables', http://dfat.gov.au/about-us/publications/Pages/trade-statistical-pivot-tables.aspx

DFAT 2016d, 'Using CHAFTA to export and import goods', http://dfat.gov.au/trade/agreements/chafta/fact-sheets/Pages/guide-to-using-chafta.aspx

DFAT 2016e, 'China Factsheet', http://dfat.gov.au/trade/resources/Documents/chin.pdf

Dhar, B 2013, 'The future of the World Trade Organization', in Baldwin, R, Kawai, S & Wignaraja, G (eds.), *The future of the world trading system: Asian Perspectives*, Centre for Economic Policy Research.

DIBP 2015a, *2014-15 Migration programme report*, https://www.border.gov.au/ReportsandPublications/Documents/statistics/2014-15-Migration-Programme-Report.pdf

DIBP 2015b, *Working holiday maker visa programme report*, http://www.border.gov.au/ReportsandPublications/Documents/statistics/working-holiday-report-dec15.pdf

DIBP 2015c, *Subclass 457 quarterly report*, June Quarter, http://www.border.gov.au/ReportsandPublications/Documents/statistics/457-quarterly-report-2015-06-30.pdf

DIBP 2016a, *Facts and statistics*, https://www.border.gov.au/ReportsandPublications/Documents/statistics/2014-15-Migration-Programme-Report.pdf

DIBP 2016b, *Subclass 457 quarterly report*, March Quarter, http://www.border.gov.au/ReportsandPublications/Documents/statistics/457-quarterly-report-2016-03-31.pdf

DIBP 2015c, *2014-15 Migration Programme Report*, https://www.border.gov.au/ReportsandPublications/Documents/statistics/student-visa-trends-2014-15.pdf

Donnan, S & Mitchell, T 2016, 'IMF sounds warning on China corporate debt', *Financial Times*, 11 June. https://next.ft.com/content/3f8dcf22-304c-11e6-bda0-04585c31b153

Dorrucci, E, Pula, G & Santabárbara, D 2013, 'China's economic growth and rebalancing', ECB Occasional Paper 142, European Central Bank, February, https://www.ecb.europa.eu/pub/pdf/scpops/ecbocp142.pdf?e627863b2fce0a26dd6c2890dae23885

Downes, P, Hanslow, K & Tulip P 2014, 'The Effect of the Mining Boom on the Australian Economy', Research Discussion. Paper, August, http://www.rba.gov.au/publications/rdp/2014/pdf/rdp2014-08.pdf

Drew G, 2015, 'Zero Carbon Australia: Renewable Energy Superpower' Beyond Zero Emissions, Canberra, http://media.bze.org.au/resp/bze_superpower_plan.pdf.

Driffield, N, Love, J, Lancheros, S & Temouri, Y 2013, 'How attractive is the UK for future manufacturing foreign direct investment?', *Foresight*, Government Office for Science, https://www.gov.uk/government/uploads/system/uploads/attachment_data/file/277171/ep7-foreign-direct-investment-trends-manufacturing.pdf

Drysdale, P 2006, 'Did the NARA Treaty make a difference?', *Australian Journal of International Affairs*, vol. 60 no. 4, pp. 490-505.

Drysdale, P 2014, 'Crossing this Chinese river needs building a large bridge', East Asia Forum, 6 January 2014, http://www.eastasiaforum.org/2014/01/06/crossing-this-chinese-river-needs-building-a-large-bridge/

Drysdale, P 2015, 'Down to the wire on the Trans-Pacific Partnership', East Asia Forum, 27 July 2015, http://www.eastasiaforum.org/2015/07/27/down-to-the-wire-on-the-trans-pacific-partnership/

Drysdale, P & Armstrong, S 2010, 'International and Regional Cooperation: Asia's Role and Responsibilities', *Asian Economic Policy Review*, vol. 5, no.2, pp. 157–173.

Drysdale, P & Dervis, K 2014, *The G20 summit at five*, Brookings Institution Press.

Drysdale, P, Armstrong, S & Thomas N (forthcoming 2016), 'Chinese ODI and the need to reform Australia's foreign investment regime', *International Journal of Public Policy*.

Drysdale, P and Zhang, X 2016, 'The Australia-China (Ao-Zhong) Commission: A preliminary proposal', *EABER Working Paper*, forthcoming

DSDBI 2014a, 'New Victoria-Jiangsu alliance to promote investment and growth', 30 July, http://dsdbi.vic.gov.au/our-department/news/new-victoria-jiangsu-alliance-to-promote-investment-and-growth

DSDBI 2014b, 'Why Victoria needs a new China Engagement Strategy', accessed 5 July 2016, http://dsdbi.vic.gov.au/our-department/strategies-and-initiatives/engaging-china-strengthening-victoria/why-victoria-needs-a-new-china-engagement-strategy

Duffy, A 2012, 'CITIC blames skills shortage and inexperience for delays', *Australian Mining*, 17 August.

East Asian Bureau of Economic Research 2015, 'Australia's foreign investment regime and the need for reform', East Asian Bureau of Economic Research Working Paper, no. 105, 11 June.

East Asian Bureau of Economic Research, 2016, 'Suggestions to improve Australia's foreign investment review framework', Submission to an Inquiry into the Foreign Investment Review Framework, Senate Economics References Committee, Parliament of Australia, March 2016.

Egan, E, Foley, M & Kus, E 2015, 'Submission to the Australia-China Joint Economic Report', Australia-China Young Professionals Initiative, 6 November.

EIA 2015, 'China factsheet', United States Energy Information Administration, 2015, https://www.eia.gov/beta/international/analysis.cfm?iso=CHN

Eichengreen, B & Mussa 1998, 'Capital Account Liberalization and the IMF', *International Monetary Fund Finance and Development Magazine*, December, vol. 35 no. 4, http://www.imf.org/external/pubs/ft/fandd/1998/12/eichen.htm

Essential Media 2013, 'Foreign Investment', 24 September, http://www.essentialvision.com.au/foreign-investment

Essential Media 2014, 'Foreign Investment', 26 August, http://www.essentialvision.com.au/foreign-investment-2

EY 2015, 'EY Global IPO Trends: 4Q', http://www.ey.com/Publication/vwLUAssets/EY-global-ipo-trends-2015-q4/$FILE/EY-global-ipo-trends-2015-q4.pdf

FASIC 2015, 'Announcement of the BHP Billiton Australia China Scholarships', http://www.fasic.org.au/images/bhp%20billiton%20australia%20china%20scholarships.pdf

Feng, Z & Huang, J 2014, 'China's Strategic Partnership Diplomacy: Engaging with a Changing World', *European Strategic Partnerships Observatory*, Working Paper 8, June.

Finsia 2014, 'The Development of Financial Services in China: The role for Australia', Financial Services Institute of Australasia, University of Sydney, November, https://sydney.edu.au/china_studies_centre/images/content/ccpublications/csc-finisa-report.pdf

FIRB 2015a, 'Australia's Foreign Investment Policy', Department of Treasury, http://firb.gov.au/files/2015/09/Australias_Foreign_Investment_Policy_December_2015_v2.pdf

FIRB 2015b, 'Foreign Government investors [GN23]', http://firb.gov.au/resources/guidance/gn23/

Florini, A 2012, 'Policy Recommendations', *IEA, World Energy Outlook 2013*, Paris 2013.

G20 India Secretariat 2014, *Regional Financial Arrangements (RFA) and Cooperation with the* IMF, G20 India Secretariat, Government of India, Ministry of Finance, Department of Economic Affairs, http://www.g20india.gov.in/finance-ifar-rfa.asp?lk=finance5

G20 2011, 'G20 Principles for Cooperation between the IMF and Regional Financing Arrangements', 15 October, http://www.g20.utoronto.ca/2011/2011-finance-principles-111015-en.pdf

G20 2014, 'G20 leaders communiqué', November 2014, http://www.g20australia.org/official_resources/g20_leaders_communique_brisbane_summit_november_2014

Garnaut, J 2014, 'Mr China No More: Clive Palmer out of Luck, Again', *The Sydney Morning Herald*, http://www.smh.com.au/federal-politics/political-opinion/mr-china-no-more-clive-palmer-out-of-luck-again-20140819-105yhb.html

Garnaut, R 1989, *Australia and the Northeast Asian Ascendancy*, Report to the Prime Minister and the Minister for Foreign Affairs and Trade, Commonwealth of Australia, Canberra.

Garnaut, R 2005, 'The emergence of substantive Sino–Australian relations, 1983-88', Paper for the Lowy Institute for International Policy, 1 April.

Garnaut, R 2012, 'The contemporary China resources boom', *The Australian Journal of Agricultural and Resource Economics*, vol. 56 no. 2, pp. 222–243.

Garnaut, R 2015, 'Australia: Energy Superpower of the Low-Carbon World', 2015 Luxton Memorial Lecture, Adelaide.

Gettler, L 2004, 'Game over: Lion quits China', *Sydney Morning Herald*, 16 September.

GFAO 2016, 'Sister Relationship, Guangdong Foreign Affairs Office, http://www.gdfao.gov.cn/Category_279/Index.aspx

Gilbert, M 2014, 'Europe's Debt Time Bomb', *Bloomberg*, 20 May, http://www.bloombergview.com/articles/2014-05-20/europe-s-debt-time-bomb

Goh, E 2007-08, 'Great Powers and Hierarchical Order in Southeast Asia: Analyzing Regional Security Strategies', *International Security*, vol. 32, no.3.

Goodman, D 1996, 'China's Provinces and Australia's States: Sister States and International Mates', in Colin Mackerras (ed.), *Australia and China: Partners in Asia*, Macmillan, Melbourne, pp. 171-195.

Government of Australia 2014, Budget Paper no. 1, http://www.budget.gov.au/2014-15/

Government of Australia 2015a, *Australia: Comprehensive G20 growth strategy*, http://www.g20.org/English/Documents/Current/index.html

Government of Australia 2015b, *Our North, Our Future: White Paper on Developing Northern Australia*, 18 June, https://www.cdu.edu.au/sites/default/files/the-northern-institute/docs/northern-australia-white-paper.pdf

Government of Australia 2015c, *Response to the Financial System Inquiry*, http://www.treasury. gov.au/~/media/Treasury/Publications%20and%20Media/Publications/2015/Government%20 response%20to%20the%20Financial%20System%20Inquiry/Downloads/PDF/Government_ response_to_FSI_2015.ashx

Government of China 2006, *Notice of the National Development and Reform Commission*, The Ministry of Commerce, the Ministry of Foreign Affairs, the Ministry of Finance, the General Administration of Customs, the State Administration of Taxation and the State Administration of Foreign Exchange on Printing and Distributing the 'Policy for the Guidance of Overseas Investment Industries', http://www.asianlii.org/cn/legis/cen/laws/cotsaofeopadtgfifemmti1503/

Government of China 2015a, *China: Comprehensive G20 growth strategy*, http://www.g20.org/ English/Documents/Current/index.html

Government of China 2015b, *Enhanced actions on climate change: China's intended nationally determined contributions*.

Government of New South Wales 2015, 'Premier hosts state dinner for Party Secretary of China's Guangdong Province', 26 May, https://www.nsw.gov.au/media-releases-premier/premier-hosts-state-dinner-party-secretary-chinas-guangdong-province

Government of South Australia 2013, South Australia's relationship with Shandong Province,

http://www.statedevelopment.sa.gov.au/investment/south-australia-china-engagement/south-australias-relationship-with-shandong-provi

Government of Victoria 2016, '*Victoria's China Strategy: Partnerships for prosperity*, http://www.dpc. vic.gov.au/images/FINAL_China_Strategy_-_English_Version.pdf

Government of Western Australia, 1997, *Chinese health sector delegation from Zhejiang visits Perth*, https://www.mediastatements.wa.gov.au/Pages/Court/1997/09/Chinese-health-sector-delegation-from-Zhejiang-visits-Perth.aspx

Greber, J 2015, 'Australia hit hardest by China investment crunch, IMF says', *The Australian Financial Review*, 21 September, http://www.afr.com/news/economy/australia-hit-hardest-by-china-investment-crunch-imf-says-20150921-gjreuu

Green, F & Stern, N 2015, 'China's 'New Normal': Better Growth, Better Climate, Policy Paper', Grantham Research Institute, LSE.

Gretton, P 2016, 'Modelling the potential impacts of economic reform in a partnership between Australia and China', East Asian Bureau of Economic Growth Working Paper 121.

Gretton, P, Gali J & Parnham N 2003, 'The effects of ICTs and complementary innovations on Australian productivity growth' Productivity Commission, July, http://www.pc.gov.au/research/supporting/ict-innovations/eictci.pdf.

Grigg, A 2015, 'Australian company is close to producing and selling gas in China's domestic market', *The Australian Financial Review*, 6 September.

Grigg, A & Murray, L 2016, 'China's $4 trillion message to short-sellers', *The Australian Financial Review*, 25 February, http://www.afr.com/markets/debt-markets/chinas-4-trillion-message-to-shortsellers-20160225-gn40lf#ixzz41EynAsYu

Groot, M 1990, 'How much? By whom? In what? Polled opinion on foreign investment, 1958–1990', *Australian Journal of International Affairs*, vol. 44, no. 3, pp. 247-267.

Gruen, D 2011, 'The macroeconomic and structural implications of a once-in-a-lifetime boom in the terms of trade', address to the Australian Business Economists Annual Conference, November.

Gruenwald, P, Conti, V & Rana, V 2016, 'How China's rebalancing shifts the ground under all of Asia-Pacific', *Standard & Poors Economic Research*, http://cdn.haymarketmedia.asia/finance-asia%2Fcontent%2FHow_Chinas_Rebalancing_Shifts_The_Ground_Under_All_Of_Asia_Pacific.pdf

Hamshere, P, Sheng, Y, Moir B, Syed, F & Gunning-Trant, C 2014, 'What China Wants', ABARES, Department of Agriculture, Forestry and Fisheries, Conference Paper 14.3, http://espas.eu/orbis/sites/default/files/generated/document/en/AnalysisChinaFoodDemandTo2050_v.1.0.0.pdf

Hanemann, T & Huotari, M 2015, 'Chinese FDI in Europe and Germany: Preparing for a new era of Chinese capital', *Rhodium Group and Mercator Institute for China Studies*, http://rhg.com/wp-content/uploads/2015/06/ChineseFDI_Europe_Full.pdf

Harris, S 2000, 'Asian Multilateral Institutions and Their Response to the Asian Economic Crisis: The Regional and Global Implications,' *The Pacific Review*, vol. 13, no. 3: p. 501.

Hatfield-Dodds, S et al. 2015, 'Australia is 'free to choose' economic growth and falling environmental pressures', *Nature*, vol. 527, pp. 49–53.

Hatzvi, E, Nixon, W & Wright, M 2014, 'The Offshore Renminbi Market and Australia', Bulletin, December Quarter 2014, http://www.rba.gov.au/publications/bulletin/2014/dec/7.html

Hawkins, A, Rahman, J & Williamson, T 2014, 'Is the global financial safety net at a tipping point to fragmentation?', *Economic Roundup* Issue 1, http://www.treasury.gov.au/PublicationsAndMedia/Publications/2014/Economic-Roundup-Issue-1/Economic-Roundup-Issue-1/Global-financial-safety-net#P8_195

Hill, H & Menon, J 2010, 'ASEAN Economic Integration: Features, Fulfillments, Failures and the Future', ADB Working Paper Series on Regional Economic Integration, no. 69.

Hirst, N 2012, 'The Reform of Global Energy Governance', *Grantham Institute for Climate Change*, Discussion paper no 3, December, https://www.chathamhouse.org/sites/files/chathamhouse/public/Research/Energy,%20Environment%20and%20Development/1212granthamreport_energygovernance.pdf

Hirst, N 2015, 'Next steps in global energy governance', in 'G20 and global governance', Blue Book of the G20 Think Tank, 2015–16, Renmin University of China.

Huang Y et al. 2011, 'Achieving capital account convertibility in China', *China Economic Journal*, vol. 4, no. 1, pp. 25–42.

Huang, Y 2016, 'Can China Rise to High Income', in Hutchinson, F & Basu Das, S (eds.), *Asia and the Middle Income Trap*, Routledge.

Hubbard, P 2015, 'Where have China's state monopolies gone?', EABER Working Paper Series, no. 115, http://www.eaber.org/system/tdf/documents/EABER%20Working%20Paper%20115%20Hubbard.pdf?file=1&type=node&id=25278&force=

Huizhou Products Expo 2015, 'Top Chinese Manufacturers in Sydney for Huizhou Products Expo', press release, *Australia–China Business Council*, 15 May, http://acbc.com.au/blog-details_120

Hulst, N 2015, 'The rise of the G20 and OECD's role', *OECD Insights*, 17 November, http://oecdinsights.org/2015/11/17/the-rise-of-the-g20-and-oecds-role/

Hurley, D 2014, National Security Lecture Series, 7 March, viewed 5 July 2016, https://www.canberra.edu.au/about-uc/media/monitor/2014/june/defence_force_chief. See also http://aus.thechinastory.org/archive/defence-and-strategic-relations/

Hurst, L 2015, 'Assessing the competitiveness of the supply side response to China's iron ore demand shock', *Resources Policy*, vol. 45, pp. 247–254.

Hurst, L 2016, *China's iron ore boom*, Routledge, London.

ICBC 2016, 'Introduction to ICBC Sydney Branch', 6 June, http://www.icbc.com.cn/ICBC/%E6%B5%B7%E5%A4%96%E5%88%86%E8%A1%8C/%E6%82%89%E5%B0%BC%E7%BD%91%E7%AB%99/en/AboutUs1/SydneyBranch/

IMF, 2009. 'Group of 20, Meeting of the Deputies'. International Monetary Fund, January 31-February 1, London. https://www.imf.org/external/np/g20/pdf/020509.pdf

IMF 2013, 'IMF Explores Ways to Enhance Cooperation with Regional Group', *IMF Survey Magazine: Policy*, 2 July, http://www.imf.org/external/pubs/ft/survey/so/2013/POL070213A.htm

IMF 2015a, 'World Economic Outlook Database October 2015', International Monetary Fund, https://www.imf.org/external/pubs/ft/weo/2015/02/weodata/index.aspx

IMF 2015b, 'Macroeconomic and reform priorities', Meetings of G-20 Finance Ministers and Central Bank Governors, 22–23 February 2014, Sydney, Australia, http://blogs.worldbank.org/developmenttalk/files/Macroeconomic_and_Reform_Priorities_0.pdf

IMF 2015c, 'Statement by Christine Lagarde on IMF Review of SDR Basket of Currencies', press release, no. 15/513, 13 November, https://www.imf.org/external/np/sec/pr/2015/pr15513.htm

IMF 2016, 'Adequacy of the global financial safety net', Washington DC. http://www.imf.org/external/np/pp/eng/2016/031016.pdf

Industry NSW 2015, 'Chinese banks choose NSW', http://www.industry.nsw.gov.au/buy-from-nsw/success-stories/chinese-banks-choose-nsw

Infrastructure Australia 2016 *Australian Infrastructure Plan*, Sydney, http://infrastructureaustralia.gov.au/policy-publications/publications/Australian-Infrastructure-Plan.aspx

Inman, P, Macalister, T, Topham, G & Sweney, M 2015, 'The UK's deals worth billions with China: what do they really mean?', *The Guardian*, 25 October, http://www.theguardian.com/business/2015/oct/24/britains-deals-with-china-billions-what-do-they-mean

IPCC 2014, 'Technical Summary', *Climate Change 2014: Mitigation of Climate Change. Contribution of Working Group III to the Fifth Assessment Report of the Intergovernmental Panel on Climate Change*.

Jara, A 2013, 'A multilateral agreement on investment: A brief reflection', in Baldwin, R, Kawai, M & Wignaraja, G, *The future of the world trading system: Asian Perspectives*, Centre for Economic Policy Research.

Jin, W & Zhang, XZ 2016, 'China's Pursuit of Environmentally Sustainable Development: Harnessing the New Engine of Technological Innovation', CCEP Working Paper no. 1601, Centre for Climate Economics and Policy, Crawford School of Public Policy, ANU.

Johnson Report 2010, *Australia as a Financial Centre*, Australian Financial Centre Forum, http://afcf.treasury.gov.au/content/final_report.asp

Karnikowski, N 2013, 'Australian tourists flock to China', Traveller (Fairfax Media), 10 November, http://www.traveller.com.au/australian-tourists-flock-to-china-2zdyc

Masahiro, K 2015, 'From the Chiang Mai Initiative to an Asian Monetary Fund', ADBI Working Paper Series, no. 527, www.adb.org/sites/default/files/publication/160056/adbi-wp527.pdf

Kearney, AT 2015, 'Asia fund passport could manage $600b by 2030: AT Kearney', Sydney Morning Herald, 3 August, http://www.smh.com.au/business/banking-and-finance/asia-fund-passport-could-manage-600b-by-2030-at-kearney-20150803-giq8cw.html

Kelly, G & La Cava, G 2014, 'Value-added trade and the Australian economy', RBA Bulletin March Quarter 2013, http://www.rba.gov.au/publications/bulletin/2013/mar/pdf/bu-0313-4.pdf

Kenny, M 2013, 'Gillard scores coup with China agreement', The Sydney Morning Herald, 10 April, http://smh.com.au/federal-politics/political-news/gillard-scores-coup-with-china-agreement-20130409-2hjin.html

Kharas, H & Gill, I 2016, 'The middle income trap turns 10', in Hutchinson, F & Basu Das, S (eds.), Asia and the middle income trap, Routledge.

King & Wood Mallesons, 2015, China Stock Connect and Mutual Recognition of Funds – latest developments in cross-border investment' Minny Siu & Hayden Flinn, 30 June, http://www.lexology.com/library/detail.aspx?g=85c1437e-34d1-43c7-b0f5-ceaaa63c4674

KPMG 2016. Demystifying Chinese Investment in Australia, http://demystifyingchina.com.au/reports/demystifying-chinese-investment-in-australia-april-2016.pdf

Kraemer, KL, Linden, G & Dedrick, J 2011, 'Capturing Value in Global Networks: Apple's iPad and iPhone', University of California, Irvine, University of California, Berkeley and Syracuse University.

Lagarde, C 2016, 'The Role of Emerging Markets in a New Global Partnership for Growth', University of Maryland, 4 February, http://www.imf.org/external/np/speeches/2016/020416.htm

Lamy, P 2013, 'Foreword', in Baldwin, R, Kawai, M & Wignaraja, G (eds.), The future of the world trading system: Asian Perspectives, Centre for Economic Policy Research.

Laurenceson, J., Burke, P. F., & Wei, E. 2015, 'The Australian public's preferences over foreign investment in agriculture', Agenda: A Journal of Policy Analysis and Reform, Vol. 22(1), 45.

LEK Consulting 2016. 'How the China tourism boom is transforming Australia'. Report for the Australia-China Business Council. http://cdn.lek.com/sites/default/files/Special_Report_China_Chinese_Tourism_in_Australia.pdf

Letts, S 2016, 'Results wrap: AMP hits record, Treasury Wine Estates profit surges and Origin sinks deeper into the red', ABC Online, 18 February, http://www.abc.net.au/news/2016-02-18/amp-posts-record-profit/7179636

Lewis, P & Woods, J, 'Our border fears speak to bigger issues', The Drum, 15 August, http://www.abc.net.au/news/2012-08-14/lewis-and-woods-boat-people/4197474

Li, J 2015, 'Chinese Medicine Expected to Benefit from China-Australia FTA', CRI English, 19 December, http://english.cri.cn/12394/2015/12/19/4204s909085.htm

Lin, M 2015, 'The Multidimensional Values of the Asian Infrastructure Investment Bank', China Today, 2 June, http://www.chinatoday.com.cn/english/columns/2015-06/02/content_690607.htm

Loubere, N 2016, 'Inside Out: Owen Lattimore on China', The China Story Journal, 8 January, https://www.thechinastory.org/2016/01/inside-out-owen-lattimore-on-china/

Lowy Institute 2015, '*Lowy Institute Poll*', *2005-2015*, http://www.lowyinstitute.org/programs-and-projects/programs/polling

Lumsden, A, Knight, L & Daveson, S 2015. 'China's One Belt One Road – A new opportunity for Australian expertise', Corrs Chambers Westgarth, 20 July, http://www.corrs.com.au/thinking/insights/chinas-one-belt-one-road-a-new-opportunity-for-australian-expertise/

Manuel, R 2016, 'China's e-commerce laws are not a 'crackdown' but closing a loophole', *The Conversation*, 14 April, https://theconversation.com/chinas-e-commerce-laws-not-a-crackdown-but-closing-a-loophole-57742

McKay, H, Sheng, Y & Song, L 2010, 'China's metal intensity in comparative perspective', in Garnaut, R, Golley, J & Song, L (eds.), *China: the next twenty years of reform and development*, http://press.anu.edu.au?p=95681

McKibbin, W 1998, 'Regional and Multilateral Trade Liberalization: The Effects on Trade, Investment and Welfare', in Drysdale, P & Vines, D (eds.), *Europe, East Asia and APEC: A Shared Global Agenda?*, Cambridge University Press, Cambridge, pp. 195–220.

McKibbin, W, Stoeckel, A & Lu, Y 2014, 'Global Fiscal Adjustment and Trade Rebalancing', *The World Economy*, vol. 37 no. 7, pp. 892–922, http://onlinelibrary.wiley.com/doi/10.1111/twec.12185/abstract

McKibbin, W and Wilcoxen, P 1999. 'The theoretical and empirical structure of the G-Cubed model', *Economic Modelling*, vol. 16, pp. 123-148.

Milman, O 2015, 'Cane toads by the million lined up for export to China as anti-cancer remedy', *The Guardian*, 26 August, http://www.theguardian.com/environment/2015/mar/26/cane-toad-venom-cancer-chinese-remedies

Minister for Immigration and Border Protection 2015, 'Work and holiday arrangement with China commences', press release, 22 September, http://www.minister.border.gov.au/peterdutton/2015/Pages/work-holiday-arrangement-china.aspx

Minister for Industry, Innovation and Science 2016, '$5.95 million for new joint research centres to strengthen innovation and science links with China', press release, 26 April, http://www.minister.industry.gov.au/ministers/pyne/media-releases/595-million-new-joint-research-centres-strengthen-innovation-and

Minister of Trade and Minister of Tourism 2015, 'New air deal with China: 2015 off to a flying start for Australian tourism', press release, 23 January.

Ministry of Commerce and Ministry of Foreign Affairs 2004, 'Notice of the Ministry of Commerce and the Ministry of Foreign Affairs about Distributing the Catalogue of Countries and Industries for Guiding Investment Overseas', http://en.pkulaw.cn/display.aspx?cgid=54037&lib=law

Monocle 2016, 'Soft power survey, 2015/2016', https://monocle.com/film/affairs/soft-power-survey-2015-16/

Montiel, P 2014, *Ten crises*. Routledge, New York.

NAB 2015, 'Unfold new opportunities in China with NAB's new Beijing branch', National Australia Bank, 17 November, http://www.nab.com.au/business-asia/expert-guidance/banking-essentials/unfold-new-opportunities-in-china-with-nabs-new-beijing-branch

New Climate Economy 2014, 'Better growth better climate', *Global Commission on the Economy and Climate*.

Ng, J 2016, 'Iron ore's big guns seize greater share of trade with China', *Bloomberg*, 26 January, http://www.bloomberg.com/news/articles/2016-01-26/iron-ore-s-big-guns-seize-greater-share-of-china-trade-amid-rout

NN Investment Partners 2015, 'Surge in emerging market capital outflows hits growth and currencies', *Financial Times*, by James Kynge & Roger Blitz, London, 18 August, http://www.ft.com/intl/cms/s/3/00b81130-45c5-11e5-af2f-4d6e0e5eda22.html#axzz3r8lRsgxx

OECD 2012, *Strategic Transport Infrastructure Needs to 2030*, Organisation for Economic Cooperation and Development, http://www.oecd.org/futures/strategictransportinfrastructureneedsto2030.htm

OECD 2013a, *China's Share of World GDP, 1980-2010: At Market and PPP Exchange Rates*, http://www.keepeek.com/Digital-Asset-Management/oecd/development/perspectives-on-global-development-2013/china-s-share-of-world-gdp-1980-2010_persp_glob_dev-2013-graph13-en#page1

OECD 2013b, *Supporting Investment in Knowledge Capital, Growth and Innovation*, http://dx.doi.org/10.1787/9789264193307-en

OECD 2014a, *Level of GDP Per Capita and Productivity*, https://stats.oecd.org/Index.aspx?DataSetCode=PDB_LV#

OECD 2014b, *FDI Regulatory Restrictiveness Index*, http://www.oecd.org/investment/fdiindex.htm

OECD 2015, *OECD Trade Facilitation Indicators*, http://www.oecd.org/trade/facilitation/indicators.htm

OECD 2016, *Trade in goods and services (indicator)*, https://data.oecd.org/trade/trade-in-goods-and-services.htm

Orton, J 2016, 'Australians are too lazy to master Chinese', *Sydney Morning Herald*, 15 March, viewed 5 July 2016, http://www.smh.com.au/national/australias-potential-in-china-lost-in-translation-20160314-gni7zt.html

Oshikawa, M 2013, 'WTO-ASEAN asymmetries: Calling for greater collaboration', in Baldwin, R, Kawai, M & Wignaraja, G (eds.), *The future of the world trading system: Asian Perspectives*, Centre for Economic Policy Research.

Pan, N & Dechian, S 2014, 'New alliance to strengthen Australia–China regional city ties', *Radio Australia*, 1 August, http://www.radioaustralia.net.au/international/2014-08-01/new-alliance-to-strengthen-australiachina-regional-city-ties/1349484-0

Pangestu, M & Nellor, D 2014, 'G20 must shape a new world trade regime', *East Asia Forum*, 17 July, http://www.eastasiaforum.org/2014/07/17/g20-must-shape-a-new-world-trade-regime/

Parkinson, M 2015, 'The Lucky Country: Has it Run out of Luck?', Griswold Center for Economic Policy Studies Working Paper no. 247, https://www.princeton.edu/ceps/workingpapers/247parkinson.pdf.

PBoC, 2015, 'Notice of the People's Bank of China (PBC) on Issues Concerning Investment of Foreign Central Banks, International Financial Institutions and Sovereign Wealth Funds with RMB Funds in the Inter-bank Market', *Notice, People's Bank of China, 14 June 2015*, http://www.pbc.gov.cn/english/130721/2813742/index.html

Pew Research Centre (2014) *Global Attitudes Survey*, 16 September 2014

Pokarier, C 2015, 'Australia's foreign investment policy: A historical perspective', EABER Working Paper Series, no. 111, http://www.eaber.org/sites/default/files/documents/EABER

Portland Communications 2016, 'The Soft power 30', http://softpower30.portland-communications.com/

Prasad, E 2015, 'The path to sustainable growth in China', Testimony to the US-China Economic and Security Review Commission, 22 April, http://www.brookings.edu/research/testimony/2015/04/22-sustainable-growth-china-prasad

Premier of South Australia 2016, 'Renewed vision for engagement with China', press release, 25 May, http://www.premier.sa.gov.au/index.php/jay-weatherill-news-releases/593-renewed-vision-for-engagement-with-china

Premier of Tasmania 2014, 'Signing up for a prosperous future', press release, 17 November, http://www.premier.tas.gov.au/releases/signing-up_for_a_prosperous_future

Premier of Victoria 2016, 'A Vision for China to Bring more Jobs and Growth to Victoria', press release, 19 April, http://www.premier.vic.gov.au/a-vision-for-china-to-bring-more-jobs-and-growth-to-victoria/

Productivity Commission 2015, *Barriers to Growth in Service Exports*, http://www.pc.gov.au/inquiries/completed/service-exports/report/service-exports.pdf

Project Atlas 2016, 'Australia's students overseas', http://www.iie.org/en/Services/Project-Atlas/Australia/Australias-Students-Overseas

Qiu, Q 2014, 'Guangdong trade delegation to visit New South Wales', *China Daily Europe*, 7 July, http://europe.chinadaily.com.cn/china/2014-07/07/content_17657599.htm

Raby, G 2011, 'What does it mean to be China Literate?', Speech to the Australian Institute of Company Directors Conference, Beijing, 18 May, http://china.embassy.gov.au/bjng/ambo110518.html

RBA 2012, 'Iron Ore Pricing', *Statement on Monetary Policy*, August, http://www.rba.gov.au/publications/smp/boxes/2012/aug/b.pdf

RBA 2016, 'Real exchange rate measures – F15', Statistical Tables, March, http://www.rba.gov.au/statistics/tables/#exchange-rates

Ren, X 2014, 'Interview: Xi's visit to strengthen strategic cooperative partnership with South Korea – ambassador', *Xinhua*, 7 March, http://english.cntv.cn/2014/07/03/ARTI1404344354269608.shtml

Rizvi, F, Louie, K & Evans, J 2016, 'Australia's Diaspora Advantage: realising the potential for building transnational business networks with Asia', Report for the Australian Council of Learned Academies, http://www.acola.org.au/pdf/saf11/SAF11%20full%20report.pdf

Roberts, I, Saunders, T, Spence, G & Cassidy, N 2016, 'China's Evolving Demand for Commodities', Conference paper in *Structural Change in China: Implications for Australia and the World*, Reserve Bank of Australia.

Robertson, A 2016, 'Investors vote to wind up AMP Capital's China Growth Fund', *ABC Online*, 28 July 2016, http://www.abc.net.au/news/2016-07-28/unit-holders-vote-to-close-amp-capital-china-fund/7670240

Rodriguez, D & Ren, S 2015. 'Which currencies have been affected by Chinese equity volatility', *Daily FX*, 10 July, https://www.dailyfx.com/forex/technical/article/forex_correlations/2015/07/09/forex-correlations-Japanese-Yen-China-300.html

Rudd, K 2008, 'Toward an Asia-Pacific Union', 4 June, viewed 5 July 2016, http://asiasociety.org/australia/kevin-rudd-toward-asia-pacific-union

Russell, C 2016, 'Australia, Brazil boost China iron ore import share, but not enough', Reuters, 27 January, http://www.reuters.com/article/us-column-russell-ironore-china-idUSKCN0V5147

Sachs, JD, Warner, A, Åslund, A & Fischer, S 1995. "Economic Reform and the Process of Global Integration" *Brookings Papers on Economic Activity* vol. 1, 25th Anniversary Issue, pp. 1-118

Schwab, K 2016, 'Global Competitiveness Report 2015-2016', World Economic Forum, Switzerland, http://www3.weforum.org/docs/gcr/2015-2016/Global_Competitiveness_Report_2015-2016.pdf

Shafik, M 2015, 'Fixing the global financial safety net: lessons from central banking', David Hume Institute, Edinburgh, Scotland, 22 September, http://www.bankofengland.co.uk/publications/Pages/speeches/2015/841.aspx.

Shambaugh, D 2004–2005, 'China Engages Asia: Reshaping the Regional Order,' *International Security*, vol. 29, no. 3, p. 68.

Sheng, Y 2016, 'Economic growth in China and its potential impact on Australia-China bilateral trade', EABER Working Paper Series, no. 122, http://www.eaber.org/system/tdf/documents/EABER%20Working%20Paper%20122%20Sheng.pdf?file=1&type=node&id=25642&force=

Slocum, Jr. JW, Conder W, Corradini, E, Foster, R, Frazer, R, Le, Di, McGuire, M, Ross, J & Scott, S 2006, 'Fermentation in the China Beer Industry', *Organizational Dynamics*, vol. 35 no. 1, pp. 32-48, doi:10.1016/j.orgdyn.2005.12.002

Smith, H 2012, 'A legal guide to investing in the UK for foreign investors', http://www.herbertsmithfreehills.com/-/media/HS/L050712154578912171416219.pdf.

Smith, M & Liew, R 2015, 'AMP's China Growth Fund under an activist cloud', *The Australian Financial Review*, 13 May, http://www.afr.com/business/banking-and-finance/financial-services/amps-china-growth-fund-under-an-activist-cloud-20150513-gh0dll

Smith, M 2015, 'AMP's leap into China, Dunne's legacy', *The Australian Financial Review*, 25 September, http://www.afr.com/business/banking-and-finance/hedge-funds/amps-leap-into-china-dunnes-legacy-20150925-gjuxwc

Somasundaram, N 2013, 'China Life in Funds Management Venture With AMP Capital', Bloomberg, 2 September, http://www.bloomberg.com/news/articles/2013-09-02/china-life-in-funds-management-joint-venture-with-amp-capital

Sonali, P 2015, 'Australian's bet on China gas begins to pay off', *Reuters*, 5 December.

Soutphommasane, T 2014, 'The Asianisation of Australia?', Speech to the Asian Studies Association of Australia Annual Conference, Perth, 10 July, https://www.humanrights.gov.au/news/speeches/asianisation-australia

State Council of the People's Republic of China 2015, *Action Plan on the Belt and Road Initiative*, http://english.gov.cn/archive/publications/2015/03/30/content_281475080249035.htm

Statistics Canada 2011, 'Immigration and Ethnocultural Diversity in Canada', https://www12.statcan.gc.ca/nhs-enm/2011/as-sa/99-010-x/99-010-x2011001-eng.cfm

Sterland, B 2013, 'Priorities for Australia's presidency of the G20 in 2014 and the role of the global financial safety net', The Shilla, Seoul, Republic of Korea, 19 December, http://www.treasury.gov.au/PublicationsAndMedia/Speeches/2013/Priorities-for-Australias-Presidency-of-the-G20.

Stubbs, R & Mustapha, J 2014, 'Ideas and Institutionalization in Asia,' in Pekkanen, SM, Ravenhill, J & Foot, R (eds.), *Oxford Handbook of the International Relations of Asia*, Oxford University Press, New York, p. 696.

Ta Kung Pao 2013, 'The ins and outs of China's partners', http://news.takungpao.com/special/partner/

Tan, S 2016, 'Chinese banks take foreign lending challenge', *The Australian Financial Review*, 11 May, http://www.afr.com/real-estate/chinese-banks-take-foreign-lending-challenge-20160602-goqp00

Teng, F and Jotzo, F 2014, 'Reaping the Economic Benefits of Decarbonization for China', *China & World Economy*, vol. 22, no. 5, pp. 37–54.

Teng, F et al. 2014, 'China', in *Pathways to deep decarbonization 2014 report*, SDSN and IDDRI, http://deepdecarbonization.org/wp-content/uploads/2015/09/DDPP_CHN.pdf

Terlato, P 2015, 'China is driving a revival for Australian tourism', *Business Insider*, 2 April, http://www.businessinsider.com.au/chinese-tourists-are-visiting-australia-in-droves-thanks-to-a-weaker-aussie-dollar-2015-4

Thomas, N 2015, 'Rhetoric and Reality – Xi Jinping's Australia Policy', *The China Story Journal*, 15 March, https://www.thechinastory.org/2015/03/rhetoric-and-reality-xi-jinpings-australia-policy/

Tourism Australia 2011, 'China 2020 Strategic Plan', Canberra, http://www.tourism.australia.com/documents/corporate/TA_China_2020_Strategic_Plan.pdf

Tourism Australia 2015a, 'Visitors by country of residence', Canberra, http://www.tourism.australia.com/images/Statistics/ABSarrivals_December_2015.pdf

Tourism Australia 2015b, 'China Market Profile 2015', Canberra, http://www.tourism.australia.com/documents/Markets/Market_Profile_2015_China.pdf

Tourism Research Australia 2014, 'Tourism Update: September Quarter 2014', Canberra, http://tra.gov.au/documents/Tourism_Update_SeptQtr2014_FINAL.pdf

Tourism Research Australia 2015, 'Tourism Forecasts', Canberra, https://www.tra.gov.au/documents/forecasts/Tourism_Forecasts_2015_FINAL.PDF

Tourism Research Australia 2016, 'Tourism Forecasts', Canberra, https://www.tra.gov.au/

Treasurer of Australia 2015a, 'Australia-China strategic economic dialogue promotes investment in regional infrastructure', joint press release with Minister for Trade and Investment, 13 August, http://jbh.ministers.treasury.gov.au/media-release/072-2015/

Treasurer of Australia 2015b, 'Statement on decision to prevent sale of S. Kidman & Co. Limited', press release, 19 November.

Treasurer of Australia, 2015c. "Australia-China strategic economic dialogue promotes investment in regional infrastructure". Joint media release with Minister for Trade and Investment. 13 August. http://jbh.ministers.treasury.gov.au/media-release/072-2015/

Treasurer of Australia 2016, 'Preliminary decision of foreign investment application for purchase of S. Kidman & Co. Limited', press release, 29 April, http://sjm.ministers.treasury.gov.au/media-release/050-2016/

UKTI 2014, 'Why overseas companies should set up in the UK', 11 April, https://www.gov.uk/government/publications/why-overseas-companies-should-set-up-in-the-uk/why-overseas-companies-should-set-up-in-the-uk

UKTI 2015, 'UKTI Inward Investment Report', https://www.gov.uk/government/publications/ukti-inward-investment-report-2014-to-2015/ukti-inward-investment-report-2014-to-2015-online-viewing

UNCTAD 2015, 'Tracing the value added in global value chains: Product level case studies in China', http://unctad.org/en/PublicationsLibrary/ditctncd2015d1_en.pdf

Universities Australia 2014, 'International Links Data', https://www.universitiesaustralia.edu.au/global-engagement/international-collaboration/international-links#.V23BHJN97pA

Urata, S 2013, 'Construction of RCEP by consolidating ASEAN+1 FTAs', in Baldwin, R, Kawai, M & Wignaraja, G (eds.), *The future of the world trading system: Asian Perspectives*, Centre for Economic Policy Research.

Uren, D 2012, *The Kingdom and the Quarry: China, Australia, Fear and Greed*, Black Inc., Melbourne.

Uren D 2015, *Takeover*, Black Inc., Melbourne.

VECCI 2015, 'China program expands to include inbound trade mission', http://www.vecci.org.au/policy-and-advocacy/news/news-articles/2015/10/22/china-program-expands-include-inbound-trade-missio

Vines, D 2015, *On concerted unilateralism: Raising the global growth rate through macroeconomic policy coordination*, Brookings Institution.

Walters, J & Kuo, Y 2016, 'China's consumers stay the (slightly lower) course', *BCG Perspectives*, Boston Consulting Group, http://www.bcg.com.cn/export/sites/default/en/files/publications/reports_pdf/BCG-Chinas-Consumers-Stay-the-Slightly-Slower-Course-June-2016_ENG.pdf

Wan, M 1995–1996, 'Japan and the Asian Development Bank,' *Pacific Affairs*, vol. 68, no. 4, pp. 509–528.

Weir, K & Walsh, G 2014, 'Internationalisation of the Renminbi: Pathways, Implications and Opportunities', Centre for International Finance and Regulation, http://www.cifr.edu.au/assets/document/CIFR%20Internationalisation%20of%20the%20RMB%20Report%20Final%20web.pdf

Weir, K & Walsh, G 2015, 'Renminbi Internationalisation and the evolution of offshore RMB centres: Opportunities for Sydney', Centre for International Finance and Regulation, https://www.industry.nsw.gov.au/__data/assets/pdf_file/0005/79574/Offshore-RMB-Report-20151104.pdf

Westpac 2016, 'Westpac in Asia', http://www.westpac.com.au/about-westpac/global-locations/westpac-in-asia/

Wilczynski, J 1965, 'The Economics and Politics of Wheat Exports to China', *The Australian Quarterly*, vol. 37, no. 2, pp. 44–55.

Wilkins, K & Zurawski, A 2014, 'Infrastructure investment in China', *Reserve Bank of Australia Bulletin June Quarter 2014*, http://www.rba.gov.au/publications/bulletin/2014/jun/pdf/bu-0614-4.pdf

Wille, K & S Waite 2016, 'Lazard, AMP, Pine River Among Firms Closing Asia Hedge Funds', *Bloomberg*, 26 February, http://www.bloomberg.com/news/articles/2016-02-25/lazard-amp-shutter-asian-hedge-funds-in-rising-wave-of-closures

World Bank 2015, 'Commodity Markets Outlook', http://www.worldbank.org/en/research/commodity-markets

World Bank 2016, 'World Development Indicators', http://data.worldbank.org/indicator/

World Nuclear Association 2016, 'Australia's Uranium', http://www.world-nuclear.org/information-library/country-profiles/countries-a-f/australia.aspx

World Steel Association 2015, 'Word Steel 2015 Steel Statistical; Yearbook', http://www.worldsteel.org/dms/internetDocumentList/bookshop/2015/Steel-Statistical-Yearbook-2015/document/Steel%20Statistical%20Yearbook%202015.pdf

WTO 2016a, 'Time series on international trade', WTO Statistics Database, http://stat.wto.org

WTO 2016b. 'China Tariff Profile', http://stat.wto.org/TariffProfile/WSDBTariffPFView.aspx?Language=E&Country=CN

WTO and OECD 2016, 'Trade in Value Added Database – October 2015', http://stats.oecd.org/Index.aspx?DataSetCode=TIVA2015_C1

Wu, H 2014, 'China's growth and productivity performance debate revisited', The Conference Board Economics Program Working Paper Series no. 14(01), https://www.conference-board.org/pdf_free/workingpapers/EPWP1401.pdf

Xinhua 2014, 'Slower CPC membership growth reflects stricter recruitment', *China Daily*, 1 July, http://usa.chinadaily.com.cn/china/2014-07/01/content_17628308.htm

Xu, B 2016, 'A silver lining to China's ageing population', *Business Spectator*, 27 January 27, http://www.theaustralian.com.au/business/business-spectator/a-silver-lining-to-chinas-ageing-population/news-story/25e58abe630815f9976763cd27a79764

Yang Y, 2000. "China's WTO Accession; The Economics and Politics." *Journal of World Trade* vol. 34 no. 4, pp. 77-94.

Yueh, L 2015, 'How a Chinese slowdown will hit global growth', World Economic Forum, 26 August, https://www.weforum.org/agenda/2015/08/how-a-chinese-slowdown-will-hit-global-growth/

Zhang, D & Freestone, O 2013. "China's unfinished state-owned enterprise reforms." *Economic Roundup* no. 77.

Zhang, Y & Wang, R 2013, 'The case for enhancing regional and global rules for investment', in Baldwin, R, Kawai, M & Wignaraja, G (eds.), *The future of the world trading system: Asian Perspectives*, Centre for Economic Policy Research.

Zhang, Y 2014, 'APEC will promote the Free Trade Area of the Asia-Pacific to become reality', *NetEase News*, 5 November, http://news.163.com/14/1105/10/AA9H4F5B00014JB6.html

Zhang, Y 2015, 'The return of China's periphery region concept and the construction of a new order', *World Economics and Politics*, 1.

Zhang, Y 2016, 'The value of One Belt One Road will come from unremitting perseverance', 3 May, http://hk.crntt.com/doc/1041/1/3/5/104113525.html

Zhao, R 2015, 'Weihai e-commerce firms' South Korea business thrives'. *China Daily*, 13 March, http://www.chinadaily.com.cn/regional/2015-05/13/content_21972332.htm

Zhong, N 2015. 'China-ASEAN trade negotiations to be concluded by year-end', *China Daily*, http://www.chinadailyasia.com/business/2015-07/30/content_15297497.html, 30 July.

Zhong, W, He, F & Wang, T 2014, 'APEC Beijing Summit: Division and Innovation', *China Foreign Exchange*, 21.

Zhou, Q 2013, 'China's 'Partners', *Southern Weekend*, 4 April.

Zogby Research Services 2015, *A Promising Partner: How Chinese Elites View Australia*, https://www.uts.edu.au/sites/default/files/How%20Chinese%20Elites%20View%20Australia%20-%20Australia-China%20Relations%20Institute%20-%20Zogby%20Research%20Services.pdf